Applied Social Science Approaches to Mixed Methods Research

Mette Lise Baran
Cardinal Stritch University, USA

Janice Elisabeth Jones
Cardinal Stritch University, USA

A volume in the Advances in Library and Information Science (ALIS) Book Series

Published in the United States of America by
    IGI Global
    Information Science Reference (an imprint of IGI Global)
    701 E. Chocolate Avenue
    Hershey PA, USA 17033
    Tel: 717-533-8845
    Fax: 717-533-8661
    E-mail: cust@igi-global.com
    Web site: http://www.igi-global.com

Copyright © 2020 by IGI Global. All rights reserved. No part of this publication may be reproduced, stored or distributed in any form or by any means, electronic or mechanical, including photocopying, without written permission from the publisher.
Product or company names used in this set are for identification purposes only. Inclusion of the names of the products or companies does not indicate a claim of ownership by IGI Global of the trademark or registered trademark.

                            Library of Congress Cataloging-in-Publication Data

Names: Baran, Mette, 1965- editor. | Jones, Janice E., 1959- editor.
Title: Applied social science approaches to mixed methods research / Mette
   Lise Baran and Janice Elisabeth Jones, editors.
Description: Hershey, PA : Information Science Reference, [2020] | Includes
   bibliographical references and index. | Summary: "This book examines
   mixed methods research from a social science approach"--Provided by
   publisher.
Identifiers: LCCN 2019023687 (print) | LCCN 2019023688 (ebook) | ISBN
   9781799810254 (hardcover) | ISBN 9781799810261 (paperback) | ISBN
   9781799810278 (ebook)
Subjects: LCSH: Social science--Research--Methodology. | Mixed methods
   research. | Applied sociology.
Classification: LCC H62 .A685 2020 (print) | LCC H62 (ebook) | DDC
   300.72/1--dc23
LC record available at https://lccn.loc.gov/2019023687
LC ebook record available at https://lccn.loc.gov/2019023688

This book is published in the IGI Global book series Advances in Library and Information Science (ALIS) (ISSN: 2326-4136; eISSN: 2326-4144)

British Cataloguing in Publication Data
A Cataloguing in Publication record for this book is available from the British Library.

All work contributed to this book is new, previously-unpublished material.
The views expressed in this book are those of the authors, but not necessarily of the publisher.

For electronic access to this publication, please contact: eresources@igi-global.com.

Advances in Library and Information Science (ALIS) Book Series

Alfonso Ippolito
Sapienza University-Rome, Italy
Carlo Inglese
Sapienza University-Rome, Italy

ISSN:2326-4136
EISSN:2326-4144

MISSION

The **Advances in Library and Information Science (ALIS) Book Series** is comprised of high quality, research-oriented publications on the continuing developments and trends affecting the public, school, and academic fields, as well as specialized libraries and librarians globally. These discussions on professional and organizational considerations in library and information resource development and management assist in showcasing the latest methodologies and tools in the field.

The **ALIS Book Series** aims to expand the body of library science literature by covering a wide range of topics affecting the profession and field at large. The series also seeks to provide readers with an essential resource for uncovering the latest research in library and information science management, development, and technologies.

COVERAGE

- Censorship
- Digital Libraries
- Cases on Library Management
- Intellectual Freedom
- Semantic Web and Libraries
- Visual Literacy
- Scholarly Communications for Libraries
- Storage Facilities
- Safety And Security in Libraries
- Managing Libraries

IGI Global is currently accepting manuscripts for publication within this series. To submit a proposal for a volume in this series, please contact our Acquisition Editors at Acquisitions@igi-global.com or visit: http://www.igi-global.com/publish/.

The Advances in Library and Information Science (ALIS) Book Series (ISSN 2326-4136) is published by IGI Global, 701 E. Chocolate Avenue, Hershey, PA 17033-1240, USA, www.igi-global.com. This series is composed of titles available for purchase individually; each title is edited to be contextually exclusive from any other title within the series. For pricing and ordering information please visit http://www.igi-global.com/book-series/advances-library-information-science/73002. Postmaster: Send all address changes to above address. © © 2020 IGI Global. All rights, including translation in other languages reserved by the publisher. No part of this series may be reproduced or used in any form or by any means – graphics, electronic, or mechanical, including photocopying, recording, taping, or information and retrieval systems – without written permission from the publisher, except for non commercial, educational use, including classroom teaching purposes. The views expressed in this series are those of the authors, but not necessarily of IGI Global.

Titles in this Series

For a list of additional titles in this series, please visit:
https://www.igi-global.com/book-series/advances-library-information-science/73002

Handbook of Research on Emerging Trends and Technologies in Library and Informatin Science
Anna Kaushik (University of Kota, India) Ashok Kumar (Maharishi Markandeshwar University (Deemed), India) and Payel Biswas (Institute of Urban Transport, India)
Information Science Reference • © 2020 • 434pp • H/C (ISBN: 9781522598251) • US $275.00

Managing and Adapting Library Information Services for Future Users
Nkem Ekene Osuigwe (African Library and Information Associations & Institutions, Nigeria)
Information Science Reference • © 2020 • 300pp • H/C (ISBN: 9781799811169) • US $185.00

Novel Theories and Applications of Global Information Resource Management
Zuopeng (Justin) Zhang (University of North Florida, USA)
Information Science Reference • © 2020 • 405pp • H/C (ISBN: 9781799817864) • US $195.00

Handbook of Research on Digital Content Management and Development in Modern Libraries
S. Thanuskodi (Alagappa University, India)
Information Science Reference • © 2020 • 395pp • H/C (ISBN: 9781799822011) • US $275.00

Building Equitable Access to Knowledge Through Open Access Repositories
Nikos Koutras (University of Antwerp, Belgium)
Information Science Reference • © 2020 • 319pp • H/C (ISBN: 9781799811312) • US $180.00

Cooperation and Collaboration Initiatives for Libraries and Related Institutions
Collence Takaingenhamo Chisita (University of South Africa, South Africa)
Information Science Reference • © 2020 • 394pp • H/C (ISBN: 9781799800439) • US $195.00

IGI Global
DISSEMINATOR OF KNOWLEDGE

701 East Chocolate Avenue, Hershey, PA 17033, USA
Tel: 717-533-8845 x100 • Fax: 717-533-8661
E-Mail: cust@igi-global.com • www.igi-global.com

Editorial Advisory Board

Roger J. Baran, *DePaul University, USA*
Todd R. Burton, *Cardinal Stritch University, USA*
Evan Diehnelt, *Cisco Systems, Raleigh, NC, USA*
Glady Van Harpen, *University of Wisconsin, Oshkosh, USA*

Table of Contents

Preface xv

Acknowledgment xxiii

Introduction xxiv

Section 1
Research Paradigms

Chapter 1
Implications of Mixing Methods: Balancing Paradigmatic and Validation
Distinctives 1
Preston B. Cosgrove, Concordia University Wisconsin, USA

Section 2
Designing a Mixed Methods Research Study

Chapter 2
Mixed Methods Research Design 26
Mette L. Baran, Cardinal Stritch University, USA

Section 3
Sampling and Data Collection in Research

Chapter 3
Considering the Source: Sampling and Data Collection in a Mixed Methods
Study 54
Mindy Crain-Dorough, Southeastern Louisiana University, USA

Section 4
Analyzing Data

Chapter 4
Analyzing Qualitative Data: Words, Words, Words! 87
Janice E. Jones, Cardinal Stritch University, USA

Section 5
Using Innovative Tools in Research

Chapter 5
Using Data, Description, and Graphics to Enrich Your Mixed Methods
Study 107
Glady Van Harpen, University of Wisconsin, Oshkosh, USA

Chapter 6
Data Speaks: Use of Poems and Photography in Qualitative Research 119
Carolyn N. Stevenson, School of General Education, Purdue University Global, USA

Section 6
Data Analysis: Examples of Research Studies Using Mixed Methods

Chapter 7
Mitigating the Effects of Social Desirability Bias in Self-Report Surveys:
Classical and New Techniques 146
Ahmet Durmaz, National Defence University, Turkey
İnci Dursun, Gebze Technical University, Turkey
Ebru Tümer Kabadayi, Gebze Technical University, Turkey

Chapter 8
Triangulation Approaches in Accounting Research: Concerns, Implications,
and Resolutions 186
Koholga Ormin, Adamawa State University, Mubi, Nigeria

Chapter 9
Beyond Statistical Power and Significance in Entrepreneurship and
Management Research 201
Pierre Sindambiwe, University of Rwanda, Rwanda & Jönköping International Business School, Sweden

Chapter 10
Using Social Media to Organize a Marginalized Community: A Case Study
Examining LGBT Military Leaders Advocating for Inclusive Service............. 216
Todd R. Burton, Cardinal Stritch University, USA

Section 7
Using Ethical Principals and Conduct in Scientific Research

Chapter 11
To Whose Benefit? At What Cost? Consideration for Ethical Issues in Social
Science Research..251
Aaliyah A. Baker, Cardinal Stritch University, USA

Section 8
Conducting Research From Start to Finish

Chapter 12
Developing the Research Study: A Step-by-Step Approach 262
Mette L. Baran, Cardinal Stritch University, USA
Janice E. Jones, Cardinal Stritch University, USA

Compilation of References 275

About the Contributors 309

Index 313

Detailed Table of Contents

Preface xv

Acknowledgment xxiii

Introduction xxiv

Section 1
Research Paradigms

Chapter 1
Implications of Mixing Methods: Balancing Paradigmatic and Validation
Distinctives 1
    Preston B. Cosgrove, Concordia University Wisconsin, USA

Much like a jigsaw puzzle box top guides one in how to connect the pieces, a research paradigm operates as a conscious or subconscious influence in conducting a research project. The promise—and challenge—of mixed methods research is that it involves the use of two box tops, and this chapter discusses the subsequent implications on the researcher. The first effect is through the need to balance the paradigmatic distinctives, requiring the researcher to identify one of four broad ways to address the paradigm divide at the heart of qualitative and quantitative research. The second effect is through the need to balance the validation distinctives. Making research credible is an essential component of any study, and the issues magnify given the stark differences between qualitative and quantitative validity orientations. Both implications reveal the level of sophistication required for the researcher when conducting a mixed methods project.

Section 2
Designing a Mixed Methods Research Study

Chapter 2
Mixed Methods Research Design 26
    Mette L. Baran, Cardinal Stritch University, USA

This chapter introduces the various design choices researchers need to decide on prior to conducting the study. The chapter starts with a detailed description of what research design is, followed by an explanation of descriptive, explanatory, or exploratory research questions. This determines what type of data will be collected. The major strategic implementation methods for quantitative, qualitative, and mixed methods are then discussed. The three strategies for mixed methods research—parallel convergent, sequential, and embedded design—are presented in detail along with the rationale for their use. Finally, in the last section, the strands or sequencing of the data collection phase of the study are explained.

Section 3
Sampling and Data Collection in Research

Chapter 3
Considering the Source: Sampling and Data Collection in a Mixed Methods Study 54
Mindy Crain-Dorough, Southeastern Louisiana University, USA

The purpose of this chapter is to describe detailed procedures for determining the data collection and sampling methods in a mixed methods study. The nuances of selecting data collection strategies and sampling techniques are explained in a practical way. The points of decision, factors to consider, and methods for weighing the advantages and disadvantages are provided along with tables that can be completed to organize the planning process. The overall design process for a mixed methods study is described to provide the context for the in-depth discussion about data collection and sampling. A fictional study is used as an example to illustrate how to apply the procedure to identify the optimal data sources for a mixed methods study.

Section 4
Analyzing Data

Chapter 4
Analyzing Qualitative Data: Words, Words, Words! 87
Janice E. Jones, Cardinal Stritch University, USA

This chapter provides an introduction to the process of qualitative analysis and uses step-by-step examples to provide an idea of how the process of qualitative analysis actually works. This chapter is intended to give the researcher a place to begin and to inspire a deeper dive into this rewarding form of data analysis. While qualitative data analysis can be time consuming, the rewards that come from immersion in the data far outweigh the time spent doing so.

Section 5
Using Innovative Tools in Research

Chapter 5
Using Data, Description, and Graphics to Enrich Your Mixed Methods Study 107
Glady Van Harpen, University of Wisconsin, Oshkosh, USA

Systems of organizing, displaying, and presenting data in studies focusing on educational research have traditionally included statistical tables and figures such as charts and graphs. This chapter provides a discussion of utilizing multiple visual methods for displaying data in an educational mixed methods study that goes beyond tables and charts. The chapter does not go into construction of visual methods but offers suggestions and ideas for graphic illustrations such as icons, emojis, or photographs to display results. The chapter calls attention to application opportunities for researchers to reflect upon prior to submitting research proposals and IRB applications.

Chapter 6
Data Speaks: Use of Poems and Photography in Qualitative Research.............119
Carolyn N. Stevenson, School of General Education, Purdue University Global, USA

Qualitative research methods provide the researcher with opportunity to share the lived experiences of participants in an authentic manner. These narratives can be enhanced through visual expression, such as use of photos, which provide another way to exercise self-expression. Found poetry has a rich history in participant-based studies, while self-studies utilize poems as an opportunity to address more philosophical or poststructuralist opportunities. These forms of data collection can provide a rich, thick description of those often overlying on the peripherals of society. By offering participants the opportunity to personally select descriptive photographs and articulate expression in their own voice through poetry, the lived experiences can authentically be displayed.

Section 6
Data Analysis: Examples of Research Studies Using Mixed Methods

Chapter 7
Mitigating the Effects of Social Desirability Bias in Self-Report Surveys: Classical and New Techniques..146
Ahmet Durmaz, National Defence University, Turkey
İnci Dursun, Gebze Technical University, Turkey
Ebru Tümer Kabadayi, Gebze Technical University, Turkey

Self-reporting is a frequently used method to measure various constructs in many areas of social science research. Literature holds abundant evidence that social desirability bias (SDB), which is a special kind of response bias, can severely plague the validity and accuracy of the self-report survey measurements. However, in many areas of behavioral research, there is little or no alternative to self-report surveys for collecting data about specific constructs that only the respondents may have the information about. Thus, researchers need to detect or minimize SDB to improve the quality of overall data and their deductions drawn from them. Literature provides a number of techniques for minimizing SDB during survey procedure and statistical measurement methods to detect and minimize the validity-destructive impact of SDB. This study aims to explicate the classical and new techniques for mitigating the SDB and to provide a guideline for the researchers, especially for those who focus on socially sensitive constructs.

Chapter 8
Triangulation Approaches in Accounting Research: Concerns, Implications, and Resolutions 186
Koholga Ormin, Adamawa State University, Mubi, Nigeria

Accounting research, like many other social science disciplines, has gradually moved from qualitative to quantitative research with an emphasis on the use of multiple evidence or methods in the conduct of research. This chapter explores the concerns and implications of triangulation in the conduct of research in the social sciences, particularly in the field of accounting. Based on evidence from existing literature, the chapter submits that triangulation is an important strategy for enhancing the quality of accounting research. Accounting researchers, like those from other social science disciplines, often adopt triangulation when investigating a complex phenomenon whereby using a single data source or method may not allow an exhaustive investigation to fully understand it, hence the inability to reach a dependable conclusion. Despite the concerns and implications of use of triangulation in accounting and social science research, the chapter concluded it is a relevant approach especially at a time when adequate evidence and analytical rigor is required to substantiate research findings.

Chapter 9
Beyond Statistical Power and Significance in Entrepreneurship and
Management Research 201
Pierre Sindambiwe, University of Rwanda, Rwanda & Jönköping International Business School, Sweden

Findings in most empirical research on entrepreneurship and management focuses on a few things: statistical representativeness of the data, the methodological rigor used for arriving at the results, and the statistical power of the results. However, both results and data are far from being free of criticism. This chapter provides a way forward that uses the mixed-methods approach without falling into the common confusion of multiple methods used in one research. It looks back at the reliance of statistical testing, null-hypothesis, and testing the statistical significance as the criteria. It explores available alternatives that can offer to overcome the problem of non-significance, rather than rejecting it as is usually done. It acknowledges some quantitative solutions like replication, conjoint, and comparative analyses and extends the use of some qualitative methods like exploratory methods, case studies, and theory development studies that offer alternatives to treating the presence or absence of significance. It discusses the concepts used and gives the limitations of the study.

Chapter 10
Using Social Media to Organize a Marginalized Community: A Case Study Examining LGBT Military Leaders Advocating for Inclusive Service 216
Todd R. Burton, Cardinal Stritch University, USA

Potential leaders within marginalized communities find it difficult to connect, learn, strategize, and support one another and build a cohesive community capable of effecting social change. This research contributes to filling a gap in empirical research on effective approaches to employing social media tools to organize and engage in social movements. The research builds on earlier studies of marginalized communities and social media to organize and engages in social movements by applying a case study design to assess how the lesbian, gay, bisexual, and transgender (LGBT) military community employed social media to organize and advocate for inclusion and end discrimination within the U.S. armed forces. Seventeen findings were identified that describe key ways the LGBT military community employed these tools to organize, identify leaders and their roles, and how online behavior affected offline advocacy.

Section 7
Using Ethical Principals and Conduct in Scientific Research

Chapter 11
To Whose Benefit? At What Cost? Consideration for Ethical Issues in Social Science Research..251
Aaliyah A. Baker, Cardinal Stritch University, USA

This chapter takes a conceptual approach to addressing issues of ethics in research with human participants. The author proposes preliminary questions at the onset of a research study that deal with the issue of addressing researcher responsibility. The chapter argues ethical considerations surround epistemology and impact when conducting mixed methods research. Moreover, defining the interaction between researchers and participants is crucial. The author challenges early career practitioners to ask the question 'To whose benefit is the research?' but more importantly 'At what cost when conducting research?' Recommendations for engaging in an applied social science methodology include understanding critical epistemological and philosophical perspectives and grappling with the potential impact and outcomes of research. This level of critical awareness enables research to display complex processes that address social, political, and moral ideals that resonate with and value human experience as knowledge.

Section 8
Conducting Research From Start to Finish

Chapter 12
Developing the Research Study: A Step-by-Step Approach 262
    Mette L. Baran, Cardinal Stritch University, USA
    Janice E. Jones, Cardinal Stritch University, USA

This chapter serves as a guideline for outlining the core characteristics of qualitative, quantitative, or mixed methods research (MMR) and the various steps researchers undertake in order to conduct a research study. While the focus is on MMR, the steps are similar for any type of research methodology. The purpose is to create a framework assisting the researcher with an outline following the seven steps to conducting research. It is important to note that MMR is not a limiting form of research. Researchers need a mixed method research question and a mixed methods purpose statement for the research project. This chapter will also help explain why MMR is one of the best approaches in answering a research question. Finally, the chapter includes a suggestion to the importance of adding a visual diagram of the mixed methods research project into the research project and into the final report.

Compilation of References 275

About the Contributors 309

Index 313

Preface

The intent of this book is to create a practical, easy-to-read and understand, user-friendly book that will reach a wide audience of those who are in the early stages of their research career. The main target is the novice researcher; for example, master or doctoral-level students committed to writing their thesis, dissertation, or scholarly articles. Typically, such students have very limited knowledge of research and little practical experience in the area. Most research books target advanced researchers and assume a fairly high level of practical research experience. This book will help to fill a void and targets beginning researchers who are committed to conducting high quality research while at the same time being novices in the area. The material in this book focuses on mixed methods research (MMR) which uses a combination of qualitative and quantitative techniques which provides for measurable statistical confidence as well as a deep understanding of the issue at hand. Mixed methods research is the technique chosen by many schools, businesses and not-for-profit organizations as it is appropriate in addressing and resolving issues that they face. The benefits of MMR include the generation of statistically accurate insights which lead to the development and implementation of effective strategy.

Graduate students and faculty can use the book as a reference and/or textbook for research courses. Graduate students, while committed to conducting high quality research, often have a limited knowledge of research planning and implementation for their thesis or dissertation. This book takes novice students through the entire research process by offering step-by-step guidance. This book is also intended for a broader audience in social and human sciences, representing many disciplines, as MMR is rapidly gaining in popularity due to the added richness in findings it affords the researcher. Faculty often ponder how to best train students in MMR. It can be a challenge since students come from a wide variety of backgrounds and arrive with various skill levels and research interests. Hence faculty may find the book useful. We encourage all graduate students to become proficient in this third research paradigm.

BOOK'S FOCUS AND EXPECTED OUTCOMES

Conducting empirical research to complete either a master's thesis or doctoral dissertation is a graduation requirement at higher education institutions today. Even accomplished students may be faced with the responsibility of conducting research for the first time, requiring them to make decisions regarding methodology and design, followed by the daunting tasks of data analysis and interpretation. Similarly, course instructors are faced with selecting teaching materials that provide the resources students need in order to learn both quantitative and qualitative methods. This can be challenging since students often like to or are required to pre-select either a quantitative or qualitative track. Likewise, advisors may be more experienced in one or the other and uncomfortable training their students in both. We need to break this trend as many issues today are highly complex and the MMR approach may be the best way to gain a complete understanding of the issue under investigation. This book demonstrates how MMR designs can address a wide array of research questions and help navigate the inexperienced researchers through the complicated mix of research decisions that must be made.

The contributors to this book are all experienced MM researchers and, combined, they walk the reader through the entire research process beginning with the need to establish an epistemological foundation to formulating the research questions, selecting the appropriate research design, collecting data, and interpreting both quantitative and qualitative findings. The final chapter includes a practical step by step outline for conducting a research study from start to finish.

ORGANIZATION OF THE BOOK

The book is organized into 12 chapters spread over eight sections which follows a natural research project outline: Research Paradigms, Designing a Mixed Methods Research Study, Sampling and Data Collection in Research, Analyzing Data, Using Innovative Tools in Research, Data Analysis: Examples of Research Studies using Mixed Methods,

Using Ethical Principals and Conduct in Scientific Research and Conducting Research from Start to Finish. A brief description of each of the chapters follows:

Preface

Chapter 1

Implications of Mixing Methods: Balancing Paradigmatic and Validation Distinctives

Much like a jigsaw puzzle box top guides one in how to connect the pieces, a research paradigm operates as a conscious or subconscious influence in conducting a research project. The promise—and challenge—of mixed methods research is that it involves the use of two box tops, and this chapter discusses the subsequent implications on the researcher. The first effect is through the need to balance the paradigmatic distinctives, requiring the researcher to identify one of four broad ways to address the paradigm divide at the heart of qualitative and quantitative research. The second effect is through the need to balance the validation distinctives. Making research credible is an essential component of any study, and the issues magnify given the stark differences between qualitative and quantitative validity orientations. Both implications reveal the level of sophistication required for the researcher when conducting a mixed methods project.

Chapter 2

Mixed Methods Research Design

This chapter introduces the various design choices researchers need to decide on prior to conducting the study. The chapter starts with a detailed description of what research design is, followed by an explanation of descriptive, explanatory, or exploratory research questions. This determine what type of data will be collected. The major strategic implementation methods for quantitative, qualitative, and mixed methods are then discussed. The three strategies for mixed methods research: Parallel Convergent, Sequential, and Embedded Design are presented in detail along with the rationale for their use. Finally, in the last section, the strands or sequencing of the data collection phase of the study is explained.

Chapter 3

Considering the Source: Sampling and Data Collection in a Mixed Methods Study

The purpose of this chapter is to describe detailed procedures for determining the data collection and sampling methods in a mixed methods study. The nuances of selecting data collection strategies and sampling techniques are explained in a practical way.

The points of decision, factors to consider, and methods for weighing the advantages and disadvantages are provided along with tables that can be completed to organize the planning process. The overall design process for a mixed methods study is described to provide the context for the in-depth discussion about data collection and sampling. A fictional study is used as an example to illustrate how to apply the procedure to identify the optimal data sources for a mixed methods study.

Chapter 4

Analyzing Qualitative Data: Words, Words, Words!

This chapter introduces the process of qualitative analysis and uses step by step examples to provide an idea of how the process of qualitative analysis works. Crabtree and Miller, 1992, note that there are many different strategies for analysis, in fact, they suggest there are as many strategies as there are qualitative researchers. This chapter is intended to give the researcher a place to begin and to inspire a deeper dive into this rewarding form of data analysis. Stake, (1995, p. 71) writes that qualitative data analysis is "a matter of giving meaning to first impressions as well as to final compilations. Analysis essentially means taking something apart. We take our impressions, our observations, apart… we need to take the new impression apart, giving meaning to the parts". While qualitative data analysis can be time consuming the rewards that come from immersion in the data far outweigh the time spent doing so.

Chapter 5

Using Data, Description, and Graphics to Enrich Your Mixed Methods Study

Systems of organizing, displaying, and presenting data in studies focusing on educational research have traditionally included statistical tables and figures such as charts, and graphs. This chapter provides a discussion of utilizing multiple visual methods for displaying data in an educational mixed methods study that goes beyond tables and charts. The chapter does not go into construction of visual methods, rather offers suggestions and ideas for graphic illustrations such as icons, emojis, or photographs to display results. The chapter calls attention to application opportunities for researchers to reflect upon prior to submitting research proposals and IRB applications.

Preface

Chapter 6

Data Speaks: Use of Poems and Photography in Qualitative Research

Qualitative research methods provide the researcher with opportunity to share the lived experiences of participants in an authentic manner. These narratives can be enhanced through visual expression such as use of photos which provide another way to exercise self-expression. Found poetry has a rich history in participant-based studies, while self-studies utilize poems as an opportunity to address more philosophical or poststructuralist opportunities. These forms of data collection can provide a rich, thick description of those often overlying on the peripherals of society. By offering participants the opportunity to personally select descriptive photographs and articulate expression in their own voice through poetry, the lived experiences can authentically be displayed.

Chapter 7

Mitigating the Effects of Social Desirability Bias in Self-Report Surveys: Classical and New Techniques

Self-reporting is a frequently used method to measure various constructs in many areas of social science research. Literature holds abundant evidence that social desirability bias which is a specific kind of response bias can severely plague the validity and accuracy of the self-report survey measurements. However, in many areas of behavioral research, there is a little or no alternative to self-report surveys for collecting data about specific constructs which only the respondents may have the information about. Thus, researchers need to detect or minimize social desirability bias to improve the quality of overall data and drawn theoretical implications. Literature provides several techniques for minimizing SDB during survey procedure and several statistical measurement methods to detect and minimize the validity-destructive impact of SDB. This study aims to explicate the extant literature on classical and new techniques for mitigating the social desirability bias and to provide a guideline for the researchers, especially for those who focus on socially sensitive constructs.

Chapter 8

Triangulation Approaches in Accounting Research: Concerns, Implications, and Resolutions

Accounting research like in many other social science disciplines has gradually move from qualitative to quantitative research with an emphasis on the use of multiple evidence or methods in the conduct of research. This current paper explores the concerns, and implications of triangulation in the conduct of research in the social sciences, particularly in the field of accounting. Based on evidence from existing literature, the paper submits that triangulation is an important strategy for enhancing the quality of accounting research. Accounting researchers like those from other social science disciplines often adopt triangulation when investigating a complex phenomenon whereby using a single data source or method may not allow an exhaustive investigation to fully understand it hence inability to reach a dependable conclusion. Despite the concerns and implications of use of triangulation in accounting and social science research, the paper concluded it is a relevant approach especially at a time when adequate evidence and analytical rigor is required to substantiate research findings.

Chapter 9

Beyond Statistical Power and Significance in Entrepreneurship and Management Research

In predicting the findings, most of empirical research in entrepreneurship and management focus on few things: "statistical representativeness" of the data, "methodological rigor" to achieve the result as well as the "statistical power" of the results. However, both results and data are far from being criticism free. This chapter provides way forward that gives rise to the mixed methods without falling into the common confusion of multiple methods used in one research. It looked back to the reliance on statistical testing, null-hypothesis and testing statistical significance as a truth criterion. It explores available alternatives that the mixed methods can offer to overcome that problem for non-significance, rather than rejecting them as usually done. It acknowledged some quantitative remedies like replication, conjoint and comparative analysis and extend using some qualitative methods like exploratory, cases studies and theory development studies that offer alternatives of treating the presence or absence of significance. Concepts are discussed, and limitations are highlighted.

Chapter 10

Using Social Media to Organize a Marginalized Community: A Case Study Examining LGBT Military Leaders Advocating for Inclusive Service

Potential leaders within marginalized communities find it difficult to connect, learn, strategize, and support one another and build a cohesive community capable of effecting social change. This research contributes to filling a gap in empirical research on effective approaches to employing social media tools to organize and engage in social movements. The research builds on earlier studies of marginalized communities and social media to organize and engage in social movements by applying a case study design to assess how the lesbian, gay, bisexual, and transgender (LGBT) military community employed social media to organize and advocate for inclusion and end discrimination within the U.S. armed forces. Seventeen findings were identified that describe key ways the LGBT military community employed these tools to organize itself, identify leaders and their roles, and how online behavior affected offline advocacy.

Chapter 11

To Whose Benefit? At What Cost? Consideration for Ethical Issues in Social Science Research

This chapter takes a conceptual approach to addressing issues of ethics in research with human participants. The author proposes preliminary questions at the onset of a research study that deal with the issue of addressing researcher responsibility. The chapter argues ethical considerations surround epistemology and impact when conducting mixed methods research. Moreover, defining the interaction between researchers and participants is crucial. The author challenges early career practitioners to ask the question 'to whose benefit is the research' but more importantly 'at what cost' when conducting research. Recommendations for engaging in an applied social science methodology include understanding critical epistemological and philosophical perspectives and grappling with the potential impact and outcomes of research. This level of critical awareness enables research to display complex processes that address social, political, and moral ideals which resonate with and value human experience as knowledge.

Chapter 12

Developing the Research Study: A Step-by-Step Approach

This chapter serves as a guideline for outlining the core characteristics of qualitative, quantitative, or mixed methods research (MMR) and the various steps researchers undertake in order to conduct a research study. While the focus is on MMR the steps are similar for any type of research methodology. The purpose is to create a framework assisting the researcher with an outline following the seven steps to conducting research. It is important to note that MMR is not a limiting form of research. Researchers need a mixed method research question and a mixed methods purpose statement for the research project. This chapter will also help explain why MMR is one of the best approaches in answering a research question. Finally, the chapter includes a suggestion to the importance of adding a visual diagram of the mixed methods research project into the research project and into the final report.

Acknowledgment

There are numerous people who contributed to this book. First, we would like to thank our Master of Educational Leadership students and Doctoral students in the Leadership for the Advancement of Learning and Service programming at Cardinal Stritch University in Milwaukee, WI. We would like to dedicate this book to all of our past, current, and future students who cross our paths and forever engage and inspire us in the inquiry of social research. You motivate us daily to become better teachers and research advisors and we thank you for the opportunity to learn along with you. As Yeats noted, "Education is not the filling of a pail but the lighting of a fire." We sincerely hope that we have inspired you to appreciate research and that you will keep perfecting your skills as scholars.

We would also like to thank our assistant editors for their time and attention to detail. We could not have completed this book without your support. Dr. Roger Baran, Dr. Todd Burton, Mr. Evan Diehnelt, Dr. Eric Dimmitt, and Dr. Glady Van Harpen, we will forever be grateful.

Finally, we must thank all of the contributors to this book for their commitment and dedication to the exciting field of mixed methods research. We are truly honored to call ourselves your colleagues.

Introduction

The question of which method—quantitative or qualitative—is superior in social science research has been heavily debated for many decades. We have now moved beyond this perennial discussion of which one is best and have accepted the mixed methods approach, which acknowledges the collection of both qualitative and quantitative data in the same study. We are still left, however, with the question regarding how best to teach novice researchers to become proficient in the mixed methods technique. As educators, we have observed both beginning masters and doctoral researchers battle with designing mixed methods research studies as well as interpreting results from the application of multiple data collection tools. This observation, apparent throughout years of working with students, led us to write this book, as limited materials on mixed methods research are available for novice researchers. As professors, teaching our masters and doctoral students research methodology, we felt it was necessary to develop comprehensive teaching materials that take students in the social and behavioral sciences through a quality Mixed Methods Research (MMR) project from start to finish.

While there are numerous definitions of MMR, we feel that Creswell's (2009) definition of this research approach "as involving philosophical assumptions, the use of qualitative and quantitative approaches, and the mixing of both approaches in a study" is precise and encompassing (p. 4).

The evolution of mixed methods research, its many contributions to the field, and its subsequent acceptance as a valid research approach, warrants our attention and requires academics to focus on the most valuable techniques for teaching the mixed methods technique. Now solidly established as the third research community, or the third methodological movement (Teddlie & Tashakkori, 2003), the mixed methods approach provides researchers with an opportunity to gain a holistic understanding of a research problem. The proposition of our experience is that students, albeit new to the research process, need to be successful in learning both quantitative and qualitative approaches.

Introduction

While some research questions can only be answered using quantitative data and others are only suited for qualitative data, one can't argue that some studies will provide more comprehensive results from a mixed methods approach. For example, a research study was undertaken for the textbook—euphemistically called the "Orange Book"—that emergency medical technicians (EMT's) must master in order to become certified. A large sample of over one thousand EMT's was selected and interviewed so that findings could be projected to the entire field of EMT's with confidence ranges established for every answer. While the book was highly rated on most attributes, a large percentage of EMT's said the book was "poorly organized". The percentage feeling this way was precisely quantified and the confidence range established since this was a quantitative study. However, no one knew how to correct the deficiency since EMT's were not asked to explain what they meant by the term "poorly organized." Was it the chapter sequence? The coordination of text with pictures, graphs and charts? The integration of footnotes and reference notes with the text? Or something else? The researchers had a precise percentage of EMT's feeling the book was poorly organized, but no one knew exactly what that meant. The solution involved going back to the sample and asking them to explain, in depth, precisely what they meant by the term "poorly organized." Hence, qualitative research was used to explain a finding from the quantitative research phase of the study. Of course, if the qualitative phase had preceded the quantitative phase, the explanation of "poorly organized" would have been covered first and then the quantitative survey would have found the precise percentage of EMT's who felt that way.

Our adage to the students that "the research question drives everything," is still very true. We note that many traditional doctoral programs still place students in either qualitative or quantitative paradigms for their initial research orientation. We believe, as Gorard and Taylor (2004) urge, that novice researchers can become imprisoned within one of these purported corners, limiting their potential to become consumers and generators of research. Hence, we concur with Teddlie and Tashakkori (2009) that it is "essential for social and behavioral scientists today to be methodologically bilingual" (p. 32). We would like to thank our students past and current for the opportunity to learn with them and to hone our own research skills in MMR as we are emerged in this journey together.

WHY CHOSE MIXED METHODS RESEARCH

Why chose Mixed Methods Research? MMR helps to improve communication across disciplines and among practitioners—which leads to better outcomes. MMR is a form of research that will greatly benefit practitioners as well as experienced researchers who want to expand their research methodology inventory. Research that has been presented primarily by quantitative research can benefit from the voice of the participants and the added value of the different perspective and exposition that qualitative research can provide. The purpose of MMR is to draw from the positive aspects of both research paradigms to better answer the research question. MMR has become a widely accepted and well-established technique used in many fields in order to enhance the proficiency, reliability and usefulness of research result. This book contributes to the understanding of MMR techniques in that we have attempted to break down the steps or decisions researchers need to consider and master in order to produce a quality study. It is our experience that the thought of conducting a study feels overwhelming to most, and in our own teaching we address these concerns and break down the research process into manageable, linear phases. Hence, the outline of our chapters follows this logical process.

The intent of this book is to create a practical, easy-to-read and understand, user- friendly book that will reach a wide audience. The main target is the novice researcher: for example, the master or doctoral-level students committed to writing their thesis, dissertation, or scholarly article. Typically, these students have very limited knowledge of research. Most books on research are highly complex and target the advanced researchers. This book will help to fill the void for researchers who are committed to conducting high quality research while at the same time being novice researchers. MMR is often used by schools, businesses and not-for-profit organizations as they strive to address and resolve questions that will impact their organizations. We hope that this book will be an excellent instructional aid for professors intending to utilize this book in a research methods course. The final chapter: Developing the Research Study, a Step by Step Approach, is a complete tool, taking students through the research process step-by-step from start to finish. This, we feel, is an excellent tool to utilize in teaching research as it highlights and prompts students to consider each important step in the research study.

Mette L. Baran
Cardinal Stritch University, USA

Janice E. Jones
Cardinal Stritch University, USA

REFERENCES

Creswell, J. W. (2009). *Research Design: Qualitative, Quantitative, and Mixed Methods Approaches*. Thousand Oaks, CA: Sage.

Introduction

Gorard, S., & Taylor, C. (2004). *Combining methods in educational and social research*. Buckingham, UK: Open University Press.

Teddlie, C., & Tashakkori, A. (2003). Major issues and controversies in the use of mixed methods in the social and behavioral sciences. In A. Tashakkori & C. Teddlie (Eds.), *Handbook of mixed methods in social and behavioral research* (pp. 3–50). Thousand Oaks, CA: Sage.

Teddlie, C., & Tashakkori, A. (2009). *Foundations of Mixed Methods Research. Integrating Quantitative and Qualitative Approaches in the Social and Behavioral Sciences*. Thousand Oaks, CA: Sage.

Section 1
Research Paradigms

Research paradigms address the philosophical dimensions of social sciences. A research paradigm is a set of fundamental assumptions and beliefs as to how the world is perceived which then serves as a thinking framework that guides the behavior of the researcher. This chapter explains the different points of view on paradigms. The historical background of mixed methods research, including the debate among the three methodology communities, is described. In addition, the nature of mixed methods and its rational is discussed.

Chapter 1
Implications of Mixing Methods:
Balancing Paradigmatic and Validation Distinctives

Preston B. Cosgrove
https://orcid.org/0000-0001-9256-0950
Concordia University Wisconsin, USA

ABSTRACT

Much like a jigsaw puzzle box top guides one in how to connect the pieces, a research paradigm operates as a conscious or subconscious influence in conducting a research project. The promise—and challenge—of mixed methods research is that it involves the use of two box tops, and this chapter discusses the subsequent implications on the researcher. The first effect is through the need to balance the paradigmatic distinctives, requiring the researcher to identify one of four broad ways to address the paradigm divide at the heart of qualitative and quantitative research. The second effect is through the need to balance the validation distinctives. Making research credible is an essential component of any study, and the issues magnify given the stark differences between qualitative and quantitative validity orientations. Both implications reveal the level of sophistication required for the researcher when conducting a mixed methods project.

DOI: 10.4018/978-1-7998-1025-4.ch001

INTRODUCTION: WHY SHOULD I CARE ABOUT RESEARCH PARADIGMS?

Consider the question: What is the most important part of putting a puzzle together? The most obvious answers always come first – start with the corner pieces, followed by locating the edges, and then grouping pieces of similar color. While you may consider yourself in command of the puzzle, a neutral observer would note something quite different: that the placement of those corners, edges, and colors was dictated in part by the image on the cover of the box top. The importance of that box top was so implicit and inherent that most do not identify it as an essential answer to the initial question, even though it controls most of our actions. You may be thinking that a puzzle *could* still be completed without a box top. A *simple* puzzle, perhaps. But what of advanced puzzles? The infamous Ravensburger puzzle with 32,000 pieces? 3D puzzles that do not fit within the confines of corners and edges? Or the set of "Impossibles" puzzles that are borderless, have irregular edges, and come with five extra pieces? Our perception of what the puzzle looks like will always influence our work to complete it.

Not significantly different from a puzzle box top, a research paradigm is a significant force in how one considers and conducts research. Before answering questions regarding potential data collection methods, or research designs (methodologies) to govern those methods, one must first consult the theoretical perspectives at hand (Crotty, 1998). The broader research *gestalts* are not a new phenomenon, and have their origins in the ancient debates among the Sophists, Socrates, Plato, and Aristotle about what constituted the pursuit and meaning of knowledge (Johnson & Gray, 2010). In this sense, "mixed methods" is not about the simple merger of words and numbers; it is the process of potentially balancing seemingly opposing paradigms, or attempting to fuse them to create a new, coherent idea. The "how" of that process is the focus of this chapter, with an emphasis on comprehending the nature of research paradigms, their role in the qualitative-quantitative debate, and how the researcher understands their function in a mixed-methods project. To pursue mixed-methods research without this foundation is akin to constructing a puzzle with no box top; and without that framing image to guide your hands as they move about the top of the table, you're lost. And there is nothing worse than an incomplete puzzle.

BALANCING PARADIGMATIC DISTINCTIVES

Tension: The Qualitative-Quantitative Debate and the Paradigm Divide

\ten(t)-shən\ noun ~ *a state of latent hostility or opposition between individuals or groups*

An examination of the tension inherent in the qualitative and quantitative debate first requires an understanding of the two terms in question. Both forms of research follow from an empirical process involving the standard collection, analysis, and interpretation of data (Leedy & Ormrod, 2010). But to describe their distinctions as a simple comparison between words (qualitative) and numbers (quantitative) is to over-generalize their fundamentally different ways of approaching the research process. Qualitative research involves emergent and inductive research designs, processes, and analyses that focus on the interpretation and meaning of phenomenon and/or participant experience in a natural setting. Conversely, quantitative research is a deductive and theory-driven approach focusing on strict measurement and control of variables within large samples and using analysis to identify statistical links among the data (Creswell, 2014; Ponterotto, 2005).

It is important to note the terminology used above. The brief descriptions articulate qualitative and quantitative *research*, not qualitative and quantitative *methods*. The distinction in terminology is critical, for as Morgan (2007) questions, is the problem "simply about how we use methods, [or does is it concern] basic issues about the nature of research" (p. 48). Biesta (2010) helps clarify by arguing that the research process or design is not innately qualitative or quantitative, but that the kinds of data obtained by a preceding method are the focus of these terms. The answer to the question then is that the crux of the dispute centers not on various methods and the corresponding types of data, but instead on the nature of social science research all together. In this context, qualitative and quantitative are clusters and categories of research designs and meanings; that is, they represent distinct approaches, or specifically paradigms (i.e. puzzle box tops) about the essence and nature of research.

The divide between paradigms was not instantaneous, but instead emerged gradually as a reaction to the dominant research archetype of positivism. (The extensive background on the historical foundations and formation of current paradigms is not revisited here, but has been documented by Johnson and Gray (2010), Teddlie and Johnson (2009a), and Teddlie and Johnson (2009b)). Positivism (or logical-positivism) represented a hyper-empiricist and deductive model of research with a belief that the natural and social world could be studied with the same approach: value-free, causal explanations, measurement of observation, and a single identifiable reality. By the mid-twentieth century, disagreements with the absolute nature of positivistic claims made it increasingly subject to critique. Phillips and Burbules (2000) explain that positivistic logic falls under the broader form of *foundationalist philosophy*, in which scholars had identified six main philosophical problems (pp. 14-25). Put simply, the attributes of positivism "[fall] short when applied to human behavior" (Mertens, 2010, p. 11). Or as Phillips and Burbules (2000) describe, ultimately, non-positivists of all stripes successfully argued that "scientists…are no less human, and no less biased and lacking in objectivity than anyone else; they work within frameworks that are just that: frameworks" (p. 1; see also Denzin, 2010). The positivist research paradigm never disappeared (and has witnessed a revival, particularly within educational research [Feuer, Towne, & Shavelson, 2002; Hammersley, 2002; Lather, 2004; Mosteller & Boruch, 2002]), but was no longer the dominant approach within the social sciences. With the reign of positivism gone, two alternative paradigms emerged. No surprise given its name, postpositivism was marked by an adherence to much of the positivistic ethos, but with modifications to many of its challenged tenets. The second approach arriving after postpositivism was constructivism (or interpretivism or naturalism), which sought to posit an understanding of research far from the positivist or postpositivist orientation.

Before a more detailed analysis of each approach, it is critical to realize how the very *understanding* of paradigm was also shifting. The historic 1962 publication of Thomas Kuhn's *The Structure of Scientific Revolutions* became responsible not only for the popularity of the term "paradigm", but also its adoption within the philosophy of science as a way to capture the various perspectives on research. Bergman (2010) remarks that, "according to Kuhn, scientific paradigms determine the kind of questions researchers ask, how these questions are to be understood, what data to collect, and how to interpret research results to derive answers to these questions" (p. 172). Despite Kuhn's (2012) admission that scholars had identified approximately two dozen ways in which 'paradigm' was used in his original text (p. 181), Morgan (2007) classified the four general versions of paradigm as understood by Kuhn: 1) Paradigms as worldviews; 2) Paradigms as epistemological stances; 3) Paradigms as shared beliefs in a research field; and 4) Paradigms as model examples (pp. 50-54). Kuhn (1962) favored the final two as appropriate understandings of paradigm, but as Morgan (2007) documents, researchers made "epistemological stances" the dominant paradigm model in the social sciences. The implication was significant, as Denscombe (2008) describes:

the focus of attention on [the philosophical] version of research paradigm both caused and reflected a shift in the nature of [the qualitative-quantitative] debate from the level of practice or outcomes to that of metaphysics. Paradigms, in this sense, concern higher level belief systems and the way these link with research questions. ...the methodological debate [shifted] from the level of research practice to the level of theoretical principles. (p. 275)

No longer were qualitative and quantitative seen simply as different research approaches; rather, they were now nested in broader paradigms conceptualized by various philosophical orientations, and as a result, research distinctions gave way to paradigm dichotomies.

Philosophical Foundations

In order to understand the nature of post-positivistic and constructivistic paradigms, we must explore the embedded philosophical foundations. Answers to the following questions help identify the core characteristics of each research paradigm:

- *Epistemology*: What is the theory of knowledge and the researcher-participant relationship?
- *Ontology*: What is the nature and role of reality?
- *Axiology*: What is the nature and role of values?
- *Causality*: What is the role and possibility of causal relationships?
- *Generalizability*: What is the role and possibility generalizing knowledge beyond the sample?
- *Logic*: What is the nature and role of theory?
- *Method*: What is the means by which the researcher gathers knowledge?

Table 1 illustrates the ways in which post-positivistic and constructivistic paradigms address these foundational questions.

Table 1. Traditional research paradigms and philosophical orientations

		Research Paradigm	
		Post-positivim	**Constructivism**
Philosophical Orientation	Epistemology	Knowledge is objectively discovered with the researcher independent of the data	Knowledge is subjectively constructed with interaction between researcher and participants
	Ontology	A single reality that is knowable based upon agreed limits of probability	Intangible realities that are holistic and context-bound
	Axiology	The influence of values in research can be checked and controlled	All research is value-bound by the context and interpretations from the researcher and participant
	Possibility for Causalities	Research can lead to an identification of causes and effects, within a specified probability	Research can make credible inferences with explanations made in the natural context
	Possibility for Generalizations	Critical to seek conditions leading to broad, context-free generalizations	Less important, with an emphasis on specific, context-bound theories
	Logic	Primarily deductive	Primarily inductive
	Methods	Primarily quantitative	Primarily qualitative

Table adapted from work by Creswell (2011), Crotty (1998), Mertens (2010), Ponterotto (2005), Teddlie and Tashakkori (2009)

It is important to know that positivism/post-positivism and constructivism are not the only research paradigms. The table above could include multiple versions of critical theory (race, pedagogy, etc.), feminist ideology, and post-modernist, among others. The paradigms in question are highlighted because they are not only the foundational philosophies behind quantitative and qualitative research, they also represent the opposing ends of a spectrum.

The qualitative-quantitative divide widened in part because of the zero-sum nature of the debate. With a theoretical/philosophical basis for paradigm, the division between the two was quickly labeled as an "incompatibility thesis" (Howe, 1988, p. 10). Incompatible could seem absolute, particularly given the arguments that research paradigms fall on a continuum (Teddlie & Tashakkori, 2009). But as Guba (1990) reminded us, answers to the kinds of questions above, "are the starting points or givens…[that] cannot be proven or disproven in any foundational sense" (p. 18). Biesta (2010) also discussed the problem of theoretically-driven understandings of paradigms by stating that they

bring under one heading a range of different ideas and assumptions that do not necessarily have to go together. This tends to make the notion of paradigm into a container concept and leads to a situation in which paradigms have to be embraced or rejected in a wholesale manner rather than letting the discussion focus on smaller elements. (p. 98)

The result has been the production of two independent box tops displaying very different pictures, with each believing they are the fulfillment of Dewey's 1966 proclamation that "we know some methods of inquiry are better than others" (p. 104).

Texture: Mixed-Methods Research as a Paradigmatic Bridge

\teks-chər\ noun ~ *something composed of closely interwoven elements*

As others in this volume describe, mixed-methods research is an alternative in the qualitative-quantitative debate. Researchers advocating this bridge refused to "reduce one's opponents to stereotyped paradigms," which, as Shadish (1995) claimed, "is an intellectually lazy solution to an intellectually important set of problems" (p. 49). While Teddlie and Tashakkori (2010) argue that there are nine broad characteristics most scholars would agree upon, mixed-methods research still lacks a common definition in several senses: When does the mixing occur in the research process? How much breadth does the mixing involve? Why is mixing being used? What is being mixed in the first place? Despite Johnson, Onwuegbuzie, and Turner's (2007, p. 123) composite definition, it is critical to understand that there is incongruity in the mixed-methods community about some fundamental components. As a result, it should not be surprising that even though mixed methods broadly helps address the qualitative-quantitative debate, there are various positions about just how that paradigmatic bridge takes shape (Shannon-Baker, 2015). The uniqueness of these stances hold implications for those considering the potential use of mixed-methods in a research project.

Bridge #1: Mixed Methods Research has its Own Distinct Paradigm

Scholars advocating this position believe that there are unique presuppositions underlying mixed methods research that do not align with post-positivism or constructivism. The most prevalent paradigm articulated is pragmatism. Historically derived from the philosophies of William James and John Dewey, pragmatism in the twentieth century moved through three periods of relevance (Maxcy, 2003), before Howe's 1988 argument for a pragmatic research approach in the social sciences signaled a rejection of the incompatibility thesis. As an alternative, the pragmatist paradigm "sidesteps the contentious issues of truth and reality, accepts, philosophically, that there are singular and multiple realities that are open to empirical inquiry and orients itself toward solving practical problems in the "real world"" (Feilzer, 2010, p. 8). The specifics of pragmatism as a distinctive paradigm are contingent on the author [see Biesta (2010); Johnson & Onwuegbuzie (2004); Teddlie & Tashakkori (2009)], but Morgan's (2007) analysis provides a general understanding of the pragmatic alternative's response to three paradigmatic dualisms: 1) an *abductive* form of logic that employs both deductive and inductive reasoning; 2) an *intersubjective* approach that rejects the near impossibility of either complete objectivity or subjectivity; and 3) *transferability* of results that moves away from the dichotomy of outcomes that are either generalizable or only context-specific. Despite claims that a pragmatic paradigm skews toward a post-positivist orientation (Giddings, 2006), it remains the dominant option for a single-paradigm approach.

But pragmatism is not the sole paradigmatic alternative for mixed methods research. Mertens' (2010) transformative paradigm has become a broadly recognize option that goes beyond the pragmatic nature described above. And as a distinct paradigm, it includes scholars whose research confronts directly social oppression in myriad ways: critical theorists, feminists, Marxists, etc. Mertens (2010) identifies four primary characteristics for the transformative paradigm: 1) it centers on the experiences of marginalized and oppressed groups; 2) it offers an analysis of how inequity is reflected in traditional demographic groups (gender, race, etc.); 3) it offers an examination of the effect of inquiry on social/political action; and 4) it's philosophical orientation is immersed in transformative theory and philosophy (p. 21). The transformative paradigm has also been adopted to address concerns that mixed-methods research lacks an advocacy purpose with an emphasis on social justice. Indeed, with its unique focus, the transformative worldview allows for a mixed-methods approach, but without losing the emancipatory inclinations traditionally located in the constructivist arena (Sweetman, Badiee, & Creswell, 2010).

The third alternative is the critical realist paradigm, although its adoption as a single mixed-methods approach is much less formal and recognized than the pragmatic and transformative. While Maxwell and Mittapalli (2010) do not think realism should constitute a distinct paradigmatic approach, they do argue that "as a philosophical perspective that validates and supports key aspects of both qualitative and quantitative approaches while identifying some specific limitations of each, realism can constitute a productive stance for mixed methods research and can facilitate a more effective collaboration between qualitative and quantitative researchers" (p. 146). Specifically, the critical realist is an ontological cousin of post-positivists, yet affirms the epistemological character of the constructivist (Krauss, 2005). Critical realism represents a definitive philosophical approach, but given that it has not been identified as a mixed methods paradigm with the same formality as pragmatism or transformative, readers should consult Maxwell and Mittapalli (2010) for a more comprehensive take.

Bridge #2: Multiple Paradigms Should be used in Mixed Methods Research

This position has been promoted primarily by Greene and Carcelli (1997), who label it as the dialectical perspective. In this approach, the differences among the various paradigms and philosophical orientations are recognized, and the researcher should ensure the integrity of any paradigm in question. That said, "[multiple paradigms] should be deliberately used both within and across studies toward a dialectical discovery of enhanced understandings, of new and revisioned perspectives and meanings" (p. 8). The dialectical approach rejects the pursuit for a solitary paradigm, and that mixed methods should take advantage of the benefits that unique research paradigms bring. Indeed, Greene (2007) has more recently stated that a mixed methods research project should involve "the planned and intentional incorporation" of diverse paradigms in the research inquiry (p. 30). Critical to this paradigmatic bridge is the ability to actively engage with and balance the tension created from the juxtaposition of contrasting ideas (Tashakorri & Teddlie. 2010, p. 811). But as Shannon-Baker (2015) observes, such tension brings benefits as well. Not only does such a stance avoid taking sides in the paradigm war, but it can "address convergent and divergent ideas… [and be] useful for studies with conflicting data sets/theoretical stances" (p. 5)

Bridge #3: Multiple Paradigms can be used as it Supports the Mixed Methods Research Design

The third bridge directs the researcher back to the research design and the type of paradigm(s) required to conduct the study. Creswell and Plano Clark (2011) serve as the advocates for this position, which is ultimately driven by the nature of the research question and the specific design. If the mixed-methods design is concurrent or parallel, a single paradigm such as transformative or pragmatic could be utilized. But in a sequential study, Creswell (2009) argues that it only makes sense for the researcher's paradigm to shift (post-positivist to constructivist, or vice-versa) depending on the data collection method. This understanding acknowledges the *potential* role of the first bridge, in contrast to the dialectical interpretation, and it only disagrees with the second bridge in that the research question/design should drive the use of multiple paradigms, and not an indiscriminating "planned and intentional" merger (Greene, 2007, p. 30).

Bridge #4: Mixed Methods Research can Operate Free from Paradigmatic Constraints

Three different perspectives form the narrative for this bridge. Argued by Morgan (2007) and Denscombe (2008), the first questions the application of philosophical orientations as the primary understanding for the concept of paradigm. As observed earlier, the adoption of a more theoretical frame for paradigm led, in part, to the incompatibility between research traditions. Morgan (2007) in particular challenged the role of epistemological influence, questioning "to what extent to metaphysical assumptions guide our research?" (p. 63). Instead, he favored Kuhn's (1962) third conceptualization focused on the shared beliefs within a field of research; or as Creswell and Plano Clark (2011) describe, paradigms as understood by the "scholarly community" (p. 46). No longer restricted by notions that particular paradigmatic assumptions govern an entire discipline, researchers can acknowledge that, practically, the social sciences has tended to concentrate on "beliefs and practices…in specific subfields" (Morgan, 2007, p. 53). Denscombe (2008) expanded the idea by advocating for "communities of practice" to determine the nature of paradigmatic assumptions. Generally credited to the work of Lave and Wegner (1991), communities of practice allow for a more malleable notion of paradigm to fit the various discipline arenas, orientations, inquiry traditions out of which research operates, which makes mixed methods research a much less paradigmatic challenge (Denscombe, 2008, p. 278).

The second perspective accepts philosophical foundations for paradigms, but rejects the fidelity and purity of a singular constructivist or post-positivist model. Maxwell and Loomis' (2003) work informs this perspective best, building off the research of McGawley (1982), Pitman and Maxwell (1990), and Sayer (1992). There is recognition of general "philosophical and methodological resonances" among various paradigmatic components, but that ultimately, they are just that: a bundle of components (Maxwell & Loomis, 2003, p. 250). While scholars can be in agreement about the holistic nature of a research paradigm, there can still be sharp disagreement about how the specific components are operationalized and the corresponding effects. The result, Teddlie and Tashakorri (2009) observe, is that mixing qualitative and quantitative does not have the dangerous philosophical consequences one might believe, because if "the two research paradigms are not 'pure' to begin with, researchers lose little when they creatively mix them" (p. 98).

The third perspective is perhaps the most radical, but also the simplest to describe. As Patton (2002) argues,

While these intellectual, philosophical, and theoretical traditions have greatly influenced the debate…[there is no need to] swear vows of allegiance to any single epistemological perspective. …Indeed, [researchers need not] be concerned about theory. …in real world practice, methods can be separated from the epistemology out of which they have emerged. (p. 136)

This stance has been labeled "a-paradigmatic" given the refusal to recognize the integrity of any philosophically-infused paradigm. Others, such as Morgan (2007), could theoretically fit here, but in those cases, the author is often questioning the utility or role of the traditionally-understood paradigm, not making an unequivocal statement similar to Patton (2002).

BALANCING VALIDATION DISTINCTIVES

/vəˈlidədē/ noun ~ *the quality of being well-grounded, sound, or correct*

Regardless of the paradigmatic bridge, there are significant implications to the blend of ontological and epistemological realities in how one understands and approaches validity. Hardly just a technique or component of the research design, validity carries its own weight, since "the crux of the issue… [is] how scientific knowledge is made credible" (Lather, 2007, p. 5161). What, then, is validity? Broadly, scholarly definitions of validity are similar and focus on importance of *inference*:

- From experimental and quasi-experimental scholars: "Validity is a property of inferences. It is not a property of designs or methods" (Shadish, Cook, & Campbell, 2002, p. 34).

- From mixed-methods scholars: "Validity refers not to the data but to the inferences drawn from them" (Creswell & Miller, 2000, p. 125).
- From qualitative scholars: "Validity is generally understood…as the trustworthiness of inferences drawn from data" (Freeman, deMarrais, Preissle, Roulston, & St. Pierre, 2007, p. 27).

The challenge arrives with the paradigmatic distinctions around what reality is, how we can know it, and the corresponding effect on what constitutes a credible inference. The following sections detail how such inferences are drawn in both postpositivist and constructivist paradigms. The goal is not to address comprehensively all validity conventions within quantitative and qualitative research. Rather—through providing some representative specifics for each—to prompt epistemological and pragmatic awareness about how a researcher has to navigate such differences in a mixed methods project.

Validation in Quantitative Research

It is essential to start with the reminder that quantitative research is not quantitative because of its method, but because of its paradigmatic foundation: Where knowledge is objectively discovered with the researcher independent of the data; where a single reality is knowable based upon agreed limits of probability; and where the influence of values can be checked and controlled. Perhaps it is unsurprising then, that for the quantitative component(s) of a mixed methods project, the researcher would follow more standardized validation processes or techniques. Included here will be an overview of two of the most common forms of quantitative research: Experimental and Survey research.

Within the various manifestations of experimental research, the randomized control trial (RCT) has long been considered the gold standard. This because as Sullivan (2011) identifies, RCTs are "quantitative, comparative, controlled experiments in which treatment effect sizes may be determined with less bias than observational trials" (p. 285). In other words, the experimental RCT allows the researcher to make causal conclusions. But in order to identify such cause and effect results, the mixed method scholar must address the classical threats to internal validity: the ability to determine if A-caused-B. First articulated by Campbell and Stanley (1963) in their landmark text *Experimental and Quasi-Experimental Designs for Research*, the threats must be mitigated to ensure the veracity of the RCTs claims to causality. Campbell and Stanley (1963) initially identified eight such threats to internal validity: history, maturation, testing, instrumentation, statistical regression, differential selection, experimental mortality, and selection-maturation interaction (p. 5), with Cook and Campbell's (1979) addition of other threats. Those interested in specifics and analysis on each threat should consult Mitchell and Jolley (2010, pp. 304-333) and Shadish, Cook, and Campbell (2002, pp. 53-62).

Internal validity is but one component within an experimental or quasi-experimental design. The mixed methods researcher also needs to be acquainted with statistical conclusion validity, construct validity, and external validity (Shadish, Cook, & Campbell, 2002, p. 38). Statistical conclusion validity involves the traditional Null Hypothesis Significance Testing and corresponding p-values and effect size indices, while Construct validity is discussed below. Most pertinent to an experiment or RCT is external validity. Where internal validity is concerned with the identification of cause-effect relationships, external validity is the extent to which the causal conclusions can be generalized to other contexts. What is critical is that "other contexts" does not simply mean other people. This is one form of external validity: population validity, where the results may hold true for participants not included in the original study. But as Johnson and Christensen (2012) assess, external validity needs to be considered from other perspectives: ecological (generalized across settings), temporal (generalized across time), treatment variation (generalized across differences in the treatment), and outcome (generalized across other, similar dependent variables) (pp. 257-260). Again, those interested in specifics and analysis on each type should consult Shadish, Cook, and Campbell (2002, pp. 83-93) and Mertens (2010, pp. 129-131).

While RCTs and other forms of experimental research may be the quantitative gold standard, survey research has become one of the most widely used forms of social science inquiry (Rea & Parker, 2014). Fundamentally a survey allows one to be able to describe, compare, explain, or test, the knowledge, opinions/attitudes, previous experiences, feelings, behaviors, or characteristics of a sample. As a result, mixed methods scholars need to understand the how and why of survey validation: either due to the necessity of developing their own instrument, or to evaluate the validity (or stated validity) of an existing instrument.

In either case, one must assess for various forms of validity within the survey (Litwin, 2003). The simplest is face validity, which is the extent to which an instrument looks like it is measuring a particular characteristic. Scholars can evaluate for face validity using content experts, survey experts, and potential participants, via respondent debriefing and cognitive interviewing (Hardesty & Bearden, 2004). Content validity must also be determined, in which the instrument should show that it fairly or comprehensively covers the domain or items that is purports to cover and that there is justification for the items included in the survey. Content validity can also be achieved using content experts, a thorough review of the literature, and/or a panel of experts (Rubio, Berg-Weger, Tebb, Lee, & Rauch, 2003). The most important type is construct validity, which is the extent to which an instrument is *actually* measuring the latent characteristics that cannot be directly observed.

As Litwin (2003) describes, "construct validity is the most valuable and yet the most difficult way of assessing a survey instrument. It is difficult to understand, to measure, and to report" (p. 41). One of the primary methods for determining construct validity is exploratory or confirmatory factor analysis. Indeed, as Thompson and Daniel (1996) state, "factor analysis and construct validity have long been associated with each other" (p. 197). The challenge is ensuring both the proper use and interpretation of the factor analysis. And as numerous scholars have argued, not only do researchers continue to engage in the questionable use of factor analysis, but also through ambiguous and arbitrary justification in the analysis of the results (Fabrigar, Wegener, MacCallum, & Strahan, 1999; Preacher & MacCallum, 2003).

This then is the quantitative validation context for the mixed methods research. Whether through experimental research, RCT, survey development and evaluation, the researcher's approach to validity must adhere to a paradigmatic reality that is objective, controlled, and deductive, with clearly defined variables, and an eye toward causality.

Validation in Qualitative Research

Similar to the last section, starting with the context of qualitative research is critical. That qualitative research is not qualitative because of its method, but because of its paradigmatic foundation: Where knowledge is socially constructed with interaction between the researcher and participant; where reality is intangible, holistic, and context-bound; and where the entire project is laden with the values of the individuals and setting. In this realm, the mixed methods researcher must be ready for a very distinct validation approach.

Perhaps the best way to introduce such differences is through metaphor. Consider the process for falling asleep. One goes through an often subconscious routine, but to fall sleep is beyond command. Sleep's arrival comes only after certain conditions are honored. As Smith (2013) describes, I must "put myself in a posture and rhythm that welcomes sleep…a kind of active welcome" (pp 65-66). Falling asleep, then, is a fitting metaphor for approaching validity in qualitative research. Unlike many quantitative methodologies, one cannot choose to "confirm" validity through techniques. And it is this lack of control that is best captured by Seale's (1999) repeated portrayal of quality in qualitative research as an "elusive phenomenon" (p. 20). The difficulty is that the literature on qualitative validity is often zero-sum in its approach: overly-dense or overly-simple (Morse, Barrett, Mayan, Olson, & Spiers, 2002). Either way, all researchers know that per Wolcott's (1990) oft-used dictum, "whatever validity is, [they] apparently 'have' or 'get' or 'satisfy' or 'demonstrate' or 'establish' it (p. 121). And to complete the metaphor, as the analysis below demonstrates, those seeking a confirmatory qualitative "validity" may never fall asleep.

Given its unique ontology and epistemology, the validation of qualitative research should follow its own path. That said, much of the discourse on qualitative validity stems from Lincoln and Guba's historic 1985 analysis of trustworthiness criteria for naturalistic inquiry. The authors took the classic validity classifications from quantitative-based research and transposed each into a more qualitatively-appropriate context:

- internal validity→credibility
- external validity→ transferability
- reliability→dependability
- objectivity→ confirmability

The authors also identified a set of specific techniques to help confirm validity within each area. For example, credibility could be achieved via prolonged engagement, triangulation, and member-checking, among other techniques. Although the eventual proposal of four criterion areas with aligned techniques has proven helpful, the origins of the framework made it susceptible to critique, given that it built from a quantitative orientation. The criticism of Lincoln and Guba's (1985) work focused on how its origins tacitly promoted the superiority of a post-positivist ontological outlook. For that was the starting point, the gold standard, by which qualitative approaches would subsequently be built and oriented. By 2001 Lincoln acknowledged they "realized [the criteria] were rooted in the concerns of positivist inquiry, but were not sure how to proceed without breaking free of those mandates" (p. 34). And eventually, Guba and Lincoln (1989) and Lincoln (1995) re-conceptualized their validity orientations within a qualitative epistemology.

The analysis of Lincoln and Guba's (1985) framework went beyond its paradigmatic origins, and the epistemic reactions focused instead on the consequences of using broad-based standards. One such response rejected the rote validity criteria, which Schwandt (1996) labeled as "criteriology." The issue was not with the techniques themselves that Lincoln and Guba had identified, but rather in a Cartesian quest for criteria that were permanent and standardized. Committing such criteriology leads to what Barbour (2001) called "a case of the tail wagging the dog" (p. 1115). A second response has been the proliferation of validity understandings from various emancipatory and deconstructive orientations (Lincoln, 2001), with the argument for validity dialogues and control to remain within paradigmatic and methodological communities (Freeman, deMarrais, Preissle, Roulston, & St. Pierre, 2007).

The theoretical and methodological challenges for the mixed methods researcher involves actually adopting a non-normative-based mindset toward qualitative validity. While the character of qualitative inquiry demands a highly-reflexive and situated validity, the enchantment with quantitative research validity approaches are ubiquitous. This, in-part, because the "regulatory validity that polices the borders between 'science' and 'not-science'" provides a clear demarcation of, and formulaic checklist for, valid research (Lather, 2001, p. 246). Broadly then, the mixed methods scholar enters a research domain controlled by positivistic orientations around the "politics of evidence" (Denzin, 2009, p. 139; St. Pierre & Roulston, 2006); and specifically, scholars will confront recommendations that persistently promote the 1985 framework or technique-only efforts.

An *a priori* set of validity techniques are not consummate with research grounded in qualitative epistemologies, and thus require an approach tailored to the study. For the mixed methods researcher, that tailoring can occur in two ways. First is through a process-orientated validation approach which is fluid and emergent compared to restrictive techniques. The distinction is not new and has its origins in Mischler's (1990) proposal to "redefine validation as [a] process(es)…rather than validity" (p. 419; see also Koro-Ljungberg, 2008). Second, the process should engage in the identification of threats to the researcher's ability to describe and interpret. The importance of qualitative description is essential to a qualitative epistemology (Merriam, 2009; Patton, 2002), with Wolcott's (2009) reminder that "description provides the foundation upon which qualitative inquiry rests" (p. 27). Similarly, qualitative inquiry has always been understood as a broad "set of complex interpretative practices" (Denzin & Lincoln, 2011, p. 6).

Focusing on one's fundamental ability to describe and interpret is then paramount. And using threat identification to those essential characteristics resists the checklist mentality of most validity classifications. Mischler (1990) argues that evaluation of the "respective threats to [validity] turned out…to be a death-blow to the typology approach" (p. 418). As a result, defaulting to criteriology is no longer a given, since the threats are always unique to specific study. As Seale (1999) observes, "the use of 'threats' requires an imaginative effort by the researcher to enter the minds of potential critics. They are devices for encouraging methodological awareness, as well as setting up an internal dialogue" (p. 39). Ultimately, threat identification is not used to arrive at a set of "correct" or formal techniques. But rather to prompt critical consideration of the hazards to a descriptive and interpretive validation process. And once potential threats are acknowledged, the researcher should find the suitable strategies, techniques, and processes to manage them. Such strategies should include, but not be limited to, traditional validity techniques. And throughout the entire process, the mixed methods scholar should embrace a reflexive posture. Reflexivity, the increased awareness to one's own subjectivity in the research process, has long been embraced in qualitative research (Finlay, 2002). And as Altheide and Johnson (1998) remark, there is now affirmation that "*how* knowledge is acquired, organized, and interpreted is relevant to *what* the claims are" (p. 486).

CONCLUSION

The preceding discussion has established the paradigmatic and validation distinctives at the heart of mixed methods research. For validity, the overview of quantitative and qualitative approaches highlights just how stark the differences are. The mixed methods researcher needs to ensure that the respective approach(es) are used accordingly during the project. The challenge is that not only are many researchers predisposed to quantitative validity classifications (Lester & O'Reilly, 2015), there continues to a widespread captivation of such orientations at the expense of qualitative processes (Lather, 2004; Stronach, 2006). As celebrated qualitative scholar Norman Denzin (2009) laments, the widespread embrace of quantitative epistemologies *within* qualitative inquiry is "like an elephant in the living room...whose presence can no longer be ignored" (p. 139). Moving forward, the mixed methods researcher needs to ensure that both quantitatively-and-qualitatively-appropriate validation approaches and processes are used within their respective parts of the project.

For the paradigmatic roots, it is critical to clarify that while a research box top dictates one's actions and decisions, the *research question* determines which paradigm the study resides in. As Bryman (2006) states, "the research question... relegates epistemological and ontological debates to the sidelines...[and] clears the path for research that combines quantitative and qualitative research" (p. 118). Or as Tashakkori and Teddlie (1998) famously described in their first book, the research question holds a "dictatorship" over everything else (p. 20). This is not to say the research question is a trump card *over* paradigms; rather that it *informs* and *drives* the type of paradigm, and corresponding methodology and methods, required to sufficiently answer the question, using one of the four bridges described above. As a result, mixed-methods research should not be chosen independent of one's research purpose because of an assumption that the approach will yield "better" conclusions. Instead, it should be selected "when the quantitative or qualitative approach, each by itself, is inadequate to best understand a research problem" (Creswell, 2014, p. 20). When this is the case, it is imperative to frame the research question appropriately so that it both addresses the research problem and directs the researcher toward a mixed-methods design (Onwuegbuzie and Leech [2006] and Plano-Clark and Badiee [2010] offer in-depth guides with recommendations, considerations, and techniques). What is missing in many research studies is an understanding of this interconnectedness throughout the entire project; or as Crotty (1998) argues, the link among epistemology (paradigm), theoretical perspective, methodology, and methods (pp. 2-3). After all, putting a puzzle together does not have to be overly strenuous, but it does require coherent planning, execution, and clear insight into the power and implications of the box top picture itself.

REFERENCES

Altheide, D., & Johnson, J. (1998). Criteria for assessing interpretive validity in qualitative research. In N. Denzin & Y. Lincoln (Eds.), *Collecting and interpreting qualitative materials* (pp. 283–312). Thousand Oaks, CA: Sage.

Barbour, R. S. (2001). Checklists for improving rigour in qualitative research: A case of the tail wagging the dog? *BMJ (Clinical Research Ed.)*, *322*(7294), 1115–1117. doi:10.1136/bmj.322.7294.1115 PMID:11337448

Bergman, M. M. (2010). On concepts and paradigms in mixed methods research. *Journal of Mixed Methods Research*, *4*(3), 171–175. doi:10.1177/1558689810376950

Biesta, G. (2010). Pragmatism and the philosophical foundations of mixed methods research. In A. Tashakkori & C. Teddlie (Eds.), *SAGE Handbook of Mixed Methods in Social & Behavioral Research* (2nd ed., pp. 95–118). Thousand Oaks, CA: Sage. doi:10.4135/9781506335193.n4

Bryman, A. (2006). Paradigm peace and the implications for quality. *International Journal of Social Research Methodology Theory and Practice*, *9*(2), 111–126. doi:10.1080/13645570600595280

Campbell, D. T., & Stanley, J. C. (1963). *Experimental and quasi-experimental designs for research*. Boston: Houghton Mifflin Company.

Cook, T. D., & Campbell, D. T. (1979). *Quasi-experimentation: Design & analysis issues for field settings*. Boston: Houghton Mifflin Company.

Creswell, J. W. (2009). Editorial: Mapping the field of mixed methods research. *Journal of Mixed Methods Research*, *3*(2), 95–108. doi:10.1177/1558689808330883

Creswell, J. W. (2014). *Research design: Qualitative, quantitative, and mixed methods approaches* (4th ed.). Los Angeles, CA: Sage.

Creswell, J. W., & Miller, D. L. (2000). Determining validity in qualitative inquiry. *Theory into Practice*, *39*(3), 124–130. doi:10.120715430421tip3903_2

Creswell, J. W., & Plano Clark, V. L. (2011). *Designing and conducting mixed methods research* (2nd ed.). Thousand Oaks, CA: Sage.

Crotty, M. (1998). *The foundations of social research: Meaning and perspective in the research process*. London: Sage Publications.

Denscombe, M. (2008). Communities of practice: A research paradigm for the mixed methods approach. *Journal of Mixed Methods Research*, *2*(3), 270–283. doi:10.1177/1558689808316807

Denzin, N. K. (2009). The elephant in the living room: Or extending the conversation about the politics of evidence. *Qualitative Research*, *9*(2), 139–160. doi:10.1177/1468794108098034

Denzin, N. K. (2010). Moments, mixed methods, and paradigm dialogs. *Qualitative Inquiry*, *16*(6), 419–427. doi:10.1177/1077800410364608

Denzin, N. K., & Lincoln, Y. S. (2011). Introduction: The discipline and practice of qualitative research. In N. K. Denzin & Y. S. Lincoln (Eds.), *The SAGE handbook of qualitative research* (4th ed.; pp. 1–19). Thousand Oaks, CA: Sage.

Dewey, J. (1966). *Logic: They theory of inquiry*. New York: Henry Holt.

Fabrigar, L. R., Wegener, D. T., MacCallum, R. C., & Strahan, E. J. (1999). Evaluating the use of exploratory factor analysis in psychological research. *Psychological Methods*, *4*(3), 272–299. doi:10.1037/1082-989X.4.3.272

Feilzer, M. Y. (2010). Doing mixed methods research pragmatically: Implications for the rediscovery of pragmatism as a research paradigm. *Journal of Mixed Methods Research*, *4*(1), 6–16. doi:10.1177/1558689809349691

Feuer, M. J., Towne, L., & Shavelson, R. J. (2002). Scientific culture and educational research. *Educational Researcher*, *31*(8), 4–14. doi:10.3102/0013189X031008004

Finlay, L. (2002). "Outing" the researcher: The provenance, process, and practice of reflexivity. *Qualitative Health Research*, *12*(4), 531–545. doi:10.1177/104973202129120052 PMID:11939252

Freeman, M., deMarrais, K., Preissle, J., Roulston, K., & St. Pierre, E. A. (2007). Standards of evidence in qualitative research: An incitement to discourse. *Educational Researcher*, *36*(1), 25–32. doi:10.3102/0013189X06298009

Giddings, L. S. (2006). Mixed-methods research: Positivism dressed in drag? *Journal of Research in Nursing*, *11*(3), 195–203. doi:10.1177/1744987106064635

Greene, J. C. (2007). *Mixing methods in social inquiry*. San Francisco: Jossey-Bass.

Greene, J. C., & Caracelli, V. J. (1997). Defining and describing the paradigm issue in mixed- method evaluation. In J. C. Green & V. J. Caracelli (Eds.), *Advances in Mixed-Method Evaluation: The Challenges and Benefits of Integrating Diverse Paradigms* (pp. 5–18). San Francisco: Jossey-Bass. doi:10.1002/ev.1068

Guba, E. C. (1990). The alternative paradigm dialogue. In E. C. Guba (Ed.), *The Paradigm Dialogue* (pp. 17–27). Newbury Park, CA: Sage.

Guba, E. G., & Lincoln, Y. S. (1989). *Fourth Generation Evaluation*. Newbury Park, CA: Sage.

Hammersley, M. (2002). *Educational research, policymaking and practice*. London: Sage. doi:10.4135/9781849209083

Hardesty, D. M., & Bearden, W. O. (2004). The use of expert judges in scale development: Implications for improving face validity of measures of unobservable constructs. *Journal of Business Research*, *57*(2), 98–107. doi:10.1016/S0148-2963(01)00295-8

Howe, K. R. (1988). Against the quantitative-qualitative incompatibility thesis or dogmas die hard. *Educational Researcher, 17*(8), 10-16.

Johnson, B., & Gray, R. (2010). A history of philosophical and theoretical issues for mixed methods research. In A. Tashakkori & C. Teddlie (Eds.), *SAGE Handbook of Mixed Methods in Social & Behavioral Research* (2nd ed.; pp. 69–94). Thousand Oaks, CA: Sage. doi:10.4135/9781506335193.n3

Johnson, R. B., & Christensen, L. (2012). *Educational research: Quantitative, qualitative, and mixed approaches* (4th ed.). Thousand Oaks, CA: Sage.

Johnson, R. B., & Onwuegbuzie, A. J. (2004). Mixed methods research: A research paradigm whose time has come. *Educational Researcher*, *33*(7), 14–26. doi:10.3102/0013189X033007014

Johnson, R. B., Onwuegbuzie, A. J., & Turner, L. A. (2007). Toward a definition of mixed methods research. *Journal of Mixed Methods Research*, *1*(2), 112–133. doi:10.1177/1558689806298224

Koro-Ljungberg, M. (2008). Validity and validation in the making in the context of qualitative research. *Qualitative Health Research*, *18*(7), 983–989. doi:10.1177/1049732308318039 PMID:18552324

Krauss, S. E. (2005). Research paradigms and meaning making: A primer. *Qualitative Report*, *10*(4), 758–770.

Kuhn, T. S. (1962). *The structure of scientific revolutions*. Chicago: The University of Chicago Press.

Kuhn, T. S. (2012). *The structure of scientific revolutions* (4th ed.). Chicago: The University of Chicago Press. doi:10.7208/chicago/9780226458144.001.0001

Lather, P. (2001). Validity as an incitement to discourse: Qualitative research and the crisis of legitimation. In V. Richardson (Ed.), *Handbook of research on teaching* (4th ed.; pp. 241–250). Washington, DC: American Educational Research Association.

Lather, P. (2004). This *IS* your father's paradigm: Government intrusion and the case of qualitative research in education. *Qualitative Inquiry, 10*(1), 15–34. doi:10.1177/1077800403256154

Lather, P. (2007). Validity, Qualitative. In G. Ritzer (Ed.), *The Blackwell Encyclopedia of Sociology* (pp. 5169–5173). Malden, MA: Blackwell Publishing. doi:10.1002/9781405165518.wbeosv001

Lave, J., & Wenger, E. (1991). *Situated learning: Legitimate peripheral participation.* Cambridge, UK: Cambridge University Press. doi:10.1017/CBO9780511815355

Leedy, P. D., & Ormrod, J. E. (2013). *Practical research: Planning and design* (10th ed.). Boston: Pearson.

Lester, J. N., & O'Reilly, M. (2015). Is evidence-based practice a threat to the progress of the qualitative community? Arguments from the bottom of the pyramid. *Qualitative Inquiry, 21*(7), 628–632. doi:10.1177/1077800414563808

Lincoln, Y. S. (1995). Emerging criteria for quality in qualitative and interpretive research. *Qualitative Inquiry, 1*(3), 275–289. doi:10.1177/107780049500100301

Lincoln, Y. S. (2001). Varieties of validity: Quality in qualitative research. In J. C. Smart & W. G. Tierney (Eds.), *Higher Education: Handbook of Theory and Research* (pp. 25–72). New York: Agathon Press.

Lincoln, Y. S., & Guba, E. G. (1985). *Naturalistic Inquiry.* Newbury Park, CA: Sage. doi:10.1016/0147-1767(85)90062-8

Litwin, M. S. (2003). *How to assess and interpret survey psychometrics* (2nd ed.). Thousand Oaks, CA: Sage. doi:10.4135/9781412984409

Maxcy, S. J. (2003). Pragmatic threads in mixed methods research in the social sciences: The search for multiple modes of inquiry and the end of the philosophy of formalism. In A. Tashakkori & C. Teddlie (Eds.), *Handbook of Mixed Methods in Social & Behavioral Research* (pp. 51–90). Thousand Oaks, CA: Sage.

Maxwell, J. A., & Loomis, D. M. (2003). Mixed methods design: An alternative approach. In A. Tashakkori & C. Teddlie (Eds.), *Handbook of Mixed Methods in Social & Behavioral Research* (pp. 241–271). Thousand Oaks, CA: Sage.

Maxwell, J. A., & Mittapalli, K. (2010). Realism as a stance for mixed methods research. In A. Tashakkori & C. Teddlie (Eds.), *SAGE Handbook of Mixed Methods in Social & Behavioral Research* (2nd ed.; pp. 145–162). Thousand Oaks, CA: Sage. doi:10.4135/9781506335193.n6

McGawley, J. (1982). *Thirty million theories of grammar*. Chicago: University of Chicago Press.

Merriam, S. B. (2009). *Qualitative research: A guide to design and implementation* (3rd ed.). San Francisco: Jossey-Bass.

Mertens, D. M. (2010). *Research and evaluation in education and psychology: Integrating diversity with quantitative, qualitative, and mixed methods* (3rd ed.). Thousand Oaks, CA: Sage.

Mishler, E. G. (1990). Validation in inquiry-guided research: The role of exemplars in narrative studies. *Harvard Educational Review*, *60*(4), 415–442. doi:10.17763/haer.60.4.n4405243p6635752

Mitchell, M. L., & Jolley, J. M. (2010). *Research design explained* (7th ed.). Belmont, CA: Wadsworth.

Morgan, D. L. (2007). Paradigms lost and pragmatism regained: Methodological implications of combining qualitative and quantitative methods. *Journal of Mixed Methods Research*, *1*(1), 48–76. doi:10.1177/2345678906292462

Morse, J. M., Barrett, M., Mayan, M., Olson, K., & Spiers, J. (2002). Verification strategies for establishing reliability and validity in qualitative research. *International Journal of Qualitative Methods*, *1*(2), 13–22. doi:10.1177/160940690200100202

Mosteller, F., & Boruch, R. F. (2002). *Evidence matters: Randomized trials in education research*. Washington, DC: Brookings Institution Press.

Onwuegbuzie, A. J., & Leech, N. L. (2006). Linking research questions to mixed methods data analysis procedures. *Qualitative Report*, *11*(3), 474–498.

Patton, M. Q. (2002). *Qualitative research & evaluation methods* (3rd ed.). Thousand Oaks, CA: Sage.

Phillips, D. C., & Burbules, N. C. (2000). *Postpositivism and educational research*. Lanham, MA: Rowman & Littlefield Publishers, Inc.

Pitman, M. A., & Maxwell, J. A. (1990). Qualitative approaches to evaluation. In M. D. LeCompte, W. L. Milroy, & J. Preissle (Eds.), *The Handbook of Qualitative Research in Education* (pp. 729–770). San Diego, CA: Academic Press.

Plano-Clark, V. I., & Badiee, M. (2010). Research questions in mixed methods research. In A. Tashakkori & C. Teddlie (Eds.), *SAGE Handbook of Mixed Methods in Social & Behavioral Research* (2nd ed.; pp. 275–300). Thousand Oaks, CA: Sage. doi:10.4135/9781506335193.n12

Ponterotto, J. G. (2005). Qualitative research in counseling psychology: A primer on research paradigms and philosophy of science. *Journal of Counseling Psychology*, *52*(2), 126–136. doi:10.1037/0022-0167.52.2.126

Preacher, K. J., & MacCallum, R. C. (2003). Repairing Tom Swift's electric factor analysis machine. *Understanding Statistics*, *2*(1), 13–43. doi:10.1207/S15328031US0201_02

Rea, L. M., & Parker, R. A. (2014). *Designing and conducting survey research: A comprehensive guide* (4th ed.). San Francisco: Jossey-Bass.

Rubio, D. M., Berg-Weger, M., Tebb, S. S., Lee, E. S., & Rauch, S. (2003). Objectifying content validity: Conducting a content validity study in social work research. *Social Work Research*, *27*(2), 94–104. doi:10.1093wr/27.2.94

Sayer, A. (1992). *Method in social science: A realist approach*. London: Routledge.

Schwandt, T. A. (1996). Farewell to criteriology. *Qualitative Inquiry*, *2*(1), 58–72. doi:10.1177/107780049600200109

Seale, C. (1999). *The quality of qualitative research*. London: Sage. doi:10.4135/9780857020093

Shadish, W. R. (1995). The quantitative-qualitative debates: "Dekuhnifying" the conceptual context. *Evaluation and Program Planning*, *18*(1), 47–49. doi:10.1016/0149-7189(94)00048-3

Shadish, W. R., Cook, T. D., & Campbell, D. T. (2002). *Experimental and quasi-experimental designs for generalized causal inference* (2nd ed.). Boston: Houghton Mifflin Company.

Shannon-Baker, P. (2015). Making paradigms meaningful in mixed methods research. *Journal of Mixed Methods Research*, *10*(4), 1–16. doi:10.1177/1558689815575861

Smith, J. K. A. (2013). *Imagining the kingdom: How worship works*. Grand Rapids, MI: Baker Academic.

St. Pierre, E. A., & Roulston, K. (2006). The state of qualitative inquiry: A contested science. *International Journal of Qualitative Studies in Education: QSE*, *19*(6), 673–684. doi:10.1080/09518390600975644

Stronach, I. (2006). Enlightenment and the "heart of darkness": (Neo)imperialism in the congo, and elsewhere. *International Journal of Qualitative Studies in Education: QSE, 19*(6), 757–768. doi:10.1080/09518390600975982

Sullivan, G. M. (2011). Getting off the "gold standard": Randomized controlled trials and education research. *Journal of Graduate Medical Education, 3*(3), 285–289. doi:10.4300/JGME-D-11-00147.1 PMID:22942950

Sweetman, D., Badiee, M., & Creswell, J. W. (2010). Use of the transformative framework in mixed methods studies. *Qualitative Inquiry, 16*(6), 441–454. doi:10.1177/1077800410364610

Tashakorri, A., & Teddlie, C. (1998). *Mixed methods methodology: Combining the qualitative and quantitative approaches*. Thousand Oaks, CA: Sage.

Tashakorri, A., & Teddlie, C. (2010). Epilogue: Current developments and emerging trends in integrated research methodology. In A. Tashakkori & C. Teddlie (Eds.), *SAGE Handbook of Mixed Methods in Social & Behavioral Research* (2nd ed.; pp. 803–825). Thousand Oaks, CA: Sage. doi:10.4135/9781506335193.n31

Teddlie, C., & Johnson, R. B. (2009a). Methodological thought before the 20th century. In C. Teddlie & A. Tashakkori (Eds.), *Foundations of mixed methods research: Integrating quantitative and quaitative approaches in the social and behavioral sciences* (pp. 40–61). Thousand Oaks, CA: Sage.

Teddlie, C., & Johnson, R. B. (2009b). Methodological thought since the 20th century. In C. Teddlie & A. Tashakkori (Eds.), *Foundations of mixed methods research: Integrating quantitative and qualitative approaches in the social and behavioral sciences* (pp. 62–82). Thousand Oaks, CA: Sage.

Teddlie, C., & Tashakkori, A. (2009). *Foundations of mixed methods research: Integrating quantitative and qualitative approaches in the social and behavioral sciences*. Thousand Oaks, CA: Sage.

Teddlie, C., & Tashakkori, A. (2010). Overview of contemporary issues in mixed methods research. In A. Tashakkori & C. Teddlie (Eds.), *SAGE Handbook of Mixed Methods in Social & Behavioral Research* (2nd ed.; pp. 1–41). Thousand Oaks, CA: Sage. doi:10.4135/9781506335193.n1

Thompson, B., & Daniel, L. G. (1996). Factor analytic evidence for the construct validity of scores: A historical overview and some guidelines. *Educational and Psychological Measurement, 56*(2), 197–208. doi:10.1177/0013164496056002001

Wolcott, H. (1990). On seeking–and rejecting–validity in qualitative research. In E. W. Eisner & A. Peshkin (Eds.), *Qualitative Inquiry in Education: The Continuing Debate* (pp. 121–152). New York: Teachers College Press.

Wolcott, H. F. (2009). *Writing up qualitative research* (3rd ed.). Thousand Oaks, CA: Sage. doi:10.4135/9781452234878

Section 2
Designing a Mixed Methods Research Study

Researchers need to make numerous methodical decisions including the research design which is the blueprint for the study. This chapter outlines the design decisions that need to be made. The design is chosen based on which strategy is best suited to answer the research question(s). The three basic mixed methods designs are discussed: Parallel Convergent, Sequential (Explanatory or Exploratory), and Embedded Design. Additional decisions need to be made about the implementation of the study including the sequencing of the data collection, weight of the two methods (quantitative and qualitative), and when and how to converge the data.

Chapter 2
Mixed Methods Research Design

Mette L. Baran
Cardinal Stritch University, USA

ABSTRACT

This chapter introduces the various design choices researchers need to decide on prior to conducting the study. The chapter starts with a detailed description of what research design is, followed by an explanation of descriptive, explanatory, or exploratory research questions. This determines what type of data will be collected. The major strategic implementation methods for quantitative, qualitative, and mixed methods are then discussed. The three strategies for mixed methods research—parallel convergent, sequential, and embedded design—are presented in detail along with the rationale for their use. Finally, in the last section, the strands or sequencing of the data collection phase of the study are explained.

INTRODUCTION

After the method for the research is determined--qualitative, quantitative or mixed methods the researcher needs to determine the design. Various designs can be employed and researchers need to determine which design bet fits the purpose of their study. Researchers need to know where the design fits in the whole research process from framing the research purpose and question(s), data collection and analysis, to finally reporting the findings. Each design has specific advantages and disadvantages. Which one the researcher selects depends on the objective of the study and the nature of the phenomenon (Hartley & Muhit, 2003). Researchers can decide to use a quantitative, qualitative, or a mixed methods design. This chapter introduces the various approaches aligned with each design.

What is Research Design?

The research design is a framework or blueprint which gives structure and direction to show how all the major parts of the research project work together to address the research question (Malhotra, 2004). It is the logical structure of an inquiry grounded in the research purpose and research question(s) (Mertens, 2005). Furthermore, Creswell (2007) refers to designs as "procedures for collecting, analyzing, interpreting, and reporting data" (p. 58). It details the procedures necessary for obtaining the information needed to structure or solve the research question(s) (Malhotra, 2004). This implies that the researcher needs to decide on the design before the study can begin.

The research design does not imply or dictate any method of collecting data or any type of data. How the data are collected is irrelevant to the logic of the design. Any research design can, in principle, use any type of data collection method and utilize either quantitative or qualitative data, as research design is different from the method by which data are collected. The main purpose of the research design is to reduce the ambiguity of research evidence providing a step by step approach to the entire research plan reducing the possibility for errors to be made.

There are numerous research designs ranging from simple in nature to overly complex; however, for the purpose of this chapter, the number of designs is limited to the three major ones in order not to overwhelm beginning researchers. Mixed methods may be the best design-approach when both quantitative and qualitative data together, will provide a richer understanding of the phenomenon being studied. So, a mixed methods research design is a procedure for mixing both methodologies in a single study to obtain evidence needed to provide a deep understanding of the research problem.

We know that the research question drives everything, including the methodology and research design. When conducting research, researchers need to follow a plan for how the study will unfold and the various steps taken from data collection tools through data analysis. The function of the design is to ensure that a blueprint is in place and that the researcher has collected enough data and analyzed the findings so that the initial research question(s) can be addressed. In other words, when designing research, one needs to ask: given this research question (or theory), what type of data will I need to collect in order to address the research objective? Researchers need to think through, carefully, what type of information is required to answer the research question(s). One can argue that the validity and reliability of the research findings are directly tied to the amount of upfront logical planning the researcher invested in the design process at the beginning.

The way in which researchers develop research designs is fundamentally affected by whether the research question is descriptive, explanatory, or exploratory as this affects what information is collected. Social researchers ask the following types of research questions:

1. What is going on (descriptive research)?
2. Why is it going on (explanatory research)?
3. How is it that it is going on? (Exploratory research)

Descriptive Research

The purpose of this research design is to observe, describe, and document aspects of events as they naturally unfold (Polit & Hungler, 1999). This is like exploratory research as there is no attempt to test hypotheses. Many scientific disciplines, especially social science and psychology use descriptive research to obtain a general overview of the subject or characteristics of an organization or community. Thus, descriptive research is playing an important role in providing data by providing a snapshot of what is going on at a specific point in time surrounding the research topic under study, focusing on the "what" is happening. As a result, descriptive research is also an effective approach to making predictions of certain outcomes, for example, how many will vote for a certain political candidate or how many will purchase a product or attend a certain university? Leedy and Ormrod (2010) posit that a descriptive approach is used in order to "see explanations and predictions that will generalize to other persons and places" (p. 95).

Descriptive studies can yield rich data that lead to important recommendations through the data collection tools of surveys, observation, interviews, and portfolio (AECT, para.20). A survey is a research study in which data are collected from the members of a sample, for the purpose of estimating one or more population parameters (Jaeger, 1997, p. 450). For certain studies, subjects can only be observed in a way as to not affect behavior. This type of research design involves observing and describing the behavior of a subject without influencing. Descriptive research has been dismissed as 'mere description' (New Your University, n.d., para. 3); however, detailed description is fundamental to the research enterprise and it has added immeasurably to the knowledge of the shape and nature of society. Good description of 'what' is going on provokes the 'why' questions of explanatory research.

Explanatory Research

Explanatory research focuses on "why" questions. This is a logical way to inquire after things become known or have been described. "For example, it is one thing to describe the crime rate in a country, to examine trends over time or to compare the rates in different countries. It is quite a different thing to develop explanations about why the crime rate is as high as it is, why some types of crime are increasing or why the rate is higher in some countries than in others;" namely, looking for the reason why a chain of events occur (New York University, n.d., p. 2). Answering the `why' questions involves developing causal explanations. Causal explanations argue that phenomenon Y (for example, level of education) is affected by factor X (for example, parental socioeconomic status).

With explanatory research a researcher conducts causal research or theory-testing. This type of research design is also known as "deductive," "hypothesis-testing," and "predictive." Deductive reasoning starts with a general theory pertaining to the research topic which is then converted into a testable hypothesis(es). This is followed by observations addressing the hypothesis(es). Trochim (2006) notes that "this ultimately leads us to be able to test the hypotheses with specific data -- a *confirmation* (or not)" of the original theory (para. 1). The idea is to test a theory by working out some of the specific implications of the theory (hypothesis) and then collecting data to see if the hypothesis is supported or not. Theory-testing often take place after exploratory work has already been done-- leading to new theory. All studies (except descriptive) are interested in causality as all theories are causal. While causality is complex, the main purpose behind theory-testing studies is basically about testing whether it's true that 'A' causes 'B' and why.

Exploratory Research

Exploratory research seeks to determine "how" is it that things are happening. This type of research design is also known as "inductive" or "theory-building" focusing on "specific observations to broader generalizations and theories" (Troachim, 2006, para. 2). In this kind of study, there is movement from specific observations to broader generalizations and theories. The researcher does not start with a theory. Instead, data are collected and analyzed, and the data are used to develop a theory. For example, a researcher may want to explore how it is that bullying does not exist in certain schools while in others it flourishes. A study may then be designed to test the theory (explanatory). So, the purpose of most exploratory studies is to develop a causal theory which can then be tested later.

Figures 1 and 2 outline the steps to designing a research study based on a deductive or inductive approach.

Figure 1. Deductive approach
Source: Trochim, 2006

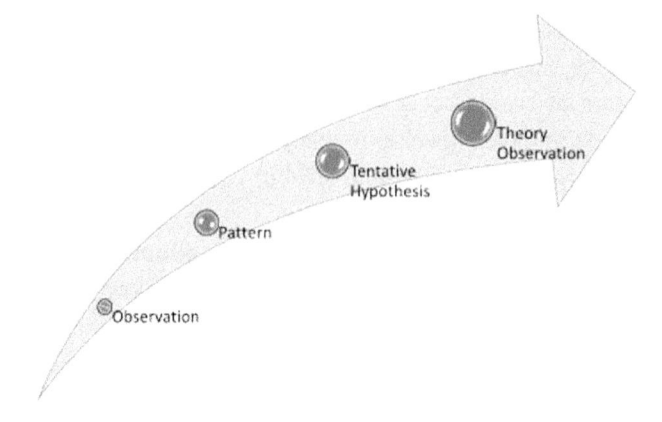

Figure 2. Inductive approach
Source: Trochim, 2006

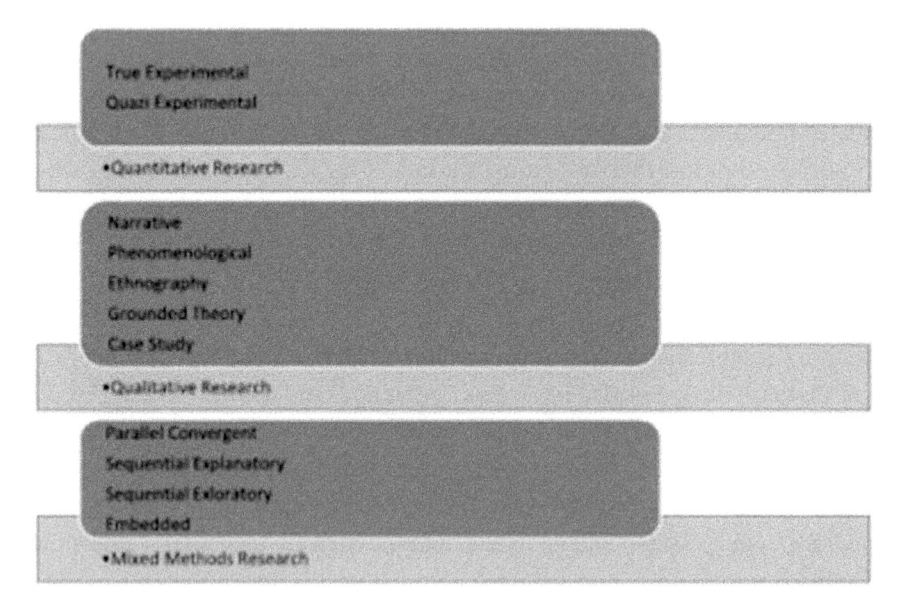

Strategies Associated with Quantitative Design

Quantitative data can be useful in obtaining generalized answers to research questions related to a large group of people. However, quantitative data often is not suitable to getting specific answers or explanations related to research questions. Quantitative research is a mode of inquiry used often for deductive research following the scientific method to test theories or hypotheses, gather descriptive information about variables, examine relationships among variables, or "to determine cause and effect interactions between variables" (Burns & Grove, 2005, p. 23). Furthermore, the authors define quantitative research as, "a formal, objective, systematic process in which numerical data are used to obtain information about the world" (p. 23). These variables are measured and yield numeric data that can be analyzed statistically. Social surveys and experiments are frequently viewed as prime examples of quantitative research and are evaluated against the strengths and weaknesses of statistical, quantitative research methods and analysis. Quantitative (mainly deductive) methods are ideal for measuring pervasiveness of "known" phenomena and central patterns of association, including inferences of causality Pasick et al., (2009). "Quantitative data have the potential to provide measurable evidence, to help establish (probable) cause and effect, to yield efficient data collection procedures, to create the possibility of replication and generalization to a population, to facilitate the comparison of groups, and to provide insight into a breadth of experiences" (U.S. Department of Health & Human Services, 2015, para. 6). Creswell (2012) noted the major characteristics of quantitative research:

1. Describing a research problem through a description of trends or a need for an explanation of the relationship among variables
2. Providing a major role for the literature through suggesting the research questions to be asked and justifying the research problem and creating a need for the direction (purpose statement and research questions or hypotheses) of the study
3. Creating purpose statements, research questions, and the hypotheses that are specific, narrow, measurable, and observable
4. Collecting numeric data from many people using instruments with preset questions and responses
5. Analyzing trends, comparing groups, or relating variables using statistical analysis, and interpreting results by comparing them with prior predictions and past research
6. Writing the research report using standard, fixed structures and evaluation criteria, and taking an objective, unbiased approach. (p. 13)

Typical quantitative approaches used in the social sciences are *descriptive, correlational*, *true experimental design* and *quasi experimental design*. The author explains the difference between true experimental design and quasi experimental design below.

True Experimental Design

True experimental design is regarded as the most accurate form of experimental research in that it tries to find support or lack thereof for a hypothesis mathematically with statistical analysis. In this design, groups are randomly selected. For an experiment to be classified as a true experimental design, it must fit all of the following criteria.

1. The sample groups must be assigned randomly.
2. There must be a viable control group.
3. Only one variable can be manipulated and tested. It is possible to test more than one, but such experiments and their statistical analysis tend to be cumbersome and difficult.
4. The tested subjects must be randomly assigned to either control or experimental groups.

Quasi Experimental Design

Quasi Experimental design involves selecting groups, upon which a variable is tested, without any random pre-selection processes. The data collection tool used is usually a survey.

Strategies Associated with Qualitative Design

Qualitative data can provide meaning and context regarding the people and environments of study but unable to provide generalized findings because the number and range of participants is low. Both methods—qualitative and quantitative-- used together, can complement each other. A salient strength of qualitative research is its focus on the contexts and meaning of human lives and experiences for the purpose of inductive or theory-development driven research. It is a systematic and rigorous form of inquiry that uses methods of data collection such as in-depth interviews, ethnographic observation, and review of documents. Qualitative (mainly inductive) methods allow for identification of previously unknown processes, explanations of why and how phenomena occur, and the range of their effects (Pasick et al., 2009). Creswell (1998) notes that: "Qualitative research is an inquiry process of understanding based on distinct methodological traditions of inquiry that explore a social or human problem. The researcher builds a complex, holistic picture, analyzes words, reports detailed views of informants, and conducts the study in a natural setting" (p. 15). Qualitative data help researchers understand processes, especially those that emerge over time, provide detailed information about setting or context, and emphasize the voices of participants through quotes and provide a depth of understanding of concepts. Typical qualitative approaches used in social science are narrative research, phenomenological research, ethnographies, grounded research, and case study.

Narrative Research

Narrative research is a form of inquiry in which the researcher studies the lives of individuals and asks one or more individuals to provide stories about their lives. This information is then retold or re-storied by the researcher into narrative chronology. In the end, the narrative combines views from the participant's life with those of the researcher's life in a collaborative narrative. Harley-Davidson collects narrative information during its annual Possee Ride from hundreds of riders who describe their experiences with their Harley. All top managers listen-in to these nightly narratives during cross-country trips lasting a week or more.

Phenomenological Research

Phenomenological research is characterized by the researcher identifying the "essence" of human experiences concerning a phenomenon, as described by participants in a study. The researcher describes and interprets the experiences of participants to understand their perspectives based on the belief that there are multiple ways of interpreting the same experience, and the meaning of that experience is what constitutes reality. Understanding the "lived experiences" marks phenomenology as a philosophy as well as a method, and the procedure involves studying a small number of subjects through extensive and prolonged engagement to develop patterns and relationships of meaning. In this process, the researcher "brackets" his or her own experiences in order to understand those of the participants in the study. This research design is focused on what is essential for the meaning of the event, episode, or interaction. Researchers studying the impact of war on soldiers find that treatment of post-traumatic-stress syndrome involves not just the soldier but the soldiers' network of family, friends and associates.

Ethnography

Ethnography is an approach in which the researcher studies an intact cultural or social group in a natural setting over a prolonged period by collecting, primarily, observational data culminating in an in-depth description and interpretation of cultural patterns and meanings. A rich description generally includes shared patterns of beliefs, normative expectations, behaviors, and meanings. The research process is flexible and typically evolves contextually in response to the lived realities encountered in the field setting. Researchers can be simply observers or observer-participants. A researcher studying sky-divers actually participated in hundreds of sky-dives in order to better understand subjects and their group culture.

Grounded Theory

Grounded theory offers the researcher an opportunity to derive a general, abstract theory of a process, action, or interaction grounded in the views of participants in a study. This process involves using multiple stages of data collection and the refinement and interrelationship of categories of information. Two primary characteristics of this design are the constant comparison of data with emerging categories and theoretical sampling of different groups to maximize the similarities and the differences of information. Hypotheses are generally developed after the research as opposed to before the research. For example, in studying the success of Indian firms researchers noticed the strong emphasis on training, development and empowerment of middle-managers, allowing them to make important tactical changes, when necessary, immediately in the field. This finding then led to a hypothesis explaining Indian-firm success due to middle-manager empowerment.

Case Study

Case study is a design in which the researcher explores a program, an event, an activity, a process, or one or more individuals in-depth. The case(s) are bounded by time and activity, and researchers collect detailed information using a variety of data collection procedures over a sustained period culminating in an in-depth analysis of one or more events, settings, programs, groups, or other "bounded systems." Creswell (1998) defines case study as "an exploration of a "bounded system or a case (or multiple cases) over time through detailed, in-depth data collection involving multiple sources of information rich in context" (p. 61). Yin (2003) describes the case study as a research strategy: "As a research strategy, the case study is used in many situations to contribute to our knowledge of individual, group, organizational, social, political, and related phenomena" (p.1). He further urges: "In brief, the case study method allows investigators to retain the holistic and meaningful characteristics of real-life events—such as individual life cycles, organizational and managerial processes, neighborhood change, international relations, and the maturation of industries" (p. 2).

Case studies are often seen as prime examples of qualitative research which adopts an interpretive approach to data, studies `things within their context and considers the subjective meanings that people bring to their situation. Yin (2003) describes the case study as a research strategy: "As a research strategy, the case study is used in many situations to contribute to our knowledge of individual, group, organizational, social, political, and related phenomena" (p.1). A further holistic case study approach was shared by Yin (2003): "In brief, the case study method allows investigators to retain the holistic and meaningful characteristics of real-life events—such as individual life cycles, organizational and managerial processes, neighborhood change, international relations, and the maturation of industries" (p. 2)

A study of Marquee nightclub in New York city, which had been successful for three times the life of a typical nightclub, highlighted the importance of personal recognition of heavy-users in order to keep revenues high.

Types of case studies:

1. Historical organizational - focus on the development of an organization over time
2. Observational - study of a single entity using participant observation
3. Life history (i.e., oral history) - a first-person narrative completed with one person
4. Situation analysis - a study of a specific event from multiple perspective
5. Multi-case - a study of several different independent entities
6. Multi-site - a study of many sites and participants with the main purpose of which is to develop theory

Rational for Mixed Methods and Sequencing of the Data Collection

Mixed Methods Research supports the use of multiple research techniques to obtain answers to the research questions and encourage researchers to have a diverse approach towards research method selections (Johnson & Onwuegbuzie, 2004; Klassen, Creswell, Clark, Smith, & Meissner, 2012; Creswell, Klassen, Plano Clark, & Smith, 2011).

Creswell and Plano Clark (2007) noted: "Mixed methods research is "practical" in the sense that the researcher is free to use all methods possible to address a research problem. It is also "practical" because individuals tend to solve problems using both numbers and words, they combine inductive and deductive thinking, and they (e.g., therapists) employ skills in observing people as well as recording behavior" (p. 10). The rationale for using mixed methods needs to fit the research purpose. Creswell (2009) indicates a mixed methods rationale leads to a better understanding of a "research problem by converging or triangulating broad numeric trends from quantitative research and the detail of qualitative research" (p. 121). A mixed methods approach provides the researcher with an opportunity to utilize both methods and provides a multitude of choices. Creswell and Plano Clark (2011) state the components needed for mixed method research: "In mixed methods research, the data collection procedure consists of several key components: sampling, gaining permissions, collecting data, recording the data, and administering the data collection" (p. 171).

Framework for Conducting Mixed Methods Research

The researcher needs to make decisions about the type of data to be collected and when in the research process it should be collected. For example, starting with quantitative data, a researcher will have the opportunity to test findings during a follow up qualitative data collection phase gaining insights that can help explain initial first phase results. Similarly, collecting qualitative data initially, especially when there may be limited understanding on a topic, will provide an opportunity to collect pertinent information about a phenomenon that will aid the researcher in designing a quantitative instrument. This is the implementation stage of the study which pertains to the order in which data are collected. Creswell (2009) asserts a strategic approach to planning for mixed methods considering four aspects: timing, weighting, mixing, and theorizing (p. 206). Within the context of a mixed methods approach, timing can be sequentially or concurrent; weight or priority may emphasize one type of study over another – qualitative over quantitative or vice versa; mixing the data, integrating, or embedding data relative to the research study and the research question(s); and, theorizing where the existence of a theory is present early in a mixed methods research study impacting the design of the study (Creswell, 2009, pp. 206-208). A credible and robust mixed methods design addresses the decisions of level of integration, priority, timing, and mixing. A systematic framework was suggested by Creswell (2003) for conducting mixed methods research. In this framework, mixed method research designs are classified according to two major dimensions:

1. Time order (Time ordering of the qualitative and quantitative phases is another important dimension, and the phases can be carried out sequentially or concurrently)

Mixed Methods Research Design

2. Paradigm emphasis (i.e., deciding whether to give the quantitative and qualitative components of a mixed study equal status or to give one paradigm the dominant status).

Two other dimensions for viewing mixed methods research are the degree of mixing and where mixing should occur (e.g., in the objective[s], methods of data collection, research methods, during data analysis, or data interpretation). Yet another important dimension is whether one wants to take a critical theory/transformative-emancipatory approach or a less explicitly ideological approach to a study. Research studies can involve mixing of qualitative and quantitative approaches in several ways. This is because there could be so many potential dimensions of classification. This key characteristic of mixed method research provides an unlimited potential for future research (Johnson & Onwuegbuzie, 2004).

Each design varies according to the implementation, priority and integration of the data collected (Cameron, 2009).

Additionally, a mixed methods approach requires a multitude of decisions as to how to design the study and how much importance and weight each approach will play in the design. Each methodology can carry equal weight or either approach can carry more weight than the other. Priority of data is "whether greater *priority* or weight is given to the quantitative data and analysis. The priority might be equal, or it might be skewed toward either qualitative or quantitative data." Priority occurs in a mixed methods study through such strategies as whether quantitative or qualitative information is emphasized first in the study, the extent of treatment of one type of data or the other and use of a theory as an inductive or deductive framework for the study.

Sequencing decisions will also need to be determined. Options include:

1. Collect both quantitative and qualitative data at the same time
2. Collect quantitative data first followed by qualitative data
3. Collect qualitative data followed by quantitative data

For example, a researcher wants to determine the impact of a reading program on student achievement and engagement. She collects pre-reading scores (quantitative data) and observes students in their classroom using the traditional reading curriculum (qualitative data). Throughout the implementation period she continues to collect weekly reading scores and observations. In addition, she conducts in-depth interviews with the teachers and parents after the program conclusion. Numerous decisions pertaining to research design had to be made. However, the decision as to the design is driven by the purpose of the study.

Finally, the researcher connects the data. The "point of interface" (Morse & Niehaus, 2009), or the point where mixing occurs, differs depending on the mixed methods design. This "point" may occur during data collection (e.g., when both quantitative items and qualitative open-ended questions are collected on the same survey), during data analysis (e.g., when qualitative data are converted or transformed into quantitative scores or constructs to be compared with a quantitative dataset), and/or during data interpretation (e.g., when results of quantitative analyses are compared with themes that emerge from the qualitative data).

Creswell and Plano Clark (2011) define the key components that the researcher needs in designing and conducting a mixed methods study:

1. Collects and analyzes persuasively and rigorously both qualitative and quantitative data (based on research questions);
2. Mixes (or integrates or links) the two forms of data concurrently by combining them (or margining them), sequentially by having one build on the other, or embedding one within the other;
3. Gives priority to one or to both forms of data (in terms of what the research emphasizes);
4. Uses these procedures in a single study or in a multiple phase of a program of study;
5. Frames these procedures within philosophical worldviews and theoretical lenses; and
6. Combines the procedures into specific research designs that direct the plan for conducting the study. (p. 5)

Types of Mixed Methods Design

The following table outlines the strategies associated with quantitative, qualitative, and mixed methods approaches (Figure 3). Four basic strategies are typically associated with mixed methods: The Parallel Convergent Design, Sequential Explanatory, Sequential Exploratory, and Embedded Design.

Figure 3.

Quantitative Research	Qualitative Research	Mixed Methods
• Descriptive • Correlational • True Experimental • Quasi-Experimental (Non-Experimental)	• Narrative • Phenomenological • Ethnography • Grounded Theory • Case Study	• Parallell Convergent • Sequential Explanatory • Sequential Exploratory • Embedded

Major Mixed Methods Data Collection & Analysis Approaches

The following sections present a detailed overview of each of the four common mixed methods designs (Creswell & Plano Clark, 2007).

The Parallel Convergent Design

In this design, quantitative and qualitative methods are simultaneously implemented in order to analyze and combine the findings of the same question into an overall interpretation. The purpose is to generate a more comprehensive understanding of the research topic by combining the two results. The researcher collects, analyzes, and merges both types of data and results at the same stage, as quantitative and qualitative data analyses are equally applied. After data interpretation, the results are compared or combined. This design can be applied across disciplines and has often been referred to by various names such as Simultaneous Triangulation (Morse, 1991), Parallel Study (Tashakkori & Teddlie, 1998), Convergence Model (Creswell, 1999), and Concurrent Triangulation (Creswell, Plano Clark, Gutmann, & Hanson, 2003).

Why use Parallel Convergent Design?

According to Morse (1991), the purpose of the parallel convergent design is "to obtain different but complementary data on the same topic" (Morse, 1991, p. 122) in order gain better understanding of the research problem. This design is efficient and provides simultaneous data collection of both quantitative and qualitative data. Each type of data can be collected and analyzed separately and independently, using their respective techniques. The parallel convergent design brings together these strengths and weaknesses to directly compare quantitative findings with qualitative findings for corroboration and validation purposes (Patton, 1990). This design can also be used by researchers to support the quantitative findings with the qualitative findings and to combine quantitative and qualitative results in order develop a more comprehensive understanding of the research problem.

This design is suitable for team research where the team includes individuals having expertise in both quantitative and qualitative research techniques. While most popular, this design is also the most challenging of the major mixed method designs. Use of this design requires much effort and expertise because of the concurrent data collection and the fact that equal priority is generally attached with each data type. To address this challenge, researchers can either form a team of individuals having expertise in quantitative and qualitative research techniques or train a single researcher in both quantitative and qualitative research techniques. Researchers need to consider the consequences of having different samples and different sample sizes when merging the two data sets. Sample sizes may vary because both data types are usually collected for different purposes. To merge two very different data sets and their results can be a daunting challenge. The research study designs should be such that quantitative and qualitative data address the same concepts so that merging of data sets is facilitated. The quantitative and qualitative results may not agree. In this case, contradictions may provide new insights into the topic. At the same time these contradictions present additional challenges to the researchers as these differences can be difficult to resolve and may require the collection of additional data. Researchers need to decide as to what type of additional data to collect or to reanalyze. This additional data could be quantitative data, qualitative data, or both. According to Clark & Creswell (2011) researchers would need to either collect additional data or reexamine the existing data to address this challenge.

Designing a Parallel Convergent Study

In the first step, both qualitative and quantitative data are collected. The researcher converges quantitative and qualitative data in order to provide a comprehensive analysis of the research problem. In this design, the investigator collects both forms of data at the same time during the study and then integrates the information in the interpretation of the overall results. For example, a researcher may want to investigate employees' overall satisfaction with a health care program. Quantitative data are collected using a close-ended instrument measuring overall satisfaction with the program. In addition, at the same time, qualitative data are collected through focus groups and in-depth interviews with a random sample of participants in order to determine what additional services and programs may be needed or desired. The findings are then converged through statistical analysis of the quantitative data as well as interview findings revealing certain themes of information to best determine the overall satisfaction levels and health care needs and preferences as

Figure 4. Steps in designing a Parallel Convergent Design study

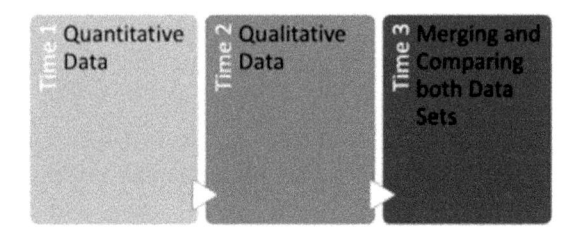

deemed by the employees. In other words, the data analysis consists of merging data and comparing the two sets of data and results as the objective is to obtain a more complete understanding of two sets of data. The same level of importance is attached to both types of data.

In the second step, a separate and independent analysis of both types of data is performed using typical analytical procedures related to each data type. In the third, step the results of both types of data analysis are validated and related. In the last and final step, the researcher interprets the results to find out whether the two results converge, diverge from each other, or relate to each other (Creswell & Plano Clark, 2007).

Sequential Procedures (Explanatory and Exploratory) Design

In this design, the researcher seeks to elaborate on or expand the findings of one method with another method. The idea is to have one dataset build on the results from the other. This is known as sequential design, and may begin by a qualitative exploration followed by a quantitative follow up or by a quantitative analysis explained through a qualitative follow up. This may involve beginning with a qualitative method for exploratory purposes and following up with a quantitative method with a large sample so that the researcher can generalize results to a population. For example, a market researcher can use focus group interview data findings from a sample of consumers to develop scales to be used in a quantitative instrument.

Alternatively, the study may begin with a quantitative method in which theories or concepts are tested, to be followed by a qualitative method involving detailed exploration with a few cases or individuals. A popular approach in the social sciences is the latter in which qualitative data help to explain in more depth the mechanisms underlying the quantitative results. A researcher exploring caretakers of cancer patient's quality of life may first start with a large sample quantitative instrument and follow up with in-depth interviews with a small sample to investigate further some of the quantitative findings to better understand the responses on the scale(s). "The straightforward nature of this design is one of its main strengths" (Creswell, 2009, p. 211).

The quantitative data collection and analysis gets priority when addressing the research questions. Once the second qualitative phase is completed, the researcher interprets the qualitative analysis results to see if they help explain the initial quantitative results. For example, a research study may seek to identify significant predictors of adolescent drug use. The researcher would first conduct a quantitative phase in which quantitative data will be collected and analyzed to identify significant predictors of adolescent drug use. This analysis may reveal some surprising findings such as some unusual association between different research variables. To gain additional insight into these results, the researcher would conduct a qualitative phase (such as detailed interviews with the adolescents) in order explain the unexpected results. Explanatory mixed method design provides a two-phase structure that is easy to implement because both phases are independent. Only one type of data is collected at a time. Due to its strong emphasis on the quantitative phase, this design is often the preferred choice of researchers. The research results can be compiled and published independently. This design is one of the emergent research designs in which the second phase of the research is built on the learning gained in the first phase of the research.

Despite its simplicity, the explanatory mixed method design has many associated challenges. This design is time consuming and implementing the qualitative phase can take considerably more time than implementing the quantitative phase. Though the qualitative phase involves few participants, the collection and analysis of qualitative data can be a lengthy process. To conduct a qualitative phase, normally an approval of institutional review board is needed. This approval can be difficult to obtain. This is because the design of the second phase is dependent on the findings of the first quantitative phase. Therefore, researcher cannot specify how participants will be selected for the second phase. One strategy to deal with this issue is that the researcher can provide a tentative design of the qualitative phase to the institutional review board and inform participants of the possibility of their participation in the second phase of the research. The researcher must decide which results of the quantitative phase would be explained further. This is difficult until the quantitative phase is completed, but the researcher may consider the significant results and strong predictors while planning the study. The selection of the sample population for the qualitative phase is another important decision. The researcher needs to come up with some criterion for this decision. For example, the researcher may use the same groups used in comparisons during the quantitative phase in order to provide the best interpretations.

Why use Sequential Explanatory Design?

Since the overall objective of sequential explanatory design is to use the qualitative phase to explain some unexpected quantitative results (Creswell et al., 2003), this method works well in situations where the researcher needs qualitative data to gain additional insight into quantitative results (whether significant or insignificant) that are surprising or outliers (Morse, 2009). This research design can also be used when group results are to be compared or when the quantitative results are to be used for purposeful sampling in the qualitative phase (Creswell, Plano Clark, et al., 2003; Morgan, 1998; Tashakkori & Teddlie, 1998).

Mixed Methods Research Design

Figure 5. Steps in Designing a Sequential Explanatory Study

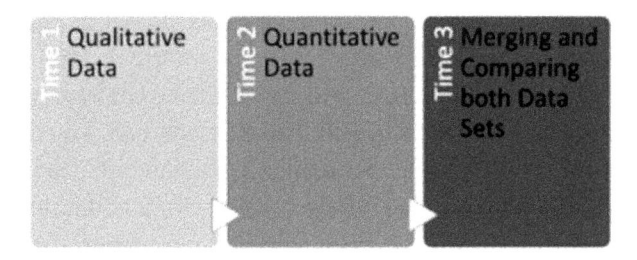

[Time 1: Qualitative Data → Time 2: Quantitative Data → Time 3: Merging and Comparing both Data Sets]

Designing a Sequential Explanatory Study

Also called the sequential model (Tashakkori & Teddlie, 1998), sequential triangulation (Morse, 1991), iteration design (Greene, 2007), and qualitative follow-up approach (Morgan, 1998), this is the most straight-forward mixed method design. It is a two-phase interactive research design that researchers use to identify cause-and-effect-relationships. The first phase is the quantitative phase and in the second qualitative phase, researchers analyzes specific results of the quantitative data to get their in-depth explanation. It is due to this focus on explaining results that we call this method the explanatory mixed method design.

In the first step of a sequential explanatory design, the researcher collects and analyzes quantitative data. In the second step, the researcher identifies specific results of quantitative analysis that warrant additional explanation. The researcher uses these results as a basis to develop or refine the qualitative research questions and decide data collection procedures. In the third step, the researcher collects and analyzes the qualitative data. In the fourth and final step, the researcher interprets the qualitative analysis results to understand how these results could provide additional insight into the results of quantitative analysis (Ivankova, Creswell, & Stick, 2006).

Figure 5 below outlines the steps in designing a Sequential study.

Sequential Exploratory Design

This research design is a two-phase sequential research design that starts with a qualitative phase. In this phase, a researcher explores a topic. The researcher uses analysis of the results of this qualitative phase to build the second quantitative phase to test or generalize the initial exploratory results. In many instances, the researcher uses results of the qualitative phase to develop a research instrument that is used for data collection in the quantitative phase. For this reason, sequential exploratory design is also called instrument development design (Creswell, Fetters, & Ivankova, 2004) or the quantitative follow-up design (Morgan, 1998).

In contrast to the sequential explanatory design, this research design begins with and lays great emphasis on the qualitative phase as shown in Figure 6. Once the quantitative phase is completed, the researcher interprets the results to see if they generalize or provide additional insight into the exploratory findings of the qualitative phase. For example, a researcher may conduct a qualitative phase to identify the possible consequences for adolescents who quit drugs. The results of the qualitative phase could provide different research variables that the researcher could use to develop a research instrument. The researcher could then use this research instrument to assess the overall frequency of these variables in a large sample of adolescents that quit drugs.

Why use Sequential Exploratory Design?

The sequential exploratory design starts with a qualitative component. The qualitative component is more significant and has greater priority in formulating the research problem and purpose. The purpose of sequential exploratory design is to generalize the initial findings from this qualitative phase. Like the sequential explanatory design, the intention of this design is to help develop or inform the second, quantitative method (Greene et al., 1989). The premise is that such exploration may be needed due to unavailability of research instruments, unknown research variables, and lack of guiding research frameworks. Since this design places great emphasis on the qualitative phase, it is well suited for studies that explore a phenomenon (Creswell et al., 2003) or when the researcher needs to develop and test a new research instrument (Creswell, 1999; Creswell et al., 2004) or to identify additional unknown research variables. This design is also suitable when the researcher seeks to test an emergent theory or to explore, in depth, a phenomenon and its associated dimensions (Morgan, 1998).

The sequential exploratory design is most useful in studies where the qualitative exploratory results are to be generalized, assessed, or tested for their applicability to a sample and a population. This design is also practical when the researcher needs to develop a new instrument through exploration. In addition, this design helps the researcher in developing a classification or typology for testing or identifying unknown variables to study quantitatively. This may lead to the discovery of additional emergent research questions based on qualitative results that cannot be answered with qualitative data alone.

Designing a Sequential Exploratory Study

There are four major steps of the exploratory mixed method design. In the first step, the researcher collects and analyzes qualitative data. In the second step, the researcher uses the results of qualitative analysis to develop the quantitative component (i.e.

Figure 6. Steps in designing a Sequential Exploratory Study

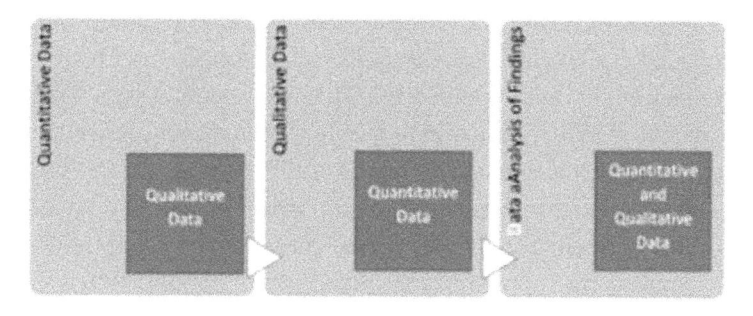

developing the quantitative research questions, developing the research instrument, and decide data collection procedures. The third step is to collect the quantitative data. In the fourth and final step, the researcher interprets the results to find out whether the results of quantitative analysis generalize or provide additional insights into the findings of qualitative analysis (Clark & Creswell, 2011). Figure 5 below outlines the steps in designing a Sequential Exploratory Design study.

The Embedded Design

A popular design in the social sciences is to use quantitative and qualitative approaches in tandem and to embed one in the other to provide new insights or more refined thinking. These designs are called embedded or nested designs. They may be a variation of a convergent or sequential design. In this form of integration, a dataset of secondary priority is embedded within a larger, primary design. An example is the collection of supplemental qualitative data about how participants are experiencing an intervention during an experimental trial. For example, mentioned previously is the study of student reading achievement and engagement after implementing a reading program. The researcher could decide to include weekly interviews with teachers during the experimental phase to discover the process being experienced by the teachers.

Alternatively, qualitative data collection may precede an experimental trial to inform development of procedures or follow an experimental trial to help explain the results of the trial. A prototype would be to conduct an intervention study and to embed qualitative data within the intervention procedures to understand how experimental participants experience the treatment. Qualitative data may be used prior to the intervention to inform strategies to best recruit individuals or to develop the intervention, during the experiment to examine the process being experienced by participants, or after the experiment to follow up and better understand the quantitative outcomes. For example, an experimental study of outcomes from an alcohol prevention program might be followed by individual interviews with participants from the experimental group to help determine why the program worked.

The embedded design combines the collection and analysis of both types of data (quantitative and qualitative) within a traditional research design. This traditional research design could either be a qualitative design (such as a case study) or quantitative (such as an experiment) (Caracelli & Greene, 1997; Greene, 2007). The traditional research design is called the primary design or primary research component and data collected is called the primary data. Either the quantitative or qualitative component can be the secondary (or supplemental) component. The collection and analysis of the secondary data set may occur before, during, and/or after the implementation of the data collection and analysis of primary research data. Both quantitative and qualitative components are implemented simultaneously. The secondary research component is embedded in the larger design of the study in order answer different research questions. Embedded mixed method research designs are suitable in cases where a single research component may not be enough to answer all the research questions (Creswell, Fetters, Plano Clark, & Morales, 2009).

One example of the embedded mixed methods design is a research study where a researcher is looking to develop peer-interventions to help adolescents develop strategies for resisting pressure to drink. In the first step, the researcher may start with a qualitative design (such as focus groups) to understand when adolescents feel pressure to drink and how they resist. Using results of this qualitative data analysis, the researcher can develop an intervention and test it with a quantitative design (such as experiment) by using a student sample.

Why use Embedded Design?

There are three different premises for use of the embedded design. First is that a single data set is not enough to answer all the research questions. Second, there may be different research questions to be answered. Third, each research question may need a different research component to be answered. A research study may be predominantly quantitative but may include some qualitative data that is needed to answer some secondary research questions. Researchers may embed qualitative data into experiment designs for a variety of reasons such as to improve research results (e.g., Donovan, Mills, Smith, Brindle, Jacoby, and Peters, 2002), examine the process of an intervention (e.g., Victor, Ross, & Axford, 2004), or to explain reactions to participation in an experiment (e.g., Evans & Hardy, 2002a, 2002b). Though the purpose of embedding qualitative data is tied to the primary purpose of the quantitative design, the qualitative data can be used to answer some questions other than the research questions sought-after by the quantitative design. This distinguishes embedded mixed method design from triangulation mixed method design. In triangulation mixed method design, the researcher uses both quantitative and qualitative methods to address a single research question.

Designing the Embedded Design Study

The purpose of embedded design is to enhance the application of a traditional research design (quantitative or qualitative). As such, the assumptions of embedded design are guided by the primary research design. The secondary or supplemental method is subservient within the primary research methodology. For example, if the primary research design were quantitative, the assumptions of embedded mixed method design would be guided by the postpositivist approach. According to this approach, a) knowledge can best be gained through a search for regularities and causal relationships among components of the social world. b) regularities and causal relationships can best be discovered if there is a complete separation between the investigator and the subject of investigation, and c) this separation can be guaranteed using the scientific method.

Similarly, if the primary research design is qualitative, the assumptions of embedded mixed method design would be guided by the constructivist approach. According to this approach, a) all knowledge is constructed and all learning is a process of that construction, b) individuals construct knowledge as part of a community but each has his/her own invisible world view that he/she believes is the same as everyone else's, and c) knowledge is content dependent so it is important to situate learning in an authentic, relevant and realistic contexts. In either case, the supplemental method is subservient within the primary research methodology.

When thinking about the procedure of embedded design, one needs to decide when supplemental data should be collected and analyzed and what could be the possible reasons to include this supplemental data in the research. This additional data collection can occur before, during, or after the primary component of the study. This decision is guided by the purpose of the supplemental component in the overall larger design of the study (Creswell, 2009). As such, the embedded mixed method design can be a one-phase or two-phase design.

In embedded design, a researcher can use either quantitative data or qualitative data as supplemental data. The most common embedded design is the one in which qualitative data is used as supplemental data. The implementation of this type of embedded design involves some important steps (Guest, Namey, & Mitchell, 2012). In the first step, the researcher designs the overall quantitative design and decides the reasons for including the supplemental data i.e. qualitative data. In the second step, the researcher collects and analyzes qualitative data to enhance the quantitative design. In the third step, the researcher analyzes the quantitative data. In the fourth and final step, the researcher interprets how the results of qualitative data analysis

Figure 7. Steps in designing an Embedded Design Study

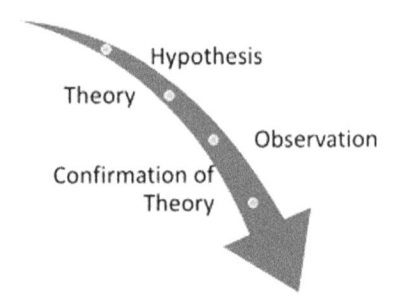

can help enhance the quantitative design and or understanding of the results of the quantitative design (Creswell, 2013).

Researchers gain many advantages by using embedded design. Researchers can save time and resources because one research component (i.e. quantitative) is given priority. By using supplemental data, the larger design of the research can be improved. Since different research components used in embedded mixed methods address different research questions, a team approach can work. Each member of a team, depending on their skills and expertise, can focus their work on a research question. Such focus also means that the results of both research components (i.e. quantitative and qualitative) can be kept and published independently. This design is particularly attractive for donor-agencies funding different research projects. Those donor-agencies unfamiliar with mixed methods research may find this design useful because of its primary focus on a traditional design that could be either quantitative or qualitative (Teddlie & Tashakkori, 2011).

Embedded design also has many associated challenges. Besides expertise in mixed methods research, a researcher also needs expertise in one of the two traditional designs (i.e. quantitative and qualitative). It is necessary for the researcher to specify the purposes of collecting supplemental data as part of the large design of the research study. These purposes can be classified as primary and secondary purposes. For example, a researcher may include supplemental data to shape the intervention or to follow up on results of the experiment. The researcher must also decide the timing of supplemental data collection (i.e., before, during, after, or some combination). This decision should be guided by the purposes of collecting supplemental data that the researcher specified earlier. Since the two research components may be used to answer different research questions, integration of results can be difficult. Contrary to the parallel convergent design, embedded design does not merge the two different data sets to answer the same research questions (Teddlie & Tashakkori, 2011; Johnson & Onwuegbuzie, 2004). Figure 7 below outlines the steps in designing an Embedded design study.

CONCLUSION

When conducting research, researchers need to follow a plan for how the study will unfold and the various steps taken from data collection through data analysis. The function of the design is to ensure that a blueprint is in place and that the researcher has collected enough data and analyzed the findings so that the initial research question(s) can be addressed. In other words, when designing research, one needs to ask: given this research question (or theory), what type of data will I need to collect in order to address the research objective? The chapter starts with a detailed description of what research design is, followed by an explanation of descriptive, explanatory and exploratory research questions. This determines what type of data will be collected.

This chapter describes the differences between research methods and designs and provides a rationale for research design. Strategies associated with quantitative and qualitative designs have been explained. In addition, a rationale for mixed methods research designs and sequencing of the data collection have been discussed. Finally, the four basic mixed methods research designs are described: Parallel Convergent, Sequential Explanatory, Sequential Exploratory, and Embedded complete with a description for selecting each type. In addition, the steps including implementation, weight of findings, and data integration are outlined.

REFERENCES

AECT. (n.d.). *The Handbook of Research for Educational Communications and Technology*. Retrieved from http://www.aect.org/edtech/ed1/41/41-01.html

Burns, N., & Grove, S. K. (2005). *The Practice of Nursing Research: Conduct, Critique, and Utilization* (5th ed.). St. Louis, MO: Elsevier Saunders.

Cameron, R. (2009). A sequential mixed model research design: Design, analytical and display issues. *International Journal of Multiple Research Approaches*, *3*(2), 140–152. doi:10.5172/mra.3.2.140

Caracelli, V. J., & Greene, J. C. (1993). Data analysis strategies for mixed-method evaluation designs. *Educational Evaluation and Policy Analysis*, *15*(2), 195–207. doi:10.3102/01623737015002195

Clark, V. L. P., & Creswell, J. W. (2011). *Designing and conducting mixed methods research*. Thousand Oaks, CA: Sage.

Creswell, J. W. (1998). *Qualitative inquiry and research design*: Choosing among five traditions. London: Sage.

Creswell, J. W. (2003). *Research design: Qualitative, quantitative and mixed methods approaches* (2nd ed.). Thousand Oaks, CA: SAGE Publications.

Creswell, J. W. (2007). *Qualitative Inquiry and Research Design: Choosing among five traditions* (2nd ed.). Thousand Oaks, CA: Sage.

Creswell, J. W. (2009). *Research design, qualitative, quantitative, and mixed methods approaches* (3rd ed.). London, UK: Sage Publications, Inc.

Creswell, J. W. (2013). *Research design: Qualitative, quantitative, and mixed methods approaches* (4th ed.). London, UK: Sage Publications, Inc.

Creswell, J. W., Fetters, M. D., Plano Clark, V. L., & Morales, A. (2009). Chapter 9, Mixed Methods Intervention Trials. In S. Andrew & E. J. Halcomb (Eds.), Mixed Methods Research for Nursing and the Health Sciences. Blackwell Publishing Ltd.

Creswell, J. W., Fetters, M. D., & Ivankova, N. V. (2004). Designing a mixed methods study in primary care. *Annals of Family Medicine, 2*(1), 7–12. doi:10.1370/afm.104 PMID:15053277

Creswell, J. W., Klassen, A. C., Plano Clark, V. L., & Smith, K. C. (2011). *Best practices for mixed methods research in the health sciences*. Bethesda, MD: National Institutes of Health. doi:10.1037/e566732013-001

Creswell, J. W., & Plano Clark, V. (2007). *Designing and Conducting Mixed Methods Research*. Thousand Oaks, CA: Sage.

Creswell, J. W., & Plano Clark, V. (2011). *Designing and Conducting Mixed Methods Research* (2nd ed.). Thousand Oaks, CA: Sage.

Creswell, J. W., Plano Clark, V. L., Gutmann, M., & Hanson, W. (2003). Advanced mixed methods research designs. In A. Tashakkori & C. Teddlie (Eds.), *Handbook of mixed methods in social & behavioral research* (pp. 209–240). Thousand Oaks, CA: Sage.

Donovan, J., Mills, N., Smith, M., Brindle, L., Jacoby, A., & Peters, T. (2002). Improving design and conduct of randomized trials by embedding them in qualitative research: Protect (prostate testing for cancer and treatment) study. *British Medical Journal, 325*, 766–769. doi:10.1136/bmj.325.7367.766 PMID:12364308

Greene, J. C. (2007). *Mixed methods in social inquiry*. John Wiley & Sons.

Greene, J. C., & Caracelli, V. J. (1997). Defining and describing the paradigm issue in mixed-method evaluation. *New Directions for Evaluation*, *1997*(74), 5–17. doi:10.1002/ev.1068

Greene, J. C., Caracelli, V. J., & Graham, W. F. (1989). Toward a conceptual framework for mixed method evaluation designs. *Educational Evaluation and Policy Analysis*, *11*(3), 255–274. doi:10.3102/01623737011003255

Guest, G., Namey, E. E., & Mitchell, M. L. (2012). Collecting qualitative data: A field manual for applied research. *Sage (Atlanta, Ga.)*.

Hartley, S., & Muhit, M. (2003). Using Qualitative Research Methods for Disability Research in Majority World Countries. *Asia Pacific Disability Rehabilitation Journal*, *103*(14).

Ivankova, N. V., Creswell, J. W., & Stick, S. L. (2006). Using mixed-methods sequential explanatory design: From theory to practice. *Field Methods*, *18*(1), 3–20. doi:10.1177/1525822X05282260

Jaeger, R. M. (1997). *Complementary Research Methods for Research in Education* (2nd ed.). Washington, DC: American Educational Research Association.

Johnson, R. B., & Onwuegbuzie, A. J. (2004). Mixed methods research: A research paradigm whose time has come. *Educational Researcher*, *33*(7), 14–26. doi:10.3102/0013189X033007014

Klassen, A. C., Creswell, J., Clark, V. L. P., Smith, K. C., & Meissner, H. I. (2012). Best practices in mixed methods for quality of life research. *Quality of Life Research: An International Journal of Quality of Life Aspects of Treatment, Care and Rehabilitation*, *21*(3), 377–380. doi:10.100711136-012-0122-x PMID:22311251

Leedy, P., & Ormrod, J. (2010). *Practical research: planning and design* (9th ed.). Boston, MA: Pearson.

Malhotra, N. K. (2004). *Marketing Research: an Applied Orientation* (4th ed.). London: Prentice-Hall International.

Mertens, D. M. (2005). *Research and evaluation in education and psychology: Integrating diversity with quantitative, qualitative, and mixed methods* (2nd ed.). Thousand Oaks, CA: Sage.

Morgan, D. L. (1998). Practical Strategies for combining quantitative and qualitative methods: Applications for health research. *Qualitative Health Research*, *8*(3), 362–376. doi:10.1177/104973239800800307 PMID:10558337

Morse, J. (1991). Approaches to qualitative-quantitative methodological triangulation. *Nursing Research, 40*(2), 120–123. doi:10.1097/00006199-199103000-00014 PMID:2003072

New York University. (n.d.). *What is Research Design? The Context of Design.* Retrieved from http://www.nyu.edu/classes/bkg/methods/005847ch1.pdf

Pasick, R. J., Burke, N. J., Barker, J. C., Galen, J., Bird, J. A., & Otero-Sabogal, R. (2009). Behavioral theory in a diverse society: Like a compass on Mars. *Health Education & Behavior, 36*(5), 11S–35S. doi:10.1177/1090198109338917 PMID:19805789

Polit, D. F., & Hungler, B. P. (1999). *Nursing Research: Principles and Methods* (6th ed.). Philadelphia: Lippincott.

Tashakkori, A., & Teddlie, C. (1998). *Mixed Methodology: Combining Qualitative and Quantitative Approaches in Applied Social Research Methods Series, 46.* Thousand Oaks, CA: Sage Publications.

Teddlie, C., & Tashakkori, A. (2011). *Mixed methods research. In The Sage Handbook of Qualitative Research.* Thousand Oaks, CA: Sage Publications.

Trochim, W. M. K. (2006). *Research Methods Knowledge Base. Deduction and Induction.* Retrieved from: http://www.socialresearchmethods.net/kb/dedind.php

U.S. Department of Health & Human Services. (2015). *The Nature and Design of Mixed Methods Research.* Retrieved from obssr.od.nih.gov/scientific_areas/methodology/mixed_methods_research/section2.aspx

Victor, C. R., Ross, F., & Axford, J. (2004). Capturing lay perspectives in a randomized control trial of a health promotion intervention for people with osteoarthritis of the knee. *Journal of Evaluation in Clinical Practice, 10*(1), 63–70. doi:10.1111/j.1365-2753.2003.00395.x PMID:14731152

Yin, R. K. (2003). *Case study research: Design and methods* (3rd ed.). Thousand Oaks, CA: Sage.

Section 3
Sampling and Data Collection in Research

This chapter explains the role of sampling in research. Sampling plays an important role in any research study and careful consideration needs to be placed on who to include as participants as part of the design process. Researchers need to determine sample sizes for the quantitative and qualitative data and whether to include the same participants for both strands of the study. In addition, decisions around random sampling or purposeful sampling must be considered.

Chapter 3
Considering the Source:
Sampling and Data Collection in a Mixed Methods Study

Mindy Crain-Dorough
Southeastern Louisiana University, USA

ABSTRACT

The purpose of this chapter is to describe detailed procedures for determining the data collection and sampling methods in a mixed methods study. The nuances of selecting data collection strategies and sampling techniques are explained in a practical way. The points of decision, factors to consider, and methods for weighing the advantages and disadvantages are provided along with tables that can be completed to organize the planning process. The overall design process for a mixed methods study is described to provide the context for the in-depth discussion about data collection and sampling. A fictional study is used as an example to illustrate how to apply the procedure to identify the optimal data sources for a mixed methods study.

INTRODUCTION

There has been much methodological literature written about mixed methods research (e.g., Fetters, Curry, & Creswell, 2013; Leech & Onwuegbuzie, 2009). The existing mixed methods literature primarily provides typologies and conceptual discussions with regard to mixed methods designs, sampling techniques, and data collection methods. This literature has been by instrumental in advancing the area of mixed methods research. Minimal detailed and practical explanation of how to navigate through the process of planning a mixed methods study is provided in the literature.

DOI: 10.4018/978-1-7998-1025-4.ch003

Some of the literature describes the steps for designing a mixed methods study (e.g., Schoonenboom, 2018), but with little intense focus on specific steps of the process.

The overall purpose of this chapter is to provide novice researchers with step-by-step instructions for one aspect of designing a mixed methods study. The focus of this chapter is the selection of the data collection and sampling methods. This aspect of the mixed methods design process is second in importance to the development of the research questions. The data collected from the study participants becomes the information used to address the research questions following data analysis. The selection begins with identifying the optimal mixed methods data sources needed to address a set of research questions. After considering the possible data collection and sampling techniques, one can plan the methods to use when obtaining the mixed methods data. This chapter unpacks the nuances of decisions to be made and describes in detail how to navigate the logistics. The selection of data collection and sampling methods is described in a practical manner that is not overly technical to meet the needs of the target audience: novice researchers, such as graduate students working on theses or dissertations; junior faculty; and, practitioners in the field conducting research to address real problems in their professional settings.

This chapter has five major sections:

- **Background:** the process for designing a mixed methods study is discussed along with an overview of each of the first four steps of the process;
- **Identifying Data Sources:** a procedure is delineated to use when identifying the optimal data sources needed to address a set of research questions;
- **Selecting Data Collection Strategies:** six data collection strategies are described along with how to weigh the advantages and disadvantages of each with regard to collecting the mixed methods data needed to address a set of research questions;
- **Developing a Sampling Plan:** a procedure to use to develop a sampling plan is described as well as various probability, purposeful, and mixed methods sampling techniques; and,
- **Discussion:** how to identify and describe the mixed methods design aligned with the data collection and sampling decisions is articulated.

BACKGROUND

In this chapter, a *study* is defined to include formal research projects, evaluations, or any other process through which data are examined and used to address questions. The term *data* is defined to include both numerical values or scores, textual material, visual material (e.g., video, photography, artwork), and other pieces of material that can be collected about a unit of analysis. A *unit of analysis* is defined as the unit for which the data are describing. This could be an individual, a group, and organization, a physical location, etc... A *mixed methods study* is defined as one that includes both quantitative and qualitative methods. Quantitative methods use numerical data and statistical analyses usually to confirm theory. Qualitative methods use non-numerical data (e.g., textual, visual) to explore and develop theory. However, qualitative methods can be used to test theory and quantitative methods can be used to develop theory. In a mixed methods study, there are two *strands*: a qualitative strand and a quantitative strand. The qualitative strand is the collection and analysis of the qualitative data. Quantitative data are collected and analyzed in the quantitative strand (Schoonenboom, 2018).

Designing a Mixed Methods Study

The methodological literature on mixed methods research provides guidelines for how to design a mixed methods study, including lists of steps to follow (e.g., Collins, Onwuegbuzie, & Sutton, 2006; Onwuegbuzie & Corrigan, 2014; Ponce & Pagán-Maldonado, 2015; Schoonenboom, 2018; Venkatesh, Brown, & Bala, 2013; Venkatesh, Bala, & Sullivan, 2016). For the purposes of this chapter, these mixed methods design processes have been sythesized and arranged into a process for novice researchers to utlize. The process is listed below:

1. **State the Purpose of the Study:** what is the reason for conducting the study;
2. **Consider the Methods from Previous Research:** what methods have others used to obtain similar data;
3. **State the Research Question(s):** what are the questions to be addressed by this study;
4. **Consider and Identify Data Sources:** what possibilities exist for obtaining data to address the research questions
5. **Consider and Select Data Collection Strategies**
6. **Consider and Develop a Sampling Plan**
7. **Select Data Analysis Techniques**
8. **Examine the Design Plan:** examine decisions for how the qualitative data will be collected and analyzed and how the quantitative methods will be collected and analyzed

When planning a study, it is good to use this order, but process can be iterative. As decisions are made, previous choices should be reconsidered to develop the best possible research plan. With any decision to be made when planning a research study, a researcher should consider the possibilities, weigh the advantages and disadvantages, and choose the best option(s) for the study. To do this well, one should understand each of the possibilities in order to maximize selection of the best choice(s). This chapter focuses on and provides details for steps 4-6. Steps 1-3 are briefly discussed in this Background section and are important consider when proceeding with selection of the study methods. Step 7 is touched on briefly in this chapter, and Step 8 is described in the Discussion section.

Purposes of a Study

Step 1 in the mixed methods design process is to state the purpose of the study, which is the reason for conducting the study. Schoonenboom (2018) differentiates between the immediate research purpose and the remote research purpose, and defines the *immediate research purpose* as what is to be accomplished by addressing the research question. Blaikie and Priest (2019) have a listing of purpose types that are designated a key verb:

Explore: to examine something new or in a new way;
Describe: to provide a detailed description of someone or some thing;
Explain: to unpack the aspects of something in an organized way;
Understand: to interpret the underlying reasons for or the meaning of something;
Predict: to use available information make determinations about future events
Change: to examine the impact of an intervention or modification on something
Evaluate: to determine the value or worth of something
Assess Social Change: to examine the consequences of something on society

A study can have more than one purpose type. The immediate research purpose is which of the purpose types will occur when the research questions are addressed. The *remote research purpose* is "the overall, larger, further-reaching purpose, which the study should contribute to achieving" (p. 1002). Maxwell (2013) calls these purposes goals: personal, practical, and intellectual goals. There are other sources that describe purpose typologies (e.g., Leech & Onwuegbuzie (2010); Newman, Ridenour, Newman, and Demarco; 2003).

A researcher planning to conduct a study can examine these typologies and consider which purposes apply to the goals of the researcher with regard to study outcomes. A study can have more than one purpose, but depending on the logistics of the methods needed to meet the purposes, multiple studies may have to be conducted. Knowing the purpose of doing the research provides the first indication of what methods to use to obtain the information needed from the study.

Methods from Previous Research

Step 2 in the mixed methods design process is to consider the methods that have been used in previous research to obtain similar data or to conduct similar studies. Elements of previous research methods to consider include sources of data, data collection instruments, sampling techniques, and ways to analyze data. In addition to being aware of existing instruments, a researcher can use the methods knowledge that others have tried and tested in order to avoid making mistakes or have misleading results. An important part of designing a study is to plan to use the methods appropriately in order to have valid results. This knowledge can also assist with developing research questions because it informs a researcher about what is possible and not possible.

Research Questions

Step 3 in the mixed methods design process is to state the research questions for the study, which are the questions to be addressed using the information obtained from the study. The research questions should include what is to be studied (i.e., variables/phenomena). Knowing what the variables/phenomena are and how these are defined conceptually are key to selecting the optimal data collection methods. When the study design is completed, the research question wording needs to be examined to ensure it is coherent with the design of the study. It should be noted that one study may not fully answer a research question, but the information can go toward an answer, but will say "answer the research question" in this chapter for ease in understanding the discussion. In this Background section, an overall process for designing mixed methods resarch was described along with the first three steps of the process. The fourth step is described in detail in the following section.

IDENTIFYING DATA SOURCES

This section of the chapter describes details regarding Step 4, identification of potential data sources needed to address the research questions for a mixed methods study. Five factors the identification process is described, including five factors to consider regarding data sources needed to address research questions. A table is provided that can be used to consider all the factors at once. A fictitious study is used to illustrate how to identify data sources using the table.

Factors to Consider

When determining the best possible data sources for addressing the research questions, five factors should be considered for each research question. The five factors are described in more detail following the listing below:

- Immediate purpose (i.e., explore, describe, explain, understand, predict, change, evaluate, or assess social impacts) (Blaikie & Priest, 2019);
- Variables/phenomena to be studied;
- Exploratory and/or confirmatory nature of the question;
- Form of data (numerical, narrative, other); and,
- Scope (i.e., breadth/depth) and goals for generalizability.

Keeping the immediate purpose in mind will help a researcher avoid getting locked into the current version of the research question wording. The wording of the research questions should be considered to be in flux until final decisions about the design are made (Ponce & Pagán-Maldonado, 2015). A research question is linked to the appropriate research methods needed to address the question. However, there could be multiple possibilities for studying the resarch question.

The variables/phenomena are the data that need to be measured or obtained in the study. A research question is exploratory in nature if the intent is to develop or expand knowledge, and a confirmatory research question seeks the testing of existing knowledge. Existing knowledge comes from the research literature and may be formal theories (Turner, Cardinal, & Burton, 2017). Typically, an exploratory research question would require qualitative methods, and a confirmatory research question would require quantitative methods. However, qualitative methods can be used to confirm (e.g., examining whether an existing theory applies to a case under study) and quantitative methods can be used to explore (e.g., descriptive studies using numerical data) (Teddlie & Tashakkori, 2009). For a study to require mixed methods, at least one question would need to be addressed using qualitative methods and at least one question would need to be addressed using quantitative methods. A question that needs to be addressed using both types of methods would be a mixed methods question (Onwuegbuzie & Leech, 2006; Ponce & Pagán-Maldonado, 2015.)

Data is usually numerical or narrative (i.e., text) in form. Other data forms include visual and audio data. The form of the data is based on the forms of data obtainable for the variables/phenomena. An awareness of how the variables/phenomena have been measured or obtained in previous studies is of benefit here. Also, knowledge of how the variables/phenomena are conceptually defined aid in identifying appropriate data sources. Whether the question is exploratory or confirmatory impacts the form of data you will need. tells you about narrative/numerical with regard to design, data collection, and analysis needs. To study a research question in a confirmatory manner, one typically would need numerical data to statistically analyze the data to confirm a hypothesis. However, narrative data can be analyzed for confirmatory purposes as well. From an exploratory perspective, numerical data can be examined, but narrative data will provide more in-depth information. At this step in the process, the consideration of the connections between the exploratory/confirmatory nature of the question and the form of the data may be premature. This can be re-examined later in the process.

Schoonenboom (2018) describes *scope* as the "reach of the conclusions that are drawn from research findings" (p. 1003). This is also described in the methodological literature as generalizability, external validity, and inference transferability (Teddlie & Tashakkori, 2009). A way to understand breadth and depth is to consider breadth as moving out horizontally from narrow to broad and depth as move down vertically from the surface to the depths. Typically, quantitative methods are considered appropriate when the scope is broad and surface-level, and qualitative methods are needed to study something narrow in an in-depth manner. Mixed methods allows one to examine breadth and depth. Scope is connected to both the remote research purpose and the exploratory/confirmatory nature of the previous research methods. Schoonenboom (2018). Turner, Cardinal, and Burton (2017) describe theoretical implications of research that are other paris of adjectives that demonstrate the spectrum for breadth/depth: generality/specificity, simplicity/complexity, and accuracy/inaccuracy. General conclusions from a study generalize to a broader context. Quantitative methods typically result in simplistic conclusions meaning explaining theory in a parsimonious way for a broad group. Studying something in-depth allows for more specific, as well as complex conclusions. Accurate theory can be applied to a broader context; whereas, thoery developed from in-depth study in narrow context will not be accurate for broad application. Onwuegbuzie, Collins, and Frels (2013) portray scope through the application of an ecological theory that describes moving from the narrow microsystem to the broad macrosystem.

A Fictional Example Study

It is helpful to use a table to examine the above factors for each research question, as shown in Table 1. In the table, each research question has a row, and there is a column for each of the five factors. An additional column is used to put ideas for potential data sources. Table 1 displays information for a fictional example study on professional development in an organization.

The example study is from the field of education, and the organization is a school district. The example will be more informative if there is context. A school district staff member chooses to conduct his dissertation on professional development for teachers.

He is aware that the school district superintendent and her staff have determined the existing professional development for teachers is not effective. Regarding Step 1, the immediate purpose is to understand the professional development needs of teachers in the school district. The remote purpose would primarily be practical as the information obtained could be used to plan the most effective professional development offerings for the teachers. A personal purpose would be met as well if the doctoral student wants to be a professional development consultant in the future. The researcher will need to also determine the immediate purposes for each of the research questions.

For Step 2, the doctoral student reviews similar studies in the literature on effective teacher professional development and meeting teachers' needs. He finds that most studies are qualitative and the research has been mostly exploratory rather than confirmatory. When he examines the data sources that have been used in the previous research, he determines that teachers, principals, central office staff, professional development providers, and teacher evaluation results have been used in previous studies. He finds a survey on effective professional development. He also recognizes that an important variable that has been considered in previous professional development research has been teachers' years of experience. The research questions for Step 3 are shown in the table, each in a separate row.

Research Question 1

Table 1 shows the results of examining Research Question 1 with regard to the five factors related to identifying data sources. In this sub-section, the details of this examination are described. When examining Research Question 1 to determine what would need to be measured or obtained, two variables are identified, teachers' areas of weakness and teachers' years of experience. Research Question 1 is both a confirmatory and an exploratory question. It is confirmatory because the question implies that teachers with different years of experience will have varying areas of weakness as opposed to there being no difference. The study results would describe whether differences exist. The question is exploratory because it is implied that the ways in which they differ are unknown.

The form of the data is based on what form of data would be obtainable for the Research Question 1 variables. Areas of weakness would be narrative data, and years of experience would be in numerical form. When considering scope, the overall immediate purpose for the study should be considered. The immediate purpose for the overall study was to understand the professional development needs of teachers in the district. The last part of the purpose indicates the scope for this research question. A broad scope is needed from the perspective of examining the district in that the results need to generalizable to the entire district. But, some depth is needed in explaining the ways the teachers differ. The immediate purpose for the research question was of use in recognizing depth is needed as well.

There are three methods to use to brainstorm potential sources of data. First, taking how the variables/phenomena are defined conceptually, one should contemplate how this variable is possibly exhibited in reality. For areas of weakness, this could be something measured in a teacher evaluation or reflected in the student test scores. Study participants could identify the areas of weakness based on their experiences, which leads to the next brainstorm methods. Next, one should consider the various individuals from whom data could be collected that would be useful in answering the research question. If the individuals are listed in the research question, they should be listed, such as teachers in this case. The perspectives of administrators could be

Table 1. Five factors to consider for each research question when identifying data sources

Research Question (RQ)	Immediate Purposes	Variables/ Phenomena	Exploratory/ Confirmatory/ Both	Numerical/ Narrative/ Both	Breadth/ Depth	Sources for Data
RQ1 - To what extent do teachers' areas of weakness vary based on years of experience?	To describe and explain ways teachers differ in areas of weakness based on years of experience	Areas of weakness; years of experience	Both – Confirmatory (do they vary) and Exploratory (in what ways do they vary)	Narrative (what the areas of weakness are); Numerical (years of experience)	Mostly breadth/ some depth	Teacher perceptions; administrator perceptions; student test scores; teacher evaluation results existing data on teacher years of experience
RQ2 - What are teachers' most preferred modes of delivering professional development?	To describe the modes and which ones are preferred	Delivery modes; Amount of preference	Both – Exploratory (what are the modes) and Confirmatory (do they differ in preference?)	Both – Compare numerical data; obtain narrative data regarding preferences	Mostly breadth/ some depth	District staff interview on current modes of delivery; teacher perceptions of preferred modes of delivery; administrator perceptions of preferred modes of delivery; feedback submitted at the end of previous professional development

Considering the Source

useful as well. Most study contexts have a structure, and considering individuals at different levels can be beneficial. Finally, one should consider possible existing data and data that would need to be collected. Sources of data for all variables/phenomena need to be considered. Years of experience could be collected from the teachers or an existing database. The potential data sources for Research Question 1 that were identified are shown in Table 1.

Research Question 2

Table 1 also shows the results of examining Research Question 2 with regard to the five factors related to identifying data sources. In this sub-section, the details of this examination are described. When examining Research Question 2 to determine what would need to be measured or obtained, two variables were identified, modes of delivering professional development and level of preference. Research Question 2 is both a confirmatory and an exploratory question. The question is exploratory if the modes of professional development cannot be determined at the beginning of the study. The question is confirmatory because it implies that teachers have preferences regarding modes of delivery. The study results would describe whether differences exist in levels of preference for the delivery modes.

The form of the data is based on what form of data would be obtainable for the Research Question 2 variables. Modes of delivery would be narrative data, and levels of preference would be in numerical. When considering scope, the overall immediate purpose for the study should be considered. The immediate purpose for the overall study was to understand the professional development needs of teachers in the district. The scope for Research Question 1 applied to Research Question 2 as well. The potential data sources for Research Question 2 that were brainstormed are shown in Table 1. In this section, a procedure was described that can be used to identify potential data sources for the research questions in a study (i.e., Step 4 of the mixed methods design process). In the next section, the information from Table 1 is used to select data collection strategies (i.e., Step 5 of the mixed methods design process).

SELECTING DATA COLLECTION STRATEGIES

This section of the chapter describes details regarding Step 5, a procedure for selecting the data collection strategies is described. The goal is to select methods to collect or obtain data from the optimal data sources needed to address the research questions in a mixed methods study. Six possible data collection strategies are described (i.e., observations, unobtrusive measures, interviews, focus groups, surveys, and tests) (Teddlie & Tashakkori, 2009). A table is provided showing the advantages and disadvantages of each data collection strategy. The fictitious study is revisited as an example of how to make decisions regarding data collection strategies. Important design considerations are described relevant to selection of data collection strategies. A discussion is provided regarding how each strategy can produce numerical data, narrative data or both (i.e., within-strategy data collection) (Ponce & Pagán-Maldonado 2015; Sandelowski, 2000). Between-strategies data collection are articulated (Teddlie & Tashakkori, 2009). In summary, this section will describe the selection of data collection strategies, including descriptions of six possible strategies, consideration of strategies needed for the potential data sources based on strengths and weaknesses, and determination of whether within- or between-strategies would be best.

Data Collection Strategies

In this sub-section, six common data collection strategies are described.

Observations

Observations as a data collection strategy involves observing and documenting the data observed. There are a couple of issues a researcher must decide upon when planning to do observations. The first is how structured the observation will be. A structured observation involves conducting the observation specifically looking for certain things. Many times the researcher checks for presence or absence of something. Often the researcher looks at frequency and duration of occurrences. These data from structured observations can become numerical data. An unstructured observation involves the researcher scripting and writing a running narrative. An observation can be somewhere in-between where certain things are observed and documented using scripting. A second issue is to consider where the data collection will fall on the participant/observer continuum, which indicates how much interaction the researcher has with the participants. This continuum ranges from the researcher being a participant in the setting to the reseracher having no interaction (e.g., observation captured through video) (Hays & Singh, 2012; Teddlie & Tashakkori, 2009).

Unobtrusive Measures

The next data collection strategy, unobtrusive measures, occurs when the researcher uses pre-existing data that were are collected anyway for some other purpose or when the researcher collects data without the participants realizing they are being studied. According to Teddlie and Tashakkori (2009), there are three kinds of unobtrusive measures: archival records, physical trace evidence, and covert/nonreactive observations. Archival records can be grouped into four types. First, written public records, which include birth and death certificates, judicial records, manuals, reports, school improvement plans. Sometimes these records may not be readily accessible, but one could obtain it without having to get permission to access it. The internet has increased access to public records considerably. Next, written private records are ones that you have to get permission to obtain and use. Examples of written private records include diaries, letters, and blogs. Another archival record type is an archived database. These databases have been obtained by others for use in natural settings, such as test data in school districts. Databases exist at the local and state levels. The federal government collects data for reporting purposes, but also for researcher use. The fourth type includes other archival data that do not fall into the other three categories, such as video of meetings and photographs (Hays & Singh, 2012; Teddlie & Tashakkori, 2009).

There are two forms of physical trace evidence: erosion and accretion. An example of erosion would be if someone could walk through a school and see wear-and-tear and use this to learn a lot about what happens in a school. Accretion is build-up, and examples include accumulation of trash and what is on the walls in a school. Covert observations occur when the researcher masks his/her identity as a researcher and/or masks the true intent of the study. A researcher could have others from a setting collect the data in a way that would seem more natural to the participants. When the researcher just observes with minimal interaction with the participants, this is a nonreactive observation (Hays & Singh, 2012; Teddlie & Tashakkori, 2009).

Focus Groups

When conducting a focus group, a researcher interviews and observes a group of six to eight participants at once. The group is typically made up of homogeneous participants but can have a heterogeneous make-up for situations where a varied group needs to be represented, such as teachers for different grade levels. The focus group is conducted by a moderator using a list of questions or just a list of topics. The session lasts no longer than two hours. Moderating a focus group is a very engaging task, so an assistant is needed to take notes and manage the recording equipment. Sometimes a third person is needed to do the observations if this is more than what the second person can manage in addition to the other tasks to perform. Usually a focus group will yield qualitative data, but sometimes quantitative data are collected. For example, the focus group could complete a short survey. One could also obtain quantitative data by counting the percent for/against something, recording the order of issues that are discussed, counting the frequency of things discussed, and obtaining demographic information (Hays & Singh, 2012; Teddlie & Tashakkori, 2009).

Interviewing

The quality of data obtained in an interview is impacted by the relationship or interaction between the interviewer and the interviewee. The established rapport and sharing of meaning are key. Unlike with a survey, in an interview the interviewer is able to probe for deeper meaning and ask clarification questions when something is unclear. Interviews are usually face-to-face but can be done by phone or using the Internet. An interview will yield qualitative data when the questions are open-ended and usually in an unstructured manner. Quantitative interviews are used when the questions are closed-ended and structured. There are five types of interviews listed below from unstructured to structured and open-ended to closed-ended:

- The informal conversational interview is just like a regular conversation with someone.
- A general interview guide approach is where the researcher uses a list of topics that the interviewee discusses in the order listed or any order.
- A semi-structured interview has actual questions written out that can be asked in any order.
- A standardized open-ended interview has open-ended questions written out and they are asked in a certain order.

A closed fixed-response interview has closed-ended questions written out and they are asked in a certain order. This is similar to reading a survey out loud to someone and is useful when participants are not able to complete a survey themselves or improving the response rate. This type of interview procedures quantitative data (Hays & Singh, 2012; Teddlie & Tashakkori, 2009).

These interview types can be combined in one interview. A common combination sequence is as follows. First, the interviewer starts with the informal conversational interview to build rapport and obtain spontaneous responses. Then, an interview guide approach is used to discuss an outline of topics still in a conversational tone. Finally, the standardized open-ended type is used to ask the interviewee the exact same things a researcher will ask all other interviewees in order to maintain some consistency across interviews (Hays & Singh, 2012; Teddlie & Tashakkori, 2009).

Surveys

With surveys, participants self-report about something (e.g., perceptions, attitudes, beliefs). A survey can be given in paper-and-pencil format where people provide their responses on a sheet of paper or a survey can be given online where people use a link to access and fill out the online survey. A quantitative survey yields numerical data using closed-ended items. Typically, Likert items are used (e.g., strongly agree to strongly disagree). There are many options for response choices. Numerical values are assigned to the responses by the researcher and are used to calculate scores for respondents. The scores indicate the level of some variable. Surveys can have other types of closed-ended items such as checklists, ratings, and demographic items. A qualitative survey yields narrative data using open-ended items. Questionnaires and surveys are usually interchangeable terms (Hays & Singh, 2012; Teddlie & Tashakkori, 2009).

Tests

Individuals complete tests to provide information on cognitive ability or knowledge of something. Tests can be norm-referenced and provide information on relative standing compared to a norm group. Tests can also be criterion-referenced and provide information on mastery of standards. Quantitative tests, or assessments, produce scores. Qualitative tests produce narrative data (e.g., rubrics, performance assessments) (Hays & Singh, 2012; Teddlie & Tashakkori, 2009).

Considering Strategy Advantages and Disadvantages

As previously stated, when planning a research study, the researcher should consider all the possibilities and then determine which would be the best choice. Tables 2 and 3 display possible data collection strategies for the two variables to be addressed for Research Question 1. The identified data sources from Table 1 were used when considering the possible data collection strategies. Some strategies are impossible or inappropriate to use for certain variables, and those are designated as "N/A" in the table. In-depth discussion of the advantages and disadvantages of data collection strategies can be found in the methodological literature (e.g., Sandelowski, 2000; Teddlie & Tashakkori, 2009).

It is important to consider the advantages and disadvantages of data strategies before considering how to integrate them in a mixed methods study. The advantages and disadvantages can be used to narrow down the options. One should rule out strategies that are not logistically possible. Compare strategies that are different ways of collecting data from the same individuals and choose the best strategies.

Table 2. Advantages and disadvantages of strategies for Research Question 1

Strategy	Teachers' Areas of Weakness	Years of Experience
Observations	Observe teachers to identify areas of weakness PRO: Able to measure areas of weakness in the natural context as they occur; Able to obtain detailed descriptions of weaknesses CON: Time-consuming; Observer needs to be trained for valid data collection: Impact of observer on natural setting	N/A
Unobtrusive Measures	Teachers' formal or informal evaluation/observation results* PRO: Pre-existing data; Could obtain multiple years of data CON: Getting access; No control over data quality	Archival data* PRO: Pre-existing data; Able to obtain multiple years of data CON: Getting access; No control over data quality
Focus Groups	Teacher or administrator focus group* PRO: Can get data from the individuals the study is about (i.e., teachers) with the benefit of a group dynamic; obtain in-depth data: able to get clarification; administrator has knowledge of entire school CON: Time-consuming; teachers may be reluctant to share in front on others; self-assessment may not be as accurate as observation; one or two participants may dominate the session; administrator is somewhat removed from the natural setting	Ask at a teacher focus group PRO: Easy to obtain if already doing the focus group for other variable CON: Only collected for a narrow group
Interviews	Teacher or school administrator interviews* PRO: In-depth discussion about areas of weakness; teacher about teacher weaknesses; administrator has knowledge of entire school; obtain in-depth data: able to get clarification; CON: Time-consuming; self-assessment may not be as accurate as observation; administrator is somewhat removed from the natural setting; impact of interviewer on results	Ask at a teacher interview PRO: Easy to obtain if already doing the interview for other variable CON: Only collected for a narrow group
Surveys	Teacher or school administrator surveys PRO: Collect data from a broader group of teachers or administrators; less time-consuming; administrator has knowledge of entire school CON: Self-assessment may not be as accurate as observation; principal is somewhat removed from the natural setting; response rate; have to be mindful of survey length; survey development may be time-consuming	Ask as a demographic item on a survey PRO: Collect from a broader group of teachers; less time-consuming CON: Asking administrator to provide it would be time-consuming for the administrator if not readily available; response rate
Tests	Student test scores* PRO: Pre-existing data; this is the outcome of teaching strengths/weaknesses CON: Getting access	N/A

Compare strategies that are doing something similar and choose the best ones. Choose the best strategies of those that would obtain a greater breadth of data and do the same for reaching more depth. The best possibilities are denoted with an asterisk in the Tables 2 and 3.

For Research Question 1, of the possible data collection strategies for measuring teachers' areas of weakness, conducting observations would be the least logistically possible. Further, the teacher evaluation results based on classroom observations are already available. The evaluation results based on observations would be more informative than a teacher survey where weaknesses would be self-reported. A better way to obtain the teachers own perceptions of their individual and collective areas of weakness, would be a focus group because it would be the most efficient way to produce in-depth data and on a broader scale, as compare to doing interviews with teachers. The same would be true for an adminstrator focus group. However, interviewing a school administrator and having a focus group with a sample of the teachers at that school could be of interest. Finally, test scores will still be considered depending on whether the data can be accessed and if the analysis of the data would not be more cumbersome than it is worth. As a result of considering the advantages and the disadvantages, the following listing displays the remaining possibilities. A notation system used by Teddlie and Tashakkori (2009) indicates the strategy type and whether qualitative or quantitative data would logistically possible as well as practical. The remaining possibilities for the teacher's areas of weakness variable include:

- Teacher evaluation results (UNOB-QUAN);
- Teacher evaluation results (UNOB-QUAL);
- Teacher focus group (FG-QUAL);
- Administrator focus group (FG-QUAL);
- Administrator interview (INT-QUAL); and,
- Student test scores (UNOB-QUAL).

For Research Question 1, of the possible data collection strategies for measuring teachers' years of experience, only one is logistically possible or worthwhile, archival data (UNOB-QUAN). A similar process of narrowing down the data collection strategies was used for the two Research Question 2 variables.

Integration of Methods

Teddlie and Tashakkori (2006) describe four stages of a mixed methods design: conceptualization, experiential (method), experiential (analysis), and inferential. Conceptualization includes the study purposes, research questions, and exploratory/

Table 3. Advantages and disadvantages of strategies for Research Question 2

Strategy	Modes of Delivery	Level of Preference
Observations	Observe the modes of delivery to be able to describe in detail* PRO: Obtain details in natural setting CON: Time-consuming; Observer needs to be trained for valid data collection; Impact of observer on natural setting	Observe various modes and collect information on teacher engagement PRO: Able to measure in the natural setting; Able to obtain detailed descriptions of level of preference CON: Time-consuming; Observer needs training; Impact of observer on natural setting
Unobtrusive Measures	Documents about the modes of delivery* (e.g., presentation materials, manuals) PRO: Pre-existing data; Could obtain details that have been captured in writing CON: Getting access	Archival data - feedback submitted at the end of previous professional development* PRO: Pre-existing data; Collected in the natural setting CON: Getting access; No control over data quality
Focus Groups	Teacher or Administrator focus groups PRO: Can get detailed descriptions of the modes of delivery from the individuals the study is about (i.e., teachers) with the benefit of a group dynamic; able to get clarification; get administrator's perspective CON: Time-consuming; teachers may be reluctant to share in front on others; one or two participants may dominate the session; teachers may not know all the details of the modes of delivery	Teacher focus group* PRO: Can get preference data from the individuals the study is about (i.e., teachers) with the benefit of a group dynamic; obtain in-depth data; able to get clarification CON: Time-consuming; teachers may be reluctant to share in front on others; one or two participants may dominate the session; Only collected for a narrow group
Interviews	District staff member interview on modes of delivery that are used*; Could interview administrators or teachers on modes of delivery PRO: In-depth discussion about modes of delivery; administrator has unique perspective; able to get clarification CON: Time-consuming; self-assessment may not be as accurate as observation; administrator is somewhat removed from the natural setting; impact of interviewer on results	Ask at an interview PRO: Easy to obtain if already doing the interview for other variable CON: Only collected for a narrow group
Surveys	Teacher or school administrator descriptions of modes of delivery PRO: Collect data from a broader group of teachers or administrators; less time-consuming; administrator has knowledge of entire school CON: Providing descriptions on a survey is time-consuming for respondents; Self-report may not be as accurate as other sources; administrators are not the professional development recipients; response rate; survey development may be time-consuming	Obtain levels of preference on a teacher survey listing modes of delivery identified using other strategies* PRO: Collect from a broader group of teachers; less time-consuming CON: Respondents may not be honest in their responses; survey development may be time-consuming
Tests	N/A	N/A

confirmatory nature of the questions. Experiential (methods) includes how the data are collected, and experiential (analysis) includes how the data are analyzed. Finally, the inferential stage includes the inferences made from the results of the study. A mixed methods study is considered fully mixed if integration of qualitative and quantitative occur at all four stages. Mixing occurs at the conceptualizaiton stage if the set of research questions is confirmatory and exploratory in nature. Mixing occurs at the experiential (method) stage if quantiative and qualitative methods are use to collect data. Mixing occurs at the experiential (analysis) stage if quantitative methods (i.e., statistical analysis) and qualitative methods (e.g., qualitative coding analysis, content analysis).

Purposes of Mixing Methods

Mixed methods research has become more prevalent in many disciplines due to the many benefits of mixing methods when studying a topic of interest. In the methodological literature, these benefits are also described as the purposes of doing mixed methods research, or in other words, the way mixing the methods will improve the way the research questions are addressed. Other names include the rationale for mixed methods and the function of the mixed methods. A study can have more than one purpose for mixing methods. The methodological literature provides typologies of these mixing methods purposes (e.g., Bryman, 2006; Greene, Caracelli, & Graham, 1989; Turner, Cardinal, & Burton, 2017). A synthesis of these purpose typologies in the methodological literature is provided below:

- Gain a more holistic understanding;
- More thoroughly study theory (development and testing);
- Breadth and depth at once;
- Convergence and divergence;
- Explain the findings of methods using the other:
- Develop one set of methods using the other;
- Offset the weaknesses of the other method;
- Obtain more diverse opinions;
- Obtain information that will be more useful.

A researcher should consider the various purpose of mixing methods possibilities for how methods can be mixed in a study. When designing a mixed methods study, one should consider each of the purposes for mixing methods and consider the contribution each would make to addressing the research questions. A mixed methods study should be done for a reason, or a purpose, and not just because it has become a popular method. One should examine the set of research questions to determine if qualitative or quantitative methods alone would provide the needed information (Venkatesh, Brown, & Sullivan, 2016).

Mixed Methods Data Collection Strategies

The six data collection strategies can produce quantitative data, qualitative data, or both. A researcher can use just one strategy and collect both types of data. This is referred to as a *within-strategy mixed methods data collection*. For example, a survey could have Likert items and open-ended items and produce numerical and narrative data. On the other hand, a researcher can use two or more strategies. This is referred to as *between-strategy mixed methods data collection* (Teddlie & Tashakkori, 2009). An example of a between-strategy mixed methods study would be a survey for numerical data and an interview for narrative data.

Certain data collection strategies are associated with quantitative methods and certain strategies with qualitative methods. Typical quantitative strategies are tests and surveys (also called questionnaires). These are often structured in format and yield numerical data. Typical qualitative strategies are interviews, focus groups, and observations. These are often unstructured in format and yield narrative data. However, a data collection strategy can be qualitative, quantitative, or have some of both.

For within-strategy mixed methods data collections, the quantitative and qualitative methods are collected at the same time, or in a parallel fashion. Quantitative and qualitative methods can be conducted sequentially, with the results of one impacting the other methods. Any of the data collection strategies can be paired in between-strategies combinations and be parallel or sequential. Some of the combinations of strategies are more common. On common between-strategies combination is pairing the quantitative survey with the qualitative interview. There are some variations of this pairing. If the survey is administered and data analyzed before conducting the interview, the survey results could be used to identify interviewees and even develop interview questions. Another variation would be to interview then survey. The survey could be developed using the interview results. A related combination would be to have a focus group and then use the focus group results to make a survey.

A study can have a quantitative observation (structured observation collecting numerical data) and a qualitative interview. In a sequential scenario, the researcher conducts the quantitative observation and then interviews the person who was observed about the results and what that person was thinking during the observation. The observation could have quantitative and qualitative data. Another combination is the pairing of the quantitative unobtrusive data strategy and the qualitative interview (e.g., an archival dataset is used along with conducting interviews. When two strategies are used sequentially, or the results of one impact the other, the design becomes more fully mixed and a researcher is better able to meet relevant purposes of mixing methods (e.g., holistic understanding). More than two strategies can be used in a study. A case study with multiple data sources is an example.

To decide on the data collection strategies for the qualitative and quantitative strands of the mixed methods study, a researcher should consider the possible pairs from the narrow list of data strategies. When choosing from the pairs, there are some ways to determine the optimal choices. The most important way is to consider how well the data collected could be used to address the research questions. If one research question is both exploratory and confirmatory in nature, a pairing needs to be identified to collect the data for that research question or a within-strategy option could be used. First, consider the efficiency of the pairing by examining (a) which are the best uses of available time and resources in the study (b)if a pairing includes a data strategy that will provide data for more than one research question, (c) one strategy uses pre-existing data, and (d) selecting strategies or even pairings that previous researchers have tried and tested.

Another important way to decide is to consider the form of data (i.e., narrative, numerical) that would result from the pairing. If a confirmatory question requires statistical analysis to best address the research question, numerical data are needed. A quantitative research design is required for that strand of the study. Options include:

- Comparative design: two or more groups are compared for differences on some variable;
- Correlational: two variables (with numerical data for both) are correlated to see if a relationship exists;
- Ex Post Facto: similar to the comparative design but the way the groups are formed naturally allows for tentative conclusions about causality; and,
- Experimental: the researcher sets up the groups (randomly is preferred) to allow for more firm conclusions about causality.

A descriptive design in which numerical data are used to describe something in detail would be used for an exploratory research question (Mills & Gay, 2015). Typically, narrative data are needed to address an exploratory question; therefore, a qualitative approach would be needed. Options include:

- Case Study: the study of something in-depth using multiple data sources;
- Narrative: the study of something using stories (e.g., as data sources, to report the results);
- Ethnography: the study of the culture, norms, and beliefs of a group;
- Phenomenology: examining the way participants make meaning from their experiences; and,

- Grounded Theory: theory is developed and refined by examining it in multiple settings.

A single data strategy would not be a case study on its own; multiple data strategies are needed. Also consider whether the pairing would produce the levels of breadth and depth needed to address the research questions and fulfill the purposes of the study (Hays & Singh, 2012).

For Research Question 1 the best option for collecting data about teachers' areas of weakness would be to use the teacher evaluation results because this one data strategy (unobtrusive measure – archival data) would provide quantitative and qualitative data that already exist. This would be a within-strategy choice. If time would permit, also using the student test data would be useful if it was examined at to determine if standards have been mastered. Patterns across teachers would indicate ways to address professional development on a broad scale. A future qualitative study could use teacher focus groups and administrator interviews and incorporate the findings from the analysis of the evaluation results into the focus group and interview questions. Why teachers have the areas of weakness and how to best address these areas of weakness could be examined. As previously mentioned, the best way to obtain the years' of experience data is to use the unobtrusive measures strategy.

For Research Question 2 the best option for collecting data about the specific modes of delivery to examine would be to use a case study approach and collect multiple data sources. A combination of the information obtained from a district staff interview, a review of relevant documents, and observation of modes of delivery would produce the best identification and descriptions of each of the modes. After identifying the modes of delivery, a survey could be developed for teachers to indicate their levels of preference. This an efficient and effective way to develop the survey, and it would provide broad information for the population of teachers in the entire district. It would be worth the addition time to examine the feedback that was obtained from professional development sessions in the past. The survey data and the feedback data can both be examined. Convergent findings would lead to more solid conclusions, and divergent findings could indicate areas of the survey or the feedback mechanisms that need to be improved. A future qualitative study could have teacher and administrator focus groups where the results from the analysis of the survey and feedback data are discussed.

As shown for the two example research questions, if more than one pairing looks ideal, prioritize and do a study using the other one at a later time. The idea is to select the pairing that will accomplish as much as possible as efficiently as possible. Often considering how to sequence and use the results of one to conduct the other strategy is an efficient and effective way to maximize the level of understanding for addressing the research questions and study purposes. In summary, when selecting a data collection strategy, identify potential data sources, consider which data collection strategies are possible, compare advantages/disadvantages of strategies, and determine which mixed methods pairing would be best. This section provided the details for Step 5, the selection of data sources.

DEVELOPING A SAMPLING PLAN

This section of the chapter describes details regarding Step 6, a procedure for developing a sampling plan.

The procedure is a set of decisions to make to determine the best sampling plan (Mills & Gay, 2015; Teddlie & Tashakkori, 2009). The procedure involves making decisions for each of the selected data collection strategies for the study. Table 1 information should also be examined (e.g., data form, scope).

Numerical Data

The considerations relevant to obtaining numerical data include:

- Considering the adequate sample size;
- Considering potential populations for sampling; and,
- Considering whether probability or non-probability sampling will be used

Explanations for each of these considerations are provided below.

Sample Size

Regarding sample size, one should consider whether the data will be statistically analyzed and how large of a sample is needed for the results to be valid. There are some rules of thumb to use as a guide and listed in most research design textbooks (e.g., Creswell & Plano Clark, 2017; Lodico, Spaulding, & Voegtle, 2010; Mills & Gay, 2015). When correlating variables, at least 30 subjects or units of analysis are needed. For statistical comparisons of groups, each group should have at least 30 units of analysis. If a researcher is validating a new instrument, the rule of thumb is to have at least 100 subjects (Bartlett, Kotrlik, & Higgins, 2001). Onwuegbuzie and Collins (2007) provide minimum sample size estimates for different research designs and approaches. There are tables accessible on the Internet that can be used to have a more accurate estimation for needed sample size that takes the size of the population into consideration. An even more accurate method is to conduct a power analysis (Faul, Erdfelder, Lang, & Buchner, 2007). This analysis combines several factors into the calculation and determines the minimum sample size to have a powerful statistical test. A power analysis calculation tool (G*Power) is available on the Internet at http://www.gpower.hhu.de/

Keep in mind that typically when surveying, a 50% response rate is the maximum achieved (Mills & Gay, 2015); therefore, whatever you minimum sample size is, administer the survey to double that number if you have no way to increase the response rate (e.g., administering to a group at a designated time). Another issue to keep in mind is that the surveys received are from those respondents who volunteered to participate. The demographics for the survey sample should be compared to the population demographics to gauge how representative the sample is of the population. There may be characteristics that differentiate the respondents and non-respondents that would bias your results (Mills & Gay, 2015; Teddlie & Tashakkori, 2009).

Population

Keep in mind that if data are accessible for an entire group or population, sampling is not required unless logistically necessary. If the population is less than 200, the entire population should be included in the study (Lodico, Spaulding, & Voegtle, 2010). Consider whether random sampling makes sense for the study. Random sampling is defined as sampling the units of the population where each member of the population has an equal probability of being selected. For a large population, a smaller yet representative sample makes the study more manageable. In statistical analysis, because of formulas used to calculate the statistics, too large of a sample can cause the research to get significant results that have no practical meaning. However, random sampling may not be possible if the researcher cannot access a list of the population. A list is needed so that a random sample can be selected and then have the data administered. If the researcher has a pre-existing data set, this would be similar to a list of the population and a random sample can be drawn from the data set and used in analyses. Random sampling is desirable because it makes sampling more objective; however, if data are yet to be collected, the random sampling could result in subjects being located at dozens of settings, or more making the study unmanageable.

Probability and Non-Probability Sampling Techniques

Because random sampling emphasizes probabilities, the variations of random sampling are referred to as probability sampling techniques (Mills & Gay, 2015). In addition to random sampling techniques, two other probability techniques are stratified sampling and cluster sampling. For stratified sampling, the population is divided into groups (or strata) based on a subgroup variable (e.g., income level of high, medium, or

Considering the Source

low). Subjects are randomly drawn from each strata either equally or in proportion to the population. For cluster sampling, a researcher identifies naturally occurring clusters (e.g., schools), and randomly samples schools to include in the study. Many studies have multiple levels of sampling (e.g., school districts, schools, classrooms), and cluster sampling is useful for randomly sampling these groups at the different levels. If random sampling is not a possibility, the researcher may purposefully select clusters. Purposeful sampling techniques will be described in the next sub-section. When a survey is administered, those that are returned make up a volunteer sample even if the survey was randomly sent to members of the population. When random sampling is used to obtain quantitative data, these are referred to as non-probability techniques. There are mixed methods sampling techniques, described further in the chapter, that can be utilized for obtaining numerical data.

Narrative Data

The considerations relevant to obtaining narrative data include:

- Consider potential data sources, including logistics and ethical issues.
- Consider purposeful sampling techniques (these sampling techniques will be described); and,
- Consider sample size/range decisions.

Explanations for each of these considerations are provided below.

First, consider the identified data sources. What logistical issues will be encountered? What ethical issues will need to be dealt with? The answers to these questions aid in weighing the advantages and disadvantages of sampling techniques, particularly purposeful sampling techniques. There are numerous purposeful sampling techniques. Hays and Singh (2012) group the purposeful sampling techniques into three categories: representativeness of the sample, description/presentation of phenomenon, and theory development and verification. A common purposeful sampling technique that provides a representative sample is maximum variation, or the selection of participants from different levels of some key variable, with goal of having contrast among participants. Two common techniques for description/presentation of the phenomenon are typical sampling (i.e., selecting an average participant/case) and extreme case sampling. A common technique for theory development and verification is criterion-based sampling, or selection participants who meet certain criteria important to studying phenomenon. Another common technique in this category is snowball sampling (i.e., participants give names for new participants).

For purposeful sampling in a qualitative strand, minimum samples sizes are ranges that depend on specifics of the study (e.g., how involved the data collection would be for each participant/case). A researcher may plan a targeted range and then make decisions once the study begins as decision factors become apparent. The range of sample sizes from previous research can serve as a guide. Also, an adequate sample size is considered to be the point of data saturation (i.e., point where data collection is producing redundant data). The specifics of this vary by study. In addition, there are mixed methods sampling techniques, described in the next sub-section, that can be utilized for obtaining narrative data.

Developing a Mixed Methods Sampling Plan

In a mixed method study, a researcher can develop a sampling plan to obtain the needed numerical data and narrative data using the identified technique as previously described. There are additional options to be considered that involve mixing methods as part of the sampling plan (Onwuegbuzie & Collins, 2007; Sharp et al, 2012; Teddlie & Tashakkori, 2009; Teddlie & Yu, 2007; Venkatesh, Brown, & Sullivan, 2016). Narrative data can be sampled using a traditionally quantitative sampling technique, for example randomly selecting participants for interviews or stratifying to purposefully sample from different subgroups. Numerical data can be sampled using traditionally qualitative techniques, purposeful sampling, as previously discussed. Narrative data can be transformed into numerical data in a process called qualitizing. Numerical data can be transformed into narrative data in a process called quantitizing. Common mixed methods sampling techniques include:

- **Sequential:** one methods results are used in the sampling for the other methods
- **Parallel:** the two methods have separate sampling entirely or one sample is used for both methods (e.g., survey with closed-ended and open-ended items)
- **Multilevel:** when sampling at different levels (e.g., districts, schools, classes) different levels can use either the probability or the purposeful sampling techniques

Returning the fictitious example, it was decided for Research Question 1 that the best option for collecting data about teachers' areas of weakness would be to use the teacher evaluation results because this one data strategy would provide quantitative and qualitative data that already exist. This would be a within-strategy choice. Also, the best way to obtain the years' of experience data was determined to be the use of archival data, another unobtrusive measures strategy. The teacher evaluation results would include quantitative and qualitative data from the formal observations.

Considering the Source

Considering the information from Table 1, breadth was considered important so the results would generalize to the entire district. With regard to sampling for this data source, a sample size decision is whether to use the evaluation results for all teachers or use a sample. The answer to this would depend on the number of teachers in the district and how involved an analysis process would be. The researcher would obtain a data set with all the evaluation results and make a determination about sampling after considering how involved the analysis would be. If a sample is taken, the researcher would likely randomly sample teachers from each school using some strata (e.g., grade level, years of experience) Random sampling would be possible because the researcher would have the entire population of scores. The researcher may decide to analyze all the quantitative data and just take a sample for the qualitative data which may have a more involved analysis process. For the years of experience variable, the researcher would obtain that with the teacher evaluation results data. It would be important to be able to link the two variables for each teacher in the analysis.

Breadth was also a priority for Research Question 2, and it was decided that a case study approach would be used in which multiple data sources would be obtained (e.g., a district staff interview, a review of relevant documents, and observation of modes of delivery). Purposeful sampling would be used to select the district staff member for the interview. The criterion-based sampling technique would be used to recruit the staff member most knowledgeable about the district professional development program. All available documents would be reviewed, but the researcher may decide to sample portions of the documents and choose random or purposeful sampling based on the document contents. Finally, for observing the professional development, the researcher's purpose is to describe each mode; therefore, typical sampling would be appropriate to see a typical delivery of a particular mode. Using the previous results, a survey will be administered that was developed for teachers to indicate their levels of preference for the modes of delivery. The survey should be sent to all teachers in the district to achieve breadth of data. The researcher would obtain all professional development feedback data. As with the sampling for

Some things to note from the sampling decisions for the example research questions. First, the data collection for each research question could be a mixed methods study on its own. The researcher may want to choose one and do the other at a later time. A second thing to note is that not all sampling decisions can be made upfront. Often a researcher has to obtain the data to get an understanding about how involved the analysis process would be. The amount of work involved in conducting a statistical analysis is often easy to gauge prior to data collection. However, this is not usually the case for qualitative data and even the format of quantitative data may not be realized until the data are obtained. This is a disadvantage of using archival data, but something that can be resolved with flexibility.

The actual sampling plan would be part of the study procedures. The ordering of data collection probably would not be in the same order as the data strategies have been described for the example study. If the it was decided to conduct separate studies for the two research questions, the data collection procedures for Research Question 1 would entail obtaining permissions to access the data, discussing what data are need (including the year's of experience), and reviewing the obtained dataset to determine whether to sample or analyze the entire dataset. For Research Question 2, permissions to conduct the study would be obtained, the district staff member interview will take place, documents about the delivery modes would likely be provided that day, a schedule of professional development sessions would be obtained, and the researcher would discuss obtaining the feedback data. The researcher would use purposeful sampling to identify a typical session of each type and conduct the observations. After identifying the types of delivery modes, the researcher would develop a survey that would be administered to all teachers. The survey would have Likert-type responses to collect preferences. An item could be included that asks the respondent to identify the two or three most preferred modes of delivery. Also, an open-ended question could ask respondents to provide feedback on what they would like to have for a professional development program. The researcher would examine the obtained sample (i.e., volunteer sample) for issues with non-response bias. The entire dataset would be analyzed.

This was an example of what to consider when developing a sampling plan (Step 6). This selection involves a lot of weighing options. It is important to keep in mind the immediate purposes, or what the researcher is trying to do in the first place. This helps eliminate some options that will not work. Also, it is important to know the boundaries for sampling. How easy/hard would it be to access potential data sources for your study? What are logistical issues you would encounter? What kinds of permissions would you need to obtain?

DISCUSSION

This last section will bring this chapter to a close. The final step of the mixed methods design process is to evaluate the design (Step 8). Most decisions regarding the methods would have been made with the exceptions of those to be decided during the study as the design emerges. The selected methods should be examined to determine coherence within the qualitative and quantitative strands with regard to providing the answers to the research questions. If changes need to be made, then make new choices. Planning a mixed methods study takes time and a great deal of intensive thinking. The researcher often gets bogged down in the pieces and parts of the study and needs to consider the bigger picture to ensure there is coherence

(Maxwell, 2013; Schoonenboom, 2018). The methods can be examined to ensure they will be conducted properly to increase inference quality. The specific mixed methods design type can be identified (Collins, Onwuegbuzie, & Sutton, 2006; Schoonenboom; 2018) and the design can be described with regard to priority, order, level of mixing (fully/partially), and type of integration (Fetters, Curry, & Creswell, 2013; Leech & Onwuegbuzie, 2009; Ponce & Pagán-Maldonado, 2015; Teddlie & Tashakkori, 2006, 2009).

Mixed Methods Designs

Teddlie and Tashakkori (2009) describe five types of basic mixed mehods designs (three are analogous to the mixed method sampling types previously mentioned. Six designs are shown because two versions of the sequential design are defined:

- **Sequential Exploratory:** qualitative methods proceed and are used to devlop quantitative methods;
- **Sequential Explanatory:** quantitative methods proceed and are explained by qualitative methods;
- **Parallel:** qualitative and quantitative methods are kept separte until the inferential stage;
- **Conversion:** qualitative data are transformed to quantitative data (i.e., quantitized) or quantitative data are transformed to qualitative data (i.e., qualitatized);
- **Multilevel:** qualitative and quantitative methods are used at different levels (e.g., districts, schools, classes);
- **Fully Mixed:** qualitative and quantitative methods are integrated at all four stages (conceptualization, data collection, data analysis, inferential) in an interative fashion.

More advanced designs include: (a) the mixed methods experimental design (b) the mixed methods case study design, and (c) the mixed methods evaluation design (Creswell & Plano Clark, 2017). A researcher should consider the priority of the methods in the study (one dominant or equal), the order (one before the other or parallel), and the stages at which the methods would be integrated (conceptualization, data collection, data analysis, inferential). A study should be considered sequential if it is necessary to the results of one method to conduct the other one. If a researcher becomes frustrated because his study is not fitting into one of the design types, this is actually a good thing because the more integrated the methods become, the inferences become more valid. More integration goes along with increased function of the mixed methods, and as a result, the purpose of mixing the methods (e.g., triangulation, explanation) could change. This should be revisited once again.

Examine the Design Plan

The chapter will end with an examination of the mixed methods design plan for the example studies (i.e., each research question is used in a separate study). For Research Question 1, the quantitative and qualitative data are collected at the same time and will likely be analyzed together. The methods are integrated at all four stages making this design fall into the fully integrated design type. The quantitative data will have higher priority in addressing the research questions. Sequencing could occur in the data analysis stage, but not data collection. The purposes of mixing methods are to obtain a more holistic understanding about teacher's areas of weakness and to offset the weaknesses of the two methods.

For Research Question 2, the qualitative and quantitative data have equal priority in addressing the research questions. The qualitative data will be collected and analyzed first and used to develop the survey for the quantitative strand. Open-ended data for one question will be collected. If the one question solicits in-depth information, the survey collection could be a parallel design. Otherwise, the overall design would be a sequential exploratory design. The purposes of mixing methods are to develop subsequent methods and to provide complementary information for addressing the research question.

REFERENCES

Bartlett, J. E., Kotrlik, J. W., & Higgins, C. C. (2001). Organizational research: Determining appropriate sample size in survey research appropriate sample size in survey research. *Information Technology, Learning and Performance Journal, 19*(1), 43.

Blaikie, N., & Priest, J. (2019). *Designing social research: The logic of anticipation.* Hoboken, NJ: John Wiley & Sons.

Bryman, A. (2006). Integrating quantitative and qualitative research: How is it done? *Qualitative Research, 6*(1), 97–113. doi:10.1177/1468794106058877

Collins, K., Onwuegbuzie, A., & Sutton, I. L. (2006). A model incorporating the rationale and purpose for conducting mixed methods research in special education and beyond. *Learning Disabilities (Weston, Mass.), 4*(1), 67–100.

Creswell, J. W., & Plano Clark, V. L. (2017). *Designing and conducting mixed methods research* (3rd ed.). Thousand Oaks, CA: Sage.

Faul, F., Erdfelder, E., Lang, A.-G., & Buchner, A. (2007). G*Power 3: A flexible statistical power analysis program for the social, behavioral, and biomedical sciences. *Behavior Research Methods, 39*(2), 175–191. doi:10.3758/BF03193146 PMID:17695343

Fetters, M. D., Curry, L. A., & Creswell, J. W. (2013). Achieving integration in mixed methods designs—Principles and practices. *Health Services Research, 48*(6pt2), 2134–2156. doi:10.1111/1475-6773.12117 PMID:24279835

Greene, J. C., Caracelli, V. J., & Graham, W. F. (1989). Toward a conceptual framework for mixed-method evaluation designs. *Educational Evaluation and Policy Analysis, 11*(3), 255–274. doi:10.3102/01623737011003255

Hays, D. G., & Singh, A. A. (2012). *Qualitative inquiry in clinical and educational settings*. New York, NY: The Guilford Press.

Leech, N. L., & Onwuegbuzie, A. J. (2009). A typology of mixed methods research designs. *Quality & Quantity, 43*(2), 265–275. doi:10.100711135-007-9105-3

Leech, N. L., & Onwuegbuzie, A. J. (2010). Guidelines for conducting and reporting mixed research in the field of counseling and beyond. *Journal of Counseling and Development, 88*(1), 61–69. doi:10.1002/j.1556-6678.2010.tb00151.x

Lodico, M. G., Spaulding, D. T., & Voegtle, K. H. (2010). *Methods in educational research: From theory to practice* (Vol. 28). John Wiley & Sons.

Maxwell, J. A. (2013). *Qualitative research design: An interactive approach* (3rd ed.). Thousand Oaks, CA: Sage.

Mills, G. E., & Gay, L. R. (2015). *Educational research: Competencies for analysis and applications* (11th ed.). Boston: Pearson.

Newman, I., Ridenour, C. S., Newman, C., & Demarco, G. M. P., Jr. (2003). A typology of research purposes and its relationship to mixed methods. In A. Tashakkori & C. Teddlie (Eds.), Handbook of mixed methods in social and behavioral research (pp. 167-188). Academic Press.

Onwuegbuzie, A. J., & Collins, K. M. (2007). A typology of mixed methods sampling designs in social science research. *Qualitative Report, 12*(2), 281–316.

Onwuegbuzie, A. J., Collins, K. M., & Frels, R. K. (2013). Foreword: Using Bronfenbrenner's ecological systems theory to frame quantitative, qualitative, and mixed research. *International Journal of Multiple Research Approaches, 7*(1), 2–8. doi:10.5172/mra.2013.7.1.2

Onwuegbuzie, A. J., & Corrigan, J. A. (2014). Improving the quality of mixed research reports in the field of human resource development and beyond: A call for rigor as an ethical Practice. *Human Resource Development Quarterly*, *25*(3), 273–299. doi:10.1002/hrdq.21197

Onwuegbuzie, A. J., & Leech, N. L. (2006). Linking research questions to mixed methods data analysis procedures. *Qualitative Report*, *11*(3), 474–498.

Ponce, O. A., & Pagán-Maldonado, N. (2015). Mixed methods research in education: Capturing the complexity of the profession. *International Journal of Educational Excellence*, *1*(1), 111–135. doi:10.18562/IJEE.2015.0005

Sandelowski, M. (2000). Combining qualitative and quantitative sampling, data collection, and analysis techniques in mixed-method studies. *Research in Nursing & Health*, *23*(3), 246–255. doi:10.1002/1098-240X(200006)23:3<246::AID-NUR9>3.0.CO;2-H PMID:10871540

Schoonenboom, J. (2018). Designing mixed methods research by mixing and merging methodologies: A 13-step model. *The American Behavioral Scientist*, *62*(7), 998–1015. doi:10.1177/0002764218772674

Sharp, J. L., Mobley, C., Hammond, C., Withington, C., Drew, S., Stringfield, S., & Stipanovic, N. (2012). A mixed methods sampling methodology for a multisite case study. *Journal of Mixed Methods Research*, *6*(1), 34–54. doi:10.1177/1558689811417133

Teddlie, C., & Tashakkori, A. (2006). A general typology of research designs featuring mixed methods. *Research in the Schools*, *13*(1), 12–28.

Teddlie, C., & Tashakkori, A. (2009). *Foundations of mixed methods research: Integrating quantitative and qualitative approaches in the social and behavioral sciences*. Thousand Oaks, CA: Sage.

Teddlie, C., & Yu, F. (2007). Mixed methods sampling: A typology with examples. *Journal of Mixed Methods Research*, *1*(1), 77–100. doi:10.1177/1558689806292430

Turner, S. F., Cardinal, L. B., & Burton, R. M. (2017). Research design for mixed methods: A triangulation-based framework and roadmap. *Organizational Research Methods*, *20*(2), 243–267. doi:10.1177/1094428115610808

Venkatesh, V., Brown, S. A., & Bala, H. (2013). Bridging the qualitative-quantitative divide: Guidelines for conducting mixed methods research in information systems. *Management Information Systems Quarterly*, *37*(1), 21–54. doi:10.25300/MISQ/2013/37.1.02

Venkatesh, V., Brown, S. A., & Sullivan, Y. W. (2016). Guidelines for conducting mixed-methods research: An extension and illustration. *Journal of the Association for Information Systems*, *17*(7), 435–494. doi:10.17705/1jais.00433

KEY TERMS AND DEFINITIONS

Between-Strategy Mixed Methods Data Collection: The use of two different data collection strategies in a mixed methods study (e.g., observations, unobtrusive measures, focus groups, interviews, surveys, tests).

Immediate Research Purpose: What the researcher aims to accomplish by conducting the study (e.g., explain the relationship of the variables in the study.

Remote Research Purpose: How the researcher intends for the study results to be used (e.g., generalizations).

Scope: The extent that the study results are far-reaching or have depth.

Strand: The collection and analysis of either quantitative or qualitative methods in a mixed methods study. There are usually two, but they can be combined into one strand.

Unit of Analysis: The unit of data used in the data analysis (e.g., individual, organization).

Within-Strategy Mixed Methods Data Collection: Using one data collection strategy to obtain both quantitative and qualitative data (e.g., a survey with closed-ended and open-ended items).

Section 4
Analyzing Data

Researchers need to consider the data analysis process, mastering both the deductive and the inductive analytical stages. There are two sources of interpretation and the researcher needs to move swiftly between a pragmatic positivist approach to a more interpretary stance relying on observations and words to better understand the context surrounding the study in order to build theory. Mixed methods researchers operate between statistical enumeration and analysis seeking to confirm hypotheses while coding qualitative data to detect patterns; hence they are required to demonstrate a repertoire for methodologies.

Chapter 4
Analyzing Qualitative Data:
Words, Words, Words!

Janice E. Jones
Cardinal Stritch University, USA

ABSTRACT

This chapter provides an introduction to the process of qualitative analysis and uses step-by-step examples to provide an idea of how the process of qualitative analysis actually works. This chapter is intended to give the researcher a place to begin and to inspire a deeper dive into this rewarding form of data analysis. While qualitative data analysis can be time consuming, the rewards that come from immersion in the data far outweigh the time spent doing so.

ANALYZING QUALITATIVE DATA: WORDS, WORDS, WORDS!

The goal of this chapter is to provide an introduction to the process of qualitative analysis and to use step by step examples to provide an idea of how the process of qualitative analysis actually works. Crabtree and Miller, 1992, note that there are many different strategies for analysis, in fact, they suggest there are as many strategies as there are qualitative researchers. This chapter is intended to give the researcher a place to begin and to inspire a deeper dive into this rewarding form of data analysis. Stake, (1995, p. 71) writes that qualitative data analysis is "a matter of giving meaning to first impressions as well as to final compilations. Analysis essentially means taking something apart. We take our impressions, our observations, apart… we need to take the new impression apart, giving meaning to the parts". While qualitative data analysis can be time consuming, the rewards that come from immersion in the data far outweigh the time spent doing so.

DOI: 10.4018/978-1-7998-1025-4.ch004

Copyright © 2020, IGI Global. Copying or distributing in print or electronic forms without written permission of IGI Global is prohibited.

Sources of Qualitative Data

Before beginning a discussion of qualitative data analysis, we must first discuss sources of qualitative data. This section is a brief overview of qualitative data collection, please further recommendations section at the end of the chapter for a more resources to help with this aspect. Most people naturally think of interviews as the most common source of qualitative data, however, focus groups, field observations, comments on surveys, historical records, and secondary data. The common thread that runs through these forms of qualitative data is words. Words of the interviewee or focus group participant who responds to an open ended question that the interviewer poses. Qualitative data is most commonly words. Patton (2002) reports that frequently the sources of qualitative date includes interviews, documents and documents which provide the researcher with a myriad of WORDS that will need to be analyzed. In quantitative analysis we would say that we are crunching the numbers, however in qualitative data analysis, we cannot crunch the words.

Normally the interviewer audio records the session, whether it be a one on one interview or a focus group of 6 to 8 people who are united by a common experience whether it be work, trauma, or illness, to name a few examples. Someone will then transcribe the session and prepare a document that has the questions asked along with the responses of the participant (See sample at end of chapter). This is a very labor intensive step of the process and if the researcher is fortunate to have grant money or other source of funding available to pay a transcriptionist they are lucky. Otherwise it is the researcher's job to listen intently to the recording and type carefully to capture each spoken word accurately. If audio recording is not possible the researcher will write down the responses that the participants have to his or her questions. If handwriting responses, it helps tremendously to prepare ahead of time with a document that is formatted with two columns, one for the actual verbatim responses and two with a place for the researcher to provide memos to him or herself, recording thoughts, feelings and/or observations (see sample at end of the chapter). Given the current state of technology, many qualitative researchers have turned to voice recordings made using their phones or tablets. Software can turn these recordings into transcripts which the researcher can use to either import into an analysis program or use to analyze the data by hand.

It is also necessary to transcribe the field notes that a researcher has taken which would include the researchers thoughts, feelings and observations of occurrences such as body language of participants or other nonverbal cues that can be seen during the interview or focus group but not seen or heard on a transcribed document (Yin, 2016). Many times a researcher will carry a special notebook specifically for field notes. These field notes can be documented by the researcher at the end of the interview, during a quiet period of reflection. Yin (2016) also discusses the importance of field notes and the importance of a researcher developing a kind of "transcribing language" (p. 170) where the researcher uses a common code such as a shorthand as it were to speed up your field note taking process. Consistency will be the key here, for example, one might use a large letter A to indicate anger. Or a large letter L for laughter. These field note images of laughter or anger will help the researcher better remember the context that is surrounding the participant's experience. Yin (2016) also describes the importance of processing the field notes as soon as possible after the interview or focus group experience as memories fade or blend together and as researchers we want the richest and most accurate data possible. Again, the benefits of technology can be seen for this important aspect of research as researchers utilize devices like their phone or tablets to record their field notes verbally versus handwritten. Field notes are important but should not be confused with field observations.

Field observations are observations made in the field by the researcher of, for example, a classroom where the researcher is purposefully observing behavior of a student or the teacher as they go about their day. A researcher making field observations will record the observation and perhaps even count the number of times, for example, the teacher says "open your books". Data that might be recorded along with the number of times the teachers says "open your books" might be tone of voice, inflection, facial expression, students body language, moans and groans of students, etc. The field observations would be transcribed in a similar fashion as mentioned previously to prepare for the data analysis.

Additionally, survey comments, or any responses on a survey to an open ended question would be handled the same way. They would be gathered, transcribed and prepared for coding. Open ended questions at the end of a survey are becoming more common as researchers understand the need for respondents to be offered an opportunity to explain themselves and/or their responses.

Historical records and secondary data will be combined here for brevity of discussion but it should be noted that they are two distinct categories of data collection. Historical records are records that have been kept usually archived of events from the past. If possible, the researcher would obtain copies however sometimes that is limited due to age of original documents, no available copier or other issue. Then the researcher will take notes on the historical document. Secondary data would be similar in that it is data that has been gathered by someone else for another purpose other than the current qualitative study. The data from secondary data could come to the researcher in an electronic format or paper depending on the original data collection project. Given the prevalence of video recordings, VLOGing, blogging and other electronic forms of communication, researchers can access a wide variety of data from a wide variety fo sources. While there may be other methods of data collection, this section was intended to provide the researcher with an overview of data collection techniques before beginning a discussion of data analysis.

Data Analysis

One of the joys of qualitative data analysis is that the process of data analysis allows the researcher to stay close to the data as he or she literally immerses themselves into the data, analyzing word for word, line for line and experience for experience. By staying close to the data, the researcher becomes sensitive to emerging themes and theories and begins to understand what is unfolding in front of them. Remembering that qualitative data analysis is not a linear process, meaning the researcher begins analyzing data after the first data gathering experience, the researcher has the benefit of beginning to understand the research and also to look for holes in the data. While in quantitative data analysis where the researcher typically waits until all of the data is gathered, authors such as Glaser and Strauss (1967) provide a framework with the constant comparison method of data analysis as a part of the Grounded Theory process of qualitative data analysis. Using the constant comparative method (Glaser and & Strauss, 1967) to analyze the data, codes are generated and utilized throughout the analysis, from the first interview through the final interview. Each incident is compared as it was discovered in the data and themes occur or emerge as they become apparent to the researcher (Glaser & Strauss, 1967; Lincoln & Guba, 1985). The categories are examined for possible relationships among the categories. So now the researcher has pages and pages of transcribed data, what will be done with it? How will the data be analyzed? Given the nature of Mixed Methods Research, data analysis is an extremely important component. As has been presented in other chapters in this book, qualitative and quantitative go hand in hand, each a necessary component of mixed methods research.

To better understand the procedure associated with qualitative data analysis, this chapter will suggest the following plan. First the researcher organizes the data that has been gathered. Second he or she immerses him or herself in the data, meaning a review of the transcripts by a careful, thoughtful reading over and over again. This leads naturally to the third step, that of generating categories or themes. Followed by, fourth, coding the data, following a coding scheme supported by the themes. Next a typical analytic procedures includes an understanding of the memoing that has taken place. Memoing is where the researcher writes notes to him or herself about the research and those memos are used to inform the analysis of the data. Memos help the researcher create meaning from the data. The researcher then will ask him or herself what other meanings could be associated or found with this data. Are there other interpretations? Finally a report is written that highlights the data analysis and the findings.

The researcher will be advised to avoid weak results. Caution will be important when considering how to address weak results from either quantitative or qualitative. It is important to remember to try not to support weak results from one methodology by adding the other methodology on top. If there are weak quantitative results, do not try to support those with qualitative results, go back and strengthen the quantitative first. Make sure the results are meaningful and accurate before adding MORE data. A helpful metaphor is building a house. A fancy roof will not be supported by a weak foundation. Both the roof and the foundation of the house needs to be strong so that the house stands safe and sound. In other words, both the quantitative and qualitative data analysis needs to be strong, complete and accurate.

Coding

In order to make sense of the data, the researcher needs to apply some coding scheme to the data in order to prepare categories and themes. By doing so, he or she utilizes some system that makes the most sense for the researcher. Some researchers use abbreviations of words, some develop a list of key words, some use numbers, some may even use colored dots to highlight the words chosen. The process of coding may take several forms, the researcher decides what works best for him or herself. The main organizational point to remember here is to be consistent, that is, take careful note of what code you are using and why. As is with anything else, the process of coding will be interrupted by other work, other commitments and life in general, so notes to oneself help keep the data analysis procedure organized, consistent and scientific in nature. Simple office tools like sticky notes, highlighters, index cards and big sheets of paper to hold the sticky notes or other creative manner to organize your quotes and other data points will make the coding easier. As the researcher begins to code the data, categories, patterns and themes will emerge from the data. This process is time consuming but very necessary. Coding is really another way to think about how the researcher will take the data and create meaning out of a large volume of words. Coding allows the researcher to organize the data. By doing so, patterns of word repetition may appear, significant phrases or ideas held by participants will rise to the surface, which in turn creates themes that the researcher will then take and compare to the next transcript, and so on and so on.

It is common practice for the researcher to develop major codes and for those major codes to have sub codes. For example, if a researcher was conducting a study on students with disabilities (see sample code book at end of chapter), possible codes and subcodes could be as follows:

Concern for safety of their children (CODE)
Potential for violence against people with disabilities (SUB CODES)

Three buses to get to school (SUB CODES)
Possible bullying (SUB CODES)
Behavior problems (SUB CODES)

Eventually the researcher will provide quotes from the participants that support each subcode. For example, "Three buses to get to school", could be supported with a quote from a mother who said "I worry all the time about Andrea, she rides three buses to get to school. She is diagnosed with LD and I worry that she will miss the bus and be stranded somewhere waiting and waiting for the next bus, what if it doesn't come? What if she doesn't understand? How will I know? I am turning into a nervous Nellie, I call the school every day to make sure that she has arrived. I don't what I will do when the day comes and I call and she is not there". By reading this quote, the reader can generate a picture in his or her own head about why the researcher chose the sub code "Three buses to get to school" and why it is falls under the Code of "Concern for safety of their children".

When reviewing the transcripts and immersing oneself in the data as codes become clear, patterns will also present themselves. Based on informed ideas and suppositions, the researcher might identify some patterns. Tentative patterns are acknowledged and continuous review of the data that has been collected will help the researcher decide if the additional data are consistent with those patterns identified. Patterns can be described and defined by examination of categories, perhaps expanding, creating new or combining existing categories to create patterns or themes.

The work done between coding and the first draft should feel a little overwhelming in that the researcher is working to exhaust his or her thinking about the data and its meaning. Themes help to summarize the findings and create categories so that eventually the data can be presented in a sensible fashion to the reader. In order to avoid losing the meaning it is important for the researcher to keep track of thoughts, feelings and comments associated with the analysis. Careful notes can help to lessen the overwhelmed feeling as the researcher knows that he or she is not losing any of the information because of the careful notes taken.

Generating Categories and Themes

The researcher begins the qualitative data analysis process by reading and reading and then reading some more. The data for qualitative research are normally pages and pages of transcription. As the data generates meaning for the researcher, the researcher seeks data that has internal convergence and external convergence to form categories (Guba, 1978). Categories need to be internally consistent yet need to be different from each other. This is called inductive analysis. Patton (2002) describes the processes of inductive analysis as "discovering patterns, themes, and categories in one's data, in contrast with deductive analysis where the analytic categories are stipulated beforehand, according to an existing framework."

The Importance of Memos and Memoing

Memos are extremely important tools to help the researcher throughout this entire process. Writing notes to oneself as ideas and insights bubble to the surface will become invaluable tools to help the qualitative researcher, take the work from basic analysis to reflective and insightful analysis of the data. Memos can become an auxiliary albeit nonexistent researcher, as they provide reminders of important data points and provide a rich context to help make sense of the words being analyzed. Birks, Chapman and Francis (2008) discuss the reflexive nature of memos to the research process and state "the interplay between researcher and data is crucial to the generation of knowledge" (p. 69). Memos are a tool to facilitate that interplay.

Offering Interpretations

As themes and categories are developed through by constant scrutiny and examination of the transcripts the researcher begins to form impressions and develop interpretations of what he or she is reading, in other words, themes emerge and the story presents itself. This allows the researcher to make meaning out of the words, to make sense of the story presenting itself and allows the lived experience of the participant to be shared with first the researcher and then eventually, the reader. At this time it is important for the researcher to ask him or herself, this question. What else could the data be telling me?

Utilizing the quotes from the interviews or focus groups to support the codes helps to answer the question, what else could the data be telling me. Observations, memoing, and field notes provide another layer to support the work. It is imperative that the researcher report evidence that is to the contrary and to provide multiple perspectives. Individual experiences may generate contradictions and tensions within the data.

Demonstrating Credibility

Throughout qualitative data analysis one will hear different terms used to describe what in quantitative analysis would be called reliability and validity. Words such as trustworthiness, credibility, and confirmability are used instead. Trustworthiness is defined by Yin (2016) as an infusion of an attitude throughout the qualitative research process that demonstrates a sense of credibility for the reader. This can be accomplished by having transparent data collection and analysis procedures that are defined for the reader without a hidden or poorly defined steps along the way. Following is a description of other steps and terms used by qualitative researchers to demonstrate credibility.

Prolonged Engagement

Qualitative research is different from quantitative in many areas but most specifically in the amount of time the researcher spends with the participants. A quantitative survey provides a snapshot in time, a one shot deal as it were. Qualitative data collection is a prolonged experience with the participants, the interviews are longer, over a longer period of time, the researcher traditionally spends more time observing, getting to know the participant and seeking to better understand each participants lived experience of the phenomenon being studied. Traditionally a qualitative researcher spends countless hours immersed in the data after spending a lot of time with the participant.

Triangulation

Thinking of a triangle, one can imagine data on each point of the triangle forming a strong bond that will ensure a tight presentation of data which will in turn inform the final report. This step in demonstrating credibility allows the reader to see, through the written explanation that the data is working together to inform the reader. Often researchers will use literature for one point, data for another and theory for the third. All three working in concert to present a uniform presentation of the findings. Yin (2006, p. 87) suggests that the researcher keep a "triangulating mind" that is, to "always seek to develop converging lines of inquiry about all of your research actions and assumptions".

Peer Review

A peer review allows peers an opportunity to review, reflect on and report about your data. A peer review may simply be colleagues or peers who are able to review the data and the findings before the final report is written. Consensus may be sought or independent review is fine as well. The important component is to ensure that this process is clearly explained in the final report. Another step in credibility that provides the reader with more confidence that the data that is informing the final report has been gathered in a scientific manner.

Negative Case Analysis

To support the rigor of the qualitative data analysis, negative case analysis provides the researcher with an opportunity to analyze data points that are different than what the researcher expected to find. These are wonderful, rich nuggets of information that challenge what the other participants are saying simply by being different. The negative cases strengthen the findings as they force the researcher to ask him or herself WHY? Why is this different? What about this participant would have made him or her say that? What is different about the lived experience of this participant? (Brodsky, 2008). Some qualitative data analysts will even go so far as to create tables with the questions, Why, What, When, Where, How and systematically address questions that may arise in regards to the data.

Researcher Bias

What does that mean in qualitative research? In qualitative research it is imperative that the researcher acknowledge any bias he or she holds before beginning the project and again during the data analysis process. By acknowledging bias the researcher is bolstering the trustworthiness of the research (Elo, Kaarlainen, Kanste, Polkki, Utriainen & Kyngas, 2014). Specifically focusing on content analysis, Elo, Kaarlainen, Kanste, Polkki, Utriainen and Kyngas (2014) provide a series of questions that the researcher can ask him or herself such as "did I lead the participant?" or "did I ask too broad of questions?" (p. 4) as the researcher is progressing through the research process. These type of questions can be asked at any time during the research process but seem to especially good after a pilot of the interview questions and again during the data analysis phase. A simple way of identifying researcher bias is for the researcher to identify blind spots, past experiences, past accomplishments, status, and values before beginning the research and reflecting on the same throughout the research process. This might the time to ask for feedback from a peer who can help assist in the identification of blind spots. A research colleague can also help in this regard by providing critical feedback by asking simple questions of the researcher. Of course, the researcher needs to have an open mind to accept critical feedback. It is always easier to find a blind spot in someone else rather than in our own self.

Another important step in addressing researcher bias is bracketing. Bracketing tasks the researcher with acknowledging ideas, values and beliefs that society takes for granted in the world we live in. The focus of bracketing is to acknowledge ideas that we know exist but that we may not be able to change. By bracketing, the researcher makes very clear first to him or herself as the researcher and then again in the written report of that data analysis what assumptions are underlying the thoughts, values and ideals that society holds.

Member Checking

An integral step in the review of the data is member checking. Member checking has been described as an opportunity for the participants in the study to review what they have said, to provide an opposing view or a clarification if needed (Miles, Huberman & Saldana, 2014). By doing this, the researcher allows for a clearer picture of the data to come forth and this step provides another level of credibility for the data. Traditionally, this step, of member checking is outlined in the procedures section and the consent documentation.

Rich, Thick Description

The researcher uses many quotes from the participants to support the themes suggested by the research. In addition, the researcher writes in vivid detail, providing and shaping a context for the reader to fully understand and visualize what is happening, what the participant is feeling, to better understand the lived experience of the participant. The reader should feel as though he or she can recreate the setting, the mood, the feel of the data gathering experience. The reader should feel as though he or she is part of the story being told. Additionally, throughout the qualitative research arena, one will hear expressions such as "I knew I had enough data when I began hearing the same thing from different participants". There is no magic number, however one will hear that the researcher has reached a point of saturation which refers to the feeling that one is reading similar experiences over at which point the researcher feels as though he or she is saturated by the data.

To summarize this section on how the researcher can demonstrate that he or she has good results, it is important to remember to accurately describe the procedures used through the study. The timing and placement of the procedures should be explained, how the data was gathered, steps in the process are clear and well defined. Additionally, the researcher has done a good job of explaining his or her bias, worldview, assumptions and epistemology and how those will be impacting the analysis of the data. Utilizing some or all of the methods described above, the researcher outlines a clear process with clear descriptions of how he or she arrived at the conclusions and findings presented in the final report.

Computer Software and Data Analysis

This chapter has focused on the more traditional way of coding data, that is, by hand, with the researcher utilizing paper and pen and assorted office supplies to organize, code and create themes out of the data. It is worthwhile to note that there are many different computer software programs available for the researcher to use.

A Google search will start the researcher on his or her path to finding a program that is both affordable and viable for the researcher. What is most important to note is that computer software programs do not do the analysis for the researcher, instead, they label and organize data which allows the researcher to search among the data points to create the themes. If there are large amounts of data, or the data collection is ongoing, a computer software program might be a great investment for the researcher to keep track of the data and ease the organization of it.

Oswald (2019) discusses his use of MAXQDA 12, which is a qualitative data analysis software package that he used to analyze, manage the data and streamline the research process. Through his description of his process the reader gains an understanding of the power that a digital tool holds for analyzing qualitative data. The important point to remember for a qualitative researcher is that whatever the tool used to analyze the data, it has to "WORK" for the researcher. It has to function in a way that makes sense of the words for the researcher.

How Will I Present my Qualitative Data?

Part of the joy of being a qualitative researcher is the freedom that comes from presenting your data in a manner that makes sense to you. One way to begin the presentation of your data might be a concept chart (see sample at end of chapter) which shows your reader how the concepts are all connected or how they fit together in your research. Another interesting tool is a flow chart (see sample at end of chapter) which demonstrates for your reader how the concepts work together through time or how they might even be steps in a process. There are a myriad of free programs online that can help the researcher create a concept map or a flow chart. In addition to the use of these tools in the data analysis portion of qualitative research, many researchers use these tools for the research design and/or the literature review. If one is not comfortable with the use of a computer to aid in the creation of these tools, a simple sketch with paper and pen works just as well. Sticky notes on pieces of paper make an excellent starting point as the sticky notes can be moved as the flow as interpreted. Another alternative method for presenting your qualitative data might be through the use of a table (see sample at end of chapter) that you make that has concepts on one axis and participants on the other, with meaningful quotes from your participants to support the identification of the concepts. All of these examples may be used with traditional written format of the presentation of the data. A recommendation that comes from years of practice is to use these graphical representations of the process or data, which ever it might be, in isolation from the rest of the data. Hang the graphical representation on the refrigerator, keep a copy on your desk or even on a mirror. The idea here is that you will look at the flow, the graph or the concept at different times and reflect on what it means, how can it be improved, or even what can be done differently. In order to answer the research question that is presented in the study, data presented will include quotes from the participants that clearly support the themes that the researcher has identified as being the most salient.

In sum, while the work needed to analyze qualitative data may seem to be more than quantitative data, the results are well worth the effort. For social scientists, sharing findings and the lived experiences of participants who might otherwise be marginalized is a noble goal. Combining the qualitative results with quantitative results will provide a richness and completeness to data that has been gathered to allow the researcher to assemble a quality mixed methods research study. Following this chapter is a list of recommended further reading along with some samples of work product using a study that focuses on parental influence on the vocational development of adolescents with a disability in an urban setting.

REFERENCES

Birks, M., Chapman, Y., & Francis, K. (2008). Memoing in qualitative research: Probing data and processes. *Journal of Research in Nursing*, *13*(1), 68–75. doi:10.1177/1744987107081254

Brodsky, A. E. (2008). Negative case analysis. In L. M. Given (Ed.), *The Sage encyclopedia of qualitative research methods*. Thousand Oaks, CA: Sage Publications.

Creswell, W. (1998). *Qualitative inquiry and research design: Choosing among five traditions*. Thousand Oaks, CA: Sage Publications.

Eisner, E. W. (1991). *The enlightened eye: Qualitative inquiry and the enhancement of educational practice*. New York: Macmillan.

Elo, S., Kaarlainen, M., Kanste, O., Polkki, T., Utriainen, K., & Kyngas, H. (2014, January-March). Qualitative content analysis: A focus on trustworthiness. *SAGE Open*, 1–10. doi:10.1177/2158244014522633

Glaser, B. G., & Strauss, A. L. (1967). *The discovery of grounded theory: Strategies for qualitative research*. Chicago, IL: Aldine Publishing Company.

Lincoln, Y., & Guba, E. (1985). *Naturalistic inquiry*. Beverly Hills, CA: Sage Publications. doi:10.1016/0147-1767(85)90062-8

Oswald, A. (2019). Improving outcomes with qualitative data analysis software: A reflective journey. *Qualitative Social Work: Research and Practice*, *18*(3), 436–442. doi:10.1177/1473325017744860

Stake, R. E. (1978). The case study method in social inquiry. *Educational Researcher*, 7(2), 5–8. doi:10.3102/0013189X007002005

Strauss, A., & Corbin, J. (1990). *Basics of qualitative research: Grounded theory procedures and techniques*. London: Sage.

Yin, R. K. (2016). *Qualitative research from start to finish*. New York, NY: Guilford Press.

ADDITIONAL READING

Miles, M. B., Huberman, A. M., & Saldana, J. (2014). *Qualitative data analysis: A methods sourcebook*. Thousand Oaks, CA: Sage Publications.

Wertz, F. J., Charmaz, K., McMullen, L. M., Josselson, R., Anderson, R., & McSpadden, E. (2011). *Five ways of doing qualitative analysis: Phenomenological psychology, grounded theory, discourse analysis, narrative research and intuitive inquiry*. New York, NY: Guilford Press.

Yin, R. K. (2016). *Qualitative research from start to finish*. New York, NY: Guilford Press.

APPENDIX

Basic Flow Chart

Figure 1. Created with Microsoft WORD, using Insert and Shapes features

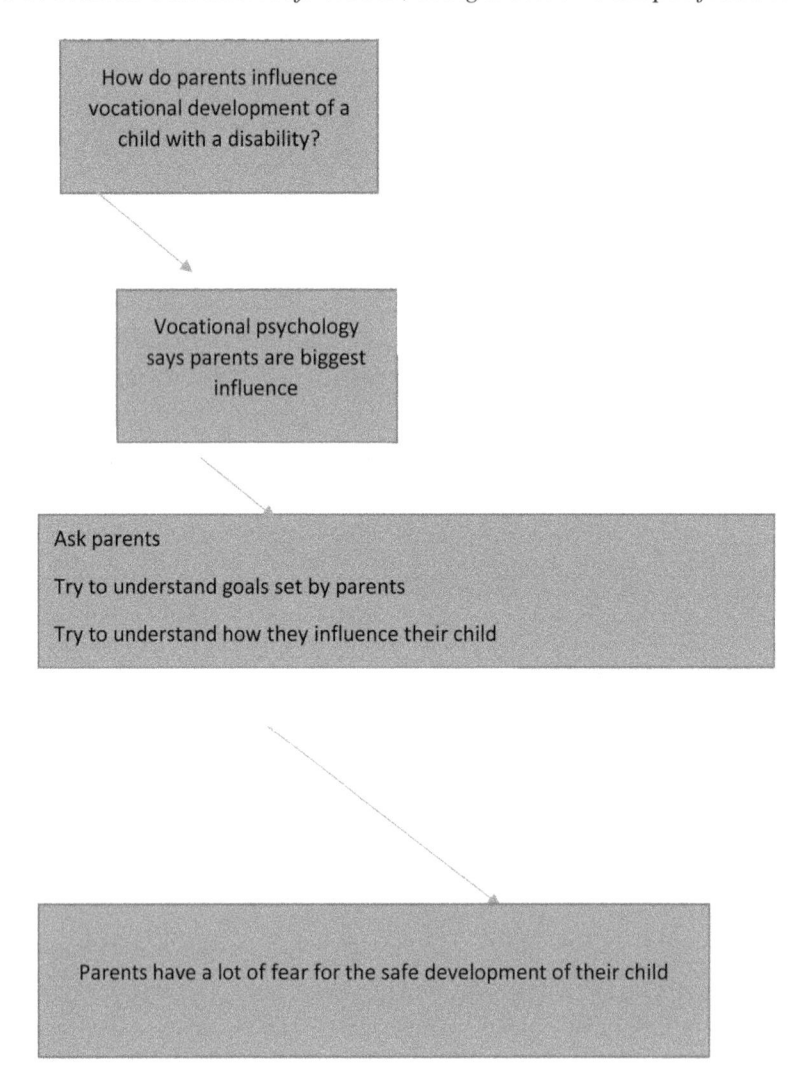

```
┌─────────────────────────────┐
│ How do parents influence    │
│ vocational development of a │
│ child with a disability?    │
└─────────────────────────────┘
              │
              ▼
      ┌──────────────────────┐
      │ Vocational psychology│
      │ says parents are     │
      │ biggest influence    │
      └──────────────────────┘
              │
              ▼
┌───────────────────────────────────────────────┐
│ Ask parents                                    │
│ Try to understand goals set by parents         │
│ Try to understand how they influence their child│
└───────────────────────────────────────────────┘
              │
              ▼
┌───────────────────────────────────────────────┐
│ Parents have a lot of fear for the safe        │
│ development of their child                     │
└───────────────────────────────────────────────┘
```

Analyzing Qualitative Data

Transcribed Interview-First question
   Interviewer comments in italics

1. When did you first find out about your son or daughter's disability? (gather information about disability specifics, strengths and needs)

First or second grade.

Did the school tell you or how did you find that out?

It was just from her behavior. The behavior problems she was having, I have two daughters who have a learning disability. I think Mindra was either, uh, uh, in first or second grade when she was tested and all of the tests and all of her M teams said she does better with one on one learning and I haven't been able to get her that. I hired well, my oldest daughter, um was getting into trouble in school, behavior problems, and she went back to school and she told the teacher that I had slapped her and the teacher called Child Protective Services

Oh dear.

And when Child Protective Services came in and saw that my youngest daughter, Mindra, was having problems with the MTeam and everything, they gave her a tutor.

Oh great.

But the tutor was only good for, I think it was, 30 days or 45 days or something like that, but after that we hired the tutor to keep coming in but it got kinda expensive, but it was like 10 dollars, but it was supposed to be like 20 dollars, and Mindra did really, really well, and the part that made me mad with the school was they seen from the time that she had the tutor and they seen she was in 2nd or 3rd grade level but she was in the 7th grade, from the time she got the tutor to the time she got the tutor again she had brought all of grades, her reading, and everything was at level. But the school board did not want to pay for her a tutor, so they would never admit it, the tutor went with me to the MTEAM meetings

Good.

The reason she scored low on the math tests one of the reasons why she scored low is because Mindra's attention span is real short. So if one of the problems in the line of problems is multiplication, Mindra did every problem like it was multiplication, so if it was two additions and two subtractions, you know they mix them up,

Sure.

The first one on the line if it was multiplication she multiplied all of them and of the second line was addition, she added all of them and that was the way she did, she multiplied all of them in a row. But she got a failing grade on the math test, and of the tutor hadn't a been there, to bring that to there attention, they would have had left that grade like that. But the tutor was there and she said, do you see what she did, she wasn't paying attention, during the first problem and she took it to the whole line, every problem, she multiplied all of them. The only thing she did differently and correctly was the division problem because the division problem looks different. So that was the only one she did absolutely right was the division problem. The multiplication, the adding, the subtraction…She has LD and ADHD.

Code Book

Career Aspirations Held by Parents for Child

Lack of information about options
Parents choosing same job they have for their child
Financial concerns
College

Concern for safety of their children

Potential for violence against people with disabilities
Three buses to get to school
Possible bullying
Behavior problems
Learned hopelessness
Marginalization
Lack of options
Lack of financial resources

Lack of support

Self reliant
Need for self advocacy on part of parents

Expert Model or deification of expert
Rely on one teacher to help
Lack of knowledge about how or where to get resources
Education professionals lack sensitivity about transition needs
Transition plans not well implemented, executed or understood
Lack of information

    Family system difficulties

Difficulties between husband and wife
Difficulties between parent and child

    Get married

From a disability perspective-someone else to look after daughter with disability
Cultural nuance-protective measure-have daughter out of "harm's way" or risk

    Ideas for vocational development

Talk to child
Help them develop goals
Responsibility
Manners
Budgeting
Being on time
Help with applications

    Parental involvement at schools

Invited to meetings
Phone calls
Emails
They haven't involved me
Need more communication

    Future Planning

Hope for independence
Need for continued involvement

Interview form for notetaking and place for memos

Participant #_____

When did you first find out about your son or daughter's disability? (gather information about disability specifics, strengths and needs)

Table 1.

Memos	Participant's Response
No eye contact Looking at floor, seems uncomfortable	First or second grade. *Did the school tell you or how did you find that out?* It was just from her behavior. The behavior problems she was having, I have two daughters who have a learning disability. I think Mindra was either, uh, uh, in first or second grade when she was tested and all of the tests and all of her M teams said she does better with one on one learning and I haven't been able to get her that. I hired well, my oldest daughter, um was getting into trouble in school, behavior problems, and she went back to school and she told the teacher that I had slapped her and the teacher called Child Protective Services.

Figure 2. Concept map

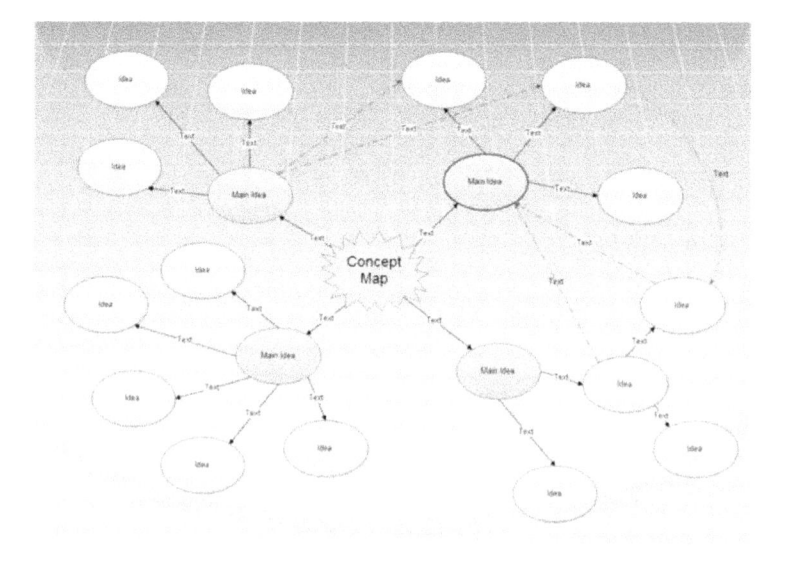

Table 2. Theme of parental involvement in school

Theme	Categories	Quotes
Parental involvement at school	Invited to meetings	"I receive invitations on slips of paper to come to meetings" "I get the announcements about meetings, I just don't go" "I have heard from the teacher about the meetings"
	Phone Calls	"I call and leave messages with his teacher" "The teacher calls me, she doesn't leave a very long message, then I have to call back and we play phone tag" "I don't have my cell phone anymore so it is hard to call me, but I use the phone at work to call"
	Emails	"I don't have the internet so I cannot get emails" "Email would be a good way to get ahold of me" "My son has an email account, I do not, but I suppose I could use his email, right?"
	They haven't involved me	"I do not think they try to involve me, I do not think they care" "I have not gotten any information from school" "I am sure the school does not want to hear what I have to say so I do not get the information about anything, anything at all."
	Need More Communication	"I would like to be involved, I do not know what to do, this school is different than the last one we were at". I think the teachers should try harder to get ahold of us parents" "I liked it better when he was little and I had to sign the assignment book, then I knew more what was going on"

Section 5
Using Innovative Tools in Research

Collecting data is critical to the design of the study and the researcher needs to determine whether the data should be collected concurrently--namely quantitative and qualitative data at the same time, or sequentially--collecting and analyzing one type of data at a time. While the traditional forms of data collection have been stable over the years--collecting archival data, surveys/questionnaires, interviews, and observation--alternative forms of data collection tools are starting to emerge. This allows the researcher to explore an issue at a more holistic level.

Chapter 5

Using Data, Description, and Graphics to Enrich Your Mixed Methods Study

Glady Van Harpen
University of Wisconsin, Oshkosh, USA

ABSTRACT

Systems of organizing, displaying, and presenting data in studies focusing on educational research have traditionally included statistical tables and figures such as charts and graphs. This chapter provides a discussion of utilizing multiple visual methods for displaying data in an educational mixed methods study that goes beyond tables and charts. The chapter does not go into construction of visual methods but offers suggestions and ideas for graphic illustrations such as icons, emojis, or photographs to display results. The chapter calls attention to application opportunities for researchers to reflect upon prior to submitting research proposals and IRB applications.

INTRODUCTION

Many research papers in the social sciences include five basic parts: (1) introduction, (2) review of literature, (3) methodology, (4) analysis, and (5) conclusions or recommendations. There are numerous sources for research methodology (Creswell, 2018; Creswell & Plano Clark, 2018; Leedy & Ormrod, 2015; Onwuegbuzie, 2007; Merriam, Yin, 2018) each with specific information on particular designs, concepts, and strategies regarding what to include within each part of the study. Furthermore, much has been written about data analysis, which is specific to the type of research

DOI: 10.4018/978-1-7998-1025-4.ch005

being conducted (quantitative, qualitative, or mixed methods). Depending on what questions the researcher is seeking to answer, in terms of quantitative or qualitative data, there is much to choose from in the literature. There is one aspect of social science research, however, which remains underdeveloped, especially in the educational fields, and that is visual data presentation.

It is safe to say that graphics have been used to visually communicate stories since humans began etching on cave walls (Samuels & Samuels, 1975). One of the first recorded uses and publications of bar chart data graphics can be traced back to the 18th century economic work of William Playfair (Ajay, 2017; Symanzik, Fischetti, & Spence, 2009). In this application, numerical data are represented by lines and special orientation rather than mathematical units. And throughout the history of commerce, charts and graphs have been used to represent all sorts of data especially related to transportation of commodities. According to Ajay (2017) "Data visualization is the presentation of data in pictorial or graphical format to understand information more easily and quickly" (p. 197). Data visualization is used in many disciplines and has many applications for presenting information, especially online.

In the field of psychology, the use of visual methods research has increased over the past thirty years (Reavey, 2011). In that same time period, educational research has relied on more traditional methods for data collection such as observation, artifact collection, and interviewing; and more traditional ways of data presentation such as tables and narrative. In traditional educational qualitative research interviews are conducted using auditory capturing devices, usually electronically, and then transcribed into text. After the transcript has been checked for accuracy against the audio source, the text is ready for analysis. Miles and Huberman (1994) "define qualitative analysis as consisting of three concurrent flows of activity: data reduction, data display, and conclusion drawing/verification" (p.10). In educational research much of the literature displays this type of narrative reporting. One concept that has been around since the end of the last century in multiple disciplines, but is still gaining traction in education research, is visualization of data through the use of infographics. Tufte's (2001) work on quantitative data visualization provides numerous examples of viewing data in graphic ways. Data visualization is commonly used in helping people understand "big data" (Mashey, 1998). In the online world of today, we view data visually presented to represent everything from weather patterns to stock market trends. In K12 through higher education teachers rely on infographics and visual data to display student achievement in meaningful and unambiguous formats. It is therefore important for researchers in educational fields to learn new and different ways to visually present data.

This chapter is not intended to deliver instruction on how to create graphics, rather it is a discussion of possible applications of and alternatives to traditional data presentation for both qualitative and quantitative research. In order to demonstrate the use of data visualization a previous study (Van Harpen, 2015) is used as an example. The original research investigated three aspects of professional learning for school leaders. First, the study examined and described the phenomenon of how secondary school leaders in small school districts and rural areas connect to information and knowledge in order to further their professional learning. Second, the study explored the extent to which technology influenced the professional learning of school leaders in small school districts, which are geographically isolated from large urban centers and institutions of higher education. Finally, the study inquired how and to what extent these school leaders perceived and accessed fellow educators, private and professional connections, and institutions of higher education, as informal communities of practice (iCoPs) and personal learning networks (PLNs), to further professional learning.

The example study (Van Harpen, 2015) in this chapter is used to illustrate and compare traditional and graphic data presentation strategies for researchers involved in educational publication. The chapter does not specifically offer readers a step-by-step instruction in creating various alternative graphics, rather examples will be shown. The example study employed a mixed method convergent parallel design (Creswell, 2014) where quantitative and qualitative methods were used to collect data from particpants. The study demonstrates how data are typically displayed in educational research using tables, figures, and quoted text. This chapter will show how these basic data displays can be graphically enhanced to provide readers with more visual enriched data. Additionally, this chapter will discuss how the concept of data visualization is useful for presenting findings after the study has been completed.

Background of the Example Study

The original mixed methods study (Van Harpen, 2015) sought to answer research questions connected to the professional learning of secondary school leaders. Specifically, the research examined and described the phenomenon of how secondary school leaders in small school districts and remote areas connect to information and knowledge in order to further their professional learning. Additionally, the study explored the extent to which technology influenced learning among school leaders in small school districts, most of whom were geographically isolated from large urban centers and institutions of higher education. Furthermore, the study examined the extent to which school leaders in small districts furthered their professional learning by utilizing fellow educators, private and professional connections, and institutions of higher education, through involvement with one another, informal communities of practice, or CoPs (Lave & Wenger, 1991), informal communities of practice iCoPs (Brown & Druid, 1991) and personal learning networks, or PLNs (Digenti,1999).

Figure 1.

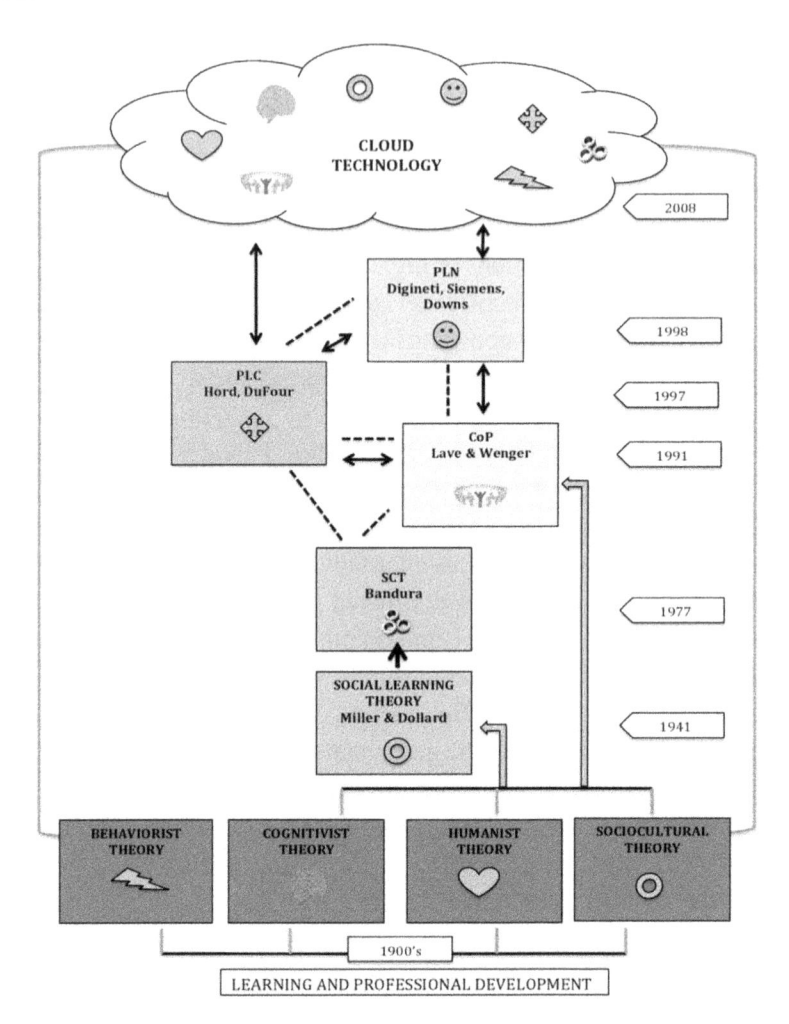

In addition to a comprehensive review of literature connected with the research topic a graphic was created to provide a visual overview of authors works along with an historical timeline. Figure 1 highlights the theoretical and contextual literature framework of the study.

Methodological Approach

Remember that a researcher considers a mixed methods approach to provide a design which allows collection of both qualitative and quantitative in order to yield "a better understanding of research problems than either approach alone" (Creswell

Using Data, Description, and Graphics to Enrich Your Mixed Methods Study

& Plano Clark, 2011, p. 5). In order to describe and understand the phenomena of continued professional learning for school leaders, occurring beyond their master's degree and/or licensure certification, a mixed method was chosen. Thus, data were gathered using quantitative and qualitative techniques and strategies.

Quantitative Methods

The quantitative portion of the study (2015) included a researcher developed survey instrument, the School Leader Professional Learning Assessment (SLPLA). The SPLA was sent electronically, via school email addresses, to the sample population in order obtain quantitative responses from participants. The quantitative data were analyzed using SPSS and inferential statistic reported on the sample population and return rates. These statistic were reported textually by Author (Name redacted)

The sample population was comprised of secondary school leaders within a unique geographic area. The SLPLA survey was electronically distributed to all of the secondary school principals in the study area (N=70). A total of n=46 school leaders completed the survey for an overall sample response rate of 65.7%. The respondents who completed the survey answered all questions including demographic data. In the sample group (n=46) there were 12 (26.1%) females and 34 (73.9%) male respondents as shown in Table 7. The breakdown of females to males in the study population (N=70) is 22 (31.42%) females to 48 (68.57%) males. Males in the sample had a higher return rate for the SLPLA at 73.9% as compared with females' return rate of 26.1%. This may indicate that female response data might be underrepresented in the study (p. 144).

Figure 2.

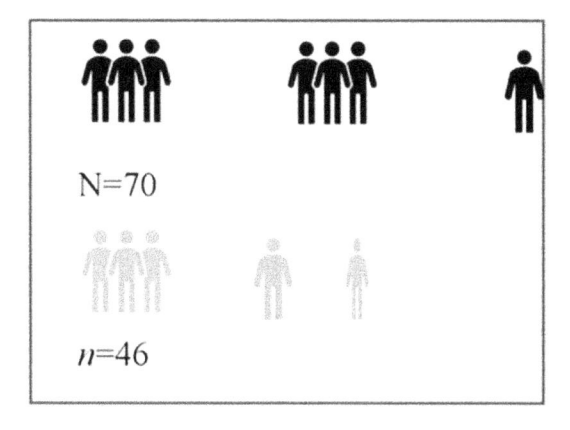

Table 1. School Leader Gender

Gender	Male	Female
	%	%
n	34 73.9	12 26.1

Now consider the same data presented in Figure 2 using icons to provide a more visual format. Just by looking at the graphic the reader can see that more than half of the sample responded. Icons can be inserted in the same way shapes and pictures are added when word-processing a document.

A second way to enliven, or possibly simplify data is to use charts. One way to do this is to take data from a computer program, such as Excel, and use the program features to create a chart or graph. In the example study, the gender of the principal respondents was reported in a typical APA table format as shown in Table 1.

Whereas, using a graphic, as shown in Figure 3, the data easily portrays the ratio of male to female respondents rounded to the nearest percent.

A third example of visually reporting quantitative data is by using photographic images. This may be considered in the research document and is especially beneficial in a personal presentation. The example study used a photographic image to convey the remoteness of the study area. In the study the same information as text states "The site was chosen due to its relative isolation from urban centers and lack of accessibility to institutions of higher education" (p. 109). While this previous statement is accurate, the following photo image, Figure 4, gives the reader an idea of what the term isolation means in context. Additionally, the graphic image may be used to interject humor.

Application opportunity. Given the previous graphic examples, think of other ways quantitative data are presented.

Figure 3.

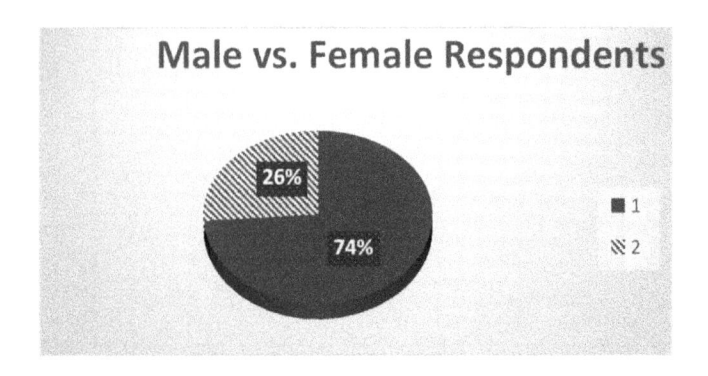

Figure 4.

Qualitative Methods

The example study used traditional qualitative methods, including personal interviews and a focus group, to gather audio data from participants. The audio data were then transcribed into text and checked for accuracy. The textual data were then visually analyzed and coded by the researcher "in order to make judgements about the meanings of contiguous blocks of text" (Ryan & Bernard, 2000, p. 780). Interview and focus group data were then visually coded and analyzed by the researcher. Descriptive codes were used as a means of "assigning units of meaning to the descriptive or inferential information complied" (Miles & Huberman, 1994, p. 56). Pattern matching (Yin, 2009, p. 136) was implemented and codes were assigned to the text based on themes related to the research questions. Interpretation of the codes led to conclusions being made, and the reporting of results. Finally, the qualitative themes were then compared with constructs from the quantitative portion of the study.

In presenting the textual data, from both the interviewees and focus groups, the researcher included individual and block quotes form the particpants. Rather than use qualitative analysis software, the author created her own tables using standard word processing in order to organize themes and patterns. Figure 5 shows how the three qualitative questions connected to themes. This table format was applied to each interviewee as well as the focus group in the data analysis section. The tables were used for individual and group data.

An additional technique to consider in presenting qualitative data is the use of participant photographs, or illustrations, along with block quotes or callouts. In graphic or web publishing callouts are graphic, often colorful, labels that call

Figure 5.

Themes and Related Questions						
SUPPORT Q#4 Composition and structure iCoPs and PLNs	Successes Q#7 (+)	ACCESS Q# 5 Preferred methods of accessing professional learning	Successes Q#7 (+)	IMPACT Q#6 iCoP and/or PLN membership on professional learning	Successes Q#7 (+)
	Challenges Q#7 (-)		Challenges Q#7 (-)		Challenges Q#7 (-)

readers' attention to text using shapes such as arrows, circles, clouds, or boxes (Bear, 2019, para. 1). Using these applications may require additional work in setting up the proposal. Check with the Institutional Review Board (IRB) process at your institution to determine how you should approach obtaining individual consent to use photographs and illustrations in your study. Furthermore, if using participant photographs or illustrations, candidate anonymity may not be possible and therefore care should be taken in to ensure particpants give consent. Therefore, whenever using photographs or illustrations of particpants and/or study sites, permission and consent MUST be addressed in your IRB proposal.

This strategy was not used in the original research, since the researchers did not obtain permission from participants to use graphic illustrations, so the researcher's image as shown in Figure 6 is used to illustrate the point.

Figure 6.

Application opportunity. Other than using software to analyze qualitative data, can you think of other ways you can visually organize qualitative data?

Converging Methods and Findings

When utilizing a convergent parallel design (Creswell & Plano Clark, 2011; Creswell, 2014) quantitative and qualitative data are analyzed separately, then merged, and in order to report the results. Figure 7 graphically displays the study design using a simple shapes, lines, and text. In the quantitative analysis section of the example study, data were presented in traditional tables as prescribed by American Psychological Association (2010) manual.

Application opportunity. How would you graphically illustrate your study design?

The final of chapter of the study focuses on summarizing, drawing conclusions, and making recommendations based on both quantitative and qualitative findings. In the example study there were three important components of school leader (SL) learning that needed to be in place in order for success: Support for SL learning, Access to learning for SL, and Impact of SL learning on their school communities. Based on these three components and nine overlapping areas connected to the research questions, conclusions were reported as a numbered list. Although using a list is good way to summarize a narrative, researchers should consider designing a representative graphic model for the study. The use of models in social sciences have been described by Lave and Charles (2000) as "simplified representations of the world: (p. 19). Although there are numerous models and representations the authors (Lave & Charles, 2000) highlight four categories: Individual Choice, Exchange, Adaptation, and Diffusion (p. 5). In the example study the researcher created a graphic model as shown in Figure 8 to highlight and illustrate study findings.

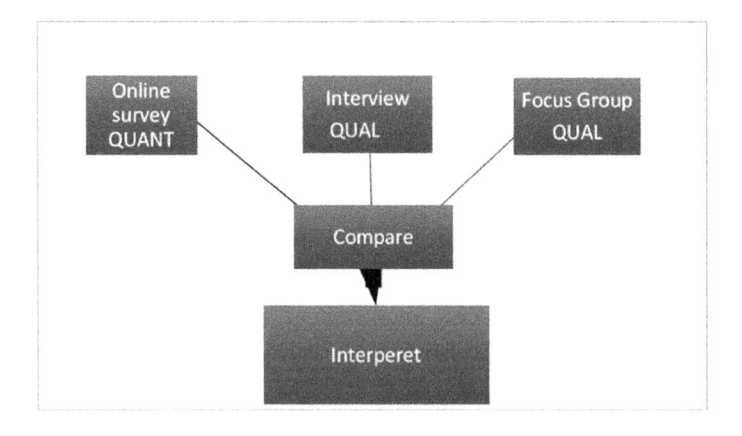

Figure 7.

Figure 8.

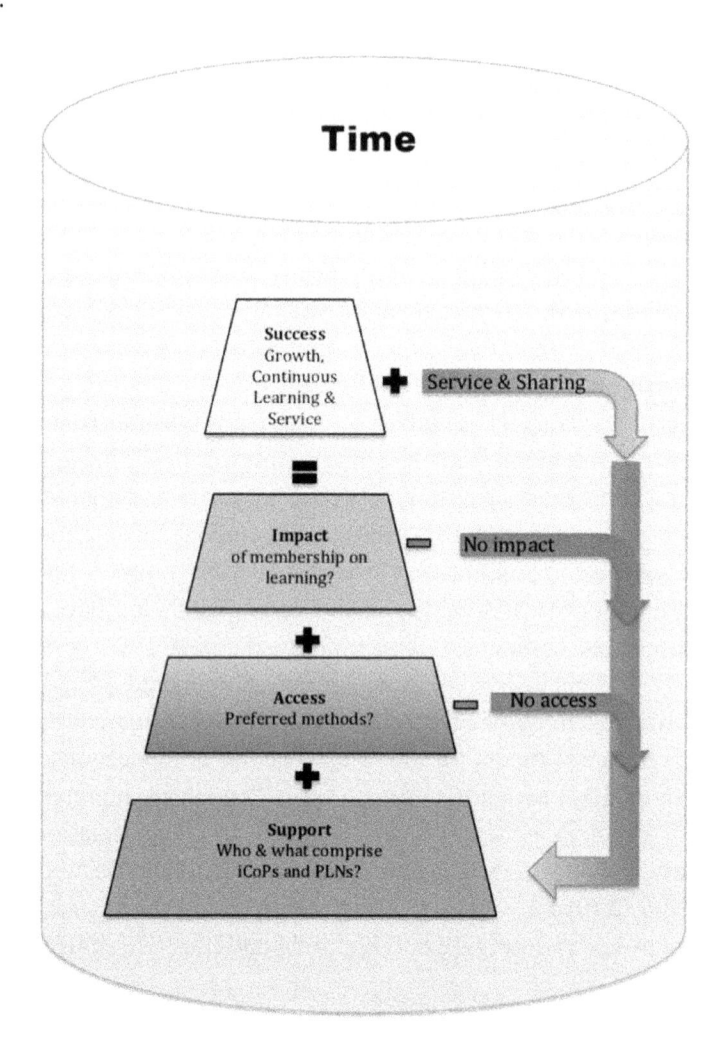

CONCLUSIONS

This chapter used an example mixed methods study to discuss how researchers in the field of education may want to propose future studies in order to organize, display, and present data in ways that are more visually interesting to readers than traditional modes such as statistical tables, charts, and graphs. Throughout the chapter examples were provided for presenting data utilizing multiple visual displays. Although the chapter does not provide step-by-step construction of the visual examples, there are several suggestions and ideas provided, as well as *application opportunities* for researchers to create their own designs.

REFERENCES

Ajay, O. (2017). *Data visualization*. Hoboken, NJ: Wiley & Sons.

Bear, J. H. (2019, January 7). *Callouts are effective in print and web design*. Retrieved from https://www.lifewire.com/call-out-in-graphic-design-1074265

Brown, J. S., & Druid, P. (1991). Organizational learning and communities of practice: Toward a unified view of working, learning, and innovation. *Organization Science*, 2(1), 40–57. doi:10.1287/orsc.2.1.40

Chenail, R. J. (2011). YouTube as a qualitative research asset: Reviewing user generated videos as learning resources. *Qualitative Report*, 16(1), 229–235.

Creswell, J. W. (2014). *Research design: Qualitative, quantitative and mixed methods approaches* (4th ed.). Thousand Oaks, CA: SAGE Publications.

Creswell, J. W., & Plano Clark, V. L. (2011). *Designing and conducting mixed methods Research* (2nd ed.). Thousand Oaks, CA: SAGE Publications.

Digenti, D. (1999). Collaborative Learning: A Core Capability for Organizations in the New Economy. *Reflections: The SoL Journal*, 1(2), 45–57. doi:10.1162/152417399570160

Lave, C. A., & March, J. G. (1993). *An introduction to models in the social sciences*. Lanham, MD: University Press of America, Inc.

Lave, J., & Wenger, E. (1991). *Situated learning: Legitimate peripheral participation*. New York, NY: Cambridge University Press. doi:10.1017/CBO9780511815355

Leedy, P. D., & Ormrod, J. E. (2013). *Practical research: Planning and design*. Boston, MA: Pearson.

Mashey, J. R. (1998). *Big data and the next wave of InfraStress* [PDF PowerPoint slides]. Retrieved from http://static.usenix.org/event/usenix99/invited_talks/mashey.pdf

Merriam, S. B., & Tisdell, E. J. (2016). *Qualitative research: A guide to design and implementation* (4th ed.). San Francisco, CA: Jossey-Bass.

Miles, M. B., & Huberman, A. M. (1994). *Qualitative data analysis: An expanded sourcebook* (2nd ed.). Thousand Oaks, CA: SAGE Publications.

Miles, Onwuegbuzie, & Collins. (2007). A typology of mixed methods sampling designs in social science research. *Qualitative Report*, 12(2), 281–316.

Reavey, P. (2011). *Visual methods in psychology: Using and interpreting images in qualitative research*. New York, NY: Psychology Press.

Ryan, G. W., & Bernard, H. R. (2000). Data management and analysis methods. In N. K. Denzin & Y. S. Lincoln (Eds.), *Handbook of qualitative research* (2nd ed.; pp. 769–802). Thousand Oaks, CA: Sage Publications, Inc.

Samuels, M., & Samuels, N. (1975). *Seeing with the minds eye*. New York, NY: Randomhouse.

Silverman, D. (2005). *Doing qualitative research* (2nd ed.). Thousand Oaks, CA: Sage Publications, Inc.

Symanzik, J., Fischetti, W. Z., & Spence, I. (2009). *Commemorating William Playfair's 250th birthday*. Utah State University.

Tufte, E. R. (2001). *The visual display of quantitative information*. Cheshire, CT: Graphics Press.

Van Harpen, G. (2015). *Connected to learn: A mixed methods study of professional learning for secondary school leaders in small districts and rural areas* (Unpublished dissertation). Cardinal Stritch University, Milwaukee, WI.

Yin, R. K. (2009). *Case study research: Design and methods* (4th ed.). Thousand Oaks, CA: SAGE Publications.

Chapter 6
Data Speaks:
Use of Poems and Photography in Qualitative Research

Carolyn N. Stevenson
School of General Education, Purdue University Global, USA

ABSTRACT

Qualitative research methods provide the researcher with opportunity to share the lived experiences of participants in an authentic manner. These narratives can be enhanced through visual expression, such as use of photos, which provide another way to exercise self-expression. Found poetry has a rich history in participant-based studies, while self-studies utilize poems as an opportunity to address more philosophical or poststructuralist opportunities. These forms of data collection can provide a rich, thick description of those often overlying on the peripherals of society. By offering participants the opportunity to personally select descriptive photographs and articulate expression in their own voice through poetry, the lived experiences can authentically be displayed.

INTRODUCTION

This chapter discusses the role of photographs and poems in qualitative research. Through use of actual student work, undergraduate student perspectives on critical social issues are presented. The presentation of the data is shown through student photographs and poems. Having an understanding of the visual means of data collection adds to the richness of the lived experiences of the participants. Use of photographs and poems provides a means for participants to express their interpretation

DOI: 10.4018/978-1-7998-1025-4.ch006

Copyright © 2020, IGI Global. Copying or distributing in print or electronic forms without written permission of IGI Global is prohibited.

of complex social issues in a visual and written format. Students also shared their lived experiences through a live classroom presentation.

Qualitative researchers need to be aware of the visual aspects of data collection and creative use of poetry to allow participants to freely document life in an urban setting and formation of self-identity. These methods allow for a more personalized approach to documenting issues related to poverty, violence, and self-understanding. It is through analysis of the photographs and poems a greater understanding of social issues in an urban setting can occur allowing qualitative researchers to gain a broader sense of social issues and ways individuals rise above environmental challenges to reach personal success.

This case study involved six undergraduate students from a small, private, urban university in Chicago, IL. The participants were instructed to use photography as a vehicle for self-expression on identity and the way they viewed their world and their communities. Participants also created poems to enhance an understanding of the way they view live in an urban setting. This chapter includes example poems, photographs, and detailed description of the social challenge faced in their individual communities.

The exploratory questions that guided the study are:

1. What elements constitute undergraduate student perspectives on social issues in their communities?
2. How can photography and poetry be used to illustrate the social issues in their communities?
3. What beliefs do these undergraduate students hold which support or negate this perspective?

Findings from this case study will assist qualitative researchers in learning more about using visual data and poetry as a means to present qualitative data. It is through the participants own perception that critical social issues in urban communities can be portrayed through the eyes of outlying, marginalized populations. Through representation of findings in a visual format serious social challenges in urban settings can be called into questions and recommendations for future change can be proposed.

CASE DESCRIPTION

The Organization

The organization selected for this case study was a four-year college in Chicago, IL. The university is a private, not-for-profit and non-denominational institution of higher learning in Chicago's South Loop. The University is accredited by the Higher Learning Commission of the North Central Association of Colleges and Schools (NCA), and provides affordable, quality higher education to students from all ethnic and socio-economic backgrounds.

Eighty percent of the university's students come from disadvantaged minority backgrounds; more than 90% of its students are first-generation college learners. More than 90% of the students come from low-income households eligible for maximum federal and state financial aid. The university's commitment to diversity and multiculturalism is consistently cited as a distinguishing feature by accreditation teams of the NCA. The University's mission fosters equal educational opportunity for all racial, ethnic, and socio-economic groups and offers programs in Liberal Arts and Sciences along with job and career related professional education geared to the service economy of modern times. The university is dedicated to serving humankind with a global, multicultural and future-oriented perspective.

The university recruits most of its students from Chicago, which has one of the largest consolidated school districts of the country, and which exemplifies social and educational problems facing youth.

The University demographics are:

- African-American students constitute 53% of the student enrollment.
- Hispanic student constitute 20% of the student enrollment.
- The majority of students are from in-state at a rate of 84%
- The overall graduation rate is 11%.
- Majority of the predominantly minority schools have a graduation rate of below 60% and a college enrollment rate of below 50% (National Center for Educational Statistics, 2019).

For this case study, photographs and poems from six participants were selected. Students were from diverse degree programs including behavioral and social science, English & Communication, Business, and Computer Science. The participants ranged between the ages of 21-38. The course assignment was given in a Group Dynamics undergraduate course offering during summer 2014 and fall 2014. All students were at the sophomore or junior level. The ethnic backgrounds included White, non-Hispanic, African American, and Hispanic. Both male and female studies agree to have their photographs and poems presented in this chapter. All of the participating students agreed to discuss their viewpoints of current social issues through a live classroom presentation. Due to space limitations, highlights of the photographs are represented in the vignettes that follow. The poems and photographs were selected based on the relevance to the topic.

Table 1. Reported annual crime in Englewood

Statistic	Englewood/100k people	Chicago/100k people	Illinois/100k people	National/100k people
Total crime	9,782 (estimate)	4,363	2,450	2,745
Statistic	Englewood/100k people	Chicago/100k people	Illinois/100k people	National/100k people
Murder	n/a	24.1	7.8	5.3
Rape	n/a	65.1	43.4	41.7
Robbery	n/a	439.3	137.2	98.0
Assault	n/a	570.4	250.4	248.9
Violent crime	3,289 (estimate)	1,099	439	383
Burglary	n/a	477.1	339.5	430.4
Theft	n/a	2,358.8	1,508.8	1,694.4
Vehicle theft	n/a	427.8	163.1	237.4
Property crime	6,493 (estimate)	3,264	2,011	2,362

Source: AeraVibes (2019).

Statement of the Problem

Literature and observation reveal that undergraduate students are concerned about social issues facing their communities, especially in an urban setting. In a large metropolitan city such as Chicago, topics such as homelessness, poverty, violence, and lack of quality education are issues challenging daily living for many individuals. For example, Englewood, one of the Southside neighborhoods in Chicago, reports 46.6% of its residents below the poverty level (City of Chicago, Data Portal, 2019). The depth of crime in this neighborhood is illustrates in Table 1. This is only one example of the neighborhoods represented in the study but highlights the reality of the magnitude of crime in the neighborhoods represented in this study.

Quality public education is a concern in Chicago. Often neighborhood schools in high poverty areas rank low in student achievement and graduation rate. Schools in Chicago are ranked from Level 1 (highest to Level 5 (lowest) in terms of quality ranking. Admission into Level 1 schools is challenging and is based on a number of factors including test scores and class rank. "In 2018 about two-thirds of district students attended a Level 1-plus or Level 1 school, including 62 percent of high schoolers. But only 45 percent of African-American students and 72 percent of Latino students filled seats at highly rated schools compared with 91 percent of white students, according to what's known as the Annual Regional Analysis," (Emmanuel, 2018).

It is reasonable to suggest there is a need for qualitative researchers to capture the lived experiences of individuals living in communities where crime and poverty are part of the natural landscape. While it apparent these social issues exit, there is a need for data to be presented through the perspectives of the individuals facing these issues on a daily basis. Through use of visual means of data collection concerns can be visually represented through photographs and telling images. Use of poetry allows a format for individuals to creatively express concerns and present social issues through their interpretation.

Purpose of the Study

The purpose of this study was to describe and explain ways photography and poetry can be used to illustrate the social issues expressed by undergraduate students. Findings of this study may assist qualitative researchers, instructors of qualitative methods, and college administrators in three ways.

The findings of the study may inform qualitative researchers, instructors of qualitative methods, and college administrators of the value of photographs and poetry in qualitative data collection and analysis. The findings may also inform current and future college administrators and qualitative research faculty members of the ways photographs and poetry can provide an authentic way of presenting data through lens of the participants—through use of visuals such as photographs and in their own voice through poetry. The study may provide the basis for greater understanding of the diversity for data collection methods in qualitative research for researchers and instructors of qualitative methods to encourage participants to express their perspectives through multiple means.

The decision to conduct a qualitative study was influenced by the characteristics of qualitative design discussed by Janesick (2011). She describes research as being alive and active. It is a way of looking at the world and interpreting the world. This study focused on qualitative methods as means to understand the multiple complexities existing in the social world (Janesick, 2011).

Qualitative research involves passion for the work. The qualitative researcher is interactive in the sense used by John Dewey (1934) when writing about artists:

An "expression of the self in and through a medium, constituting the work of art, is itself a prolonged interaction issuing from self with objective conditions, a process in which both of them acquire form and order they did not first possess." (p. 65)

This immersion into the research process actively involves the qualitative researcher in the quest for gaining a deeper understanding of the social phenomena. A case study was selected for this study. Case studies involve an in-depth study of this bounded system and rely on a number of data collection materials. The cases used in this study were four faculty members teaching in an online format from four generation. The study sought to gain understanding of the perspectives of faculty members on working with multigenerational employees and students.

According to Yin (2003) "the distinctive need for case studies arises out of the desire to understand complex social phenomena" because "the case study method allows investigators to retain the holistic and meaningful characteristics of real-life events" (p.2) such a social problems, for example. In fact, case studies seem to be the preferred strategy when "how or "why" questions are being posed, when the investigator has little control over events, and when the focus is on a contemporary phenomenon within some real-life context (Yin, 1981).

A case study approach was selected for this study to gain an in-depth understanding of undergraduate student perspectives on social issues facing their communities. Willig (2008) asserts, case studies "are not characterized by the methods used to collect and analyze data, but rather its focus on a particular unit of analysis: a case" (p. 74). Stake (2005) argues that the topic of the case can be an individual, but not the means by which the individual engages in a particular practice. He writes, "A doctor may be a case. But his or her doctoring probably lacks the specificity, the boundedness to be a case" (p. 444).

Presentation of the individual cases provides the reader the opportunity to gain understanding of the views, observations, and opinions of the individual undergraduate student participant perspectives on social issues. Actual photographs and poems from the undergraduate students were used in the case studies as an attempt to portray the participant as an individual entity.

Data Collection

Interviews, researcher reflective journal, observations, researcher field notes, documents, artifacts, and transcripts were collected. At least two in-depth interviews were conducted with the participants. In an attempt to gather the rich, descriptive information required for qualitative research, semi-structured interviews with open-ended questions were used. The first step in the data collection process was conducting interviews with the study participants. The information qualitative researchers seek to gain is rich, thick descriptions of the participants in their social setting. Thus, open-ended questions were used to elicit the most complete and thorough responses from the participants.

The nature of qualitative research is flexible, as participants are being studied in their social setting. While variables in the social world cannot be controlled, the researcher can follow a format to help ensure items such as equipment are functioning.

In addition to interviews, participant observation was used to supplement the data collected in the interviews. Janesick (2011) alludes to observation as the immersion into the social setting which allows the researcher to begin to experience the experiences of the participants. The researcher observed each participant at least one time. Settings for potential observations included faculty in their offices, department meetings, and faculty interaction with others at the institution.

Observations also provided a check as to the credibility of the other data collected. Observations do require a series of planned steps. There are limitations as to the amount of information individuals reveal in the interview. Observations served as a means for verifying that the participants' actions match their words.

Document and artifact analysis, researcher field notes, and a researcher reflective journal also served as other sources of data for this case. The researcher gathered documents and artifacts from all participants as an attempt to further understand selected faculty member perspectives on working with multi-generational administrators, students, and faculty. Field notes consisted of supporting interview and observation notes. Format for the field notes collected during interviews and observations followed suggestions provided by Janesick (2011). A researcher's reflective journal was also kept as another means of data collection. The reflective journal served as means for the researcher to express emotions, ideas, and reactions to the study. During the data analysis stage, the reflective journal provided another resource for identifying emerging themes and sub themes.

The Role of the Researcher

The researcher's role (full participant or observer), issues of entry, reciprocity, personal biography and ethics (i.e., informed consent, privacy, etc.) must be taken in account during the research process. In this case study, the role of the qualitative researcher was to adhere to the possibility of neutrality (Silva, 2008).

The role of the researcher in this case study follows that of a non-participant observer (Creswell, 1994; Cohen and Manion, 1989). This means that the role as researcher and observer was clearly known by all the participants. The researcher did not interact as a participant in the development, delivery, or activities of this class. Researcher presence was kept as passive as possible, except when needed to actively pursue additional information from one of the participants. At times this policy of non-interference restricted observations and abilities to seek out more information which imposed another limitation of the research method, but it also preserved the natural setting for these observations.

Participant Selection

Six university students attending a small, private college in Chicago, Illinois were selected for this study. The university has approximately 500 full-time students is mainly a computer school. More than 90% of the university students are first generation college students and receive some form of financial aid. The university is primarily a minority serving institution with a strong social justice mission to serve the under-served. The six participants all were enrolled in a Group Dynamics course in Summer 2014 and Fall 2014. With informed consent, the participants agreed to share the results of a class projects involving caputring a social issue facing their community. Requirements for the assignment included creating a poem and use of photography to represent the issue and the participants' reflective thoughts and opinions on the issue.

Following the recommendations of Janesick (2011), the researcher relied on collection and analysis of various forms of data. Each pre-university student was interviewed at least two times for a total of eight formal and informal interviews. The university students were audiotaped for the formal interviews. Data was also collected from three observations, eleven documents and artifacts, and sixteen researcher reflective journal entries.

The university students were selected because of the representation of an urban population, their willingness to talk about their experiences, and their ability to provide their poems and photographs which represented diverse perspectives. Each participant was a full-time student, came from diverse socio-economic backgrounds, and the same university in Chicago, Illinois.

There were three males and three females selected for this study. Terrance and Delano were African American males. Jacqueline was a Hispanic female. Tanieka and Sierra were African American females. James was a White, non-Hispanic male. All of the participants were selected because of their willingness to participate in the study, their interest in photography as a means for promoting awareness of social issues, and their connection to the other university students selected for the study. Each participant agreed to use their actual first names in the study. Table 1 shows the basic profile of each participant.

Each participant discussed his or her perspectives on social issues facing their community and the need for change.

Table 2. Case ordered matrix, participant characteristics

University Student	Gender	Age
Terrance	Male	Early 20's
Delano	Female	Early 30's
James	Female	Mid 30's
Jacqueline	Female	Early 20's
Sierra	Female	Early 20's
Tanieka	Female	Later 30's

Data Speaks

Presentation of the Data

All six participants agreed to share their reflective poems and photographs as a means for representing a social issue in their community. The students were assigned a project for a Group Dynamics course and also presented their material to a class of fifteen other students. The researcher served as their instructor for the course. Following are the actual poems and photographs presented by the university students which capture the social issues faced by students today.

Awoken by: Terrance

When sleeping there is Chaos that fills
Of constant war that seems everlasting
An empire soiled with blood and grief.
Stretching beyond the lengths and depths of the earth.
Who will take on the evils of the world?
To clench and grasp by the throat of opportunity.
There is nothing that will stop he who will go and take what is his.

By: Delano

I bet God can get you out
Of This mess,
If anybody believe he
deliver scream "YES"

Figure 1.

Figure 2.

Street Life
Think back when was running
In the streets
All the things we did up under the
Sun it wasn't sweet
We were robbers
We were killers
We were thieves
So called Chiefs had us on dark corners,

Figure 3.

Figure 4.

*They programmed our minds had us doing what they wanted.
We were doing everything you can name from A-Z.
Blind to the facts
Lost in Misery
Looking for a way to turn but marked but marked by the beast.
WE were Robots that were Ran by thoughts.
But not aware of the road that we were about to cross.
Then all of a sudden disaster strikes and we end up getting cursed for what we thought was right.
What you get when you live as a misfit
IN and out of trouble like you some type of dip stick
What you get when you live as a misfit
IN and out of trouble like you some type of dip stick
All the blessings God had for us we missed it
Cause we chose to do a bid instead of receiving it
Same people you thought were your back bone
It's the same people that talking about you back home
He ain't this He ain't gone never be that
Prime Example look where he putting himself at
I bet God can get you out
Of This mess,
If anybody believe he*

Figure 5.

Deliver scream "YES"
I bet God can get you out
Of This mess,
If anybody believe he
Deliver scream "YES"

Black Queens by: Sierra

Dark Skinned vs. Light skinned when will this battle between us Black Queens ever end. Don't look at me like I am your enemy because I am your sister. Don't want to hurt you, don't want to abuse you, I'm sorry if the light color of my skin has taken some confidence away from you.

But, you have hurt me too! Calling me light bright like as if my skin is white making me seem like I'm not black see that's not even right. You think I'm boogie and mean right off the back yet you don't take the time to get to know me, not realizing that I am still black!

Your mind is still stuck on slavery days, saying how you were the field nigga and I was the house nigga. (Scratching my head) **AIN'T WE STILL SLAVES!** *Why does is matter who was outside or who was inside. But if you want to know the truth I would rather be outside, so that I would not be used as a comfort girl for white men to come inside.*

Stripping me of my innocence. Blossoming my flower before its time, constantly going in and out of me not realizing what he's doing to my body is a crime. But baby girl this was you too! You experienced the same pain I do. So you see, you are me, and I am you. Stop letting people divide us, because I am no more than you.

I am sorry for that person that called you dark night, saying how they was glad they child came out light so they won't be dark like you. **IGNORANCE!** *Please don't let that ignorance make you start resenting me. I know they told you my skin was fair!? But I was never the fairest in the land because I am still you, you are still me. Fairness was not in my pigmentation, I wasn't fair enough. The Cinderella movie was still sitting in my living room.*

Please stop letting people fool you. When I saw the movie Dark Girls my heart started crying. See my family is different shades of beautiful blackness and we have never discriminated against each other, so please understand that this dark skin and light skin nonsense comes as a surprise to me. Because I will never let someone disrespect you or me.

I am so sorry for that ignorant man and female that called you dirty and ugly and made you feel like you were below the ground. But sweetie, you are a Queen pick up that crown! For you to feel like I am more than you is blasphemy. I am you and you are me. I'm tired of us trying to compete like we are in a race.

What if my DARK BROWN sisters were the eyes, my CARAMEL sisters were the ears, my BROWN skinned sisters were the lips and my RED BONE sisters were the nose.

WHY ARE WE TRYING TO BE LIKE EACH OTHER WHEN WE ARE APART OF THE SAME FACE?! SO LET US EMBRACE EACH OTHER WITH OUR LONG ARMS AS OUR BACKS STAND STRONG AND WE SHOW LOVE LIKE NO ONE HAS EVER SEEN BECAUSE WE ARE SISTERS, AND MOST IMPORTANTLY BEAUTIFUL BLACK QUEENS!

Social Issues: Chicago by: Jacqueline

Our Youth
Wanderers of night and day
Walking the streets with no direction.
Confused and misguided
In need of love and affection.
A repeated cycle with no end

Figure 6.

Uneducated minds full of rage.
Choosing wrong over right
Ending up in a cage.
The Forgotten
There is no place to call home
The nights are long and the floor is cold.

Figure 7.

Data Speaks

Figure 8.

Digging through trash
To hopefully find some gold.
A lost soul who has given up
Jobless and full of hunger.
Still living but in the dark
Full of pain and yet to suffer.
The Beast
Planted in every city and every country
Destroying all businesses in its path.
Conveniently making profits
While workers exploited feeling wrath.
Taking over the world
Remaining in the one percent.
The rest of society fighting for one cent.
Bad Economy
Empty rooms full of dust
Wooden windows all around.
No solution it's time to go
Vacant buildings all over town.
The American dream gone bad
Life savings thrown away.
Memories left behind
You can start again they say.

Figure 9.

The Hurt of Knowledge Locked Away by: James

In a time when our communities are hurting
Rich, pale men, hiding in their towers
Miserly not in their expenditures, but in their opportunities
Our people struggling
Our communities drying up
Empty lots where business used to be
Empty schools where children used to learn
Knowledge locked away, like trusts reserved for those with;
Knowledge stolen that could have enriched the victim
Knowledge of our path sadly unavoidable in its absence
Our mistakes unlearned, unchanged, repeated and magnified
Even our childhood games tell of what's to come
If only we could see through the conditioning
A child without training, learning, growth
An adult lost and struggling
Those who have, wielding their knowledge as power
Spewing their lies as truth
Manipulating the uninformed, the uneducated

Data Speaks

Figure 10.

Figure 11.

Texas and its textbooks across the land
The loss of Franklin
The absence of ethnicity's contribution
A dark labor, a dark time, a sad truth
Let us tear down their towers

Figure 12.

Figure 13.

Let us build living, breathing monuments to knowledge
Beautiful and redeeming
Filled with light hearts, laughing voices, and eager minds
Their minds, laughter, and ingenuity will change our future
They will change our nation
They will change our hearts
Let the misers keep their opportunities,
The educated will make their own
Knowledge free from its cell, given to the young

Data Speaks

Figure 14.

Hurt no longer felt or feared
A nation, a people; strong enough to stand again

The Future of Our City by: Tanika

The fear of rejection in a city of so much class...
The same rejection our ancestors dealt with in the past....
Having so little resources' provided is an issue in our communities...
Poverty on the rise which to most is no surprise you see...

Figure 15.

Figure 16.

Figure 17.

Just one change/chance to act fast for our future....
We'll reach the goals that were set for us to nurture...
As long as we come together and pave a positive way...
Our children's children will want to stay!

Data Speaks

Figure 18.

Major Themes

The topics of poverty, violence, and lack of quality education were major themes that emerged from the study. All of the participants expressed a need for safer communities with a strong call to action to stop the violence. The participants talked about the lack of quality public education and discussed ways that education can make a positive change in the lives of the youth and the future of the community. Homeless and poverty were major themes that they discussed wanting to do more to help their communities and provide a brighter future for youth.

FUTURE RESEARCH DIRECTIONS

Findings of this study revealed that regardless of race or age, there is a need to reduce the amount of violence and poverty in the city. Lack of quality education is an area that needs to be addressed. It is through education and sense of purpose urban youth can have hope for a brighter future.

Higher education can be an agent for change. Future research needs to be conducted on ways higher education can be affordable and accessible to all individuals. Research findings related to the ways participants use their knowledge to benefit the community is needed. In addition to completing a course project, actually following up with having students complete a service learning component would be a benefit to the students and the community. Identification of issues is the first step; creating an action plan for improvement would lead to positive change.

Qualitative researchers should also consider using poems and photography in their research projects when appropriate. The poems allow participants to have their voices heard in a creative manner. Photographs create an outlet for viewing issues through their own lens and capture images participants may not be able to articulate through spoken word. The visual representation allows the reader to see the actual settings as though being a first-hand observer.

EPILOGUE AND LESSONS LEARNED

After conducting this student the researcher learned the strong desire for university students to have their voices heard about social issues facing their communities. While students are willing to talk about these issues, the students found the use of poems and photography a more creative approach to sharing their views. All six of the participants enjoyed working on the project and expressed a strong desire to create change in their communities. The reflective poetry allowed students to express their concerns with a heighten level of passion—one that is often times not easy to articulate though conversation alone. Photography also allows the visual representation of the social issues through actually capturing the image of people and scenery depicting challenges in urban communities.

REFERENCES

AeraVibes. (2019). Retrieved from: https://www.areavibes.com/chicago-il/englewood/crime/

City of Chicago Data Portal. (2019). *Selected socioeconomic indicators 2008–2014*. Retrieved from: https://data.cityofchicago.org/Health-Human-Services/Englewood/b352-9cxu

Cohen, L., & Manion, L. (1989). *Research methods in education* (3rd ed.). London, UK: Routledge.

Creswell, J. W. (1994). *Research design: Qualitative and quantitative approaches*. Thousand Oaks, CA: Sage.

Dewey, J. (1934). *Art as experience*. New York: Minton, Malach, and Co.

Emmanuel, A. (2018). *Chicago releases school ratings: Few make the top tiers*. Retrieved from:https://chalkbeat.org/posts/chicago/2018/10/26/chicago-releases-school-ratings-fewer-make-the-top-tiers/

Janesick, V. J. (2011). *Stretching exercises for qualitative researchers* (3rd ed.). Thousand Oaks, CA: Sage. doi:10.1177/136078041101600402

Kiersz, A. (2018). *Every U.S. state ranked from worst to best*. Retrieved from: https://www.businessinsider.com/state-economy-ranking-q1-2018-2#36-illinois-16

National Center for Educational Statistics. (2019). *College navigator*. Retrieved from: https://nces.ed.gov/collegenavigator/?q=East+West+University&s=all&id=144883#expenses

Silva, C. N. (2008). Review: Catherine Marshall & Gretchen B. Rossman (2006). Designing Qualitative Research [20 paragraphs]. Forum Qualitative Sozialforschung / Forum: Qualitative. *Social Research*, *9*(3), 13. Retrieved from http://nbn-resolving.de/urn:nbn:de:0114-fqs0803137

Stake, R. E. (1995). *The Art of Case Study Research*. Thousand Oaks, CA: SAGE.

Willig, C. (2008). *Introducing qualitative research in psychology: Adventures in theory and method*. London: Open University Press.

Yin, R. K. (1981). The case study crisis: Some answers. *Administrative Science Quarterly*, *26*(1), 58–65. doi:10.2307/2392599

Yin, R. K. (2003). *Case study research, design and methods* (3rd ed.; Vol. 5). Thousand Oaks, CA: Sage.

ADDITIONAL READING

Butler-Kisber, L. (2010). *Qualitative inquiry: Thematic, narrative and arts-informed perspectives*. London: Sage. doi:10.4135/9781526435408

Cahill, C. (2007). The personal is political: Developing new subjectivities through participatory action research. *Gender, Place and Culture*, *14*(3), 267–292. doi:10.1080/09663690701324904

Case, K. A., Iuzzini, J., & Hopkins, M. (2012). Systems of privilege: Intersections, awareness, and applications. *The Journal of Social Issues*, *68*(1), 1–10. doi:10.1111/j.1540-4560.2011.01732.x

Cousik, R. (2016). Research in special education. In K. T. Galvin & M. Prendergast (Eds.), *Poetic inquiry II—Seeing, caring, understanding. Using poetry as and for inquiry* (pp. 227–236). Rotterdam: Sense Publishers. doi:10.1007/978-94-6300-316-2_22

Dumenden, I. E. (2016). "If you believe, if you keep busy, you can develop yourself": On being a refugee student in a mainstream school. In K. T. Galvin & M. Prendergast (Eds.), *Poetic inquiry II—Seeing, caring, understanding. Using poetry as and for inquiry* (pp. 227–236). Rotterdam: Sense Publishers. doi:10.1007/978-94-6300-316-2_17

Faulkner, S. L., & Nicole, C. (2016). Embodied poetics in mother poetry. In K. T. Galvin & M. Prendergast (Eds.), *Poetic inquiry II—Seeing, caring, understanding. Using poetry as and for inquiry* (pp. 81–97). Rotterdam: Sense Publishers. doi:10.1007/978-94-6300-316-2_6

Fenge, L.-A., Hodges, C., & Cutts, W. (2016). Performance poetry as a method to understand disability. Forum Qualitative Sozialforschung / Forum: Qualitative. *Social Research*, *17*(2), 11. doi:10.17169/fqs-17.2.2464

Galvin, K. T., & Prendergast, M. (2016). Introduction. In K. T. Galvin & M. Prendergast (Eds.), *Poetic inquiry II—Seeing, caring, understanding. Using poetry as and for inquiry* (pp. xi–xvii). Rotterdam: Sense Publishers. doi:10.1007/978-94-6300-316-2

Gaventa, J., & Cornwall, A. (2015). Power and knowledge. In H. Bradbury (Ed.), *The Sage handbook of action research* (pp. 172–189). London: Sage. doi:10.4135/9781473921290.n46

Happel-Parkins, A., & Azim, K. A. (2017). She said, she said: Interruptive narratives of pregnancy and childbirth. Forum Qualitative Sozialforschung / Forum: Qualitative. *Social Research*, *18*(2), 9. doi:10.17169/fqs-18.2.2718

Haynes, C., Stewart, S., & Allen, E. (2016). Three paths, one struggle: Black women and girls battling invisibility in U.S. classrooms. *The Journal of Negro Education*, *85*(3), 380–391. doi:10.7709/jnegroeducation.85.3.0380

Hordyk, S. R., Soltane, S. B., & Hanley, J. (2014). Sometimes you have to go under water to come up: A poetic, critical realist approach to documenting the voices of homeless immigrant women. *Qualitative Social Work: Research and Practice*, *13*(2), 203–220. doi:10.1177/1473325013491448

Jewkes, Y. (2011). Autoethnography and emotion as intellectual resources: Doing prison research differently. *Qualitative Inquiry*, *18*(1), 63–75. doi:10.1177/1077800411428942

Kagan, C., Burton, M., Duckett, P., Lawthom, R., & Siddiquee, A. (2011). *Critical community psychology*. Oxford: BPS Blackwell.

Moriarty, J. (2013). Leaving the blood in: Experiences with an autoethnographic doctoral thesis. In Nigel P. Short, Lydia Turner & Alec Grant (Eds.), Contemporary British autoethnography (pp.63-78). Rotterdam: Sense Publishers.

Rapport, F., & Hartill, G. (2016). Making the case for poetic inquiry in health services research. In K. T. Galvin & M. Prendergast (Eds.), *Poetic inquiry II—Seeing, caring, understanding. Using poetry as and for inquiry* (pp. 211–226). Rotterdam: Sense Publishers. doi:10.1007/978-94-6300-316-2_16

Roffee, J. A., & Waling, A. (2016). Rethinking microaggressions and anti-social behaviour against LGBTIQ+ youth. *Safer Communities*, *15*(4), 190–201. doi:10.1108/SC-02-2016-0004

Sjollema, S., & Yuen, F. (2017). Evocative words and ethical crafting: Poetic representation in leisure research. *Leisure Sciences*, *39*(2), 109–125. doi:10.1080/01490400.2016.1151845

Sjollema, S. D., & Bilotta, N. (2017). The raw and the poignant: Using community poetry in research. *Journal of Poetry Therapy*, *30*(1), 1567–2344. doi:10.1080/08893675.2016.1256466

KEY TERMS AND DEFINITIONS

Action Research: Inquiry or research in the context of focused efforts to improve the quality of practice and is typically designed and conducted by practitioners who analyze the data to improve their own practice.

Case Study: Attempts to shed light on a phenomenon by studying in depth a single case example of the phenomena. The case can be an individual person, an event, a group, or an institution.

Confidentiality: To respect the confidential nature of the information gathered during the research and preserve the anonymity of participants.

Consent: The informed consent of participants and respect the right of respondents to refuse involvement. Must understand the nature of the project, the procedures that will be used and the use to which the results will be put.

Ethnography: Focuses on the sociology of meaning through close field observation of socio-cultural phenomena. Typically, the ethnographer focuses on a community.

Document Analysis: Looks for occurrences of specific words or phrases in a document or interpret text to seek nuances of meaning and to consider context.

Field Observation: The observation of participants in their natural setting. Observation can be direct or indirect, participatory, or non-participatory.

Framework Analysis: Where the objectives of the investigation are set in advance and shaped by the information requirements of the funding body; the thematic framework for the content analysis is identified before the research commences (a priori).

Grounded Theory: Aims to generate a theory that is 'grounded in' or formed from the data and is based on inductive reasoning. This contrasts with other approaches that stop at the point of describing the participants' experiences. In terms of data analysis grounded theory refers to coding incidents from the data and identifying analytical categories as they emerge from the data, rather than defining them a priori.

Holistic: Exploration of a research question multi-dimensionally, exhaustively and in its entirety, preserving the complexity of human behavior.

Transferability: The ability to apply the results of research in one context to another similar context. Also, it refers to the extent to which a study invites readers to make connections between elements of the study and their own experiences.

Triangulation: The process by which the area under investigation is looked at from different perspectives. These can include two or more methods, sample groups or investigators. It is used to ensure that the understanding of an area is as complete as possible or to confirm interpretation through the comparison of different data sources.

Validity: Asks whether the interpretation placed on the data accords with common sense and is relatively untainted with personal or cultural perspective.

Section 6
Data Analysis: Examples of Research Studies Using Mixed Methods

In this section, four studies are used as innovative examples of how researcher use mixed methods to provide holistic interpretations of phenomena. Mixed methods researchers need to be experienced in three types of data analysis strategies. This chapter provides examples of innovative mixed methods research studies combining the use of inductive and deductive logics. The strength of a mixed methods approach is that it provides ample opportunities for researchers to be creative and eclectic in their approach, examining an issue from various angles using a myriad of data collection tools and data analysis techniques.

Chapter 7

Mitigating the Effects of Social Desirability Bias in Self-Report Surveys:
Classical and New Techniques

Ahmet Durmaz
https://orcid.org/0000-0002-9287-4375
National Defence University, Turkey

İnci Dursun
https://orcid.org/0000-0002-9856-3914
Gebze Technical University, Turkey

Ebru Tümer Kabadayi
Gebze Technical University, Turkey

ABSTRACT

Self-reporting is a frequently used method to measure various constructs in many areas of social science research. Literature holds abundant evidence that social desirability bias (SDB), which is a special kind of response bias, can severely plague the validity and accuracy of the self-report survey measurements. However, in many areas of behavioral research, there is little or no alternative to self-report surveys for collecting data about specific constructs that only the respondents may have the information about. Thus, researchers need to detect or minimize SDB to improve the quality of overall data and their deductions drawn from them. Literature provides a number of techniques for minimizing SDB during survey procedure and statistical measurement methods to detect and minimize the validity-destructive impact of SDB. This study aims to explicate the classical and new techniques for mitigating the SDB and to provide a guideline for the researchers, especially for those who focus on socially sensitive constructs.

DOI: 10.4018/978-1-7998-1025-4.ch007

INTRODUCTION

Surveys are a widespread method of data collection for quantitative research. In this method, self-reported measures are often and sometimes inevitably used to measure participants' attitudes, beliefs, feelings, values, intentions, behaviors, personalities, and many other directly unobservable constructs within the context of social science research. However, the vulnerability of these kinds of measures to response bias is still a matter of debate today. Response biases are non-relevant sources of systematic error and need to be controlled or registered by researchers before, during or after the application of self-report surveys. Among these biases, social desirability bias (SDB hereafter) is considered as the most complicated and pervasive bias especially while measuring socially sensitive constructs.

Social desirability generally refers to the "tendency for an individual to present him/her, in a way that makes the person look positive with regard to culturally derived norms and standards in test-taking situations" (Ganster, Hennessey and Luthans, 1983). It subsists especially in sensitive questions which are designed to explore potentially embarrassing and invasive matters and yields a high level of non-response rates and intense underreporting (Tourangeau & Smith, 1996). More specifically, SDB is considered as an evident threat to the validity of research which involves measurement of self-report scales, since it may "(a) produce spurious results; (b) hide real results (suppression); and (c) moderate relationships" (Ganster et al., 1983). Due to its not only validity-destructive impact and but also obscure and intricate nature (King & Bruner, 2000), SDB has received the attention of personality researchers and behavioral scientists since the 1930s (Paulhus, 2002). But it was first Edwards (1957) who enunciated the plight as "social desirability bias" and provided the very first scale to the literature. Since then, many methods and scales have been suggested to mitigate social desirability bias and its effects. Today, many researchers utilize these measurement or attenuation methods to identify and manage social desirability bias in order to improve the overall quality of their data-set and the deductions drawn from them.

Because of the extensive cluster of contentious subjects that have accumulated throughout the years, this study aims to explicate the extant literature, provide a clear guideline for young researchers and bring upon an invigorated impetus to current research by introducing some classical and new techniques for mitigating the social desirability bias. In this context, the current chapter is composed of the following sections;

- SDB and its relation with sensitivity,
- impacts of SDB on the accuracy of measurements,
- techniques for attenuating the SDB,

- SDB measurement methods,
- and finally conclusion and further research.

SOCIAL DESIRABILITY BIAS

Social Desirability Bias and the Role of Sensitivity

Self-reporting is a commonly used method for data collection in many areas of behavioral science research because it is a convenient, easy-to-use and effective measurement instrument of the directly unobservable constructs (Jo, 2000) and often because there is no practical alternative (Bradburn, Sudman, Blair & Stocking, 1978). In this method, participants are asked to answer questions which might disclose information about their personalities, attitudes, values, lifestyles, beliefs, feelings, behavior, etc. This method stands on the assumption that respondents tell the truth while giving the answers. However, the method is often criticized because self-reports are prone to have various kinds of response biases including deviant responding, careless responding, consistent responding, omitting items, acquiescence (tendency to agree), and extremity bias (tendency to use extreme ratings) and socially desirable responding (Paulhus, 1991) which decrease the quality of the data. Among the biases encountered in self-report surveys, social desirability bias has received the most attention due to its obscure and intricate nature (King & Bruner, 2000). Here, social desirability refers to "need for social approval and acceptance and the belief that this can be attained by means of demonstrating culturally acceptable and appropriate behaviors" (Marlowe & Crowne, 1964). SDB on the other hand, represents the systematic measurement error caused by this need for social approval.

SDB is mostly explained by the term "sensitivity" (Näher & Krumpal, 2012). In many areas of behavioral research, some measurement items are designed to explore sensitive matters regarding ethical conduct (Schoderbek & Deshpande, 1996) or cultural norms (Hult, Keillor & Lafferty, 1999). In their study, Tourangeau and Yan (2007) delineate the structure of sensitivity in three categories, namely, intrusion, threat of disclosure and social desirability. The first term, *intrusion,* refers to questions that are considered to be invading the privacy of respondents. These questions are so sensitive that, regardless of what the correct answer is or the other situational factors are, respondents basically feel offended or think that the context of these questions should not be a subject of research. The second factor is the *threat of disclosure* which is pertinent to the possible consequences of disclosure of honest answers to an unknown third party. When respondents feel that their confidentiality is in jeopardy, relative sensitivity increases and they prefer to shun from answering questions in order to protect their privacy. The final aspect of sensitivity is actually closely related to the conventional concept of *social desirability*. Sensitivity, in this case, varies according to the conformity between the context of a question and the degree of endorsement of it by social norms (Tourangeau & Yan, 2007). Sensitive questions cause disturbances, seen as an invasion of privacy, and heighten concerns about the disapproval of others or probable consequences for reporting honestly. As a result, and also in line with most of the literature, researchers encounter high non-response rates and intense biased reporting (Tourangeau & Smith, 1996).

When questions are socially sensitive, respondents - specifically those who have a high need for social approval - are likely to answer the questions in a certain fashion to adjust their image and look good (Paulhus, 1991). This certain way of "looking good" depends on the type of sensitive question. Bradburn et al. (1978) argue that there are "two kinds of sensitive questions which might lead respondents to distort their responses: (1) anxiety-arousing questions about, for example, behaviors that are illegal, contra-normative or not usually discussed in public without some tension, and (2) questions about highly desirable or socially condoned behavior". Consequently, respondents distort their responses by overreporting socially desirable behaviors such as voting (Bradburn et al., 1978) or religious attendance (Presser & Stinson, 1998), and underreporting socially undesirable notions like neuroticism or materialism (Mick, 1996). Similarly, literature reviews list some of the sensitive constructs which are subject to misrepresentations such as attendance in educational programs, seat belt use, environmentally responsible behaviors, charity contributions, income, bankruptcy, crime victimization, illicit drug use, alcohol consumption, drunken driving, and arrests (Peterson & Kerin, 1981; Krumpal, 2013).

For understanding the misrepresentations in social desirability, a two-factor model is often used which distinguishes the response distortion that is formed through lying (other-deception) or self-deception (Paulhus, 1984; Nederhof, 1985). Accordingly, when respondents encounter a socially sensitive question, they may simply lie to elude experiencing negative emotions such as shame or embarrassment (Schaeffer, 2000) or to falsify their true positions in order to manage their impression (Brenner & DeLamater, 2014). In concordance, it is asserted that misreporting on sensitive questions is partially under the respondent's voluntary control, rather than a wholly automatic nonconscious process (Holtgraves, 2004). On the other side, the automatic process wherein respondents are not aware of their misreporting is called self-deception. Self-deception is a self-description that respondents actually believe to be true (Paulhus, 1984).

Impact of Social Desirability Bias on the Accuracy of Measurements

Cote and Buckley (1988) state that the measure of a construct is composed of three types of variance including trait variance, method variance, and random error variance. In measurements, trait variance explains the main notion behind the construct which is being measured, whereas method variance shows the amount of variance attributable to the methodological issues such as systematic measurement error or common method error. Trait variance and method variance intrinsically affect the observed relationships between variables (Cote & Buckley, 1988).

SDB can be an agent of intervention to the relations between variables that leads to unwarranted theoretical or practical conclusions as a source of systematic measurement error (Fisher, 1993) and naturally as a source of method variance. Therefore in measurements, SDB might distort the true relationships between variables. The types of distortion induced by social desirability bias are identified as (Ganster et al., 1983);

- Spuriousness, misleading evaluation of entire measurement,
- Suppression, masking the relationships between variables,
- Moderation, altering the relationships between other variables.

In spuriousness case, SDB may be correlated with both predictor and criterion variables, causing an unintended increase in the value of the correlation between these variables. This artificial observed correlation between the variables is actually caused by the variables' shared variance with SDB rather than an existing relationship (Lönnqvist, Paunonen, Tuulio-Henriksson, Lönnqvist & Verkasalo, 2007). Partialling out of social desirability from dependent and independent variables is a controlling method of spuriousness effect. However, partialling out the effect of SDB by using partial correlation or multiple regression techniques may degrade the relationship if not remove it totally. (Ziegler & Buehner 2009).

In the suppression case, Zerbe and Paulhus (1987) state that the effect is the opposite of the spuriousness effect and the possible relationship between two variables remains undetected, because SDB masks the true relation. Therefore, if social desirability is controlled for, dependent and independent variables might this time produce a boosted partial correlation (Zerbe & Paulhus, 1987). Though it should be noted that necessary statistical methods for discovering suppressor effects are challenging (Conger & Jackson, 1972).

The final effect is the moderation effect which alters the dependent variable based on the level of interaction between an independent variable and SDB. By using hierarchical multiple regression analysis, the significance of moderation effect can be observed (Nederhof, 1985). If partialling out the SDB results in decreased predictor value, SDB is accounted as a mediator variable in the structural path. Moreover, if SDB contributes to one of the indicators and not to the others then it will be treated as error variance in terms of the correlation (Lönnqvist et al., 2007). On the other hand, Zerbe and Paulhus (1987) argue that moderation of correlation between variables has two distinct frameworks termed as "form" and "degree". They state that by using hierarchical multiple regression analysis, Ganster et al. (1983) only measured the "form". However, to measure the moderation of "degree" one needs to compare subgroups formed on the basis of scores derived from the moderating variable (Zerbe & Paulhus, 1987).

Methods of Coping with Social Desirability Bias

As indicated in the previous section, SDB has been a major threat to self-report survey procedures. Thus, researchers need to understand the sources and detection methods of SDB in order to measure or mitigate its validity-distorting impacts. SDB has particularly perturbed personality researchers in the field of psychology (Paulhus, 1991). One of the first systematic efforts directed to resolve the issue was presented by Meehl and Hathaway (1946). However, it was first Edwards (1957) who enunciated the plight as social desirability bias and provided the very first scale to the literature. Since then, there has been an ever-increasing interest for manipulative and deteriorative impacts of SDB and for the methods that mitigate them. Literature provides two groups of techniques to cope with SDB including (1) preventive methods which focus on preventing or at least minimizing SDB during the data collection process and (2) deductive and reparative methods which aim to detect, measure, and capture spuriousness, suppression and moderation effects of social desirability. According to the needs of their study, researchers can implement a mixture of methods that are discussed in the following sections. The distinction between situational and personal determinants of SDB is critical for researchers while choosing the right method for coping with it. Nederhof (1985) indicates that situational determinants, mainly related with other-deception (lying) can be prevented or reduced by methods used by researchers during data collection process, whereas personal determinants, associated mainly with self-deception are less easily controlled and in most cases, can only be detected or measured, but not be prevented or reduced.

Methods for Minimizing Socially Desirable Responding

The Bogus Pipeline Procedure

The 'bogus pipeline' procedure which was introduced by Jones and Sigall (1971) refers to any technique utilized to make respondents believe an objective instrument such as biochemical test or lie detector is being used during an interview session to identify false responses. According to empirical evidence, bogus pipeline procedure increases respondents' proclivity to report discreditable information more accurately (Akers, Massey, Clarke & Lauer, 1983; Roese & Jamieson, 1993). The procedure relies on the principle of lowering subjects' embarrassment threshold with the help of such an instrument. Thus, their responses are expected to be less confounded with SDB than the standard self-reports are (Paulhus, 1991). According to Krumpal (2013), bogus pipeline increases respondent's perceived misreporting costs. Therefore, instead of being revealed as a liar involved in socially undesirable activities, respondents prefer to simply admit doing a frowned-upon behavior like deceit or stealing.

Efficacy of bogus pipeline procedure in identifying SDB has been documented in several attitude areas (Paulhus, 1991). However, this procedure is not an absolute incentive for accurate responding to socially undesirable questions. In congruence, extant literature provides conflicting results. Whereas research conducted by Roese and Jamieson (1993) presents reduced socially desirable responding for bogus pipeline procedure, studies conducted by Campanelli, Dielman and Shope (1987) and Aguinis, Pierce and Quigley (1995) revealed contrasting results. However, it would be prudent to state that these divergent results might also be stemming from disparate samples chosen and surveyed in each study.

However, it must be noted that methods like bogus pipeline are criticized for arising serious ethical issues since they are usually deceptive in nature and violate professional codes of conduct. By using these techniques, respondents are misled to believe in the ostensible effect of the instrument being used by the researcher, although its actual purpose is entirely different (De Jong, Pieters & Fox, 2010).

Assuring Confidentiality and Anonymity of the Respondent

In self-report surveys, privacy is a key factor especially when the research focus on sensitive topics. Privacy of respondents is manipulated by two most frequently used guarantees: anonymity and confidentiality. According to Ong and Weiss (2000) anonymity refers to a condition in which the researcher does not know the identity of the respondent whereas confidentiality refers to an agreement that no traceable information of the respondent will be revealed and only the researcher will know the response. In short, this commonly used experimental paradigm involves manipulating whether opinions are expressed privately or publicly (Ong & Weiss, 2000). Confidentiality and anonymity assurances stimulate respondents to give honest answers to embarrassing or even harmful questions (Richman, Kiesler, Weisband & Drasgow, 1999; De Jong et al., 2010). There have been a plethora of empirical applications to test this phenomenon, either confirming or refuting it (Ong & Weiss, 2000; Krumpal, 2013; Roxas & Lindsay, 2012).

Because the lack of privacy increases respondent's reluctance to self-report norm-violating behavior, many researchers include confidentiality assurances in introduction sections in their questionnaire forms (Krumpal, 2013). However, it must be noted that too intricate confidentiality assurances might produce unintended effects and raise suspicions and concerns about who might process the data (Singer, Hippler &Schwarz, 1992). Such that, in three experimental studies, Singer et al. (1992) found that elaborate data protection assurances produce higher nonresponse rates compared to concise and simple assurances. Hence, researchers ought to assess the correct degree of confidentiality statements in their questionnaires.

On the other hand, because sustaining a certain level of anonymity is strongly advised to mitigate SDB, researchers apply techniques such as computerized-survey, randomized response or removal of the interviewer to maintain anonymity and further induce cooperation (Ong & Weiss, 2000). Many researchers aver that anonymously collected self-report information may be less propensive to bias (Richman et al., 1999; Lajunen & Summala, 2003; Mühlenfeld, 2005; Bell & Naugle, 2007). However, there also others who propound otherwise (Lelkes, Krosnick, Marx, Judd & Park, 2012; Dodou & de Winter, 2014). As a result, the issue of anonymity is still a matter of debate and should be handled carefully.

The Randomized Response Technique

The randomized response technique which was first introduced by Warner (1965), attempts to preserve the privacy of a respondent via randomization mechanism. The rationale behind this method is that the respondent uses a randomizing device at will and select the questions of his/her choice. Generally, desirability-loaded question (e.g., Have you ever stole an object?) is asked along with an irrelevant and benign question (Have you ever written a poem?). Only the respondent knows the outcome of the randomizing device and whether they answered to the sensitive question or not. Because the interviewer is not aware which question is being answered, the given answer does not expose respondent's anonymity and thus, pressure on responding to socially sensitive questions is mitigated (Krumpal, 2013).

A comprehensive meta-analysis performed by Gerty, Hox and Heijden (2005) avers that randomized response methods produce significantly more valid and robust estimates than conventional data collection methods of face-to-face and self-administered surveys do. However, one shortcoming of the procedure is that only the aggregate-level inferences can be obtained from the responses of the whole sample (De Jong et al., 2010). (For detailed information on the technique and development presented in the literature see Krumpal, 2013)

Indirect Questioning

A frequently used procedure to prevent SDB during data collection involves obtaining data about interviewee but from another individual nominated by either respondent or interviewer. This particular method has been given disparate terms in the literature such as proxy subjects (Sudman & Bradburn, 1974), nominative technique (Sirken, 1970), inferred valuation (Norwood & Lusk, 2011) but involves similar operationalization in each of them. As indicated above, maintaining the anonymity of respondents is a very crucial factor for minimizing SDB in self-report surveys (Willis & Sirken, 1994; Ong & Weiss, 2000; Hancock & Flowers, 2001). In congruence, indirect questioning method enables the preservation of subject anonymity (Fisher, 1993) and minimizes respondents' own discomfort. During the implementation of indirect questioning, respondents are asked about what "others" think about a sensitive issue. Respondents may find it easier to express their attitudes and opinions (Jo, Nelson & Kiecker, 1997) because the interviewer interested in those "others" about whom the embarrassing or incriminating information is being provided (Lee, 1993). However, evidence provided by Sudman and Bradburn (1974) suggests that whereas satisfactory results are obtained while measuring behaviour, the attitudes might prove problematic to measure. Therefore technique should be exercised with caution (Nederhof, 1985).

Refining Socially Sensitive Item Wordings

Researchers can provide a more comfortable and private interview atmosphere to respondents with an insightful configuration of the design and context of their surveys. Consequently, respondents' subjective perceptions of negative outcomes associated with truthfully responding to sensitive questions are mitigated (Krumpal, 2013). According to the hypothesis set forth by Näher and Krumpal (2012), question wordings defined by its appropriateness and context alters respondents' answers. Thus, while measuring sensitive topics, researchers often use "unthreatening, euphemistic, familiar and forgiving words or phrases" (Krumpal, 2013) to extenuate the concerns in admitting behaviours or attitudes regarding a taboo.

By manipulating the wording, researchers may also modify the level of anonymity. For instance, embedding personal statements such as "I would ..." to a sensitive question can give rise to respondent's feelings of jeopardy. But constructing context with wordings such as "A typical university student would .... " can disperse the focus of respondents and render them apt to express themselves conveniently (Fisher, 1993). This procedure is also known as "loading strategy" in survey methodology suggesting a technique in which researchers can obtain somewhat more honest answers if "forgiving-wording (forgives the behavior in question by acknowledging that it is done by everybody or is appreciated by authorities etc.) is used (Näher & Krumpal, 2012). Nonetheless, literature provides inconsistent results regarding the effect of item wording on social desirability (Tourangeau & Smith, 1996; Tourangeau & Yan 2007; Näher & Krumpal, 2012). As a consequence, the procedure is still under debate today and requires further evidence.

Another issue is that, when a sensitive topic is the case, apart from item wordings, designing answers congruently is also crucial. For example, by providing 5-point Likert scale instead of a dichotomous response set, respondents will have an opportunity to tell the truth with more room of freedom (Grimm, 2010). Also, it must be noted that not only sensitive questions but also some benign and irrelevant survey items might elicit socially desirable responses. The preliminary revision or elimination of these socially desirable survey items is feasible with a scrupulous statistical evaluation (Nederhof, 1985).

Data Collection Mode

In literature, the data collection mode is presumed to be one of the substantial factors explaining the level of respondents' reluctance to disclose sensitive information in self-report surveys (Holbrook, Green & Krosnick, 2003; Tourangeau & Yan 2007; Krumpal, 2013; Roxas & Lindsay, 2012). The salient disparity among the different modes is whether the questions are interviewer-administered or self-administered since interviewers' presence, expectations combined with the sensitivity of a survey might affect SDB considerably during data collection (Brenner & DeLamater, 2014). Even bystanders such as a spouse or a sibling have a significant impact on respondents' answers (Aquilino, 1997; Aquilino, Wright & Supple, 2000). These factors may seriously distort answers given to sensitive questions (Krumpal, 2013).

Many studies show that removing the presence of the interviewer seems to reduce subjective probabilities of emotions like embarrassment and feelings of jeopardy, thus stimulating respondents to generate more honest answers to sensitive questions (Lautenschlager & Flaherty, 1990; Tourangeau & Smith, 1996; Presser & Stinson, 1998; Booth-Kewley, Larson & Miyoshi, 2007; Heerwegh, 2009; Roxas & Lindsay, 2012). On the other hand, a number of studies provide converse findings. These studies posit that statistical difference between any mode of survey is insignificant (Hancock & Flowers, 2001; Wilkerson, Nagao & Martin, 2002; Dodou & de Winter, 2014).

Other researchers focus on the impact of using computers in survey studies assuming that computers reduce social context cues, increase self-absorption (Sproull & Kiesler, 1986), thus they may provide a greater sense of privacy and reduce SDB. However, according to evidence acquired through a comprehensive meta-analysis and presented by Richman et al. (1999), paper-and-pencil and computer surveys give similar mean results in many testing situations. They contend that essential difference stems from whether a bystander or an interviewer is present or not. More intriguingly they found that being able to backtrack previous answers can significantly attenuate social desirability, along with confidentiality assurances. Similarly, Dodou and de Winter (2014) provide a more recent meta-analysis which showed that social desirability in offline, online, and paper surveys is practically the same.

Selecting Interviewers

In the previous section, the effect of interviewer on the respondent was mentioned. In concordance with this conditional assumption, there are also other factors affecting the whole procedure associated with the interviewer such as; interviewers' own feelings, state of their mind and their relation to the interviewee. These factors can pose problems for valid data collection and also cause a notable impact on the answers given to sensitive questions (Tourangeau & Yan, 2007; Krumpal, 2013).

When a potentially embarrassing topic is involved, the subjective understanding of respondents drives them to gain social approval of the interviewer (Krumpal, 2013). Thus, while collecting sensitive data, interviewers frequently attempt to build a cordial atmosphere to acquire more valid responses (Nederhof, 1985). However, studies show that the situation is not as simple as it seems. For example, according to King and Bruner (2000), when respondents' perceived social distance is similar to the interviewer, the interview process will probably be more biased. Previous studies confirm this assertion and aver that lesser social distance between interviewer and interviewee produces more dishonest answers (Hyman, 1954; Williams, 1964). On the other hand, research made by Dohrenwend, Colombotos & Dohrenwend (1968) presents intriguing results. They deduce that acquiring honest answers is hampered by both small and large social distance disparities. One crucial averment is that when the objective social distance is negligible, bias contamination in the data is actually attributed to the interviewer attitude, rather than perceived status similarity. Therefore, Dohrenwend et al. (1968) suggest that an intermediate social range should be sought while collecting data regarding sensitive topics.

Another aspect of interviewer effect emanates from the state of the interviewer. Hyman (1954) hypothesized that too much intrusiveness can alter respondents' orientation in the direction of the interviewer. In addition, Hox et al. (2002) propound that interviewer's feelings of discomfort and embarrassment pertinent to asking a specific question can significantly affect the course of the data collection process. This contention is also closely related to Fowler and Mangione (1990)'s assumption in which the correlation is underlined between respondent's proclivity to alter answers with the interviewer's relation to the topic of the survey. Accordingly, when survey questions directly related to the interviewer, respondents might distort answers to avoid insulting the interviewer.

Forced Choice Items

Forced-choice items are one of the earliest (Humm & Wadsworth, 1935) developed methods of coping with SDB (Nederhof, 1985). The simple rationale behind this technique is to make respondents to choose between two answers. For example, Humm-Wadsworth temperament scale (Humm & Wadsworth, 1935) includes forced-choice items such as: "Do you like to meet people and make new friends?" or "Do you ever have to fight against bashfulness?". These questions have dichotomous answers that compel respondents to choose between. Answers can range from single-word forms like "yes and no" to long statements such as: "I steal money or I steal candy".

According to Edwards (1957), the forced-choice technique might mitigate the effects of social desirability. Moreover, he constructed the widely-known Edwards Personal Preference Schedule (EPPS) scale concordantly. However, this method is not without criticisms. Nederhof (1985) reifies these problems under three topics.

- Unrealistic and probably antagonizing choice wordings may cause missing data problems.
- Due to dichotomous form of the answers, varying social desirability levels for every individual cannot be observed.
- Finally, highly contrasting answers might preclude obtaining quantitatively valuable statistical results.

Mentioned shortcomings of the forced-choice method are corroborated by Ray (1990). But, several studies with contradicting results (Jackson, Wroblewski & Ashton, 2000; Christiansen, Burns & Montgomery, 2005) might offer better insight on social desirability for practitioners of the method since they possess valuable statistical results.

Measurement Techniques

Researchers can use one or a combined form of methods listed above to prevent the respondents from presenting themselves in a socially desirable fashion. However, it is not always possible to control SDB during data collection. For self-report surveys, where SDB cannot be prevented, efforts can be directed to registering the distorting effect of SDB on the validity of the research. Aware of the threat that SDB poses, researchers can measure SDB in order to perform following procedures,

- ensure that content variables have discriminant validity,
- verify that content variables are free of SDB contamination,
- extract individual differences (Paulhus, 1991).

Assessment of social desirability for each item or scale is a cumbersome procedure. There is no absolute measurement of social desirability because it is not feasible to control every cognitive function and psychological factor during data collection. In addition, controlling or partialling out SDB after it occurs is often not recommended because the procedure might distort the validity of the data (Paulhus, 2017). However, there have been several methods and scales produced in order to identify the desirability ratings on the item or scale level. In the following subsections, these methods are explicated.

SDB Scales

With a need to discriminate between "the effects of item content and respondents' urge to present themselves in a socially desirable (or undesirable) light" (Crowne & Marlowe, 1960) researchers can use multi-item SDB scales in self-report surveys. Although the technique is contentious due to being devoid of exact detection of the contamination (Paulhus, 1991, 2002), a plethora of researchers have used or considered using it owing to its convenience. These studies often use various relationship calculations including regression, correlation, covariation and factor analyses in their methodology to single out the SDB in data (Fisher, 2000). Coherently, many of these studies offer deductions of significant or insignificant relationships between social desirability scales and behaviour or attitude models (King & Bruner, 2000). Consequently, the intrinsic rationale behind the use of SD scales is to capture this systematically formed divergence in which individuals deny undesirable items and claim desirable items. This divergence causes item's desirability to precede its accuracy (Paulhus, 2002).

Various calculations with SDB measures can be employed while testing content measures in terms of SDB contamination. The most common and simplest usage for identifying desirability is the confirmation of discriminant validity between a content scale and SDB scale (King & Bruner, 2000). In this procedure, a researcher basically administers SDB measures along with the content measures and hopes to obtain low intercorrelation (Paulhus, 1991). The common consensus is that subjects who respond desirably on an SDB scale are expected to be responding desirably on other measures included in the same survey form (Paulhus, 2017). Hence, low intercorrelations denote SDB-free content scales. This method also resembles factor analytic techniques which involve the elimination of the highest-loading items during scale construction. If a measure of SDB is administered along with the other content items, the highest-loading items on other variables might be considered to be apt for socially desirable responding (Morf & Jackson, 1972). Therefore, the procedure may be used to build SDB-free constructs (Paulhus, 1991).

In one of the recent studies in which comparative and correlational explorations are integrated and investigated, researchers enunciate that social desirability can be modeled statistically by calculating spurious mean differences between groups and constructs with longitudinal research design and structural equation modeling (Ziegler & Buehner 2009). Even though results offer promising support for the brand new introduced model, theoretical context has been criticised because SDB was being reduced to a simple faking notion (Paunonen & LeBel, 2012).

Further implementation of this statistical technique involves regression analysis. If a substantial correlation is found between SDB scale and content variable, regression analysis can be used to determine the amount of SDB related variance from residuals (Fisher, 2000). Intercept term (residual) in the regression equation intrinsically demonstrates targeted value score when SDB (the independent variable) is null (Fisher & Katz, 2000). Subsequently, SDB can be partialled out and SDB-corrected measures can be acquired by the use of canonical or partial correlations (King & Bruner, 2000). This method is also employed in order to identify spuriousness or suppression effects of social desirability between constructs (Ones, Viswesvaran & Reiss, 1996; Li & Bagger, 2007). Additionally, the moderation effect of SDB scales can be predicted or measured by direct regression analyses (Randall & Fernandes, 1991; Hebert, Clemow, Pbert, Ockene and Ockene, 1995).

To measure or control SDB by statistical means, various scales have been introduced since the 1930s. In the following subsections, scales which were developed to measure SDB in behavioral and attitudinal contexts are discussed briefly, starting from Crowne and Marlowe (1960) scale (MCSD) which is one of the earliest developed scales and also has gained wide acceptance (Nederhof, 1985; King & Bruner, 2000).

Marlowe-Crowne SD Scale

Even though several SD scales were set forth during the earlier stages in which social desirability was being defined such as Edward's (Edwards, 1957) or Wiggin's SD scale (Wiggins, 1959), the measure that gained the most widespread popularity is the Marlowe-Crowne SD scale (MCSDS) (Crowne and Marlowe, 1960, 1964). This scale has 33 true-false questions such as "I have never intensely disliked anyone" or "I am sometimes irritated by people who ask favors of me". Additionally, a number of short forms of MCSD scale were also proposed by Strahan and Gerbasi (1972), Greenwald and Satow (1970), Reynolds (1982) and Ballard (1992) in order to minimize respondent fatigue. According to Paulhus (2017), MCSD scale owes its far-reaching substance to its solid construct validity and scrupulously done research.

Van de Mortel (2008) suggests that people who score high on an SD scale are in need for social approval and are more likely to avoid the disapproval of others. On the other hand, average or low scorers are considered free of bias (Paulhus, 2017). Because there hasn't been a conclusive categorization generated to differentiate between both types of social desirability scorers for MCDS (Edens, Buffington, Tomicic & Riley, 2001), researchers frequently prefer the examination of intercorrelations between content and MCSD scales (King & Bruner, 2000). However, Andrews and Meyer (2003) delineate mean scores on the MCSDS for respondents who are faking good and are being honest as 24 and 15, respectively. Moreover, Edens et al. (2001) in their study, obtained internal consistency value of .83 and posited it as the honest response condition.

The dispute over social desirability scales, MCSD in particular, is not limited to the categorization of respondents. There is still an ongoing debate about the dimensionality of social desirability. Therefore, in order to elucidate this argument, many studies were conducted and conclusions were drawn to determine the dimensions of social desirability.

Multi-Dimensional Structure of Social Desirability Bias and Balanced Inventory of Desirable Responding

Contentions about the validity of SDB measures were started even after the propoundment of popular MCSD. Due to low intercorrelations among several other well-known instruments, a number of early researchers (Wiggins, 1959; Messick, 1960; Jackson and Messick, 1961) called into question the unidimensionality of social desirability. In addition, factor analyses were revealing two independent clusters. Wiggins (1964) was the first to define these distinct clusters as Alpha and Gamma. According to Paulhus (2002), conscious decision making is the key difference between Alpha and Gamma factors of SDB. In Alpha case, respondent deliberately alters his/her choices, whereas respondent is oblivious of his/her responses in Gamma case. Paulhus (1984, 1986, 1991, 2002) presented a series of studies in order to reveal a two-dimension model in social desirability structure. In these studies, several scales including Marlowe-Crowne SD scale were used to measure the tendency of SDR. In figure 1, these scales plotted on a two-dimension plane can be seen. A more robust and clear cut model presented by Paulhus (1984) showed that two-factor SD model which consists of self-deception and impression-management dimensions produced much better fit results. These two factors were later expounded thoroughly by Zerbe and Paulhus (1987). However, there are also contradicting voices in the air presenting an alternative approach to impression-management construct but partially fail to deliver the desired solution (Uziel, 2010).

In two-factor model, self-deception is over-favorable but honest self-descriptions that respondent actually believes to be true and subsists in factors such as anxiety or self-esteem (Zerbe & Paulhus, 1987). Respondents tend to underreport sensitive or

Figure 1. Factor loadings of six SD scales
Source: (Paulhus, 1984)
ESD: Edward's SD scale, SDQ: Self-Deception Questionnaire, MC: Marlowe-Crowne SD scale, LIE: MMPI Lie Scale, ODQ: Other-Deception Questionnaire, WSD: Wiggin's SD scale.

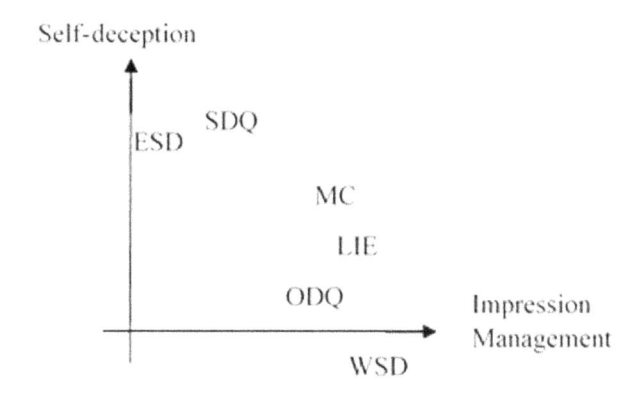

embarrassing behaviors (e.g., illicit drug use and other illegal activity) as a result of self-deception (Brenner & DeLamater, 2014). It is not advised to remove this form of SDB because it may negatively impact the validity of content measures (Fisher, 2000). On the other hand, term impression management represents a conscious presentation of oneself in an assenting light. A person who is deliberately and dishonestly falsifying test responses to create a positive impression is an example of such propensity (Zerbe & Paulhus, 1987). People tend to overreport positively viewed, socially desirable or normative behaviors (e.g., voting, consuming healthy food or physical exercise) in order to manage their impression (Brenner & DeLamater, 2014). Impression management also positively correlates with lie measures, confirming its motivation for social approval (Milfont, 2009).

Recently a new explanation to deliberate misreporting associated with impression management was introduced by Brenner and DeLamater (2014) in which it is averred that definitions in *identity theory* (McCall & Simmons, 1966; Stryker, 1968) can more suitably depict the false self-reporting than impression management can. According to the theory, respondent's identity is evoked depending on the prominence and salience of the situational parameters (Brenner, Serpe & Stryker, 2014). However, the theory's assumed relation to impression management needs further investigation.

Although the level of awareness (nonconscious and conscious) was at the center of interest for a long time, researchers have recently shifted their focus on an entirely different concept in which SDR may be manifested, namely agentic and communal structures (Steenkamp, De Jong & Baumgartner, 2010). Whereas some people demonstrate SDR in agency-related domain, which is associated with dominance, assertiveness, control, influence, autonomy, mastery, uniqueness, independence,

Figure 2. Two-Tier Structure of SDB
Source: Paulhus, 2002

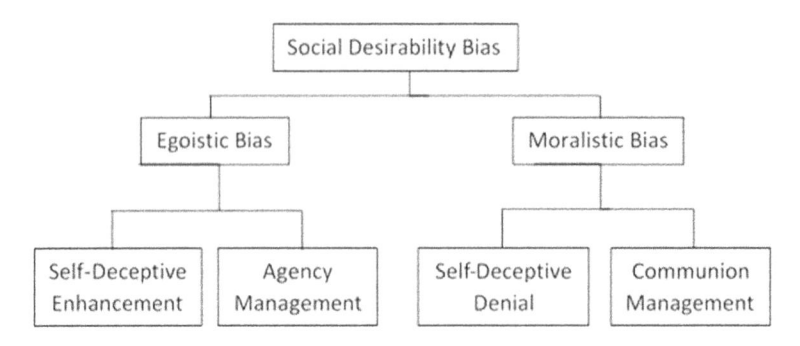

```
                    Social Desirability Bias
                    /                      \
             Egoistic Bias            Moralistic Bias
             /        \                /         \
     Self-Deceptive  Agency      Self-Deceptive  Communion
      Enhancement   Management      Denial       Management
```

status, and power also termed as "egoistic response tendencies", others exhibit SDR in communion-related domain, which involves belonging, intimacy, affiliation, nurturance, connectedness, approval, and love also termed as "moralistic response tendencies" (Paulhus & John, 1998). This process of reasoning resulted in the most recent and intricate conceptualization of SDB which was proposed by Paulhus (2002).

In this two-tier system, egoistic bias which is also associated with *Alpha type* bias represents the enhancement process of one's intellectual and social status. It involves *Agency Management*, the promotion of assets such as competence, physical prowess, fearlessness or intelligence. Besides, moralistic bias which is a manifestation of *Gamma bias* is the self-deceptive tendency and denial of non-normative attributes. *Communion Management* term on this construct defines excuse-making or damage-control behaviours (Paulhus, 2002). In recent years, Trapnell and Paulhus (2012) and Vecchione, Alessandri & Barbaranelli (2013) presented the scope and measurement methods for this agentic and communal-focused structure. The structure proposed by Paulhus (2002) can be seen in figure 2.

Probably the most important product of this entire division process of the SDB is no doubt the Balanced Inventory of Desirable Responding (BIDR) scale which has been widely used in a variety of empirical studies. BIDR scale was first introduced by Paulhus (1988). This 40-item, two-factor scale is also known as Paulhus Deception Scales and regularly updated through validity and reliability tests. The latest BIDR version was presented by Paulhus in 1998.

The BIDR scale development process was actually inspired by the Self Deception Questionnaire (SDQ) and Other Deception Questionnaire (ODQ) created by Sackeim and Gur (1978). But Paulhus (1984)'s factor analysis with several well-known SD scales robustly showed that two-factor model namely, self-deception and impression management, could better interpret the social desirability than the previously proposed scales could (Holden & Fekken, 2017). BIDR scale also shows significant validity (Kroner & Weekes, 1996; Lanyon & Carle, 2007) and delivers acceptable test-retest correlation levels (Lönnqvist et al. 2007; Vispoel & Kim, 2014) and internal consistency reliabilities (Holden, Starzyk, McLeod & Edwards, 2000; Li & Bagger, 2007). Moreover, even Sackeim, one of the co-creators of other/self-deception questionnaire, recommended using the BIDR scale after its introduction (Paulhus & Reid, 1991).

Other SDB Scales

Marlowe-Crowne SD scale and Balanced Inventory of Desirable Responding scale have been frequently used by researchers due to their well-established theoretical background. Hence, for the most part of the studies regarding desirable responding,

Table 1. Other SDB Scales

Name of The Scale	Source
Minnesota Multiphasic Personality Inventory (MMPI) Test-Taking Attitude (K) scale	Meehl and Hathaway, 1946
MMPI Lie (L) scale	Hathaway and McKinley, 1951
California Psychological Inventory	Gough, 1957
Edwards's SDB Scale	Edwards, 1957
Wiggin's Social Desirability Scale	Wiggins 1959
Repression-Sensitization scale	Byrne, 1961
Facilitation - Inhibiatation scale	Ullmann, 1962
The Eysenck Personality Inventory	Eysenck and Eysenck, 1964
SDB Scale for Children	Crandall, Crandall and Katkovsky, 1965
Personality Research Form	Jackson, 1967
Censure Avoidance	Allaman, Joyce and Crandall, 1972
16-PF Scale	Winder, O'Dell and Karson, 1975
Approval Motivation Scale	Larsen, Martin, Ettinger and Nelson, 1976
Attribution and Denial	Jacobson, Kellogg, Cauce and Slavin, 1977
Other/Self-Deception Questionnaire	Sackeim and Gur, 1978
RD16	Schuessler, Hittle and Cardascia, 1978
Comrey Personality Scales	Comrey, 1980
Differential Personality Questionnaire	Tellegen, 1982
Basic Personality Inventory	Jackson, 1996
SDS – 17 Scale	Stöber, 2001
Six-Dimension SDB Scale	Lee and Sargeant, 2011

they have been used as instruments to identify and estimate SDB. However, apart from these scales, various other personality and desirability questionnaires were developed for identifying this fashion of responding. The current state of the scales propounded by researchers is presented in Table 1.

Validation and Comparison Methods for Detecting SDB

For an in-depth and precise analysis of social desirability, Krumpal (2013) delineates two statistical control methods; validation studies and comparative studies. In validation studies, researchers possess both survey response and the true status of each individual. Thus, they can compare social desirability both in individual and aggregate level. Examples to such studies in which individual responses were compared with data obtained anonymously from sources (e.g. administrative records) are given by Hebert et al. (1995) and Brenner and DeLamater (2014).

When external validation is not available due to absence of such data or data protection rules, researchers can implement comparative study method in which data is obtained through two different experimentally created survey conditions and finally compared. According to desirability or undesirability of behaviour models inherent in the survey items, mean values are expected to deviate (Krumpal, 2013). For further comprehension of the method, studies presented by Doyle and Aboud (1995), Crutzen and Göritz (2010) and Simoni, Frick and Huang (2006) can be examined.

Response Latency Measurement

Response latency measurement is a distinct form of SDB measurement in self-report surveys. The method is based on a system which records response times of subjects and analyses the data in order to detect dissimulation. Within this framework, subjects' responses to the items are collected through the use of a computerized procedure and latencies are then standardized with the standard deviations and means of the scores derived from subjects answer times (Holden & Kroner, 1992). Differential item response latencies acquired during application process are used to distinguish honest and faking conditions. Generally, answers with shorter response times are considered honest.

This method was first proposed by Popham and Holden (1990) in pursuit of assessing a social desirability scale through measurement of response latencies. Afterwards, Holden, Kroner, Fekken and Popham (1992) suggested that these latencies can also be used to identify faking on self-report inventories. Literature generally offers studies of response latency applications in the clinical field. For example, findings from the studies presented by Holden and Kroner (1992) and

Holden and Lambert (2015) offer significant results in detection of faking good, bad and standard responding. Because of these promising findings, this technique is open to further examination and implementation in other disciplines.

Another type of response latency measurement is the Implicit Association Test (IAT). The procedure requires participants to distinguish between certain concepts and finally compares response times (Greenwald, Poehlman, Uhlmann & Banaji, 2009). It was initially developed to measure implicit attitudes but has received a significant level of attention. Slabbinck and Kenhove (2010) assert that IAT is immune to socially desirable responding, confirming that it is suitable for testing desirable response tendencies. Moreover, Egloff and Schmukle (2002) report that IAT is suitable for predicting social desirability measures.

The Over-Claiming Technique

Over-claiming is the propensity to claim knowledge over nonexistent terms or subjects. The term originated from the study of Phillips and Clancy (1972), who examined the effects of social desirability in consumer surveys. However, it was Paulhus, Harms, Bruce and Lysy (2003) who systematically developed the term into a method of capturing SDR. In this technique, a distinct survey comprising items from various topics is administered to respondents. Some of these items in the survey consist of real and existing terms or statements, but others are composed of non-existing materials in order to serve the needs of the procedure. Naturally, while respondents answering these questions, it is expected from them to deny the non-existing statements. However, if the respondent were to claim knowledge over non-existing items it would constitute the over-claiming (Paulhus et al., 2003). As a result, SDB is determined through these items with non-existing, unreal statements. Although many researchers (Mesmer-Magnus, Viswesvaran, Deshpande & Joseph, 2006; Kam, Risavy & Perunovic, 2015) adapt the technique for predicting social desirability, there are others (Ludeke & Makransky, 2016) asserting that it lacks the required validity and scants adequate empirical support. Future explorations on the technique will probably shed light on the validity and applicability of the method.

Unmatched Count Technique (List experiment)

The unmatched count technique was developed as an alternative to Randomized Response Technique in order to provide privacy, especially to the respondents of sensitive surveys (Krumpal, 2013). The other names which refer to the same method in the literature are 'Block total response' (Smith, Federer & Raghavarao, 1974), 'item count technique' (Tsuchiya, 2005), 'unmatched block count' (Dalton, Daily &

Wimbush, 1997), 'unmatched count technique' (Dalton, Wimbush & Daily, 1994) and 'survey list experiment' (Kuklinski et al., 1997).

The method begins with assigning respondents randomly into control and treatment groups (Krumpal, 2013). Then, these two groups are administered the same benign questions (n questions), except that the treatment group receives one additional sensitive question placed among other innocuous questions (n+1 questions). When this socially undesirable or potentially sensitive statement is included in the list along with more normative statements, it is expected from respondents to honestly agree or disagree with the socially undesirable statement without revealing their response by only counting their answers (Krumpal, 2013). Four questions below can be examples of the item count technique.

- Have you been to a café, bar or restaurant during the last two years? (administered to both groups)
- Have you ever ordered dinner with a drink alongside it during the last two years? (administered to both groups)
- Have you ever deliberately left a restaurant or café without paying the bill? (sensitive question, treatment group only)
- Have you paid a bill over 50 dollars in a restaurant during the last five years? (administered to both groups)

By implicitly counting the number of statements that respondents agree with, theoretically, a difference of means occurs between the two groups' responses. So, a researcher can basically infer the proportion of the total sample that agrees with the sensitive statement from the difference (Knoll, 2013).

Factor Mixture Models

"Factor mixture models" which was first introduced by Yung (1997) under the name "finite mixtures of CFA", upgrades common factor analysis by including a latent categorical variable that represents the number of disparate populations present in the sample data. Factor mixture models have drawn a significant amount of attention in recent years, particularly in the field of psychology. However, it was first Leite and Cooper (2010) who proposed using the technique to identify group membership stemming from SDB. The method seems promising and applicable but holds various disadvantages such as being computationally expensive, error-prone or having model identification problems (Terzi, 2017).

Factor mixture models can be utilized to discriminate heterogeneous populations and are especially useful when a researcher hypothesizes that unobserved memberships of multiple response styles are present in the population (Lubke & Muthén, 2005).

Although there can be multiple classed models, the basic form of this technique is based on single-class two models in which the target populations are defined and differentiated. In the first model, the focal variable is not predicted by the cross-loadings of SDB variable, meaning that respondents do not demonstrate social desirability bias. In the latter model, the focal variable is cross-loaded with SDB variable, indicating that individuals' responses to the focal scale are affected by SDB (For details see Leite & Cooper, 2010). As a result, homogenous populations are identified by these models.

Social Desirability Index

The concept of item desirability (also known as item specific social desirability rating (ISSDR)), is based on a method in which desirability of items are rated by individuals on a pre-determined scale. These individuals are asked to assess how desirable or undesirable the content of items is. Alternatively, researchers can also utilize the judgments of experts to elicit item specific desirability ratings. However, data gathering and estimating the ISSDR is a cumbersome method, because it doubles the time required for completing the research (Nederhof, 1985). Gittelman et al., (2015), Bradburn et al., (1979) and Sudman and Bradburn (1974) are some of the studies in which social desirability index is estimated.

In their study, Sudman and Bradburn (1974) estimated social desirability ratings by simply requesting subjects to rate survey questions on a 3-point scale (no possibility, some possibility, or strong possibility). Later, adopting a different perspective, Bradburn et al. (1979) directed two types of sensitivity ratings to respondents and finally integrated responses to constitute an "acute anxiety" scale, which can be used for measuring to what extent a question poses a threat to an interviewee (Tourangeau & Yan, 2007). However, the scale didn't quite gain traction. Gittelman et al. (2015), employed a different but intriguing approach. After acquiring ISSDR and true desirability variations, they simply utilized regression and standardization analyses to evaluate the magnitude and direction of social desirability.

DISCUSSION AND FUTURE RESEARCH DIRECTIONS

Self-report surveying is a widely used method of data collection in the area of social sciences. Nonetheless, SDB, a data corrupting factor in self-report studies, is rarely checked and has mostly been neglected by researchers (King & Bruner, 2000). This chapter provides a succinct review on the background of SDB, conventional and contemporary techniques which are used to prevent, measure and adjust the impact of SDB. In this context, as prevention methods bogus pipeline procedure, assuring confidentiality and anonymity, randomized response technique, refining socially sensitive item wordings, choosing the right data collection mode and interviewer, indirect questioning, forced-choice items, stress minimization, and as measurement methods employing SDB scales, validation and comparison studies, response latency measurement, over-claiming technique, list experiment, factor mixture models, social desirability index along with their statistical control procedures are examined in terms of effectiveness, advantages, disadvantages and their role in providing a suitable solution to SDB predicament.

Inferences can be drawn from a large number of studies that provide knowledge on developing and validating the best methods of coping with SDB. However, there are still a number of unsettled issues about the structure of SDB that drive the whole concept to become more complicating and challenging. The latest structure of SDB was presented by Paulhus (2002) which consists of two dimensions: Egoistic Response Tendencies and Moralistic Response Tendencies with agentic and communal aspects. The theory receives confirmations (Steenkamp et al., 2010), improvements (Paulhus, 2018) and moreover, acceptable validity and reliability scores (Vecchione et al., 2013). However, there are still uncharted fields regarding social desirability to be researched. The strength of SDB is affected by various personal values and traits (Paulhus, 2002). How these traits and values diversify and intertwine constitutes a major conundrum for future research. There are contrasting results on the theoretical background of personality traits and values. Additionally, supportive empirical evidence for some of these traits, values and interactions among them is tenuous (Steenkamp et al., 2010; Dodaj, 2012).

Cultural and demographic factors altering the core of desirable responding are also open to further empirical research, because there are only a handful of dedicated studies that focus on these factors or takes them into consideration (Keillor, Owens & Pettijohn., 2001; Lalwani, Shavitt & Johnson, 2006; Detrick & Chibnall, 2008; Tellis & Chandrasekaran, 2010; Shulruf & Dixon, 2011). Hence, literature is nowhere near possessing a full-fledged systematic approach. Furthermore, discerning substantive and stylistic variance in the context variables catalysed by social desirability is still a problematic issue despite simply yet rationally developed approaches (Connelly & Chang, 2016). Procedures that effectively detect and separate style from substance remain elusive especially not while the question of consciousness persists.

Another unsettled issue in SDB literature is the efficiency of the offered SDB scales. During the period when SDB scales were deemed unidimensional, many validation studies between scales were producing inconsistent correlation scores. Low intercorrelation values among these well-known scales such as Edwards's SD scale, the Marlowe-Crowne SD scale or Wiggins's SD scale were disturbing (Paulhus & Trapnell, 2008). However, after the introduction of two-dimension SDB scales (Sackeim & Gur, 1978; Paulhus, 1988), the subject of debate shifted towards the issue of substantive versus stylistic variance. In practice, the main goal of using SDB scales has been to discern individual response style differences. But there is a longstanding concern that assessment of response styles interferes with the substance which is also claimed to reflect deeper psychological meanings in the constructs of interest (Fisher, 2000). Because SDB scales contain both stylistic and substantive variance, a correlation between an SDB scale and a content variable may signify confounding, but not necessarily (Steenkamp et al., 2010). If the correlation is not defined exclusively in terms of content versus style comparison by the researcher, then the entire assessment process might be considered void (Paulhus, 2017). Therefore, single evidence is rarely conclusive in detecting the confounding (Steenkamp et al., 2010).

As expressed by Paulhus (2002), presenting a single calculation of relationship (e.g. correlation) between SDB and target scale is debatable. However, almost all of the studies consider this simple procedure adequate, assent to it and finally derive conclusions from it. In addition, if the influence of a SDB is a focal point in research, partialling out or controlling SDB can prove to be a significant drawback (Zerbe & Paulhus, 1987). Especially, partialling out SDB from measures of substantive marketing variables often has limited usefulness (Steenkamp et al., 2010), if not results in validity distortion effects (Paulhus, 2017). Hence, more intricate follow-up experimental procedures are needed to establish whether scores on content variables are contaminated (Steenkamp et al., 2010).

According to Fisher (2000), there are also logical and physical barriers hampering the success of the entire SDB scale implementation process. These issues are presented below.

- SDB scales are too long for implementation or to be comprehended by respondents.
- Some of the items of SDB scales are too sensitive or offensive for respondents to answer.
- Items of SDB scales are too general to be analysed and categorized.

On the other hand, many analysts and researchers state that despite the significant correlations with SDB scales, the validity of common personality test instruments such as Big Five measures changes little when SDB is controlled. Consequently, they argue that whether concerns over SDB are exaggerated (Paulhus, 2017).

Even today a consensus has not been constituted regarding the nature of SDB constructs and their relationship with other most commonly used measures. Controlling for SDB or partialling it out poses uncertain risks because it is unclear what is being controlled or partialled out. Today, Marlowe and Crowne's (1964) need for approval and Paulhus's (1991) Impression Management and Self-Deception

Enhancement scales are the most widely-known models. Despite their well-established structure and numerous confirming validation studies, dimensionality of these scales or whether scores derived from them can be used by those who are interested in validating their own measures or not is still a matter of dispute (Leite and Beretvas, 2005).

CONCLUSION AND RECOMMENDATIONS

SDB plagues the validity and accuracy of the self-report measurements. Therefore, researchers ought to use a mixture of prevention, minimization, measurement and adjustment techniques. However, none of these techniques are free of disadvantages and thus, they should be implemented with caution. For example, preventive methods can be beneficial as the first line of precaution for SDB but they may eventually lead some ethical issues, boomerang effect, ineffective measurement of content variables, etc. More particularly, establishing an experimental research design with manipulation of item wordings or implementation of distinct modes of survey administration in order to provide an artificially created environment for stimulating SDB, currently poses uncertain risks due to contrasting results in the literature as stated in the previous sections. While adopting such a design, researchers should not solely rely on one of these procedures and expect concrete results. Since desirable responding tests are mostly applied to undergraduate students, currently there is no systematic and comprehensive analysis available that explores which test condition or type of wording affects which homogenous groups in particular. Additionally, assurances of anonymity and confidentiality should be overseen with utmost care on account of the conversing results presented by a number of studies on the subject.

On the other hand, the accuracy of the SDB measurement methods is also called into question. In self-report surveys, the popularity of MCSD scale and its usage are still persevering as a classical technique for measuring SDB effect. However, there is abundant research showing that two dimensions of SDB act independently and differently from one another (Perinelli & Gremigni, 2016) in disparate testing conditions. Hence, researchers are encouraged to implement the two-dimension SD scale while identifying the effects of SDR (Steenkamp et al., 2010).

As for the new measurement methods such as social desirability index and over-claiming technique, they might offer desirable solutions to the SDB predicament. On one hand, measuring social desirability index requires substantial effort albeit, it may be an effectual instrument for detecting the strength and direction of the bias. Over-claiming technique, on the other hand, might return notable results with lesser work during the application. Both of these methods require further research in order to claim their role in the literature.

Finally, researchers even who attained an acceptable measurement of SDB should be very careful while conducting statistical control procedures. Because the impact of SDB on the relationships between variables has vital importance, it should be well registered and documented. The importance of this impact is twofold. First, it helps us to understand the nature of the effects caused by SDB and secondly, it provides us the necessary statistical information to reach deductions. However, as important as they are, most of the studies have failed to include and report the nature of interactions (spuriousness, suppression and moderation) between SDB measures and various context variables. These terms are of significant importance in defining the classification of the effects caused by SDB. Thereby, it would be prudent to explain and report the type of effect in future correlational or exploratory studies inquiring SDB.

REFERENCES

Aguinis, H., Pierce, C. A., & Quigley, B. M. (1995). Enhancing the validity of self-reported alcohol and marijuana consumption using a bogus pipeline procedure: A meta-analytic review. *Basic and Applied Social Psychology*, *16*(4), 515–527. doi:10.120715324834basp1604_8

Akers, R. L., Massey, J., Clarke, W., & Lauer, R. M. (1983). Are self-reports of adolescent deviance valid? Biochemical measures, randomized response, and the bogus pipeline in smoking behavior. *Social Forces*, *62*(1), 234–251. doi:10.2307/2578357

Allaman, J. D., Joyce, C. S., & Crandall, V. C. (1972). The antecedents of social desirability response tendencies of children and young adults. *Child Development*, *43*(4), 1135–1160. doi:10.2307/1127504 PMID:4643767

Andrews, P., & Meyer, R. G. (2003). Marlowe–Crowne social desirability scale and short form C: Forensic norms. *Journal of Clinical Psychology*, *59*(4), 483–492. doi:10.1002/jclp.10136 PMID:12652639

Aquilino, W. S. (1997). Privacy effects on self-reported drug use: Interactions with survey mode and respondent characteristics. *NIDA Research Monograph*, *167*, 383–415. PMID:9243571

Aquilino, W. S., Wright, D. L., & Supple, A. J. (2000). Response effects due to bystander presence in CASI and paper-and-pencil surveys of drug use and alcohol use. *Substance Use & Misuse*, *35*(6-8), 845–867. doi:10.3109/10826080009148424 PMID:10847214

Ballard, R. (1992). Short forms of the Marlowe-Crowne social desirability scale. *Psychological Reports, 71*(3), 1155-1160.

Bell, K. M., & Naugle, A. E. (2007). Effects of social desirability on students' self-reporting of partner abuse perpetration and victimization. *Violence and Victims, 22*(2), 243–256. doi:10.1891/088667007780477348 PMID:17479559

Booth-Kewley, S., Larson, G. E., & Miyoshi, D. K. (2007). Social desirability effects on computerized and paper-and-pencil questionnaires. *Computers in Human Behavior, 23*(1), 463–477. doi:10.1016/j.chb.2004.10.020

Bradburn, N. M., Sudman, S., Blair, E., Locander, W., Miles, C., Singer, E., & Stocking, C. (1979). *Improving interview method and questionnaire design: Response effects to threatening questions in survey research*. San Francisco: Jossey-Bass.

Bradburn, N. M., Sudman, S., Blair, E., & Stocking, C. (1978). Question threat and response bias. *Public Opinion Quarterly, 42*(2), 221–234. doi:10.1086/268444

Brenner, P. S., & DeLamater, J. D. (2014). Social desirability bias in self-reports of physical activity: Is an exercise identity the culprit? *Social Indicators Research, 117*(2), 489–504. doi:10.100711205-013-0359-y

Brenner, P. S., Serpe, R. T., & Stryker, S. (2014). The causal ordering of prominence and salience in identity theory: An empirical examination. *Social Psychology Quarterly, 77*(3), 231–252. doi:10.1177/0190272513518337 PMID:27284212

Byrne, D. (1961). The repression-sensitization scale: Rationale, reliability, and validity 1. *Journal of Personality, 29*(3), 334–349. doi:10.1111/j.1467-6494.1961.tb01666.x PMID:13689584

Campanelli, P. C., Dielman, T. E., & Shope, J. T. (1987). Validity of adolescents' self-reports of alcohol use and misuse using a bogus pipeline procedure. *Adolescence, 22*(85), 7. PMID:3591505

Christiansen, N. D., Burns, G. N., & Montgomery, G. E. (2005). Reconsidering forced-choice item formats for applicant personality assessment. *Human Performance, 18*(3), 267–307. doi:10.120715327043hup1803_4

Comrey, A. L. (1980). *Handbook of interpretations for the Comrey Personality scales*. San Diego, CA: EdITS.

Conger, A. J., & Jackson, D. N. (1972). Suppressor variables, prediction, and the interpretation of psychological relationships. *Educational and Psychological Measurement, 32*(3), 579–599. doi:10.1177/001316447203200303

Connelly, B. S., & Chang, L. (2016). A meta-analytic multitrait multirater separation of substance and style in social desirability scales. *Journal of Personality*, *84*(3), 319–334. doi:10.1111/jopy.12161 PMID:25565409

Cote, J. A., & Buckley, M. R. (1988). Measurement error and theory testing in consumer research: An illustration of the importance of construct validation. *The Journal of Consumer Research*, *14*(4), 579–582. doi:10.1086/209137

Crandall, V. C., Crandall, V. J., & Katkovsky, W. (1965). A children's social desirability questionnaire. *Journal of Consulting Psychology*, *29*(1), 27–36. doi:10.1037/h0020966 PMID:14277395

Crowne, D. P., & Marlowe, D. (1960). A new scale of social desirability independent of psychopathology. *Journal of Consulting Psychology*, *24*(4), 349–354. doi:10.1037/h0047358 PMID:13813058

Crowne, D. P., & Marlowe, D. (1964). *The approval motive*. New York: John Wiley & Sons.

Crutzen, R., & Göritz, A. S. (2010). Social desirability and self-reported health risk behaviors in web-based research: Three longitudinal studies. *BMC Public Health*, *10*(1), 720. doi:10.1186/1471-2458-10-720 PMID:21092267

Dalton, D. R., Daily, C. M., & Wimbush, J. C. (1997). Collecting" sensitive" data in business ethics research: A case for the unmatched count technique (UCT). *Journal of Business Ethics*, *16*(10), 1049–1057. doi:10.1023/A:1017917904743

Dalton, D. R., Wimbush, J. C., & Daily, C. M. (1994). Using the unmatched count technique (UCT) to estimate base rates for sensitive behavior. *Personnel Psychology*, *47*(4), 817–829. doi:10.1111/j.1744-6570.1994.tb01578.x

De Jong, M. G., Pieters, R., & Fox, J. P. (2010). Reducing social desirability bias through item randomized response: An application to measure underreported desires. *JMR, Journal of Marketing Research*, *47*(1), 14–27. doi:10.1509/jmkr.47.1.14

Detrick, P., & Chibnall, J. T. (2008). Positive response distortion by police officer applicants: Association of Paulhus Deception Scales with MMPI-2 and Inwald Personality Inventory Validity scales. *Assessment*, *15*(1), 87–96. doi:10.1177/1073191107306082 PMID:18258735

Dodaj, A. (2012). Social desirability and self-reports: Testing a content and response-style model of socially desirable responding. *Europe's Journal of Psychology*, *8*(4), 651–666. doi:10.5964/ejop.v8i4.462

Dodou, D., & de Winter, J. C. (2014). Social desirability is the same in offline, online, and paper surveys: A meta-analysis. *Computers in Human Behavior*, *36*, 487–495. doi:10.1016/j.chb.2014.04.005

Dohrenwend, B. S., Colombotos, J., & Dohrenwend, B. P. (1968). Social distance and interviewer effects. *Public Opinion Quarterly*, *32*(3), 410–422. doi:10.1086/267624

Doyle, A. B., & Aboud, F. E. (1995). A longitudinal study of White children's racial prejudice as a social-cognitive development. *Merrill-Palmer Quarterly*, *41*, 209–209.

Edens, J. F., Buffington, J. K., Tomicic, T. L., & Riley, B. D. (2001). Effects of positive impression management on the Psychopathic Personality Inventory. *Law and Human Behavior*, *25*(3), 235–256. doi:10.1023/A:1010793810896 PMID:11480802

Edwards, A. L. (1957). *The Social Desirability Variable in Personality and Assessment and Research*. Ft Worth, TX: Dryden Press.

Egloff, B., & Schmukle, S. C. (2002). Predictive validity of an implicit association test for assessing anxiety. *Journal of Personality and Social Psychology*, *83*(6), 1441–1455. doi:10.1037/0022-3514.83.6.1441 PMID:12500823

Eysenck, H. J., & Eysenck, S. B. G. (1964). *The manual of the Eysenck Personality Inventory*. London: Univ. of London Press.

Fisher, R. J. (1993). Social desirability bias and the validity of indirect questioning. *The Journal of Consumer Research*, *20*(2), 303–315. doi:10.1086/209351

Fisher, R. J. (2000). The future of social-desirability bias research in marketing. *Psychology and Marketing*, *17*(2), 73–77. doi:10.1002/(SICI)1520-6793(200002)17:2<73::AID-MAR1>3.0.CO;2-L

Fisher, R. J., & Katz, J. E. (2000). Social-desirability bias and the validity of self-reported values. *Psychology and Marketing*, *17*(2), 105–120. doi:10.1002/(SICI)1520-6793(200002)17:2<105::AID-MAR3>3.0.CO;2-9

Fowler, F. J. Jr, & Mangione, T. W. (1990). *Standardized survey interviewing: Minimizing interviewer-related error* (Vol. 18). Newbury Park, CA: Sage Publications. doi:10.4135/9781412985925

Ganster, D. C., Hennessey, H. W., & Luthans, F. (1983). Social desirability response effects: Three alternative models. *Academy of Management Journal*, *26*(2), 321–331.

Gerty, J. L. M., Hox, J. J., & Heijden, P. (2005). Meta-analysis of randomized reponse research: 35 years of validation studies. *Sociological Methods & Research*, *33*(3), 319–348. doi:10.1177/0049124104268664

Gittelman, S., Lange, V., Cook, W. A., Frede, S. M., Lavrakas, P. J., Pierce, C., & Thomas, R. K. (2015). Accounting for social-desirability bias in survey sampling: A model for predicting and calibrating the direction and magnitude of social-desirability bias. *Journal of Advertising Research*, *55*(3), 242–254. doi:10.2501/JAR-2015-006

Gough, H. G. (1957). *Manual for the California Psychological Inventory*. Palo Alto, CA: Consulting Pschologists Press.

Greenwald, A. G., Poehlman, T. A., Uhlmann, E. L., & Banaji, M. R. (2009). Understanding and using the Implicit Association Test: III. Meta-analysis of predictive validity. *Journal of Personality and Social Psychology*, *97*(1), 17–41. doi:10.1037/a0015575 PMID:19586237

Greenwald, H. J., & Satow, Y. (1970). A short social desirability scale. *Psychological Reports*, *27*(1), 131–135. doi:10.2466/pr0.1970.27.1.131

Grimm, P., (2010). Social desirability bias. *Wiley International Encyclopedia of Marketing*.

Hancock, D. R., & Flowers, C. P. (2001). Comparing social desirability responding on World Wide Web and paper-administered surveys. *Educational Technology Research and Development*, *49*(1), 5–13. doi:10.1007/BF02504503

Hathaway, S. R., & McKinley, J. C. (1951). *MMPI Manual*. New York: Psychological Corporation.

Hebert, J. R., Clemow, L., Pbert, L., Ockene, I. S., & Ockene, J. K. (1995). Social desirability bias in dietary self-report may compromise the validity of dietary intake measures. *International Journal of Epidemiology*, *24*(2), 389–398. doi:10.1093/ije/24.2.389 PMID:7635601

Heerwegh, D. (2009). Mode differences between face-to-face and web surveys: An experimental investigation of data quality and social desirability effects. *International Journal of Public Opinion Research*, *21*(1), 111–121. doi:10.1093/ijpor/edn054

Holbrook, A. L., Green, M. C., & Krosnick, J. A. (2003). Telephone versus face-to-face interviewing of national probability samples with long questionnaires: Comparisons of respondent satisficing and social desirability response bias. *Public Opinion Quarterly*, *67*(1), 79–125. doi:10.1086/346010

Holden, R. R., & Fekken, G. C. (2017). Balanced Inventory of Desirable Responding. Encyclopedia of personality and individual differences, 1-4.

Holden, R. R., & Kroner, D. G. (1992). Relative efficacy of differential response latencies for detecting faking on a self-report measure of psychopathology. *Psychological Assessment*, *4*(2), 170–173. doi:10.1037/1040-3590.4.2.170

Holden, R. R., Kroner, D. G., Fekken, G. C., & Popham, S. M. (1992). A model of personality test item response dissimulation. *Journal of Personality and Social Psychology*, *63*(2), 272–279. doi:10.1037/0022-3514.63.2.272

Holden, R. R., & Lambert, C. E. (2015). Response latencies are alive and well for identifying fakers on a self-report personality inventory: A reconsideration of van Hooft and Born (2012). *Behavior Research Methods*, *47*(4), 1436–1442. doi:10.375813428-014-0524-5 PMID:25381021

Holden, R. R., Starzyk, K. B., McLeod, L. D., & Edwards, M. J. (2000). Comparisons among the holden psychological screening inventory (HPSI), the brief symptom inventory (BSI), and the balanced inventory of desirable responding (BIDR). *Assessment*, *7*(2), 163–175. doi:10.1177/107319110000700208 PMID:10868254

Holtgraves, T. (2004). Social desirability and self-reports: Testing models of socially desirable responding. *Personality and Social Psychology Bulletin*, *30*(2), 161–172. doi:10.1177/0146167203259930 PMID:15030631

Hox, J., De Leeuw, E., Couper, M. P., Groves, R. M., De Heer, W., & Kuusela, V. (2002). The influence of interviewers' attitude and behavior on household survey nonresponse: An international comparison. *Survey Nonresponse*, 103-120.

Hult, G. T. M., Keillor, B. D., & Lafferty, B. A. (1999). A cross-national assessment of social desirability bias and consumer ethnocentrism. *Journal of Global Marketing*, *12*(4), 29–43. doi:10.1300/J042v12n04_03

Humm, D. G., & Wadsworth, G. W. Jr. (1935). The Humm-Wadsworth temperament scale. *The American Journal of Psychiatry*, *92*(1), 163–200. doi:10.1176/ajp.92.1.163 PMID:14838148

Hyman, H. H. (1954). *Interviewing in social research*. Chicago: Chicago University Press.

Jackson, D. N. (1967). *Manual for the personality research form*. University of Western Ontario.

Jackson, D. N. (1996). *Basic Personality Inventory manual* (2nd ed.). London, Canada: Sigma Assessment Systems.

Jackson, D. N., & Messick, S. (1961). Acquiescence and desirability as response determinants on the MMPI. *Educational and Psychological Measurement*, *21*(4), 771–790. doi:10.1177/001316446102100402

Jackson, D. N., Wroblewski, V. R., & Ashton, M. C. (2000). The impact of faking on employment tests: Does forced choice offer a solution? *Human Performance*, *13*(4), 371–388. doi:10.1207/S15327043HUP1304_3

Jacobson, L. I., Kellogg, R. W., Cauce, A. M., & Slavin, R. S. (1977). A multidimensional social desirability inventory. *Bulletin of the Psychonomic Society*, *9*(2), 109–110. doi:10.3758/BF03336944

Jo, M. S. (2000). Controlling social-desirability bias via method factors of direct and indirect questioning in structural equation models. *Psychology and Marketing*, *17*(2), 137–148. doi:10.1002/(SICI)1520-6793(200002)17:2<137::AID-MAR5>3.0.CO;2-V

Jo, M. S., Nelson, J., & Kiecker, P. (1997). A model for controlling social desirability bias by direct and indirect questioning. *Marketing Letters*, *8*(4), 429–437. doi:10.1023/A:1007951313872

Jones, E. E., & Sigall, H. (1971). The bogus pipeline: A new paradigm for measuring affect and attitude. *Psychological Bulletin*, *76*(5), 349–364. doi:10.1037/h0031617

Kam, C., Risavy, S. D., & Perunovic, W. E. (2015). Using Over-Claiming Technique to probe social desirability ratings of personality items: A validity examination. *Personality and Individual Differences*, *74*, 177–181. doi:10.1016/j.paid.2014.10.017

Keillor, B. D., Owens, D., & Pettijohn, C. (2001). A Cross—Cultural/cross national Study of Influencing Factors and Socially Desirable Response Biases. *International Journal of Market Research*, *43*(1), 1–19. doi:10.1177/147078530104300101

King, M. F., & Bruner, G. C. (2000). Social desirability bias: A neglected aspect of validity testing. *Psychology and Marketing*, *17*(2), 79–103. doi:10.1002/(SICI)1520-6793(200002)17:2<79::AID-MAR2>3.0.CO;2-0

Knoll, B. R. (2013). Assessing the effect of social desirability on nativism attitude responses. *Social Science Research*, *42*(6), 1587–1598. doi:10.1016/j.ssresearch.2013.07.012 PMID:24090853

Kroner, D. G., & Weekes, J. R. (1996). Balanced Inventory of Desirable Responding: Factor structure, reliability, and validity with an offender sample. *Personality and Individual Differences*, *21*(3), 323–333. doi:10.1016/0191-8869(96)00079-7

Krumpal, I. (2013). Determinants of social desirability bias in sensitive surveys: A literature review. *Quality & Quantity, 47*(4), 2025–2047. doi:10.100711135-011-9640-9

Kuklinski, J. H., Sniderman, P. M., Knight, K., Piazza, T., Tetlock, P. E., Lawrence, G. R., & Mellers, B. (1997). Racial prejudice and attitudes toward affirmative action. *American Journal of Political Science, 41*(2), 402–419. doi:10.2307/2111770

Lajunen, T., & Summala, H. (2003). Can we trust self-reports of driving? Effects of impression management on driver behaviour questionnaire responses. *Transportation Research Part F: Traffic Psychology and Behaviour, 6*(2), 97–107. doi:10.1016/S1369-8478(03)00008-1

Lalwani, A. K., Shavitt, S., & Johnson, T. (2006). What is the relation between cultural orientation and socially desirable responding? *Journal of Personality and Social Psychology, 90*(1), 165–178. doi:10.1037/0022-3514.90.1.165 PMID:16448316

Lanyon, R. I., & Carle, A. C. (2007). Internal and external validity of scores on the Balanced Inventory of Desirable Responding and the Paulhus Deception Scales. *Educational and Psychological Measurement, 67*(5), 859–876. doi:10.1177/0013164406299104

Larsen, K. S., Martin, H. J., Ettinger, R. H., & Nelson, J. (1976). Approval seeking, social cost, and aggression: A scale and some dynamics. *The Journal of Psychology, 94*(1), 3–11. doi:10.1080/00223980.1976.9921389

Lautenschlager, G. J., & Flaherty, V. L. (1990). Computer administration of questions: More desirable or more social desirability? *The Journal of Applied Psychology, 75*(3), 310–314. doi:10.1037/0021-9010.75.3.310

Lee, R. M. (1993). *Doing research on sensitive topics*. London: Sage Publications.

Lee, Z., & Sargeant, A. (2011). Dealing with social desirability bias: An application to charitable giving. *European Journal of Marketing, 45*(5), 703–719. doi:10.1108/03090561111119994

Leite, W. L., & Beretvas, S. N. (2005). Validation of scores on the Marlowe-Crowne social desirability scale and the balanced inventory of desirable responding. *Educational and Psychological Measurement, 65*(1), 140–154. doi:10.1177/0013164404267285

Leite, W. L., & Cooper, L. A. (2010). Detecting social desirability bias using factor mixture models. *Multivariate Behavioral Research, 45*(2), 271–293. doi:10.1080/00273171003680245 PMID:26760286

Lelkes, Y., Krosnick, J. A., Marx, D. M., Judd, C. M., & Park, B. (2012). Complete anonymity compromises the accuracy of self-reports. *Journal of Experimental Social Psychology*, *48*(6), 1291–1299. doi:10.1016/j.jesp.2012.07.002

Li, A., & Bagger, J. (2007). The Balanced inventory of desirable responding (BIDR) a reliability generalization study. *Educational and Psychological Measurement*, *67*(3), 525–544. doi:10.1177/0013164406292087

Lönnqvist, J. E., Paunonen, S., Tuulio-Henriksson, A., Lönnqvist, J., & Verkasalo, M. (2007). Substance and style in socially desirable responding. *Journal of Personality*, *75*(2), 291–322. doi:10.1111/j.1467-6494.2006.00440.x PMID:17359240

Lubke, G. H., & Muthén, B. (2005). Investigating population heterogeneity with factor mixture models. *Psychological Methods*, *10*(1), 21–39. doi:10.1037/1082-989X.10.1.21 PMID:15810867

Ludeke, S. G., & Makransky, G. (2016). Does the Over-Claiming Questionnaire measure overclaiming? Absent convergent validity in a large community sample. *Psychological Assessment*, *28*(6), 765–774. doi:10.1037/pas0000211 PMID:26372263

McCall, G. J., & Simmons, J. L. (1966). *Identities and Interactions*. New York: Free Press.

Meehl, P. E., & Hathaway, S. R. (1946). The K factor as a suppressor variable in the Minnesota Multiphasic Personality Inventory. *The Journal of Applied Psychology*, *30*(5), 525–564. doi:10.1037/h0053634 PMID:20282179

Mesmer-Magnus, J., Viswesvaran, C., Deshpande, S., & Joseph, J. (2006). Social desirability: The role of over-claiming, self-esteem, and emotional intelligence. *Psychological Science*, *48*(3), 336–356.

Messick, S. (1960). Dimensions of social desirability. *Journal of Consulting Psychology*, *24*(4), 279–287. doi:10.1037/h0044153

Mick, D. G. (1996). Are studies of dark side variables confounded by socially desirable responding? The case of materialism. *The Journal of Consumer Research*, *23*(2), 106–119. doi:10.1086/209470

Milfont, T. L. (2009). The effects of social desirability on self-reported environmental attitudes and ecological behaviour. *The Environmentalist*, *29*(3), 263–269. doi:10.100710669-008-9192-2

Morf, M. E., & Jackson, D. N. (1972). An Analysis of Two Response Styles: True Responding and Item Endorsement 1. *Educational and Psychological Measurement*, *32*(2), 329–353. doi:10.1177/001316447203200210

Mühlenfeld, H. U. (2005). Differences between talking about and admitting sensitive behaviour in anonymous and non-anonymous web-based interviews. *Computers in Human Behavior*, *21*(6), 993–1003. doi:10.1016/j.chb.2004.02.023

Näher, A. F., & Krumpal, I. (2012). Asking sensitive questions: The impact of forgiving wording and question context on social desirability bias. *Quality & Quantity*, *46*(5), 1601–1616. doi:10.100711135-011-9469-2

Nederhof, A. J. (1985). Methods of coping with social desirability bias: A review. *European Journal of Social Psychology*, *15*(3), 263–280. doi:10.1002/ejsp.2420150303

Norwood, F. B., & Lusk, J. L. (2011). Social desirability bias in real, hypothetical, and inferred valuation experiments. *American Journal of Agricultural Economics*, *93*(2), 528–534.

Ones, D. S., Viswesvaran, C., & Reiss, A. D. (1996). Role of social desirability in personality testing for personnel selection: The red herring. *The Journal of Applied Psychology*, *81*(6), 660–679. doi:10.1037/0021-9010.81.6.660

Ong, A. D., & Weiss, D. J. (2000). The impact of anonymity on responses to sensitive questions 1. *Journal of Applied Social Psychology*, *30*(8), 1691–1708. doi:10.1111/j.1559-1816.2000.tb02462.x

Paulhus, D. L. (1984). Two-component models of socially desirable responding. *Journal of Personality and Social Psychology*, *46*(3), 598–609. doi:10.1037/0022-3514.46.3.598

Paulhus, D. L. (1986). Self-deception and impression management in test responses. In Personality assessment via questionnaires (pp. 143-165). Springer. doi:10.1007/978-3-642-70751-3_8

Paulhus, D. L. (1988). Balanced inventory of desirable responding (BIDR). *Acceptance and Commitment Therapy Measures Package*, *41*, 79586–79587.

Paulhus, D. L. (1991). Measurement and control of response bias. In Measures of personality and social psychological attitudes (pp. 17-59). San Diego, CA: Academic Press. doi:10.1016/B978-0-12-590241-0.50006-X

Paulhus, D. L. (1998). *Paulhus deception scales (PDS): the balanced inventory of desirable responding-7: user's manual*. North Tanawanda, NY: Multi-Health Systems.

Paulhus, D. L. (2002). Socially desirable responding: The evolution of a construct. In The role of constructs in psychological and educational measurement (pp. 49-69). Erlbaum.

Paulhus, D. L. (2017). Socially desirable responding on self-reports. Encyclopedia of Personality and Individual Differences, 1-5.

Paulhus, D. L. (2018). The Big Two dimensions of desirability. In Agency and communion in social psychology (pp. 79-89). Routledge. doi:10.4324/9780203703663-7

Paulhus, D. L., Harms, P. D., Bruce, M. N., & Lysy, D. C. (2003). The over-claiming technique: Measuring self-enhancement independent of ability. *Journal of Personality and Social Psychology*, *84*(4), 890–904. doi:10.1037/0022-3514.84.4.890 PMID:12703655

Paulhus, D. L., & John, O. P. (1998). Egoistic and moralistic biases in self-perception: The interplay of self-deceptive styles with basic traits and motives. *Journal of Personality*, *66*(6), 1025–1060. doi:10.1111/1467-6494.00041

Paulhus, D. L., & Reid, D. B. (1991). Enhancement and denial in socially desirable responding. *Journal of Personality and Social Psychology*, *60*(2), 307–317. doi:10.1037/0022-3514.60.2.307

Paulhus, D. L., & Trapnell, P. D. (2008). Self-presentation of personality. Handbook of Personality Psychology, 19, 492-517.

Paunonen, S. V., & LeBel, E. P. (2012). Socially desirable responding and its elusive effects on the validity of personality assessments. *Journal of Personality and Social Psychology*, *103*(1), 158–175. doi:10.1037/a0028165 PMID:22564012

Perinelli, E., & Gremigni, P. (2016). Use of social desirability scales in clinical psychology: A systematic review. *Journal of Clinical Psychology*, *72*(6), 534–551. doi:10.1002/jclp.22284 PMID:26970350

Peterson, R. A., & Kerin, R. A. (1981). The quality of self-report data: review and synthesis. In Review of marketing, (pp. 5-20). AMA.

Phillips, D. L., & Clancy, K. J. (1972). Some effects of "social desirability" in survey studies. *American Journal of Sociology*, *77*(5), 921–940. doi:10.1086/225231

Popham, S. M., & Holden, R. R. (1990). Assessing MMPI constructs through the measurement of response latencies. *Journal of Personality Assessment*, *54*(3-4), 469–478. doi:10.1080/00223891.1990.9674012 PMID:2348336

Presser, S., & Stinson, L. (1998). Data collection mode and social desirability bias in self-reported religious attendance. *American Sociological Review*, *63*(1), 137–145. doi:10.2307/2657486

Randall, D. M., & Fernandes, M. F. (1991). The social desirability response bias in ethics research. *Journal of Business Ethics*, *10*(11), 805–817. doi:10.1007/BF00383696

Ray, J. J. (1990). Acquiescence and problems with forced-choice scales. *The Journal of Social Psychology*, *130*(3), 397–399. doi:10.1080/00224545.1990.9924595

Reynolds, W. M. (1982). Development of reliable and valid short forms of the Marlowe-Crowne Social Desirability Scale. *Journal of Clinical Psychology*, *38*(1), 119–125. doi:10.1002/1097-4679(198201)38:1<119::AID-JCLP2270380118>3.0.CO;2-I

Richman, W. L., Kiesler, S., Weisband, S., & Drasgow, F. (1999). A meta-analytic study of social desirability distortion in computer-administered questionnaires, traditional questionnaires, and interviews. *The Journal of Applied Psychology*, *84*(5), 754–775. doi:10.1037/0021-9010.84.5.754

Roese, N. J., & Jamieson, D. W. (1993). Twenty years of bogus pipeline research: A critical review and meta-analysis. *Psychological Bulletin*, *114*(2), 363–375. doi:10.1037/0033-2909.114.2.363

Roxas, B., & Lindsay, V. (2012). Social desirability bias in survey research on sustainable development in small firms: An exploratory analysis of survey mode effect. *Business Strategy and the Environment*, *21*(4), 223–235. doi:10.1002/bse.730

Sackeim, H. A., & Gur, R. C. (1978). Self-deception, self-confrontation, and consciousness. In Consciousness and self-regulation (pp. 139-197). Springer. doi:10.1007/978-1-4684-2571-0_4

Schaeffer, N. C. (2000). Asking questions about threatening topics: A selective overview. In The science of self-report: Implications for research and practice (pp. 105-121). Erlbaum.

Schoderbek, P. P., & Deshpande, S. P. (1996). Impression management, overclaiming, and perceived unethical conduct: The role of male and female managers. *Journal of Business Ethics*, *15*(4), 409–414. doi:10.1007/BF00380361

Schuessler, K., Hittle, D., & Cardascia, J. (1978). Measuring responding desirably with attitude-opinion items. *Social Psychology*, *41*(3), 224–235. doi:10.2307/3033559

Shulruf, B., Hattie, J., & Dixon, R. (2011). Intertwinement of individualist and collectivist attributes and response sets. *Journal of Social, Evolutionary, & Cultural Psychology*, *5*(1), 51–65. doi:10.1037/h0099275

Simoni, J. M., Frick, P. A., & Huang, B. (2006). A longitudinal evaluation of a social support model of medication adherence among HIV-positive men and women on antiretroviral therapy. *Health Psychology*, *25*(1), 74–81. doi:10.1037/0278-6133.25.1.74 PMID:16448300

Singer, E., Hippler, H. J., & Schwarz, N. (1992). Confidentiality assurances in surveys: Reassurance or threat? *International Journal of Public Opinion Research*, *4*(3), 256–268. doi:10.1093/ijpor/4.3.256

Sirken, M. G. (1970). Household surveys with multiplicity. *Journal of the American Statistical Association*, *65*(329), 257–266. doi:10.1080/01621459.1970.10481077

Slabbinck, H., & Kenhove, P. V. (2010). *Social desirability and indirect questioning: New insights from the Implicit Association Test and the Balanced Inventory of Desirable Responding*. ACR North American Advances.

Smith, L. L., Federer, W. T., & Raghavarao, D. (1974). *A Comparison of Three Techniques for Eliciting Answers to Sensitive Questions*. Academic Press.

Sproull, L., & Kiesler, S. (1986). Reducing social context cues: Electronic mail in organizational communication. *Management Science*, *32*(11), 1492–1512. doi:10.1287/mnsc.32.11.1492

Steenkamp, J. B. E., De Jong, M. G., & Baumgartner, H. (2010). Socially desirable response tendencies in survey research. *JMR, Journal of Marketing Research*, *47*(2), 199–214. doi:10.1509/jmkr.47.2.199

Stöber, J. (2001). The Social Desirability Scale-17 (SDS-17): Convergent validity, discriminant validity, and relationship with age. *European Journal of Psychological Assessment*, *17*(3), 222–232. doi:10.1027//1015-5759.17.3.222

Strahan, R., & Gerbasi, K. C. (1972). Short, homogeneous versions of the Marlow-Crowne social desirability scale. *Journal of Clinical Psychology*, *28*(2), 191–193. doi:10.1002/1097-4679(197204)28:2<191::AID-JCLP2270280220>3.0.CO;2-G

Stryker, S. (1968). Identity salience and role performance: The relevance of symbolic interaction theory for family research. *Journal of Marriage and the Family*, *30*(4), 558–564. doi:10.2307/349494

Sudman, S., & Bradburn, N. M. (1974). *Response effects in surveys: A review and synthesis (No. 16)*. Chicago, IL: Aldine.

Tellegen, A. (1982). *Brief manual for the Differential Personality Inventory* (Unpublished manuscript). University of Minnesota, Minneapolis, MN.

Tellis, G. J., & Chandrasekaran, D. (2010). Extent and impact of response biases in cross-national survey research. *International Journal of Research in Marketing*, *27*(4), 329–341. doi:10.1016/j.ijresmar.2010.08.003

Terzi, T. (2017). *Detecting semi-plausible response patterns* (Doctoral dissertation). The London School of Economics and Political Science (LSE).

Tourangeau, R., & Smith, T. W. (1996). Asking sensitive questions: The impact of data collection mode, question format, and question context. *Public Opinion Quarterly*, *60*(2), 275–304. doi:10.1086/297751

Tourangeau, R., & Yan, T. (2007). Sensitive questions in surveys. *Psychological Bulletin*, *133*(5), 859–883. doi:10.1037/0033-2909.133.5.859 PMID:17723033

Trapnell, P. D., & Paulhus, D. L. (2012). Agentic and communal values: Their scope and measurement. *Journal of Personality Assessment*, *94*(1), 39–52. doi:10.1080/00223891.2011.627968 PMID:22176265

Tsuchiya, T. (2005). Domain estimators for the item count technique. *Survey Methodology*, *31*(1), 41–51.

Ullmann, L. P. (1962). An empirically derived MMPI scale which measures facilitation-inhibition of recognition of threatening stimuli. *Journal of Clinical Psychology*, *18*(2), 127–132. doi:10.1002/1097-4679(196204)18:2<127::AID-JCLP2270180206>3.0.CO;2-V PMID:13923691

Uziel, L. (2010). Rethinking social desirability scales: From impression management to interpersonally oriented self-control. *Perspectives on Psychological Science*, *5*(3), 243–262. doi:10.1177/1745691610369465 PMID:26162157

Van de Mortel, T. F. (2008). Faking it: Social desirability response bias in self-report research. *The Australian Journal of Advanced Nursing*, *25*(4), 40–48.

Vecchione, M., Alessandri, G., & Barbaranelli, C. (2013). Measurement and application of egoistic and moralistic self-enhancement. *International Journal of Selection and Assessment*, *21*(2), 170–182. doi:10.1111/ijsa.12027

Vispoel, W. P., & Kim, H. Y. (2014). Psychometric properties for the Balanced Inventory of Desirable Responding: Dichotomous versus polytomous conventional and IRT scoring. *Psychological Assessment*, *26*(3), 878–891. doi:10.1037/a0036430 PMID:24708082

Warner, S. L. (1965). Randomized response: A survey technique for eliminating evasive answer bias. *Journal of the American Statistical Association*, *60*(309), 63–69. doi:10.1080/01621459.1965.10480775 PMID:12261830

Wiggins, J. S. (1959). Interrelationships among MMPI measures of dissimulation under standard and social desirability instruction. *Journal of Consulting Psychology*, *23*(5), 419–427. doi:10.1037/h0047823

Wiggins, J. S. (1964). Convergences among stylistic response measures from objective personality tests. *Educational and Psychological Measurement*, *24*(3), 551–562. doi:10.1177/001316446402400310

Wilkerson, J. M., Nagao, D. H., & Martin, C. L. (2002). Socially Desirable Responding in Computerized Questionnaires: When Questionnaire Purpose Matters More Than the Mode 1. *Journal of Applied Social Psychology*, *32*(3), 544–559. doi:10.1111/j.1559-1816.2002.tb00229.x

Williams, J. A. Jr. (1964). Interviewer-respondent interaction: A study of bias in the information interview. *Sociometry*, *27*(3), 338–352. doi:10.2307/2785623

Willis, G. B., & Sirken, M. G. (1994). *The cognitive aspects of responses to sensitive survey questions*. Cognitive Methods Staff working paper series, US Department of Health and Human Services, Centers for Disease Control and Prevention, National Center for Health Statistics.

Winder, P. (1975). New Motivational Distortion Scales for the 16 PF. *Journal of Personality Assessment*, *39*(5), 532–537.

Yung, Y. F. (1997). Finite mixtures in confirmatory factor-analysis models. *Psychometrika*, *62*(3), 297–330. doi:10.1007/BF02294554

Zerbe, W. J., & Paulhus, D. L. (1987). Socially desirable responding in organizational behavior: A reconception. *Academy of Management Review*, *12*(2), 250–264. doi:10.5465/amr.1987.4307820

Ziegler, M., & Buehner, M. (2009). Modeling socially desirable responding and its effects. *Educational and Psychological Measurement*, *69*(4), 548–565. doi:10.1177/0013164408324469

Chapter 8
Triangulation Approaches in Accounting Research:
Concerns, Implications, and Resolutions

Koholga Ormin
Adamawa State University, Mubi, Nigeria

ABSTRACT

Accounting research, like many other social science disciplines, has gradually moved from qualitative to quantitative research with an emphasis on the use of multiple evidence or methods in the conduct of research. This chapter explores the concerns and implications of triangulation in the conduct of research in the social sciences, particularly in the field of accounting. Based on evidence from existing literature, the chapter submits that triangulation is an important strategy for enhancing the quality of accounting research. Accounting researchers, like those from other social science disciplines, often adopt triangulation when investigating a complex phenomenon whereby using a single data source or method may not allow an exhaustive investigation to fully understand it, hence the inability to reach a dependable conclusion. Despite the concerns and implications of use of triangulation in accounting and social science research, the chapter concluded it is a relevant approach especially at a time when adequate evidence and analytical rigor is required to substantiate research findings.

INTRODUCTION

Validity and reliability are fundamental criteria upon which the quality of any research finding is adjudged. Validity is the extent to which a measure reflects the phenomena being studied and reliability is the extent to which studies are

DOI: 10.4018/978-1-7998-1025-4.ch008

replicable (Ibiamke & Ajekwe, 2017). These two concepts mean different things in quantitative and qualitative research. In quantitative research, validity entails the extent to which an instrument actually measures what it intends to measure and how well it does measure it (Smith, 1990) and reliability concerns replicability or repeatability of results (Golafshani, 2003) while in qualitative research validity has to do with the quality of findings and reliability is about dependability of study findings (Golafshani, 2003; Bashir, Afzal & Azeem, 2008). Broadly, in qualitative research, validity and reliability concerns the issues of trustworthiness, dependability, credibility, transferability, and confirmability (Ibiamke & Ajekwe, 2017; Fusch, Fusch & Ness, 2018).

The qualitative nature of research which most social science researches takes poses problems of validity and reliability. Shenton (2004) for example pointed out that positivist researchers who operate on the belief that reality is 'out there' and exists independently of the researcher have often questioned the trustworthiness of qualitative research. The standardization of research design in the natural sciences and the selection of samples base on randomization according to the National Child Care Information Center (NCCIC, 2011) make these issues less problematic in pure sciences research than social sciences. Social science research designs are flexible and the selection of sample is more purposively done than drawn randomly (Shenton, 2004), therefore, tend to be associated with the problems of validity and reliability.

Social science researches which main element is human beings and involve the study of attitude, perception, feelings, behavior and other such qualitative attributes necessarily needs to meet these two criteria (i.e. validity and reliability). Generally, every research method, be it in terms of data collection or analysis has attendant strengths and weaknesses. Each data collection method including the questionnaire, interview, and observation as well as research designs like survey, case-study, experimental, historical design, etc or more broadly, qualitative and quantitative research, has its own weaknesses. Research findings and results are thus affected to some extent by the weaknesses associated with the research approach adopted by the researcher.

Over the years, to overcome the weaknesses associated with the use of particular or single research approach, a combination of approaches has been proposed. Such a strategy to research is known as "triangulation". The Wikipedia encyclopedia (2011) explains triangulation to mean the use of more than two methods in a study with a view to double or triple check results. In other words, it is the utilization of multiple research methodologies by a researcher in the study of a phenomenon of interest. The objective of triangulation approach is to validate the findings of research as posited in the Wikipedia explanation. This view has however been contested by other scholars on the grounds of paradigm divided (see Burrell & Morgan, 1979).

In particular, Burrell and Morgan (1979) argued that inter-paradigmatic journeys by researchers is rare. Notwithstanding, triangulation as a research strategy is stated to aim at enriching understanding of a phenomenon under examination (Hoque, Covaleski & Gooneratne, 2013) hence research quality.

This paper examines triangulation approaches as an evolving trend to research specifically within the domain of social science research. It specifically explores the meaning, forms, concerns and implications of triangulation to accounting research as well as proposes ways to resolve the contentious issues surrounding its use by accounting researchers. The paper is theoretical in nature therefore relies on previous published articles to deductively infer conclusion.

CONCEPT OF TRIANGULATION

Bazeley (2004) maintains that the term triangulation originally is conceived as the conduct of parallel (duplicate) studies utilizing multiple methods to achieve the same purpose, in order to provide corroborative evidence for the conclusions arrive at. However, in recent times; Bazeley (2004) stated that the term is loosely used as a synonym for mixed methods research; a view shared by Modell (2009). In its original sense which Denzin (1989) popularized; triangulation was seen as a strategy of validation of research results or findings. This is the same perspective which the earlier cited explanation by the Wikipedia encyclopedia took. According to the source, triangulation in qualitative research increases the credibility and validity of results.

Rothbaner (2008) opined triangulation to mean a multi-method approach to data collection and data analysis. On their part, O'Donoghue and Punck (2003) view the concept as a method of cross-checking data from multiple sources to search for regularities in the research data. Similarly, Shenton (2004) puts it as the use of different methods, especially observation, focus groups and individual interviews. Sandelowski (1995) cited in Johnstone (2007) contends that triangulation is appropriate in research only when data from one source is used to collaborate data from another source, and when such convergent and consensual validity is of importance.

Arnold (2006), however, retains triangulation as the use of recursive approach between the case study and survey methods. In a more broader perspective, NCCIC (2011) described triangulation as an approach that adopts multiple data sources such as archival, interview, video; multiple informants; and multiple methods like participant observation, focus groups etc, in order to confirm or validate research findings. In a similar line of reasoning, Murphy (1989) in Charoenruk (2009) posited the concept to relate to data, investigator, theory, and methodological issues by way of utilizing more than one approach.

It should be noted that the apparent different conception of triangulation by authors as from the foregoing hinges on its different forms. For instance, O'Donoghue and Punck (2003), Shenton (2004), and Rothbaner (2008) view of the concept relates to the data form; Arnold (2006) looks at it only from the methodological perspective; while Bazeley (2004), NCCIC (2011), and Murphy (1989) considered it more broadly from all the forms. Authors tend therefore to conceive the concept within the context of their research concern. Irrespective of these differences, it is quite clear from some of the considered definitions above (see Bazeley, 2004; NCCIC, 2011) that triangulation mainly serves the purpose of validating research findings. This understanding about the use of triangulation in research is however disputed by some scholars.

Forms of Triangulation

Triangulation as a research strategy has different forms, depending in the context within which it is utilized by the researcher. There are four identified forms of triangulation, namely; data triangulation, investigator triangulation, theory triangulation, and methodological triangulation (Denzin, 1978). Each of these forms of triangulation is examined in turn.

Data triangulation involves the exploration of different data sources in the conduct of a study. It consists of a mixture of qualitative and quantitative methods such as interviews, detailed observations and shadowing, documentary evidence and questionnaires that yield rich source of field data (Hopper & Hoque, 2006). Data is the issue in this form of triangulation. The relevant question to determine the use of this form of triangulation is: has a study used more than one data source to explain or examine a phenomenon? If the answer is 'yes', then the study could be said to involve data triangulation. The concern is not on the instrument or technique used in collecting data but the type of data. Hopper and Hoque (2006) pointed out that this form of triangulation makes it possible for a researcher to tap from the strong points of each type of data, cross-check data collected by each method as well as collect information that is available only through particular techniques.

Investigator triangulation involves use of multiple researchers in an investigation (Denzin, 1978). This implies deploying more than one investigator in data collection or analysis. This form of triangulation is useful because it provides opportunity to corroborate the findings (accounts) of different investigators hence greater understanding of the phenomenon under study. Pratt and Woods (2006) reiterated that the corroboration of investigators' account could facilitate closer interrogation of data which may necessitate a revisit to site to collect more data that ensures more accurate development of theory.

Theory triangulation involves the utilization of more than one theoretical scheme in the interpretation of the phenomenon being examined (Denzin, 1978). This form of triangulation according to Rothbaner (2008) is useful in examining dissonant data, but not relevant in the area of increasing validity of findings. Hopper and Hoque (2006) identified four opportunities that this form of triangulation offers accounting researchers. These include: allowing a researcher to build a wider explanation of the phenomenon, and helping uncover the deviant or off-quadrant dimensions of a phenomenon. It enables a researcher build in avenues of testing a whole range of plausible theoretical interpretations and permits individual learning in the field. It also has the advantage of creating theory from extant situations. However, the effective use of this form of triangulation requires a researcher to be well grounded in different theoretical approaches. Hoque, Covaleski and Gooneratne (2013) and Modell (2015) have promoted the debate on theoretical triangulation in accounting research.

Methodological triangulation on the other hand involves the use of more than one method to gather research data. This may include the use of interviews, observation, questionnaire, and documents. It is possible that with a particular method, there can be variations, for example; with interview, a researcher may use both conversational interviewing and structural interview questions. This form of triangulation must not be confused with data triangulation because whereas data triangulation focuses on the type of data, methodological triangulation emphasizes on the method or technique used to generate data. Rothbaner (2008) also posited this form of triangulation to mean a combination of sampling methods to collect data from different kinds of informants or from the same people but at different times and in the same place. This explanation reinforces the earlier assertion that combining methods; whether for data collection, sampling or analysis of data, is what this form of triangulation is concerned with.

The Concerns of Triangulation in Research

A review of literature shows several arguments about triangulation approaches to research. This argument is basically derived from the aim or objective of the use of triangulation in research. While there are those in support of the research approach, there is also a school of thought that is against triangulation in research. This subsection considers some of these concerns.

Initially, triangulation was thought of as a validation strategy in research. It was popularized from this ideology. This is obvious from most of the existing definitions on the concept. Specifically, Golafshani (2003) argued triangulation typically as a strategy for improving validity and reliability of research or evaluation of findings. More recently, this fact has come under dispute. Fielding and Fielding (1986) and

Flick (1992) all argued that triangulation does not validate research. They maintain that each source or method used in research must be understood on its own terms, meaning that, different sources employed in a study are not likely to yield completely the same outcomes due to differences in underlying assumptions thus may simply not be reinforcing each other. This practically is undisputable. Therefore, the essence of the research strategy according to Jick (1979) and Mark, Feller and Button (1997) rather, is to add depth to a study and may be useful for understanding the processes which occur in the study.

Rothbaner (2008) also wrote that triangulation is often employed by researchers to allow them identify, explore, and understand different dimensions of the units of the study, thereby strengthening their research findings and enriching their limitations. As documented by Johnstone (2007), Denzin who popularized the approach (Bazeley, 2004) shifted from the validity idea to proposing that by using a combination of methods in a study of a phenomenon, any bias in a particular data source, investigator, or method, would be neutralized. This is made possible by the evidence from the several sources used. This as further stated tends to give greater confidence in the conclusion reached by the researcher.

Aligning with the foregoing, Charoenruk (2009) clearly submitted that the aim of triangulation is to enhance understanding of complex phenomenon and not criteria-based validation, in which agreement among different sources confirms validity. With respect to the combination of qualitative and quantitative approach to organizational research, Charoenruk (2009) emphasized that the use of several methodologies may help to create a balance in the knowledge needed to develop organizational research both as a science and an art. Similarly, Olsen (2004) argued triangulation as not just aiming at validation which many authors dispute but more at deepening and widening ones' understanding. According to Pratt and Woods (2006), the use of several methods increases the chances of depth and accuracy.

The most controversial contention about triangulation approach is drawn from the paradigms perspective in research. There is the school of thought which argues that researchers cannot belong to more than one paradigm; notable among this school are Burrell and Morgan (1979). Based on this school of thought, the use of qualitative and quantitative approaches to research is not compatible in the conduct of a research due to philosophical differences underlining each approach. This then restricts the use of some methods with others, for example, structured questionnaire and interview. But triangulation encourages the use of cross-methodological approaches, techniques and sources.

The idea of paradigm divided as advocated by Burrell and Morgan (1979) restricting triangulation in research has since been contested. Jick (1979) contended that qualitative and quantitative methods in research rather than being construed as rival camps should be viewed as complementary. Yeasmin and Rahman (2012) stated that recently the position is that qualitative and quantitative approaches to research should not be taken to be separate but as having equal status and being interactive. Hayashi, Abib and Hoppen (2019) would therefore maintained that quantitative studies are not better than qualitative studies nor qualitative better than quantitative studies, noting that they are merely different and complementary. This implies that the two are interactive and can be adapted to a large extent in the same study. Olsen (2004) unambiguously submitted that there is no contradiction between the mixing of approaches, pointing out the possibility of bringing the two together as a means to shed light on any chosen social research problem.

Another practical concern with the use of triangulation in research is derived from the fact that the researcher will have to contend with a longer time conducting research and bear higher cost than would be the case where a single approach is utilized. The fundamental challenge may lay in the large amount of evidence (data) available to the researcher. By utilizing multiple methods and sources, the data generated is often very large that managing it may pose a problem. With large evidence obtained from the field, expertise knowledge may become a prerequisite for sorting and analysis. It may become inevitable where the researcher is not versed in analysis to contract out the different aspects (Olsen, 2004; Rothbaner, 2008). Despite the associated problem of overwhelming data, there are meta-analysis studies such as Stavros and Westberg (2009) and Tijjani (2010) that have successfully used mixed methods. Stavros and Westberg (2009) used the approach to illustrate the relationship marketing theory. Hussein (2009) proposed the use of triangulation to study welfare offered by employers to employees in companies in Tanzania. Tijjani (2010) employed mixed methods in the study of share valuation and stock market analysis in emerging markets using Nigeria as a case study whereby secondary data, questionnaire and interview were utilized as complementary methods.

Notwithstanding these concerns, the triangulation approach has evolved and it specifically assists researchers cancel out the limitations associated with the use of particular research approach while tapping the strengths from the combined approaches utilized. This assertion is apparent in Murphy (1989) in Charoenruk (2009) who concluded that triangulation does not only maximize the strengths and minimize associated weaknesses of every approach, but further strengthens results and contributes to the development of both theory and knowledge. It is therefore pertinent to point out that though there is no consensus among researchers on the subject of triangulation, its relevance is not in doubt and its limitation is also obvious. Its adoption in any research is dependent on the extent to which a researcher deems it useful in enriching research and sees the choice of methods compatible.

Implications of Triangulation to Social Science Research

Generally in the research literature, triangulation is accepted to help overcome the limitations associated with the use of each of the separate methodologies in the conduct of research. In social science research especially in terms of data collection and analysis, it is also agreed to provide better observation of the phenomenon in the data (Charoenruk, 2009). Studies conducted using triangulation approach, available literature show provide a richer and deeper understanding of the phenomenon examined. This is because it provides opportunity for comparison of evidence from the multiple sources used. To this end, the approach is useful for social science research where behavioral issues are often investigated. There is however a debate according to Rothbaner (2008) among researchers as to the degree to which triangulation strategies allow for comparison and integration of evidence from multiple methods of data collection and multiple analytical perspectives. These are some of the positive implications of the triangulation approach to research.

On the contrary, triangulation also has negative implications. It increases the length of time required to complete a study as well as cost involved. The use of more than one method in the conduct of research especially where the methods cannot be utilized simultaneously, but in succession, definitely implies that longer time will be required to complete the research. Rothbaner (2008) posited that the use of multiple methods of inquiry and team investigations may lead to very high cost of conducting research thereby making some research impracticable. Every research method has a cost associated with using it. The accumulated cost of these different methods may therefore be overwhelming.

Writing on the implications of triangulation approaches to accounting research, Hopper and Hoque (2006) noted that triangulation (theory-triangulation and data-triangulation) fundamentally have the danger of using theories and methods with different philosophies. The different philosophies of the combined theories and methods as stated could create theoretical and methodological opportunism and incoherence. The paradigmical divide argued by some researchers for instance is against the mixture of positivist methods or approaches with interpretative methods. Because the philosophical assumptions underpinning these methods differ, it means that the corroboration among methods which triangulation provide may well be considered erroneous. Despite these implications, Hopper and Hoque (2006) were of the view that they do not undermine the fundamental objectives of triangulation as a research strategy but rather are practical difficulties which need to be overcome.

Effective use of Triangulation in Accounting Research

There are three identified approaches in accounting research; qualitative, quantitative and mixed approaches (Ibiamke & Ajekwe, 2017). The distinction between qualitative and quantitative research is advanced to rest in the use of narratives than numbers or open-ended questions as against closed-ended questions respectively. The mixed approach combines the qualitative and quantitative approaches in the same study. The use of mixed approach in the conduct of research is also known as triangulation.

The triangulation of research methods or data which is commonly found in accounting research could be complex and challenging. The appropriate use and particularly sequential use of mixed methods to maximize its merits in research is something that novice researchers are shown to find difficult (Fusch, Fusch & Ness, 2018). Jick (1979) noted that one of the underlying problems affecting use of mixed method research is the failure of authors and researchers to explain the why of this approach in greater details by indicating how convergent data are collected and interpreted.

This subsection of the paper provides some insights on the effective use of triangulation especially to graduate students of accounting and other social sciences where the approach has been widely advocated but at the same time contested. In particular, the subsection demonstrates to the novice accounting researcher how to effectively do methodological triangulation (i.e use of multiple methods of data collection) in a particular study. Fusch, Fusch and Ness (2018) on methodological triangulation noted that it makes the researcher to consider a phenomenon in more than one way thereby mitigating any potential to see the data from just one point. Methodological triangulation has two aspects; within-method triangulation and between-method or cross-method triangulation. Triangulation of techniques of the same approach such as interview, focused groups and observation as methods of data collection is described as within-method triangulation while a combination of quantitative and qualitative techniques such as questionnaire and interview is between method triangulation (Fusch, Fusch & Ness, 2018). The focus here is on between method triangulation.

To start with, the effective use of triangulation requires that the choice of methods or instruments of data collection or evidence gathering should be congruent and produce comparable data (Jick, 1979). In other words, complementarity of the methods or instruments should be considered and evaluated before deciding on combining the same for research purpose. This is largely ensured where the methods or instruments are oriented towards achieving the same objective. For instance, questionnaire, interview and observation could effectively be combined in a research as each may serve to enrich the data collected from the other. However, depending on the phenomena of study, the instruments will necessarily need to be deployed in a sequence to ensure that complementarity is achieved. The sequence could begin with questionnaire administration followed by interview and observation or begin with observation to questionnaire administration to the conduct of interview.

Fielding (2012) noted that the commonest mixed method design involves the combination of survey and interview. That is, the use of questionnaire and interview in the same research. The effective use necessarily requires that interview be designed and follow after the questionnaire as a means of probing issues raised on the questionnaire. However, Fusch, Fusch and Ness (2018) stated that conventionally, the use of mixed methods study should begin with the use of qualitative methods to identify and narrow down the problem, then, followed by quantitative method to answer the research questions or hypotheses. But depending on the type of research, the process could be reversed. This is why Hussein (2009) concluded that the nature of the research influences the use of and how triangulation is applied.

Notwithstanding the appeal of triangulation, the use of secondary data which is extracted from annual reports and accounts in accounting research may not in all cases also warrant the use of questionnaire or interview as doing so may create divergent findings than complementarity in findings. This could be so because of the bias responses that are likely to be generated from the respondents who may be speaking from individual experiences and thinking. In many instances therefore, data from annual reports and accounts should be considered authentic and superior to produce more reliable findings regarding the financial performance of organizations hence may not require further probing using interview or questionnaire.

However, were the accounting researcher is conducting a study on say Corporate Social Responsibility (CSR) behavior and the financial performance of organizations, the nature of the phenomena under study may well warrant the use of both annual report and accounts data and questionnaire. The combination of methods will become ideal because whereas data on CSR commitment will be available from the annual report and accounts, the source may not sufficiently disclose CSR motivations of the organizations therefore making use of structured questionnaire becomes relevant too. Again, in accounting, the effectiveness of a policy could be interrogated using mixed methods such as interview, observation and review of performance records of organization(s) affected by such policy. Such a combination of methods gives a more comprehensive and accurate conclusion regarding the effectiveness of the policy. What should be understood here is that where a phenomenon has different dimensions and the research objective is to examine these different dimensions and one method or technique cannot effectively support the realization of the objective, then, the use of multiple methods in the study becomes pertinent.

It is important to point out that judgment of the researcher is critical in deciding the congruence and appropriateness of use of triangulation in accounting research.

Jick (1979) posited that whereas statistical tests can be applied to a particular method to determine its suitability in research context, there are no formal tests that can be conducted to decide between the use of different methods in research, thereby leaving it to researchers' judgment.

When triangulating research methods, the researcher should endeavor to subject the instrument, that is, the developed questionnaire or planned interview to expert's scrutiny to ensure that all the domains of the phenomena of study are sufficiently covered or represented on the instrument and that the items are geared towards obtaining complementary data to be collected using other instruments. The emphasis here is the logical arrangement and comprehensiveness with which the instruments are developed. Doing this ensures content validity.

Ibiamke and Ajekwe (2017) suggested that in accounting research, due to the fact that most concepts are not directly observable and lack consensus definition, the onus is on the researcher to clearly provide a theoretical definition and select indicators that thoroughly cover the domain and dimensions of the concept under study. Also, to ensure that empirical results are consistent with theoretical expectations which construct validity is about, when triangulation is adopted, the researcher should endeavor to anchor the study on more than one theory. Pulling more than one theory to explain a study allows for construct validity which may be elusive where only one theoretical framework is adopted.

With respect to analysis of data generated using methodological triangulation, to attain valid statistically conclusion, efforts should be made by the researcher to ensure that the assumptions of the statistical techniques selected for data analysis is satisfied in the data generated from the methods. Ibiamke and Ajekwe (2017) opined statistical conclusion validity as the extent to which a study's conclusion about the relationships from the data are reasonable, credible or believable. Finally, at the interpretation stage of the data, the concern should be that of identifying issues of congruence and trying to explain variations and possible reasons for such variations. This enriches understanding of the phenomena being studied.

There is no doubt that the use of methodological triangulation in research may end up producing divergent results in some cases. But Jick (1979) remark is very relevant in such a situation. Jick (1979) pointed out that it is not always that the use of multiple methods in the study of the same phenomena will produce consistent results, where there is divergence; it should rather be perceived as an opportunity for enriching the explanation. Jick explained further that in looking for explanation of divergent results, it is likely the researcher will uncover results that were hitherto not envisaged within the context. In the situation of divergent results, it should be seen only as a call for further investigation by applying other techniques that help in probing the difference and reconciling as appropriate by the researcher. Therefore, were questionnaire and interview methods are utilized in a study; the accounting researcher should be able to compare the similarities in responses generated. Any dissimilarity should be subjected to further interrogation which may produce more enriching finding about the phenomena.

The bottom line that the accounting researcher needs to note here is that the ability to justify and make clear the use of methodological triangulation in research is important. In addition, the methods being combined should be properly managed. The novice accounting researcher also needs to understand that the synthesization of methods in a particular research necessarily should be a well thought out thing involving the fitness of methods to investigate a phenomena, the methods compatibility, how the weakness of use of one method could be neutralized by adopting others and the ability to apply the methods in a logical manner.

CONCLUSION

This paper shows that triangulation is one of the strategies for enhancing the quality of accounting research. It is primarily aimed at collecting multiple evidences so as to assist the researcher gain a more complete and accurate understanding of a phenomenon of interest. Social science researchers including those in the accounting, economics, business management, marketing and others disciplines often adopt triangulation when investigating a complex phenomenon that applying one source or method may not allow an exhaustive investigation to fully understand it hence inability to reach dependable conclusion. In fact, accounting research in some cases is characterised by behavioral and financial data which need to be properly integrated through triangulation for reliable research conclusion.

While there are limitations associated with triangulation and arguments about its application to research as discussed in this paper, the relevance of the approach especially at a time when adequate evidence and analytical rigor is required to substantiate research findings cannot be overemphasized. This paper is of the view that to effectively use triangulation in accounting research, the researcher should apply the methods and sources creatively in sequence, such that one provides impetus to others to be employed. Semi-structured interviews, for example, should be used before the administration of questionnaire. In doing so, the former will provide insights into what caliber of questions the latter should contain. Additionally, and very importantly too, the choice of different methods and sources to be used in investigating a phenomenon should be made after a careful consideration of the congruence of their philosophical underpinnings. This is essential for a valid, reliable and critic-free corroboration of evidence generated from the multiple sources and methods.

REFERENCES

Arnold, V. (2006). Behavioral research opportunities: Understanding the impact of enterprise systems. *International Journal of Accounting Information Systems, 7*(1), 7–17. doi:10.1016/j.accinf.2006.02.001

Bashir, M., Afzal, M. T., & Azeem, M. (2008). Reliability and validity of qualitative and operational research paradigm. *Pakistan Journal of Statistical and Operation Research, IV*(1), 35–45. doi:10.18187/pjsor.v4i1.59

Bazeley, P. (2004). Issues in mixing qualitative and quantitative approaches to research. In R. Buber, J. Gadner, & L. Richards (Eds.), *Applying qualitative methods to marketing management research* (pp. 141–156). Palgrave Macmillan.

Burrell, G., & Morgan, G. (1979). *Sociological paradigms and organizational analysis*. Ashgate Publishing Limited.

Charoenruk, D. (2009). *Communication research methodologies: qualitative and quantitative methodology*. Available From: http://utcc2.utcc.ac.th/localuser/amsar/PDF/documents49/quantative and qualitative methodologies.pdf

Denzin, N. K. (1989). *The research act: a theoretical introduction to sociological methods* (2nd ed.). Sage.

Denzin, N. K. (1989). *The research act* (3rd ed.). Englewood Cliffs, NJ: Prentice Hall.

Denzin, N. K. (2006). *Sociological methods: a source book* (5th ed.). Chicago: Aldine Publication Company.

Fielding, N. G. (2012). Triangulation and mixed methods designs: Data integration with new research technologies. *Journal of Mixed Methods Research, 6*(2), 124–136. doi:10.1177/1558689812437101

Fielding, N. G., & Fielding, J. L. (1986). *Linking data: the articulation of qualitative and quantitative methods in social research*. Beverly Hills, CA: SAGE. doi:10.4135/9781412984775

Flick, U. (1992). Triangulation revisited: Strategy of validation or alternative? *Journal for the Theory of Social Behaviour, 22*(2), 175–197. doi:10.1111/j.1468-5914.1992.tb00215.x

Fusch, P., Fusch, G. E., & Ness, L. R. (2018). Denzin's paradigm shift: Revisiting triangulation in qualitative research. *Journal of Social Change, 10*(1), 19–32.

Golafshani, N. (2003). Understanding reliability and validity in qualitative research. *Qualitative Report, 8*(4), 597–607.

Hayashi, P., Abib, G., & Hoppen, N. (2019). Validity in qualitative research: A processual approach. *Qualitative Report*, *24*(24), 98–112.

Hopper, T., & Hoque, Z. (2006). Triangulation approaches to accounting research. In Z. Hoque (Ed.), *Methodological issues in accounting research: theories, methods and issues* (pp. 562–569). London: Spiramus Press.

Hoque, Z., Covaleski, M. A., & Gooneratne, T. N. (2013). Theoretical triangulation and pluralism in research methods in organizational and accounting research. *Accounting, Auditing & Accountability Journal*, *26*(7), 1170–1198. doi:10.1108/AAAJ-May-2012-01024

Hussein, A. (2009). The use of triangulation in social science research: Can qualitative and quantitative methods be combined? *Journal of Comparative Social Work*, *1*, 1–12.

Ibiamke, A., & Ajekwe, C. C. M. (2017). On ensuring rigour in accounting research. *International Journal of Academic Research in Accounting. Finance and Management Sciences*, *7*(3), 157–170.

Jick, T. D. (1979). Mixing qualitative and quantitative methods: Triangulation in action. *Administrative Science Quarterly*, *24*(4), 602–611. doi:10.2307/2392366

Johnstone, L. P. (2007). Weighing up triangulating and contradictory evidence in mixed methods organizational research. *International Journal of Multiple Research Approaches*, *1*(1), 27–38. doi:10.5172/mra.455.1.1.27

Mark, M. M., Feller, I., & Button, S. B. (1997). Integrating qualitative methods in a predominantly quantitative evaluation: a case study and some reflections. In J. Green & V. Caracelli (Eds.), Advances in mixed-methods evaluation. New directions for evaluations. San Francisco, CA: Jossey-Bass Publishers. doi:10.1002/ev.1071

Modell, S. (2009). In defence of triangulation: A critical realist approach to mixed methods research in management accounting. *Management Accounting Research*, *20*(3), 208–221. doi:10.1016/j.mar.2009.04.001

Modell, S. (2015). Theoretical triangulation and pluralism in accounting research: A critical realist critique. *Accounting, Auditing & Accountability Journal*, *28*(7), 1138–1150. doi:10.1108/AAAJ-10-2014-1841

National Child Care Information Center. (2011). *Qualitative research assessment tool*. Available From: http://www.researchconnections.org/childcare/datamethods/downloads/qualitativeresearchassesstool.pdf

O'Donoghue, T., & Punck, K. (2003). *Qualitative educational research in action: doing and reflecting*. London: Falmer Press. doi:10.4324/9780203506301

Olsen, W. (2004). Triangulation in social research: qualitative and quantitative methods can really be mixed. In M. Holborn (Ed.), Development in sociology. Causeway Press.

Pratt, N., & Woods, P. (2006). *Qualitative research*. University of Plymouth. Available from: http://www.edu.plymouth.ac.uk/resined/qualitative%20methods%202/qualrshm.htm

Rothbaner, P. M. (2008). *Triangulation*. Available From: http://www.sage-ereference.com/research/Article_n468.html

Shenton, A. K. (2004). Strategies for ensuring trustworthiness in qualitative research projects. *Education for Information, 22*(2), 63–755. doi:10.3233/EFI-2004-22201

Smith, J. (1990). Alternative research paradigms and the problem of criteria. In E. G. Guba (Ed.), *The paradigm dialogue* (pp. 167–187). Newbury Park, CA: SAGE.

Stavros, C., & Westberg, K. (2009). Using triangulation and multiple case studies to advance relationship marketing theory. *Qualitative Market Research, 12*(3), 307–320. doi:10.1108/13522750910963827

Tijjani, B. (2010). *Share valuation and stock market analysis in emerging markets: the case of Nigeria*. Adamu Joji Publishers.

Wikipedia. (2011). *Triangulation: Social science*. Available From: http://en.wikipedia.org/wiki/triangulation_(social_science)

Yeasmin, S., & Rahman, K. F. (2012). Triangulation research method as the tool of social science research. Bangladesh University of Professionals Journal, 1(1), 154-163.

Chapter 9
Beyond Statistical Power and Significance in Entrepreneurship and Management Research

Pierre Sindambiwe
University of Rwanda, Rwanda & Jönköping International Business School, Sweden

ABSTRACT

Findings in most empirical research on entrepreneurship and management focuses on a few things: statistical representativeness of the data, the methodological rigor used for arriving at the results, and the statistical power of the results. However, both results and data are far from being free of criticism. This chapter provides a way forward that uses the mixed-methods approach without falling into the common confusion of multiple methods used in one research. It looks back at the reliance of statistical testing, null-hypothesis, and testing the statistical significance as the criteria. It explores available alternatives that can offer to overcome the problem of non-significance, rather than rejecting it as is usually done. It acknowledges some quantitative solutions like replication, conjoint, and comparative analyses and extends the use of some qualitative methods like exploratory methods, case studies, and theory development studies that offer alternatives to treating the presence or absence of significance. It discusses the concepts used and gives the limitations of the study.

DOI: 10.4018/978-1-7998-1025-4.ch009

INTRODUCTION: ISSUES WITH STATISTICAL SIGNIFICANCE TESTING

In this chapter, the researcher revises the heavy reliance on statistical significance as a truth criterion and explore available alternatives that mixed methods can offer to overcome this problem. According to Schmidt (1996), statistical significance is not an appropriate approach and relying on it leads to slow development of cumulative knowledge in psychology making it something that needs to be replaced. Similarly, in predicting the findings most of the empirical research on entrepreneurship and management, like research in many other social sciences, focuses on a few things: *statistical representativeness* of the data, methodological *rigor* to arrive at the results, and the *statistical power* of the results. However, both results and data are far from being criticism free as noted by Schmidt (1996). According to Bettis, Ethiraj, Gambardella, Helfat, & Mitchell (2016), statistical methods have been common in many fields since the 1950s, but reliability of statistical tests is questionable, and therefore, scholars need appropriate knowledge about the use and interpretation of statistics.

There is a need to know the meaning of the significant results as well as the reasons for the non-significance of some of the results.

The author discusses the following three points, as well as their respective problems with statistical representativeness, methodological rigor, and statistical power. This chapter also discusses the way forward to go beyond statistical power and recognition of non-significance in entrepreneurship and management research.

(1) *Issues of assumption of randomness and statistical representativeness of the data that directly affect the interpretation of the results:* One issue related to the assumption of randomness and the statistical representativeness of the data that affects the interpretation of the results directly is the assumption of randomness in most quantitative research (Shaver, 1993) but the results do not always take care of the theoretical relevance and theoretical representativeness of the data (Davidsson, 2004). Theoretical relevance of the sample is needed to enrich the applied theory instead of just representative sampling and its associated significance testing or statistical power. It is not easy to find an empirical population that is theoretically relevant that exists in one place at one time so that we can sample it probabilistically based on certain predictions (Davidsson, 2004). It is a challenge to define such a category of the population, entirely or as a sample that gives the assurance that the results have the validity for the entrepreneurship phenomenon. Both simple random and stratified sampling should be supplemented with clear reasons for representing a phenomenon that theory tries to explain, rather than proving its statistical representativeness. It

is not solely statistical validity or representativeness of the sample that will give power to the results, but its impact on the studied phenomenon that will.

(2) *Issue of methodological rigor for achieving the results: Lack of precision in the formulation of the null-hypothesis that affects the interpretation of the results directly:* Another issue is related to the *methodological rigor* for arriving at the results, that is, lack of precision in formulating the null-hypothesis that affects the results' interpretation directly. Researchers put the theory at risk of falsification very early in designing and setting *directional predictions* such as two variables will be positively or negatively related (Edwards & Berry, 2010: 668). Instead, researchers in entrepreneurship and management fields are advised to predict propositions with meaning other than deviations from zero. D*irectional predictions* can easily lead to biased results when the test whether there is a case or not. At the end of mission, it misses the opportunity to contribute to the theory development.

(3) *Issue of statistical power that diminishes the results' impact: Presence or absence of significance:* Another issue is related to the statistical power or significance that diminishes the impact of the results is the presence or absence of significance. According to Davidsson (2004), Hubbard and Lindsay (2013), and O'Boyle Jr, Rutherford & Banks (2014) there is a general tendency to insist on the strengths of a relationship without checking their consistency with theory. Contradictory or non-significant results have lower chances to be published and their theoretical implications are ignored. A genuine statistical relationship matters in entrepreneurship research and researchers, editors, and reviewers invest much effort in a 'genuine relationship' with less focus on its rigor and relevance. This may lead to publication bias through suppression of non-significant or counterintuitive findings without knowing why and how they are non-significant, which may lead to the development of a new theory (Kepes et al., 2014; O'Boyle et al., 2014; Van Burg & Romme, 2014).

Even though they might interpret the results, entrepreneurship and management researchers need to go beyond statistical significance or theory testing alone as if it was the ultimate finality so that the lack of significance or its presence represents the effects of its absence or presence.

Theoretical development and/or methodological rigor must prevail over accuracy in statistical testing. Without rigor in the methodology, there will also be a problem of robust conclusions to guide future trustworthy research and evidence-based management research and practices (Kepes et al., 2014; Van Burg & Romme, 2014). Publications are / or may be biased because of suppression of non-significant or counterintuitive findings in entrepreneurship research (O'Boyle et al., 2014). However, the absence of significance in data gathered from a given population will not be treated as having failed to test the theory as such because it does not necessarily guarantee the absence of effect in the field. Instead it reflects the absence of effect within a small population that is selected, and it cannot fit all sizes and all fields. Each deviation must be investigated separately, but not rejected because of non-significance. There has to be a reason for rejecting it. Such a rejection of a non-significant test or failure to publish the findings because of non-significance prevents researchers from advancing theory and knowledge in management and entrepreneurship fields. "Exclusion of studies with counter-or null relations hampers our ability to build approach appropriate theory" (O'Boyle et al., 2014: 9). Such a bias constitutes a threat to theory building and development as well as a threat to evidence-based practices and research which has an impact and makes a meaningful contribution for practitioners.

Some remedies like replication, conjoint and comparative analyses remain applicable in quantitative field research per see but extending them using some qualitative methods like exploratory methods, cases studies, and theory development offer alternatives to treating the presence or absence of significance. Such an extension from the quantitative results to a qualitative application makes the mixed methods approach effective without falling into the confusion of multiple methods used in one research.

This chapter provides the way forward that leads to the mixed-methods approach or simply going beyond statistical testing and null-hypothesis testing and investigating the reasons for non-significance rather than rejecting the null-hypothesis.

WAY FORWARD FOR SIGNIFICANCE TESTING IN ENTREPRENEURSHIP AND MANAGEMENT RESEARCH

Ensuring Theoretical Representativeness For Theoretical Significance

According to Davidsson (2004), one way of dealing with representativeness issues and arriving at practical results is determining the case/or population included in the data matrix that goes beyond statistical representation or an assumption of randomness to ensure that it is good enough to bring something new to theory that the researcher is testing or developing. That is theoretical representativeness instead of statistical representativeness.

Theoretical representativeness must be ensured at different levels of an analysis, that is, individual, venture, firm, industrial, special unit, and regional and national levels (Davidsson, 2004). Heterogeneity across firms, sizes, and nations exists and what is meaningful for one category does not necessarily apply in other contexts while statistically it might be important. Some statistics can be just in terms of numbers without being less associated with economic values like a large number of start-ups or self-employed people with less contributions to GDP while with technology intensity in other countries these numbers may contribute more financially and/ or economically when one considers their employment or social impact, or regional development brought about by a few firms. Statistical significance without meaning is just numbers.

Ensuring Precisions in The Results Through Propositions Development

As contradictory or non-significant results have lower chances of being published Schwab et al., (2011) showed how weak predictors led to rejections. This is because editorial and review processes insist on methodological precisions that make predictions stronger and convincing enough to yield robust tests results like size and confidence intervals, hypotheses, and metrics. According to Edwards and Berry (2010), it is better to predict more meaningful propositions other than directional predictions. This can be achieved through: First, null-hypothesis set as a range (not points) with upper and lower limits; second, the proposition should be stated as a comparison; third, not only do the propositions need to be stated as 'deviation from zero' but they also need to be supplemented by non-zero quantities that specify range of allowable values, also known as the 'good- enough belt'; fourth, there is a need for developing "contingent predictions that identify factors that influence the form and magnitude of the relationships of the theory" (Edwards and Berry, 2010: 677), whereby:

- First, null-hypothesis is set as a range (not points) with upper and lower limits. For example, 'X is positively related to Y within a correlation greater than ... [lower limit] and less than ... [upper limit]';
- Second, the proposition should be stated as a comparison. This has the advantage of measuring the relationship not only greater than zero, but also larger than another relationship. For example, the relationship between 'X and Y' is larger than the relationship between 'W and Y' beyond or within the lower and upper limits set (see previous example);
- Third, not only do the propositions need to be stated not as 'deviations from zero' but they also need to be supplemented by non-zero quantities that specify the range of the allowable values, also known as the 'good-enough belt.' For example, 'X is positively related to Y with a correlation within the good-enough belt (specify them) surrounding the correlation (noted)'; and

- Fourth, there is a need for developing "contingent predictions that identify factors that influence the form and magnitude of the relationships of the theory" (Edwards and Berry, 2010: 677). For example, 'X has a positive relationship with Y that increases as the level of moderator Z increases.'

By doing so, many methodological issues are ensured in advance and it promises good and stronger results which are easy to understand and interpret.

Non-Significance Treatment Null-Hypothesis Significance Testing

It is observed that academics persist with null-hypothesis significance testing (Shaver, 1993) which impedes the development of a strong theory that predicts anything other than what the null hypothesis predicts, that must differ from zero. This has undermined scientific progress in entrepreneurship and management research, leading to an inertia in methodological practices (Edwards & Berry, 2010: 684). Such an increasing consideration of statistically significant results turns people away from negative results in entrepreneurship and management research.

Negative results are rejected simply because they do not support theory (Edwards & Berry, 2010: 681) while researchers, actors, and reviewers encourage such a practice to legitimize theory rather than testing whether a given theory is valid or not. Failure to support the proposed hypothesis should not be considered as 'not working.' It might have more to do with the research's conception, design, and execution rather than the construct itself. In theory testing, researchers insist on statistics in the results matrix, looking for significance or non-significance of theoretical constructs/variables in the model. Non- significant variables are ignored in further analyses and interpretations. This has its own implications because some extant literature might have found them significant under different circumstances, which means that non-significance is related to and has significance for the sample only and is not always non- significant in all datasets. It is hard to prove that if a given variable has non-significance in your data and, it will have non-significance in other data outside your population or a kind of worldwide non-significance. To prove this, one must verify the results in the population under study (internal replication, internal validity) and different populations to compare the results (external replication, external validity). If the results of both the replications do not support each other, then significance or non-significance has to do with the associated context.

Researchers interpret wrongly a non-significance as theory (O'Boyle et al., 2014). Results contradicting existing theory can lead to a new theory, so it is not advisable to reject non-significance results for the sake of rejecting the null-hypothesis but a new window should be opened for advancing theory. What is found significant only for your data and to your context and what is found non-significant must be investigated further. There must be a reason behind the non- significance in your tests. "There is often significance in non- significance" (O'Boyle et al., 2014:9). Besides replication for verifying the results as one more way of remediating this issue is to go for mixed-methods, encouraging a *contextual study* or *exploratory*, *qualitative*, and *theory development studies* as well as a *case study design* capable of building a counterbalance and theory contest.

MIXED-METHODS AND REPLICATION: BEYOND FINDINGS AND STATISTICAL SIGNIFICANCE

Replication

As mentioned earlier, the power of statistical tests does not reside in their statistical significance as if it was an end, but in its power to represent "a certain size in the theoretically relevant population" (Davidsson, 2004: 175). To do so, a verification is needed, preferably a condition for all the results before being published (Shaver, 1993) but few researchers reach that level simply because of strong incentives for innovations and weak incentives for confirmations (Open Science Collaboration, 2012: 657). Replication and reproducibility as well as generalizability of findings are concerns in many disciplines (Open Science Collaboration, 2015). Since the sample represents a certain size of the population, the power of statistical significance testing is seen through the lens of its capacity of being replicated, that is, to be right for the same or original population, internal validity or on a targeted similar sample or population which is external validity or generalizability (Kepes et al., 2014). Many terms are used here to talk about replication, reproducibility, and generalizability. This needs to be done with caution because some findings are statistically significant at a certain level but fail to verify the predicted relationship when replicated or verify some but not all the predicted relationships (Edwards & Berry, 2010; Hubbard & Lindsay, 2013). This is where the problem of statistical significance lies in terms of replicability: whether the presence or absence of significance means the presence or absence of the relationship as well as its effects on the sample/ population (Davidsson, 2004; Hubbard & Lindsay, 2013; Kepes et al., 2014; O'Boyle et al., 2014; Van Burg & Romme, 2014*)*. In fact, lack of significant results will not be taken as proof of the non-existence of an effect, that is, as firm evidence against the theory (Davidsson, 2004: 183), as closer observations of the sample/population being re-used may give different results.

People need to look back at where the research started and think of its replicability in the same population or other similar populations. This is where the second problem of statistical significance lies in terms of replicability: when researchers stop with statistical significance testing only and forget why they were doing what they were doing (Davidsson, 2004; Hubbard & Lindsay, 2013; Kepes et al., 2014; O'Boyle et al., 2014; Van Burg & Romme, 2014). If the statistical significance cannot be replicated in a theoretically relevant population, then measures need to be taken for the research to yield its intended impact, otherwise successful theory testing or statistical significance is not the ideal teller of expected truth. Entrepreneurship and management quantitative researchers need to do justice to themselves by just stopping and asking themselves one question: "what am I doing?" If the answer is the intended impact, then it is worth looking at the population again, if there is a certain theoretical relevance of the selected population or sample then they need to look forward at how to verify the obtained results and predictions for that very population or sample or even others or what is called replication. Such a backward and forward exercise can compensate for the efforts made. The findings need to have a meaning regarding the sample and population. Without extra effort beyond statistical significance testing or theory testing, without replication of the results, the impact cannot be ensured. In other words, stopping at theory testing alone or doing only statistical significance testing would be wasting the researcher's efforts and readers' time.

INCLUDING THE RESEARCH'S CONTEXT IN THE ANALYSIS

According to Schwab et al., (2011), most research results are superficial and illusive because of little knowledge of the study's variables or context and therefore the relationship between the context of the study and its research findings. This exercise comes after the hypothesis significance tests. It can establish the relevance of each metric for the dependent variable. Such a description will establish the significance of the variables, for whom they are relevant, and at what cost. Such a contextual inclusion and control of the context (Chlosta, 2016) in the model helps understand other related variables as well as the contextual influence that they bring because of the stable and changing contexts of entrepreneurs. These contextual factors include the gender of the entrepreneur (social context), region where the venture is founded (spatial context), and when (temporal) it happens as well as how they influence the variables in entrepreneurship research. The context is divided into social context, spatial context, institutional context, and business or temporal context of the business (Welter, 2011; Zahra & Wright, 2011). The business context is made of industry and market; the social context is made of networks, household, and family; the spatial context includes the geographic environment; and the institutional context includes culture and society, as well as political and economic systems (Welter, 2011). The context can provide both opportunities and/or liabilities for entrepreneurs depending on which context one is referring to (Colli, 2012).

CONJOINT AND COMPARATIVE ANALYSES

We have seen that comparison is one way of ensuring the robustness of the findings by measuring at least two different relationships instead of just measuring whether the relationship between the two variables is different from zero (Edwards & Berry, 2010). It has also been highlighted that the findings need to be compared with one another due to the differences in the entrepreneurs' contexts if one wants to grasp the reality in quantitative entrepreneurship research. According to Bygrave (2007), entrepreneurs are just outliers while quantitative entrepreneurship research is all about the central tendency. A random sample of entrepreneurs that researchers use fails to get extremes like full time or part time entrepreneurs, entrepreneurs with or without employees, and many others. Talking of entrepreneurs should go hand in hand with comparing their entrepreneurial motives (antecedents) and outcomes, with a focus on why, when, and how questions instead of comparing entrepreneurs and non-entrepreneurs based on their attributes and behaviors (Davidsson, 2004). Such a comparison of attributes and behaviors may lead to the mistake of studying individual and situational attributes of entrepreneurial motives and outcomes while entrepreneurs' attributes or situations cannot help researchers in understanding how, when, and why entrepreneurs start or quit a business. Therefore, comparing the findings helps to arrive at some conclusions because the significant results may have been for just one category of entrepreneurs. As they are different categories in the variables, a conjoint analysis and ANOVA tests, help to know which variable is more or less significant thus helping in drawing the conclusions (Shepherd & Zacharakis, 1998).

EXPLORATORY, QUALITATIVE, AND THEORY DEVELOPMENT STUDIES

Without advocating for qualitative research as an alternative for quantitative research, most of the recommendations made earlier can be better understood if significant tests are supplemented by a qualitative analysis (O'Boyle et al., 2014) like mixed methods. This will allow following-up those variables that are non-significant while they were probably linked to the context and may have significance in other circumstances. To do so, once statistical tests show non-significant variables or counterintuitive ones, a new window should be opened and using exploratory, qualitative, and theory development studies may reveal more information on non-significant variables as well as their contexts once the study shifts from quantitative to qualitative research.

Coming back to the debate on the relationships between quantitative and qualitative methods and how they can cohabitate in mixed-methods research, some authors like Daft (1983), Morgan and Smircich (1980), and Siggelkow (2007) advocate the qualitative approach when it comes to studying social phenomena. For instance, Morgan and Smircich (1980) explored debates between the dichotomies between quantitative / qualitative methods which took place during the 1960s, 1970s, and 1980s. They concluded that the dichotomy of quantitative/qualitative research is a matter of an ideological debate of minor significance. According to Morgan and Smircich (1980), both approaches (quantitative / qualitative) are empirical and are based on methods and only differ in the way that they look at a social phenomenon. The difference should be an understanding of the underlying assumptions of each of these methods and how they treat the issue of knowledge about the social world: objectively or subjectively. In this continuum from subjectivity to objectivity, different researchers from different backgrounds (quantitative/qualitative view) analyze and give meaning to the social world and social reality but the issue is how they study it or the methodology that they use. The objectivist view of the social world emphasizes the importance of studying the nature of relationships among elements constituting the structure, while the subjectivist's view of the social world emphasizes the importance of understanding the process through which human beings concretize their relationships with their world and the external environment.

The concept of qualitative methods is discussed by different authors at times alluding to a comparison with pre-existing and dominant quantitative methods used in social sciences. In fact, according to Morgan and Smircich (1980), the quantitative methods study the social reality by manipulating data through sophisticated quantitative approaches for statistical significance and relationships of elements that have to be abstracted from their context (objectivism) which can be done in a partial or limited way, leading to a partial role in analyzing and understanding the process of social change. Criticizing quantitative methods, researchers also show that scientists need to change from being limited to being external observers (objectivity) to being investigators from within the subject of the study (subjectivity) and supplementing quantitative research with techniques appropriate for that task (rather than studying the statistical significance of the relationships). Different techniques such as participant observations, content analysis, in-depth interviewing, biography, and a linguistic analysis can be used for this. The qualitative method investigates by going beyond a general understanding of the phenomenon and following the subjects under study closely in their real-life settings to come up with concrete explanations rather than a general explanation of the phenomenon. This approach does not exclude the other research approaches of empiricism but starts from where it is necessary and goes further in elaborating on existing theoretical knowledge and providing new explanations for new social phenomena.

CASE STUDY

Another way of extending the quantitative method is by using a case study approach; this helps illustrate or verify the findings and conclusions.

To understand what a case is one needs to understand the types of cases studies. According to Stake (1995), a case study may be intrinsic or an instrumental study depending on the researcher's interest. A researcher is interested in a case not because s/he would be able to learn about other cases or about some general problem, but because s/he wants to learn about that particular case. If we have an intrinsic interest in the case, and we may call our work an *intrinsic case study*. Sometimes, case studies are used for understanding something else other than the case, A case study approach then is instrumental in accomplishing something other than understanding a particular case, and we may call our inquiry an *instrumental case study*. This kind of case study may push the researcher to elaborate on and compare the phenomena case by case. So, we may feel that we should choose several cases to study rather than just one, where there will be important coordination between the individual studies. Then, we may call this a *collective case study*.

The allocation of attention to contexts (issues) will be based partly on the distinction between intrinsic and instrumental purposes of the case study. "The more the case study is an intrinsic case study the more attention needs to be paid to the contexts. The more the case study is an instrumental case study, certain contexts may be important, but other contexts important to the case are of little interest to the study" (Stake, 1995: 64). This is probably where the choice of a case in entrepreneurship and management case studies will be decided depending on the researcher's interest based on the context. The choice is made depending on whether the case is to be an intrinsic case study or an instrumental case study. A firm may be unique in its settings and therefore attract the attention of the researcher as a 'single case' while a firm may be similar to many firms so the researcher can choose it alone or together with many others (multiple cases) to investigate a given phenomenon that the firms share.

However, qualitative researchers in entrepreneurship and management studies present almost the same limitations as other fields. The limitations are set regarding the sample size, or "representativeness" (Humphreys, 2013:24), plus the issue of "generalizability" (for example, Cater III, 2012: 166; James Cater III & Beal, 2014). According to Meneses, Coutinho & Carlos Pinho (2014), a small sample from the same region may lead to problems of generalization.

These problems are not specific to entrepreneurship and management research. According to Siggelkow (2007), researchers using case studies face two challenges and feel obliged to explain or defend themselves against why they use too small a sample as well as the challenge of *'no representativeness'* of the case. However, Stake (1995) provides an explanation for this because even for collective case studies selection by sampling of attributes should not be the highest priority. The representativeness of a small sample is difficult to defend. The essence is the reason why you chose it instead of its representativeness. The reason or the selection criterion of a case should be to maximize what we can learn; if we can, we need to pick cases which are easy to get to and hospitable to our inquiries, perhaps for which a prospective informant can be identified along with actors (the people studied) being willing to comment on certain draft material (Stake, 1995).

Another challenge in the case study approach is the 'lack of generalizations.' However, according to Stake (1995) people should not worry about this issue because the real business of a case study is 'particularization,' not generalization. We take a particular case and come to know it well, not primarily about how it is different from others but what it is and what it does. Still if the findings of a case can be observed in other similar cases it is already a generalization (Petite generalization) as per Stake (1995).

IMPLICATIONS, LIMITATIONS, AND FUTURE RESEARCH AGENDA

This chapter considered the problems directly associated with statistical significance. It identified a need to know the meaning of the significant results as well as the reasons for non-significant results and how to go beyond them. The chapter touched on the problems of statistical representativeness, methodological rigor, and statistical power, and discussed their problems and way forward going beyond statistical power and recognizing non-significance in entrepreneurship and management research. The author acknowledges that other issues are pertinent too in an analysis such as research design, theoretical sensitivity, and data collection, but these were not the focus in this chapter. There is also a need to go for point estimates and interval confidence, meta-analyses (Schmidt, 1996), as well as systematic reviews and evidence-based management that are also good alternatives but not discussed in this chapter as they do not involve mixed-methods directly. Research can look into each level. Statistical representativeness of the data as well as its methodological rigor need similar attention to have a broader picture of how to answer the research question, have a valid generalization, and for addressing the different issues affecting the strengths of the results of entrepreneurship and management research.

As a way forward and a solution provided in this chapter, an analysis also needs to be carried out through replication at different levels of the analysis and comparing the units of analysis to understand to what extent theory testing is significantly different in one unit of analysis and in others as well as their implications. Conjoint analysis and ANOVA tests (see for example Shepherd & Zacharakis, 1998) are also good alternatives. Researchers can also perform a cross-sectional comparison (Davidsson, 2004, pp. 70-71) and then interpret the existing differences among groups using the same units of analysis like self-employed compared to owner-managers or successful ventures. Apart from replication and comparison, some authors also advocate a contextual analysis of non-significant constructs as well as a case study design and exploratory, qualitative, and theory development studies to understand the how, when, and why questions that are not captured by statistical significance tests in entrepreneurship and management research.

REFERENCES

Bettis, R. A., Ethiraj, S., Gambardella, A., Helfat, C., & Mitchell, W. (2016). Creating repeatable cumulative knowledge in strategic management: A call for a broad and deep conversation among authors, referees, and editors. *Strategic Management Journal*, *37*(2), 257–261. doi:10.1002mj.2477

Bygrave, W. D. (2007). The entrepreneurship paradigm (I) revisited. Handbook of qualitative research methods in entrepreneurship, 1748.

Cater, J. J. III. (2012). The Pierre Part store: A case study. *Journal of Family Business Management*, *2*(2), 166–180. doi:10.1108/20436231211261899

Chlosta, S. (2016). *Getting into methodological trouble. In A Research Agenda for Entrepreneurship and Context* (pp. 109–119). Cheltenham, UK: Edward Elgar. doi:10.4337/9781784716844.00013

Colli, A. (2012). Contextualizing performances of family firms: The perspective of business history. *Family Business Review*, *25*(3), 243–257. doi:10.1177/0894486511426872

Daft, R. L. (1983). Learning the craft of organizational research. *Academy of Management Review*, *8*(4), 539–546. doi:10.5465/amr.1983.4284649

Davidsson, P. (2004). *Researching entrepreneurship*. New York: Springer.

Edwards, J. R., & Berry, J. W. (2010). The presence of something or the absence of nothing: Increasing theoretical precision in management research. *Organizational Research Methods*, *13*(4), 668–689. doi:10.1177/1094428110380467

Hubbard, R., & Lindsay, R. M. (2013). From significant difference to significant sameness: Proposing a paradigm shift in business research. *Journal of Business Research*, *66*(9), 1377–1388. doi:10.1016/j.jbusres.2012.05.002

Humphreys, M. M. (2013). Daughter succession: A predominance of human issues. *Journal of Family Business Management*, *3*(1), 24–44. doi:10.1108/20436231311326472

James Cater, J. III, & Beal, B. (2014). Ripple effects on family firms from an externally induced crisis. *Journal of Family Business Management*, *4*(1), 62–78. doi:10.1108/JFBM-02-2013-0006

Kepes, S., Bennett, A. A., & McDaniel, M. A. (2014). Evidence-based management and the trustworthiness of our cumulative scientific knowledge: Implications for teaching, research, and practice. *Academy of Management Learning & Education*, *13*(3), 446–466. doi:10.5465/amle.2013.0193

Meneses, R., Coutinho, R., & Carlos Pinho, J. (2014). The impact of succession on family business internationalisation: The successors' perspective. *Journal of Family Business Management*, *4*(1), 24–45. doi:10.1108/JFBM-01-2013-0004

Morgan, G., & Smircich, L. (1980). The case for qualitative research. *Academy of Management Review*, *5*(4), 491–500. doi:10.5465/amr.1980.4288947

O'Boyle, E. H. Jr, Rutherford, M. W., & Banks, G. C. (2014). Publication bias in entrepreneurship research: An examination of dominant relations to performance. *Journal of Business Venturing*, *29*(6), 773–784. doi:10.1016/j.jbusvent.2013.10.001

Open Science Collaboration. (2012). An open, large-scale, collaborative effort to estimate the reproducibility of psychological science. *Perspectives on Psychological Science*, *7*(6), 657–660. doi:10.1177/1745691612462588 PMID:26168127

Open Science Collaboration. (2015). Estimating the reproducibility of psychological science. *Science*, *349*(6251), aac4716. doi:10.1126cience.aac4716 PMID:26315443

Schmidt, F. L. (1996). Statistical significance testing and cumulative knowledge in psychology: Implications for training of researchers. *Psychological Methods*, *1*(2), 115–129. doi:10.1037/1082-989X.1.2.115

Schwab, A., Abrahamson, E., Starbuck, W. H., & Fidler, F. (2011). Perspective—Researchers should make thoughtful assessments instead of null-hypothesis significance tests. *Organization Science*, *22*(4), 1105–1120. doi:10.1287/orsc.1100.0557

Shaver, J. P. (1993). What statistical significance testing is, and what it is not. *Journal of Experimental Education*, *61*(4), 293–316. doi:10.1080/00220973.1993.10806592

Shepherd, D. A., & Zacharakis, A. (1999). Conjoint analysis: A new methodological approach for researching the decision policies of venture capitalists. *Venture Capital: An International Journal of Entrepreneurial Finance*, *1*(3), 197–217. doi:10.1080/136910699295866

Siggelkow, N. (2007). Persuasion with case studies. *Academy of Management Journal*, *50*(1), 20–24. doi:10.5465/amj.2007.24160882

Van Burg, E., & Romme, A. G. L. (2014). Creating the future together: Toward a framework for research synthesis in entrepreneurship. *Entrepreneurship Theory and Practice*, *38*(2), 369–397. doi:10.1111/etap.12092

Welter, F. (2011). Contextualizing entrepreneurship—Conceptual challenges and ways forward. *Entrepreneurship Theory and Practice*, *35*(1), 165–184. doi:10.1111/j.1540-6520.2010.00427.x

Zahra, S. A., & Wright, M. (2011). Entrepreneurship's next act. *The Academy of Management Perspectives*, *25*(4), 67–83. doi:10.5465/amp.2010.0149

Chapter 10

Using Social Media to Organize a Marginalized Community:
A Case Study Examining LGBT Military Leaders Advocating for Inclusive Service

Todd R. Burton
Cardinal Stritch University, USA

ABSTRACT

Potential leaders within marginalized communities find it difficult to connect, learn, strategize, and support one another and build a cohesive community capable of effecting social change. This research contributes to filling a gap in empirical research on effective approaches to employing social media tools to organize and engage in social movements. The research builds on earlier studies of marginalized communities and social media to organize and engages in social movements by applying a case study design to assess how the lesbian, gay, bisexual, and transgender (LGBT) military community employed social media to organize and advocate for inclusion and end discrimination within the U.S. armed forces. Seventeen findings were identified that describe key ways the LGBT military community employed these tools to organize, identify leaders and their roles, and how online behavior affected offline advocacy.

INTRODUCTION

This chapter demonstrates how case study research employing content and social network analysis can provide a framework to explore inter-group dynamics of a social movement.

DOI: 10.4018/978-1-7998-1025-4.ch010

Copyright © 2020, IGI Global. Copying or distributing in print or electronic forms without written permission of IGI Global is prohibited.

The purpose of this research was to identify how social media tools connect and organize members of a marginalized community. The research question asks: How did the LGBT military community employ social media tools to organize and advocate to seek inclusion and an end to discrimination within the U.S. armed forces?

- How did the online LGBT military community develop/organize?
- How were leaders of online groups identified and what was their role?
- How did online behavior affect offline behavior/advocacy?

The case study examines how LGBT military personnel used social media to organize online during the effort to end DADT and the following effort to end the ban on transgender military service.

BACKGROUND

Potential leaders within marginalized communities find it difficult to connect, learn, strategize, and support one another and build a cohesive community capable of effecting social change (Arredondo, 2008). Further research can demonstrate the value of these tools and to identify how communities have most effectively employed social media to advance their social cause. As social media tools have become commonly available and accessible, they have the potential to facilitate connections and allow individuals to connect and organize for collective social action (Delany, 2016; Garrett et al., 2012; Obar, Zube, & Lampe, 2012).

The theoretical framework focuses on the intersection between social movement theory as described in Blumer's four-phase model defining the lifecycle of a social movement (Della Porta & Diani, 2006) and the emerging field of social media research, assessed against a series of four factors identified by Fulton (2013) in her assessment of the group OutServe as key to effective organizing online. Figure 1 depicts the interaction between these factors and processes.

Social movement theory, as articulated by Blumer (1969), in his seminal work "Collective Behavior" and later expanded on by other researchers (Della Porta & Diani, 2006) describes four phases through which a social movement progresses: emergence, coalescence, bureaucratization, and decline as depicted in Table 1.

As social media tools have become broadly accessible and widely adopted, they provide new ways for organizers of social movements to facilitate work towards changing their status. Allsop (2016) describes three distinct perspectives on the effectiveness of social media for political organizing. Skeptics view social media as an army of armchair "slacktivists" who do not convert interest to action (Gladwell, 2010; Lewis, Gray, & Meierhenrich, 2014; Lievrouw, 2011; Rutledge,

Figure 1. Theoretical framework

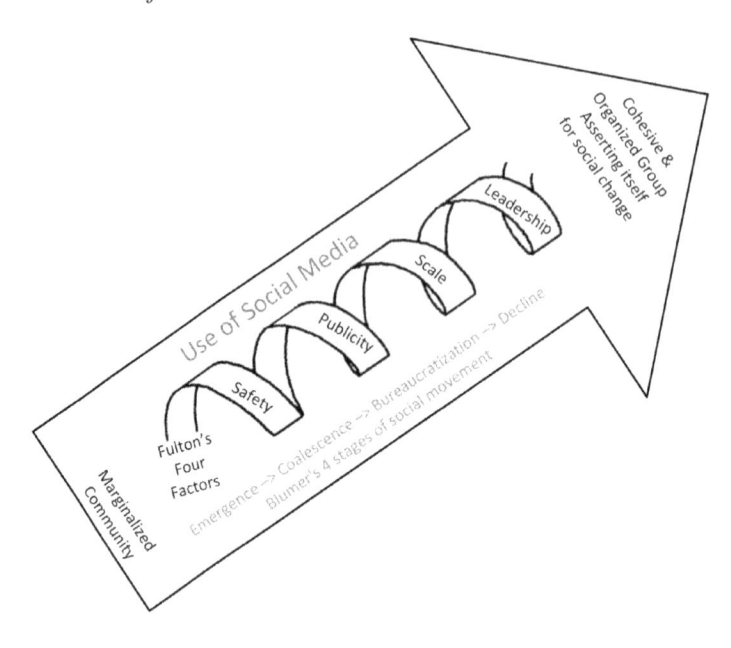

Table 1. Stages of a social movement

Stage	Characteristics
Emergence	• Unorganized • Discontent with the status quo • Little effort to work together • Increased stress • Increased media coverage
Coalescence	• "Individuals participating in the mass behavior of the preceding stage become aware of each other" (Hopper, 1950) • Emergence of leaders and strategy • Focalized collective action • Identification of opposition
Bureaucratization	• Clear discontent • Formalized roles and organizational structures • Access to political elites • Sustainable effort • Coalition-based strategies
Decline	• Repression, co-option, success, failure, establishment within the mainstream
(Blumer, 1969; Christiansen, 2009; Della Porta & Diani, 2006; Hopper, 1950; Macionis, 2001; Melluci, 1995; Miller, 1999)	

2010). On the opposite end of the spectrum from the slacktivists are the paradigm shifters who view social media as transformative and radically changing the world of politics (Dobusch & Schoeneborn, 2015; Gainous & Wagner, 2013; Gerbaudo, 2018; Harfoush, 2009; Kahn & Kellner, 2004; Lewis et al., 2014; Morozov, 2011; Obar & Wildman, 2015; Onuch, 2015b; Shirky, 2011; Tapscott, 2008; Tatarchevskiy, 2011). Allsop's (2016) third camp takes the middle ground, arguing that social media facilitates action by adding value to traditional political tactics and techniques but is not adequate to effect social change without also employing more traditional offline organizing activities (Gerbaudo, 2018; Onuch, 2015a, 2015b; Valenzuela, 2013).

Fulton's (2013) case study of the group OutServe exemplifies this middle-ground perspective, as she describes how a small group used Facebook to create an online "queer space" — a closed/protected environment for LGBT Servicemembers to communicate and collaborate while still engaging in traditional advocacy for inclusive service. She identified four key factors (safety, publicity, scale, and leadership) that were critical to the success of the LGBT military movement. This effort expands on that theoretic work to empirically examine the efforts of the LGBT military community activities online during each of the four phases of a social movement lifecycle.

RESEARCH APPROACH

This study applied a multiple-method single case study design. Data were analyzed using social network and content analysis techniques. The case study sought to:

- Develop the case history and provide a detailed understanding/chronology of major activities and milestones.
- Determine, through content analysis, what was happening in order to identify key themes and approaches to the use of social media.
- Identify, through social network analysis, the structure, growth, and interactions between the organizations engaged in advocacy.
- Produce a taxonomy of the LGBT military movement's organizational structure.
- Identify interactions between online activities and traditional advocacy through semi-structured interviews with key decision-makers.

The case study process was iterative with the case history development, interviews, and analysis of the content informing the need for additional data collection.

Case Study Design

Selection and Description of the Case

The LGBT military experience is an appropriate case study for identifying how marginalized communities organize online because it provides a contemporary example of a mature social movement in which a marginalized community has experienced each stage of development.

In assessing the appropriateness of the case, it is first necessary to demonstrate that the LGBT military community is an appropriate group to model marginalized community behavior. Wald's (2000) book chapter describing the context of gay politics examines this question and assesses that

> . . . attempts by gays to alter their status through political means gives us the opportunity to study how small, weak and despised groups can use political means to challenge larger and stronger political forces who enjoy the support of entrenched social values. (p. 6)

Mucciaroni (2011) expands on this assertion, arguing that "studies of LGBT politics address basic, longstanding issues in political science, including how democratic regimes cope with the challenges posed by social diversity and how minorities and excluded groups induce the majority to address their claims for recognition, freedom, and equality" (p. 18).

The LGBT military community is particularly useful as a case study of marginalized communities online because it has gone through the full life-cycle of a social movement (emergence, coalescence, bureaucratization, and decline) as described by Della Porta and Diani (2006), thereby bounding the case within the theoretical framework. LGBT military members began the process of *emergence* as they began to gather together in online communities in about 2009. The community *coalesced* as the movement gathered steam and grew into an organization needing centralized leadership and organizational structure. The movement *bureaucratized* as they grew and began working with professional staff, organized chapters and forums, and gained a public voice in the debates on changes to policy and law. Finally, they experienced *decline* as they achieved success and began the process of operating within a mainstream (i.e., legal to serve) environment.

These experiences were ripe for study, as they provided a rich context of data over an extended timeframe. The experiences of movement leaders in effecting social action online provide an in-depth examination of how social media platform usage contributed to the accomplishment of a social movement's objectives.

Figure 2. Research plan flowchart

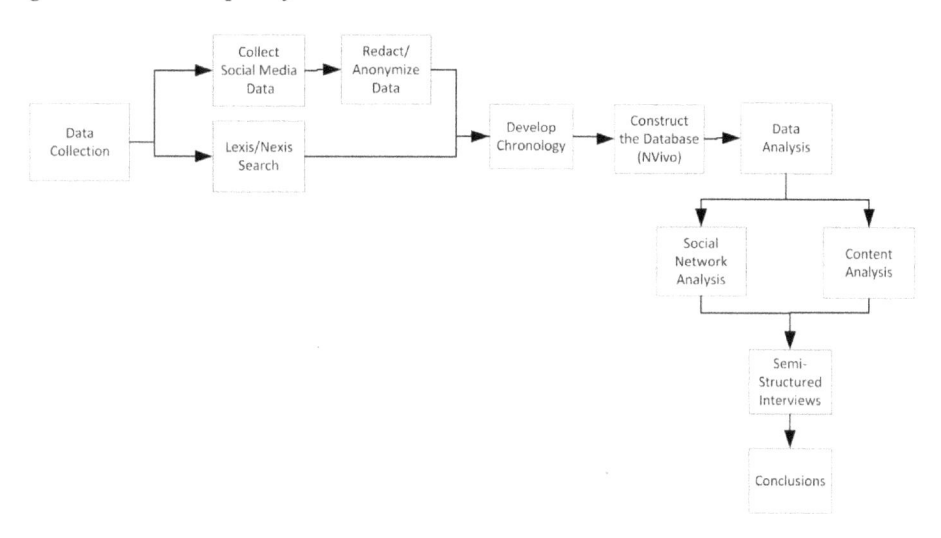

Research Plan

Analysis of this case required collection from multiple sources of data, including historical documents, news media coverage, interview transcripts, and social media online postings. Data collection was an iterative process as interviewees and content analysis identified additional source material to build out the case. Data collection involved online database searches for news coverage of LGBT military activities as well as the gathering of public and private social media posts from Facebook and Twitter. The flowchart in Figure 2 depicts this methodology.

DATA COLLECTION

Step 1: Database Searches

The researcher developed a detailed chronology of LGBT military community activities from the inception of online collaboration through the current efforts to achieve full inclusion and acceptance of LGBT Servicemembers. This phase focused on collecting and organizing publicly available documents including newspaper articles, press interviews, speeches, event transcripts, and social media posts on Facebook pages and Twitter feeds (Table 2).

Database records include news articles and transcripts, web postings, interview transcripts, historical records, and case notes pertaining to that particular event. The data were identified through:

- Lexis/Nexis® Academic and LexisNexis Academic (Broadcast) database searches provided access to full-text articles, transcripts, and legal filings from over 17,000 sources (LexisNexis, 2018). Database searches targeted names of the various organizations involved in advocacy work related to LGBT military service as outlined in Table 2.
- The EBSCO Information Services LGBT Life with full-text database provided access to full text for more than 140 LGBT journals, magazines, regional newspapers, monographs and books (EBSCO Information Services, 2018).

Step 2: Gathering Social Media Content

Facebook Group Data

Facebook does not provide a direct tool means to download data from groups, and researchers must rely on a third-party vendor to scrape the data into a format that is useful for analysis. Grytics (https://grytics.com/) provided such a tool that provided the researcher with an Excel compatible file from the "OutServe-SLDN Network" Secret Facebook Group (https://www.facebook.com/groups/OutServe/).

The researcher anonymized the data set to ensure that group participants could not be identified in accordance with the Institutional Review Board approval requirements. Using Microsoft Excel, the researcher deleted columns in the report that identified the individual poster prior to conversion of the data into a .pdf format. This procedure removed the bulk of the personal identifiers but did not anonymize data that in the post/comment itself. Those data were anonymized via redaction during the analytic process. The total data set includes 51,316 rows of data yielding a 583-page PDF document for coding. An excerpt of the data is depicted in Figure 3.

Facebook Page Data

Birdsong Analytics (www.birdsonganalytics.com) was used to develop a spreadsheet of posts and responses [N= 17,108] to the OutServe public Facebook page (https://www.facebook.com/OutServe.SLDN/). Facebook automatically redacted personal identification data. Birdsong Analytics also provided empirical data on user interactions with the page. An example of the data incorporated into the NVIVO database is depicted in Figure 4. It should be noted that after the generation of this data set, Birdsong Analytics ceased operations due to changes in the way Facebook allows third-party vendors to access data.

Table 2. Database search results

Source	Articles	Pages (.pdf)
LEXIS/NEXIS Academic		
OutServe	271	1,623
AMPA	160	710
AVER	90	327
DoD Pride	8	15
MPFC	26	62
SLDN	107	203
SPARTA	90	1,182
	848	*4,122*
LEXIS/NEXIS Academic (Broadcast)		
OutServe	7	59
AMPA	8	86
AVER	1	9
DoD Pride	9	13
MPFC	102	715
SLDN	—	—
	127	*882*
EBSCO LGBT Life w/ Full Text		
OutServe	20	47
AMPA	366	112
AVER	1	3
DoD Pride	2	2
MPFC	223	605
SLDN	291	220
OutServe	20	63
	923	*1,735*
Summary		
News articles	1,898	6,519
Facebook group posts	51,316	9,141
Facebook public page posts	17,108	592
Twitter posts	3,208	199
Total Data Set	**73,530**	**16,451**

Figure 3. Sample Facebook group data

Comment_date	Post_content	Comment_text	Comment_likes
2010-12-31 21:13:20	Kinda funny I post a picture to keep everyone in good spirits for the new year with all the things that have happened for us in 2010 and they get deleted. Regardless, Happy New Year people, thanks for this group, thanks for your commitment to the armed services and lets kick ass in 2011!	haha i dug the pic. happy new year	0
2010-12-31 21:20:20	Kinda funny I post a picture to keep everyone in good spirits for the new year with all the things that have happened for us in 2010 and they get deleted. Regardless, Happy New Year people, thanks for this group, thanks for your commitment to the armed services and lets kick ass in 2011!	lol	0
2010-12-31 21:24:06	Kinda funny I post a picture to keep everyone in good spirits for the new year with all the things that have happened for us in 2010 and they get deleted.. Regardless, Happy New Year people, thanks for this group, thanks for your commitment to the armed services and lets kick ass in 2011!	LOL....	0
2010-12-31 22:09:23	Kinda funny I post a picture to keep everyone in good spirits for the new year with all the things that have happened for us in 2010 and they get deleted. Regardless, Happy New Year people, thanks for this group, thanks for your commitment to the armed services and lets kick ass in 2011!	Ok, well since you don't approve of those then I don't approve of the 90 something friend requests and the many messages I get saying they liked the picture, I just figured with this invite(you invited me not the other way around) came a little sense of humor and a little bit of freedom but your the boss, I am not aware of the delete procedures so go get em tiger..	0

Twitter Data

The researcher employed Markitics Technologies' Twitter account analytics insights report and their Export Tweet tool (https://www.exporttweet.com/) to download Twitter feed data for the account @OutServeSLDN, yielding a spreadsheet containing tweets for the entire history of the feed [N=3208] along with a report the empirical data on user interactions. Sample data is depicted in Figure 5.

Historical Documents

In addition to the social media and news reporting, the researcher used primary source material including speeches, event transcripts, email records, and items publicly posted on the internet. These include records identifying organizational structure and leadership of LGBT military organizations, annual reports, fact sheets, copies of letters to policymakers (members of Congress and the executive branch), event planning documents and agenda, presentations, government reports, and legal filings.

Figure 4. Sample Facebook page data

29/11/2016	11/29/2016 Tuesday	17:50:11 Outserve - SLDN	No donation is too small or too large, every donation counts towards the fight for LGBT military equality. All donations will go to building our legal services and future programs. https://www.outserve-sldn.org/news/319457/GivingTuesday---The-Most-Wonderful-Day-of-the-Year.htm Today is #GivingTuesday! Our goal today is to reach 100 donors who will help us secure the necessary financial support to continue to advocate, protect and defend the LGBT military community. Click here to make a donation
29/11/2016	11/29/2016 Tuesday	16:30:49 Outserve - SLDN	https://www.outserve-sldn.org/news/319457/GivingTuesday---The-Most-Wonderful-Day-of-the-Year.htm
28/11/2016	11/28/2016 Monday	15:15:10 Outserve - SLDN	Ducking work for some Cyber Monday shopping? Support OutServe-SLDN while you get your shop on via Amazon Smile: http://smile.amazon.com/ch/52-1845000 OutServe-SLDN wishes you and your family a very Happy Thanksgiving.
24/11/2016	11/24/2016 Thursday	15:13:56 Outserve - SLDN	https://www.outserve-sldn.org/news/319097/Thankful.htm

Figure 5. Sample Twitter feed data

Tweet Id	Is Retweet	Is Reply	Tweet Time	Tweet Day	Tweet Mo	Tweet Text	Tweet Retweet Count	Tweet Favorite Count
1.02E+18	Yes	No	7/18/2018 20:26	Wednesda	July	"The order comes in our case with @OutServeSLDN, representing @HRC, @LGBTMilPartners, @GenderJusticeWA & 9 individuals. Read it here: https://t.co/lebyYxPCIa https://t.co/APPkmLk2lA"	6	25
1.02E+18	No	No	7/18/2018 18:45	Wednesda	July	"BREAKING: Today, in our case with @LambdaLegal, the U.S. Court of Appeals for the Ninth Circuit denied yet another attempt by the Trump Administration to implement its discriminatory plan to ban transgender people from serving openly in the U.S. Armed Services. #TransMilitary"	14	36
1.02E+18	Yes	No	7/18/2018 18:43	Wednesda	July	"BREAKING: Another court has blocked implementation of the attempted Trump-Pence #transgender military ban. @HRC is proud to be an organizational plaintiff, along with @LGBTMilPartners and @GenderJusticeWA, in the case brought by @LambdaLegal/@OutServeSLDN. https://t.co/TGsvDP5KXa"	307	822

Step 3: Interviews with Key Leaders and Activists

Interviews are particularly crucial in analysis of LGBT military behavior online. Much of the empirical data such as strategy and planning sessions for lobbying Congress and DoD are confidential to the participants and inaccessible to the researcher. Talking with the people involved in the process, those who were in the room when decisions were made, is the only way to properly assess the case. Interviews with key leaders also provides an evaluative aspect to the analysis. The perspectives provide a unique voice about the successes and failures of the various techniques used in achieving the movement's policy objectives. The researcher conducted a series of responsive semi-structured interviews with LGBT military leaders, social media moderators, and organization members to identify perspectives about core activities during the seminal events across the life cycle of the movement, especially with respect to the relationship between social media, traditional advocacy campaigns, and the use of social media.

Interviewees were selected using a purposeful sampling approach, with carefully selected key leaders in LGBT military advocacy, to gain a broad cross-section of the movement. Interviewees were identified from among the organizational founders, current and former board members, and prominent activists. Interviewees were asked to offer further recommendations of colleagues who ought to be interviewed to fill out the details of the case (snowball sampling). This phase focused on key stakeholders who were involved in the public advocacy campaigns and included professional staff, major public "faces" of the movement, and other key personnel as identified during phase one. Each interviewee signed an informed consent form agreeing to participate and acknowledging that their comments were for attribution.

Table 3. Interview protocol

Protocol/Questions	Alignment to Research sub-questions
Introduce the purpose of the study/research question	
Introduce protocol/verbally confirm informed consent	
What was your role? How did you get involved? When?	2
Let's talk about Facebook groups. How were they organized? Please describe the organizational structure of the group(s) you were involved with	1,2
Sue Fulton identified four core factors: (Safety, Publicity, Scale, Leadership). - How important were each of these? - Did this change as the groups got larger? - What additional factors would you identify?	1,2,3
Talk to me about the online leaders. - How were they identified? What was their role?	2
For each core event in which the interviewee participated: - What happened? Please describe the event. - What was happening offline? (Who, what, where, how) - What was happening online? (Who, what, where, how)? - How were the online/offline efforts coordinated/ synchronized? Probes: Was this effective? What went right? What would you do differently?	1,2,3
I'm looking to talk to the principal actors. Who else do you think I should interview?	2
Is there anything you would like to add?	1,2,3
Research Sub-questions: 1) How did the online LGBT military community develop/organize? 2) How were leaders of online groups identified and what was their role? 3) How did online behavior affect offline behavior/advocacy?	

The responsive semi-structured interviewing process used the protocol described in Table 3, which provided the researcher with flexibility for adjusting and changing the interview questions during the interview to delve into a particular topic raised during the conversation (Rubin & Rubin, 2011). Interviews were conducted in-person and via online video calls and recorded for transcription. For follow-up questions, interviewees were asked to expand on their responses or provide additional material via email or Facebook Messenger. Interviewees were each provided with a copy of the transcript and offered the opportunity to provide additional material or clarify their responses to the interview questions for member checking.

Step 4: Database Design

Data were converted to PDF Files [$N=31$] using Adobe Acrobat and imported into a NVIVO Version 12.2.0 Plus Edition (QSR International, 2018) database. Files

Figure 6. NVIVO database structure

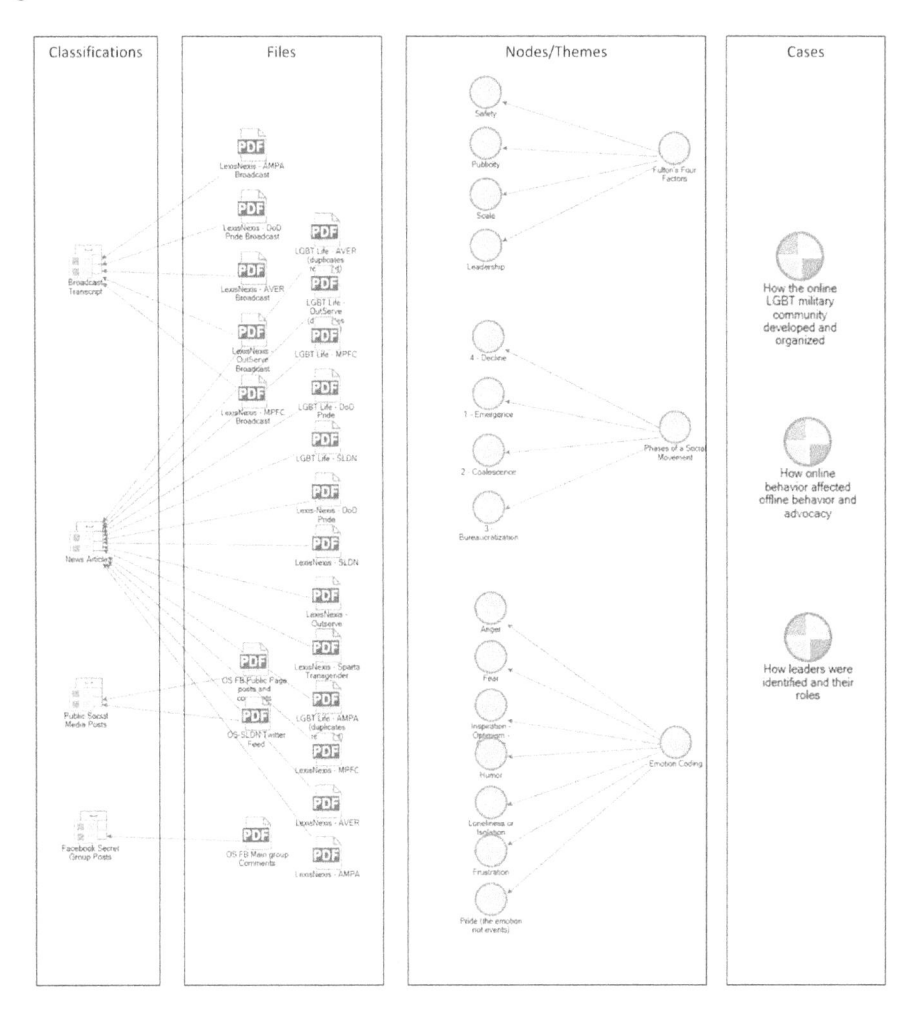

were organized within the database using one of the following file classifications: Broadcast Transcript, Facebook Secret Group Posts, Interview, News Article, or Public Social Media Post. Figure 6 depicts this database structure.

ANALYSIS

Analysis focused on identifying the structure and relationships between the LGBT community members using content analysis and social network analysis to describe online and offline activity.

Figure 7. Codebook

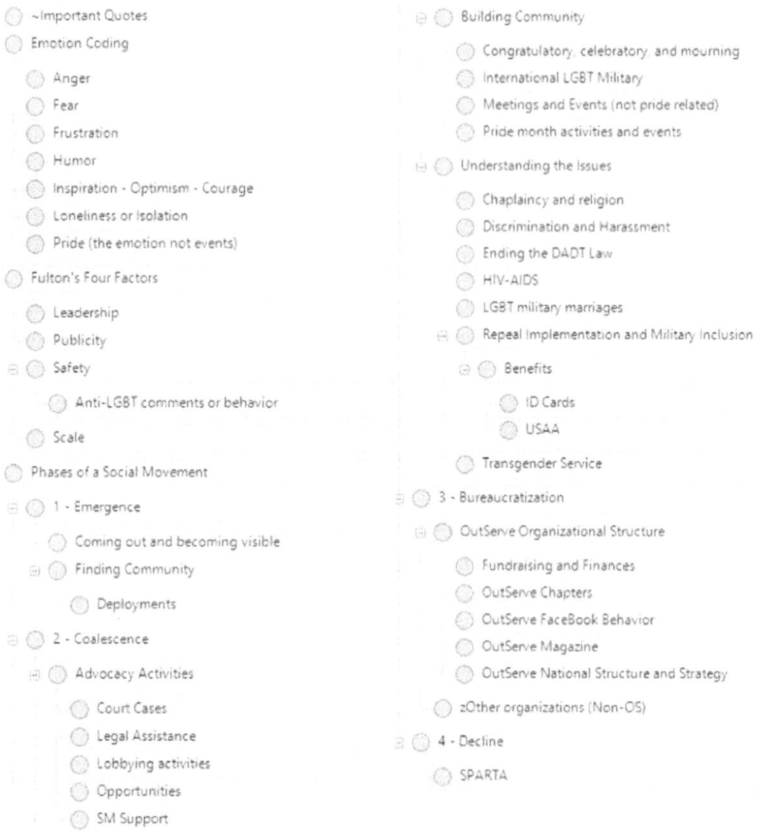

- ~Important Quotes
- Emotion Coding
  - Anger
  - Fear
  - Frustration
  - Humor
  - Inspiration - Optimism - Courage
  - Loneliness or Isolation
  - Pride (the emotion not events)
- Fulton's Four Factors
  - Leadership
  - Publicity
  - Safety
    - Anti-LGBT comments or behavior
  - Scale
- Phases of a Social Movement
  - 1 - Emergence
    - Coming out and becoming visible
    - Finding Community
      - Deployments
  - 2 - Coalescence
    - Advocacy Activities
      - Court Cases
      - Legal Assistance
      - Lobbying activities
      - Opportunities
      - SM Support
- Building Community
  - Congratulatory, celebratory, and mourning
  - International LGBT Military
  - Meetings and Events (not pride related)
  - Pride month activities and events
- Understanding the Issues
  - Chaplaincy and religion
  - Discrimination and Harassment
  - Ending the DADT Law
  - HIV-AIDS
  - LGBT military marriages
- Repeal Implementation and Military Inclusion
  - Benefits
    - ID Cards
    - USAA
  - Transgender Service
- 3 - Bureaucratization
  - OutServe Organizational Structure
    - Fundraising and Finances
    - OutServe Chapters
    - OutServe FaceBook Behavior
    - OutServe Magazine
    - OutServe National Structure and Strategy
  - zOther organizations (Non-OS)
- 4 - Decline
  - SPARTA

Content Analysis

Data were coded within NVIVO in order to identify themes from the data. A codebook was developed based on the theoretical framework for this study, e.g., Fulton's four factors and the four phases of a social movement (Della Porta & Diani, 2006; Fulton, 2013), and created as nodes within NVIVO. These codes focused on four phases (emergence, coalescence, bureaucratization, and decline), four factors (safety, publicity, scale, and leadership), and participant emotions. Additional codes were identified and nodes added during the coding process as issues and recurring themes became apparent. Emotion coding captured the state of mind of individuals participating in conversations and the tone of particular news articles or quotes contained therein.

Coding

A multi-stage process was used to code the data. Because of the large size of the data set (16,451 pages saved as PDF files), the researcher depended heavily on the spread coding capability within NVIVO. An initial series of keywords were used to identify particular terms across the files in the database, and text queries were used to generate report delineating where the words appeared across the database. These reports were then individually coded to the appropriate node. Keywords included: pride, coming out, marriage, benefits, deployment, magazine, ID Cards, DEERS (Defense Enrollment Eligibility Reporting System — the DoD personnel database), membership, trans or transgender, Board of Directors, SPARTA, anyone, HIV or AIDS or Truvada or Prep, discharge, leadership, and USAA. In most cases, the text search parameter included stemmed words and synonyms with the results spread to a broad context to include the entire paragraph in the search results.

Descriptive coding was used to summarize basic topics within the data (e.g.' safety, publicity, scale, leadership); process coding focused on the actions of the participants (e.g., building personal networks, sharing information, calls to action); and emotion coding was used to describe states of mind (e.g.' anger, fear, loneliness) (Miles, Huberman, & Saldaña, 2013). NVIVO word mapping, spread coding, and query tools were employed extensively to assist in the coding process.

Second cycle coding focused on identifying the core themes in order to condense the data into a smaller number of analytic units and to develop a cognitive data map (Miles et al., 2013). NVIVO nodes (codes) were sorted into a logical structure that organizes data, creates conceptual clarity, provides prompts for rich coding, and helps identify patterns using the catalog tree function within the database (Bazeley & Jackson, 2013).

The analysis looked across the data sets during second cycle coding using NVIVO analytic tools including cross-tabulation and cluster analysis of themes/codes by source in order for the researcher to easily identify cross-cutting issues among the sources. Coding was an iterative process and the catalog tree evolved as additional themes were identified during first and second cycle coding.

In total, the researcher coded 24,406 items to particular nodes in the database with many of the items coded relating to more than one node. For example, a quote from a person angry about the lack of benefits for a spouse was coded at both the 'Anger' and the 'Benefits' nodes. In total, the researcher coded 57,012 items across the files in the NVIVO database. Deliberate and detailed analytic memoranda were compiled throughout the coding process to track completed actions and maintain consistency.

Themes

Nodes were then sorted into themes. Themes identified include:

- The most prevalent theme reflects coalescence, the second phase of a social movement, with three major subcomponents: understanding the issues, building community, and advocacy activities.
- Bureaucratization represented the second most prevalent theme, with coding that reflects internal organizational factors such as chapter structure, the national organization, roles and missions, fundraising, and group norms.
- Fulton's (2013) four factors represented the third major theme. Leadership figured most prominently alongside safety and publicity. Fulton's fourth factor, scale, was not a major topic of conversation within the data coded.
- Emotion coding reflects the researcher's perception of the individual authors' state of mind identified fear, anger, and loneliness as prominent factors.
- There was also a great deal of material coded relative to the decline of the organization and the challenges presented as the repeal of the DADT policy was implemented while the transgender ban remained in effect.

A summary of coding and themes is depicted below in Table 4.

Descriptive Analysis

After completion of the coding and identifying themes, the researcher conducted a deep dive into each of the themes to develop insights into specific language used by participants in the social media groups and the media reporting. An example of this can be found in the first finding (of seventeen) in the study:

Finding 1.1: Loneliness and isolation. *Many servicemembers experienced a sense of isolation. Prior to joining a social media secret group, they were disconnected from the other LGBT Servicemembers and had no way to find community. Social media provided a means to overcome this loneliness and begin to build personal networks.*

DADT was a very isolating experience for the LGBT personnel who served in the military. Empirically, this can be shown within the emotion coding, where 77 instances were identified where a Servicemember expressed concern about being isolated and alone. The word cloud generated by NVIVO (Figure 8) depicts the 1000 most frequent words to appear within this code and shows the type of language used by members experiencing these emotions.

Almost all of these coded references appeared in the OutServe secret group [$N=68$] but references also appeared in comments to public social media posts, with interviews conducted by this researcher, and in a television interview with

Table 4. Coding Summary (By node and theme)

Name	Files	References Coded
Emotion Coding		
Anger	2	97
Fear	5	217
Frustration	3	52
Humor	1	72
Inspiration, optimism, or courage	5	56
Loneliness or isolation	3	74
Pride (the emotion not events)	5	60
Fulton's four factors		
Leadership	8	754
Publicity	13	238
Safety	5	113
Anti-LGBT comments or behavior	10	210
Scale	3	35
Phases of a social movement		
1 - Emergence	3	3
Coming out and becoming visible	16	501
Finding community	4	370
Deployments	3	664
2 - Coalescence		
Advocacy activities		
Court cases	19	5206
Legal assistance	9	117
Lobbying activities	14	295
Opportunities	2	21
SM support	7	44
Building community		
Congratulatory, celebratory, and mourning	16	1303
International LGBT military	5	42
Meetings and events (not pride related)	11	300
Pride month activities and events	14	981
Understanding the issues		
Benefits	10	958
ID Cards	5	90
USAA	2	122

continued on following page

Table 4. Continued

Name	Files	References Coded
Emotion Coding		
Chaplaincy and religion	4	232
Discrimination and harassment	20	3444
Ending the DADT law	12	415
HIV-AIDS	6	316
LGBT military marriages	9	1558
Repeal implementation and military inclusion	7	102
Transgender Service	17	2138
3 - Bureaucratization		
OutServe organizational structure		
Fundraising and finances	3	296
OutServe chapters	3	1341
OutServe Facebook behavior	1	148
OutServe magazine	6	571
OutServe national structure and strategy	7	377
Other organizations	8	44
4 - Decline	4	252
SPARTA	3	68

Figure 8. Loneliness and isolation word cloud

an unidentified Servicemember appearing on the Rachel Maddow show. He asked viewers to imagine:

. . . being told that they can't be seen with their spouse in public or if they are, they're constantly wondering, you know, how many — I'm constantly with this person, what are people going to start saying? I can't show any affection in the supermarket, not even at home, because who knows if somebody might — my next-door neighbor's military or knows someone who knows someone. So, you're just — it's a very — emotional strain to constantly live that life. So, again, I equate it to, if you would ask a heterosexual couple to completely hide every aspect of their relationship at work and in their personal life and then have them tell me if that works for them. And nobody would say it would work for them. (Anonymous Maddow Guest, 2010)

Social media posts ranged from the "is anyone one out there" type of post described extensively later in the section on finding community, to the anguished cry of a lonely Servicemember who posted to the OutServe secret group:

Why is it so difficult being a part of the LGBT community? It is so easy to feel alone and invisible online or even in public. . . . Why is it that when you could use the support, you are only left to fall into the sea of simulation and wander through the forest of illusion alone? . . . The worst thing about being in a new place is trying to find your place, while, if you actually care to be social, it sucks when you are trying to find it alone. Been deployed for just over two weeks and a part of OS for almost 2 weeks, and whilst I've got decent self-esteem and confidence, finding where I fit in and coming up empty takes a small chunk little by little. (Redacted, 2011)

These feelings of isolation were particularly identifiable within the transgender military community after the repeal of DADT. These members were still excluded from open service while their LGB brethren were largely able to be more open. Sheri Swokowski (2018) described the impact of this isolation and how she "suppressed my individual feelings, sacrificed my authenticity for the three and a half decades that I was in the military in order to be the best soldier, commander, director that I could be." These feelings were also expressed by the other interviews that this researcher conducted with transgender military activists. They each also expressed firm beliefs that social media provides a critical tool to bring their community together, especially for isolated individuals outside large military enclaves like the National Capital Region, Norfolk, Virginia, or San Diego, California (Beck, 2018; Dremann, 2018; Simpson, 2018).

OutServe executive director and former Guam Chapter Leader Andy Blevins described the environment that many Servicemembers faced and the value that Facebook secret groups provided to isolated troops:

When we first founded OutServe, it was really that sense of security and community that we couldn't get anywhere else. We couldn't talk to our family about it, because we were afraid they were going to get questioned on our next security clearance application. We couldn't talk to people in our unit about it, because they were mandated to tell on us if we did. We couldn't go to any service providers, because . . . I did go to a service provider. They contacted my command. We all knew that that was going to happen out there, so we felt alone. (Blevins, 2018)

Social Network Analysis

Social Network Analysis focused on identifying and mapping organizational structure of the LGBT military community, both online and offline. This effort focuses on identifying relationships between the organizations and how they interacted. This analysis provided crucial insights as to the scale aspect in the theoretical framework. Social network analysis is based on the premise that an organization (or movement) is not a singular entity, but rather is a web of interconnected organisms (Scott & Carrington, 2011). The approach provides insight into how the members of a widely dispersed movement like the LGBT military organized itself to accomplish their advocacy objectives. Scott and Carrington (2011) describe a four-step process for discovery and mapping of a social network from internet data:

1. Node discovery: identifying the key actors (groups).
2. Co-reference and alias resolution: resolving ambiguities.
3. Tie discovery: Determining connections between nodes.
4. Relationship and role identification.

NVIVO Plus 12.0 was employed to map out the organizational structure of the movement. Each Facebook group was created as a case within the NVIVO database and then hierarchically aligned within the case structure. A project map was then generated to depict the overall online structure of the movement. Organizationally, these groups established presence both in public and private online spaces. Subgroups (chapters and forums) largely operated in the closed/secret Facebook presence with the overarching organizations also establishing a public presence on Facebook and Twitter as well as organizational websites.

Social network analysis identified both the public structure (Facebook Pages and Twitter Feeds), as well as the private/closed or secret groups that have been publicly

Using Social Media to Organize a Marginalized Community

acknowledged (i.e., the main groups and subordinate chapters) and the traditional advocacy organizations/people involved in the effort to achieve LGBT military inclusion. This organizational structure was informed by the results of phase one and iteratively confirmed and expanded during the interviews. With respect to the online Facebook Groups, the social network analysis only operated to the organizational level and did not seek to identify any particular individuals involved beyond the public spokespeople. Secret groups that have not been publicly acknowledged are excluded from the analysis. The resulting analytic product includes a map of the organizational structure online and the relationships to online activities as well as a narrative description of the coalition(s) that were involved throughout the lifecycle of the LGBT military advocacy effort.

The social network analysis diagram (Figure 9) depicts the organizational structure of the LGBT military movement within the Facebook environment. The clusters represent each of the major groups and their subordinate groups.

Figure 9: Social network analysis

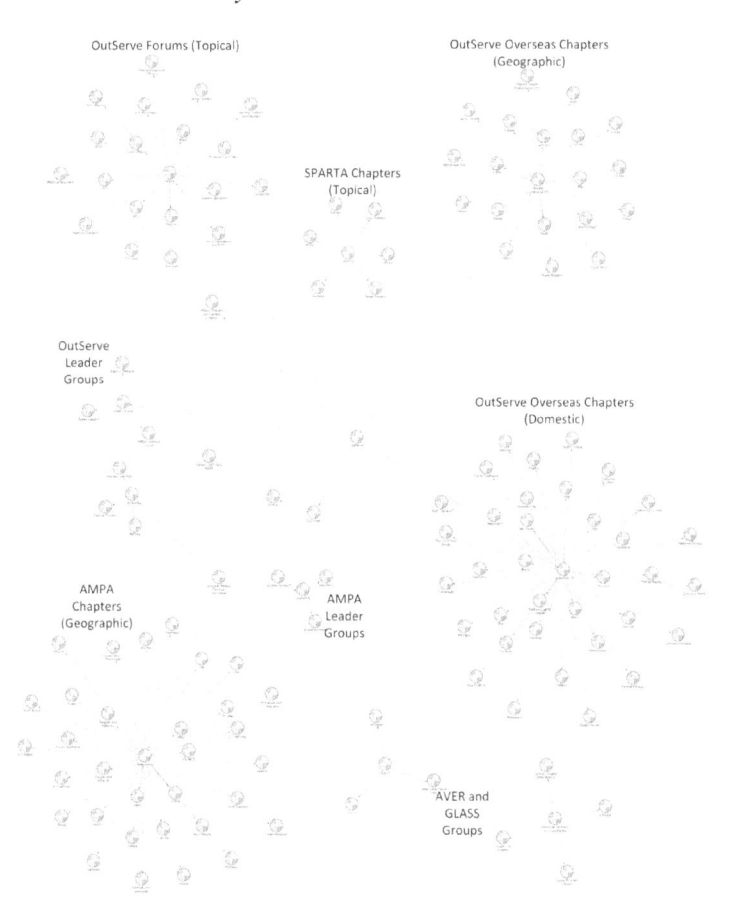

Among the groups involved in the social movement, OutServe developed the most complex online presence. The social network analysis diagram below depicts the multiple organizational levels that include:

- Geographic based chapters formed both within and outside the continental United States,
- Forums represented the various interests and equities within the community. Structurally, these groups exist online as Facebook Secret Groups with varying levels of online public activities and real-world participation depending on time, circumstances, and the ability to identify effective leaders.
- Leadership coordinating groups provided a space distinct from the rank and file membership for the organizational leaders to discuss strategies and to collaborate on programs.

AMPA also has a well-developed organizational structure with a similar geographic, topical, and leadership structure online. Ashley Broadway-Mack, the president of AMPA, described the organizational construct:

Veterans, Veterans' spouses, that's our main group. Then we're broken down into 40 plus networks. Those networks can be location based, so we have one for the DMV. You know obviously, Virginia, Maryland, and DC. We have different regions. The smaller areas, like we have combined Georgia and Alabama together because of kind of how the bases are. Then we have OCONUS locations that can be what we call an AMPA Italy or AMPA Germany, AMPA Japan, and Korea and what not. Then we also have an additional private network for those members, because we are a family organization, for those members who have children. (Broadway-Mack, 2018)

Blake Dremann (2018) attributes the importance of segmentation to the difficulty in managing a group larger than about 200 members. He says that his group (SPARTA) is currently too large and that it is very difficult to manage the conversations and keep conflict from getting out of hand. They've organized into constituent groups and have some local chapters in large military enclaves, but have not yet established a large subordinate structure to their main Facebook group.

Leader groups were organized by OutServe to coordinate activities once the group scaled in size and chapters/forums began to proliferate. These included Facebook groups for the board of directors to collaborate, for leaders of each chapter, and for a military advisory council composed of senior leaders and charged with providing advice to the board.

Summary of Findings

The findings are organized based on the theoretical framework's construct of Blumer's four stages of a social movement: emergence, coalescence, bureaucratization, and decline (Della Porta & Diani, 2006). Some of these findings can be linked to more than one of the three research sub-questions:

- How did the online LGBT military community develop/organize? [RQ1]
- How were leaders of online groups identified and what was their role? [RQ2]
- How did online behavior affect offline behavior/advocacy? [RQ3]

Table 5 summarizes the findings outlined in the chapter above and aligns them to these three research questions:

Bias and Validity

Researcher Bias

Maxwell's chapter on validity in his book "Qualitative Research Design: An Iterative Approach" (2013) defines researcher bias as a major concern in qualitative research. "Selection of data that fit the researcher's existing theory, goals, or preconceptions, and the selection of data that 'stand out' to the researcher" (p. 124) are the core concerns and are impossible to eliminate. He proposes instead that these biases need to be acknowledged and examined during analysis. In the case of this research effort, the researcher served on active duty as a closeted LGBT Army officer, was an early OutServe member, donated to organizations seeking repeal of the ban on LGBT Service, and maintains personal connections with many of the individuals involved in the social movement.

Reactivity

Maxwell (2013) further warns that the influence of the researcher can affect outcomes. The interviewer always influences the responses of the individual being interviewed. In the case of LGBT military organizations, the interviewees selected are likely to tend towards overstating their contributions to the social movement's success as they view the movement through the lens of their own participation. The responsive semi-structured interview process used in this study is particularly susceptible to reactivity as it offers the researcher the opportunity to ask leading questions and influence the answers of the participants. Following the interview protocol carefully and member checking were essential to reducing this potential threat.

Table 5: Summary of findings

1	Finding	RQ
	**1. Emergence**	
11	*Loneliness and isolation:* Many Servicemembers experienced a sense of isolation. They were disconnected from the other LGBT Servicemembers and had no way to find community. Social media provided a means to overcome this loneliness and begin to build personal networks.	1, 3
12	*Safety and fear:* The idea of fear and the possibility that a LGBT Servicemember's sexual orientation or gender identity might be revealed was a prevalent theme on social media. Safety was viewed as a necessary element for organizing – even after repeal. Vetting of members in online groups was viewed as a challenge – particularly as a group scaled in size.	1, 3
.3	*Coming out and becoming visible:* Social media provided a venue for closeted LGBT Servicemembers to discuss how to come out and acknowledge their sexual orientation/gender identity to family, friends, coworkers, and bosses.	1, 3
14	*Finding community:* Members viewed social media as a useful mechanism to link individual members of a marginalized community together – but leaders viewed these conversations as distracting from other efforts. Moderation and establishing workarounds and formation of local sub-communities were identified as effective, though not perfect, options.	1, 2, 3
	2. Coalescence	
21	*Sharing stories:* Participants frequently shared stories about major accomplishments, celebrations, and life events. These posts generated numerous comments in which the participants offered congratulations, shared similar experiences, and offered encouragement/suggestions. Similarly, for tragic events, participants posted their memories about those in the community affected, offered condolences, and shared in grief.	1, 3
22	*Real-world events:* Moving outside social media and meeting face-to-face was a major recurring topic of discussion, with members posting about event opportunities, sharing successes, and discussing the various norms pertaining to them.	1, 3
23	*Publicity:* Organizational leaders focused more on public messaging, both through public social media and traditional media, in order to spread messaging about organization activities. Leaders viewed this approach as more effective in advocacy than they did in speaking to private/secret group members because the public approaches allowed for broader reach.	1, 2, 3
24	*Recruitin voices*: Organizational leaders used social media to identify individuals willing to publicly advocate for the LGBT community inside the Pentagon, on Capitol Hill, in the courts, and in the media.	2, 3
25	*Understanding issues:* Social media participants spent a great deal of time discussing, in detail, the issues surrounding LGBT military service, both to gain a better understanding of the state of bureaucratic play in Washington DC and the courts, and to argue for/against particular courses of action.	3
26	*Advocacy:* Organizations depended primarily on traditional lobbying techniques to influence policies with respect to LGBT military inclusion. These included lobbying members of congress and the executive branch, impact litigation, collaboration with other interest groups, and grass-roots activities such as letter writing and petitions. Public social media was largely viewed by organization leaders as useful and secret groups often shared these public postings, but neither was seen as a primary tool for seeking changes to policy or law.	2, 3

continued on following page

Table 4. Continued

1	Finding	RQ
\multicolumn{3}{c}{**1. Emergence**}
\multicolumn{3}{l}{3. Bureaucratization}
31	*Online organizational structure:* Within the LGBT military community, scale is can be viewed as both a function of size and one of dispersion. Chapters, forums, and other subgroups were a defining characteristic of the major LGBT military organizations online activity. This bureaucratic organization was viewed by leaders as critical to the organization's ability to grow and operate.	11
32	*Leader identification:* Finding good leaders is viewed as a key concern for organizational success – especially at the local level. Senior leadership in the organizations view identifying, training, and supporting these key team members as essential elements for organizational success. Humility, an understanding and commitment to the organization's mission, and the ability to commit enough time to be effective were identified as the most important criteria for selecting effective leaders. Anger and a sense of duty were commonly cited by leaders as reasons why they stepped up.	22
33	*Formal leader roles:* Formal leadership roles included chapter leaders, who served at the grass-roots level, a diverse board of directors who provided organizational oversight at the national level and raised funds, and professional staff.	22
34	*Informal leader roles:* Leadership is more than just positional, and the LGBT military groups depend on members to step up and take on leadership roles outside the formal structure. Assuming these informal roles are individuals who act as public voices to the media and to policymakers, people who serve as mentors for both leaders and individual members, and people who spend their energy organizing events.	2
35	*Leadership and social media:* . Organization leaders had a mixed perspective with respect to the role of social media in actually managing their organization. Some viewed is as an essential tool, while others were more skeptical and tried to identify other ways to collaborate with colleagues. The social media environment provides a venue for significant 'armchair quarterbacking' and criticism from the rank and file. Leaders found this dialogue frustrating, but ultimately healthy.	1, 2, 3
\multicolumn{3}{l}{4. Decline}
41	*Splinter groups:* As the LGB community began to assimilate and live openly within the broader military community, the transgender community was left behind and felt unserved by the existing organizational structure (OutServe/SLDN). Infighting and a lack of resources drove the transgender members away from the group and led to the formation of a new organization and social media secret group.	1,2,3
42	*Social meia decline and resurgence:* Postings in the OutServe secret social media group saw a dramatic decline following the implementation of DADT repeal and the availability of benefits for spouses following the Supreme Court decision on marriage equality. Leaders attribute this both to success (people moving on) and to a lack of emphasis on providing engaging content.	1,2,3

Descriptive Validity

Descriptive validity relates to the factual accuracy of the case description (Lincoln, 2001). The primary challenge in this particular study is the lack of access to the full scope of the data online. Much of the information posted to secret Facebook groups is inaccessible to this researcher due to privacy concerns. The data contained within many social media platforms are proprietary to both the owners of the social media platforms and to group members. While access to these data through automated social network analysis tools could provide an important avenue for data triangulation and serve as a rich environment for research and analysis, these data are unavailable. The analysis is, therefore, largely dependent on public speech acts and redacted postings in private/secret web forums.

Social media is only one tool available to the social movement. Social movements do not exist in an online vacuum, and it may be difficult to ascertain causality between online and "real-world" actions. There are a large number of online groups. The researcher only has access to a small set of these groups. The results of the analysis will, therefore, be limited to only those available data and may not reflect the full scope of the movement.

Furthermore, much of the work in advocacy campaigns involves legal proceedings and confidential communications between advocates for LGBT inclusion and Members of Congress, Defense Department leadership, the White House, and between coalition members on strategy. Many of these communications are closely and privately held and are not available to the researcher. Interviews sought to draw out much of these data but may not reflect the full range of communicative activity during the advocacy effort.

Validity Strategies/Techniques

The abovementioned threats to validity require the author to extensively and explicitly address the topic and describe the multiple validity strategies/techniques the researcher employed throughout data collection and analysis to ensure the results are defensible. Techniques included the use of a thick-rich description, multiple forms of triangulation, member checking, peer debriefing, and the preparation of an audit trail through maintenance of detailed analytic memos.

Thick-rich description. (Onwuegbuzie & Leech, 2007) describe this technique as "an important way of providing credibility of findings by collecting rich and thick data, which correspond to data that are detailed and complete enough to maximize the ability to find meaning" (p. 244). In order to achieve this, the researcher used historical data, social media transcripts, and interview results in the NVIVO database.

Using Social Media to Organize a Marginalized Community

These data were then coded the data to identify themes and organized to provide an in-depth description of the social movement's online and offline activities.

Triangulation of Data Sources. "Triangulation involves the use of multiple and different methods, investigators, sources, and theories to obtain corroborating evidence" (Onwuegbuzie & Leech, 2007). Within this study, interviewees were recruited via purposeful sampling that ensures inclusion from the breadth of the movement's activists. The interview and social media transcripts are cross-referenced to historical data and compared to the comments from individual actors and the public record. NVIVO analytic tools allow the cross-tabulation of codes and themes across the data set to triangulate and verify that themes are indeed cross-cutting. Social network analysis provides another avenue for data triangulation by describing in detail the key online nodes and their interrelationships (Marin & Wellman, 2011).

Member checking and peer debriefing. These approaches allow the voice of the study group to play a major role in the analytic process, and peer debriefing brings in the perspectives of other scholars with expertise in the subject matter and methodology (Onwuegbuzie & Leech, 2007). Interviewees were provided a copy of the transcription in order to review and validate their inputs and the semi-structured interviews. Interviews were conducted after analysis of the social media content, allowing the researcher to gain member insights into initial analysis and helping to determine the findings. Other scholars and researchers with interest in the LGBT military movement were also asked to review and provide feedback on the results.

Audit trail. "Leaving an audit trail involves the researcher maintaining extensive documentation of records and data stemming from the study" (Onwuegbuzie & Leech, 2007). The researcher compiled a detailed a detailed chronology of communicative events. Analytic memos were prepared within NVIVO and Evernote to document the data collection and analysis process. Copies of the database including all transcripts and anonymized social media content are available to document the findings contained within this study.

IMPLICATIONS AND RECOMMENDATIONS

These findings inform social movement theory and fill a gap in understanding about how members of a marginalized community leverage social media technology to better organize into a social movement capable of advocating for a change to their status in society. These conclusions must be taken in the context of the environment in which the research occurred. This case study focused on the activities of military personnel who identify as LGBT and who participated in social media groups during the period leading up to the repeal of bans to LGBT military service. The experiences of this particular community may not be directly comparable to the experiences of other marginalized groups. Study findings have particular implications for practice and research, as well as related leadership, learning and service.

Implications for Leadership

Organizations Need to Identify Formal And Informal Leaders

This study identified the importance of identifying and fostering individuals to operate in both formal and informal leadership roles. Formal roles include chapter leaders, who served at the grass-roots level, a diverse board of directors who provided organizational oversight at the national level and raised funds, and professional staff. Informal roles include individuals who act as public voices to the media and to policymakers, people who serve as mentors for both leaders and individual members, and people who spend their energy organizing events. Within the social media context, the moderators and group administrators (primarily the volunteer chapter leaders) served as key gatekeepers, helping new members find the group, welcoming new members, helping them become comfortable within the group, and assisting them to connect with other people in their local area or to people within their particular subgroup through a network of chapters and forums. Future research would be valuable to examine in greater detail each of these roles and the characteristics of the successful leadership practitioners in the social media context.

Social media adds value to traditional organizing and advocacy, but is not adequate to effect social change without traditional real-world activities.

Traditional advocacy efforts such as lobbying and strategic litigation remained important tools and require expertise beyond that which can be found within the social media groups. This affirms the results of earlier research (Earl & Garrett, 2016; Gerbaudo, 2018; Obar et al., 2012; Puranam, Alexy, & Reitzig, 2014) arguing that while social media provide very different opportunities for organizations to reach supporters and spread their message, they do so within the broader context of more traditional approaches. The research demonstrates through content analysis and interviews with key players the added value that social media provides for the traditional organizing approaches.

Implications for Learning

Learning about Issues Related To The Movement

Within the context of this research, content analysis identified that social media participants spent a great deal of time discussing, in detail, the issues surrounding LGBT military service, both to gain a better understanding of the state of bureaucratic play in Washington, DC and the courts, and to argue for/against particular courses of action. Social media provided a venue for members to discuss the implications of the news stories, personal experiences, and activities occurring in the real-world. The social media environment allowed members to learn from each other the state of the bureaucratic play related to repeal of DADT as well as the day to day challenges of LGBT military service. This research suggests an opportunity for organization leaders to actively engage with members on events and issues relevant to their social movement. Social media presents an opportunity for education and professional development within the context of discussing the social movement.

Implications for Practice

Online and real-world efforts to organize and advocate for the LGBT military community are intertwined and interdependent Those who believe that social media is paradigm shifting argue that the tools are transformative and radically change the world of politics, while skeptics argue that the commitment of online activists is soft and seldom leads to major social change (Allsop, 2016). This analysis demonstrates a more nuanced perspective and builds on the work of those arguing that these tools are important but not adequate to effect social change by themselves. Leaders of other marginalized communities can learn from the experiences of the LGBT military community with respect to bringing people together in a common forum and to learn about issues affecting the community to which they belong. This research demonstrates the importance of traditional organizing and advocacy techniques as well as the benefits of face-to-face interaction at the grass-roots level.

FUTURE RESEARCH DIRECTIONS

Content Analysis of Other Social Movements Could Be Used To Validate Findings

This study builds upon the study of social movements by applying detailed content analysis of social media data in a manner that might be applied by other researchers in examining social movements operating in emerging social media environments like Instagram or online collaborative gaming. Application of these qualitative analysis methods to identify codes and themes from the transcripts of social media conversations occurring over the lifecycle of an organization provides a wealth of rich, thick data from which to draw out a series of key factors for success.

Quantitative Analysis

Metadata contained within social media platforms includes a vast array of quantitative data relative to the groups and pages that was not accessible to this researcher. Access to these data through automated social network analysis tools, combined with additional content analysis within this data set could provide further insights into the findings of this study. Companies are increasingly limiting the availability of such data, both in response to user demands for privacy and because the data is a valuable proprietary asset. Collaboration with these companies to gain access to the data might be required by future researchers.

Quantitative data gained through the surveying of leaders and/or members of the social media groups could provide additional information into their perspectives on the role of social media in their individual activism that might add significant insight and further detail into the findings of this study.

These data are ripe for future analysis.

The data set contains a great deal of information about a social movement across time. Future research using this data set might focus on comparing it to other models or frameworks, the application of machine learning to dig deeper into the coding and theme identification, and the extension of the social network analysis to a deeper level focusing on individual interactions between participants.

Social Media Is A Rapidly Evolving Technology

While Facebook and Twitter remain the most prevalent sites in use today, other platforms, like Instagram, are gaining ground, and new generations of users are making different choices as to their preferred site. Future research needs to follow this pattern and look to where the users are going to be operating in the future.

CONCLUSION

The purpose of this research was to identify how a social movement uses social media tools such as Facebook secret groups and pages to connect and organize members of marginalized groups. This research begins to fill a gap in the scholarly record in understanding how the members of a marginalized community leverage social media technology to better organize into a social movement capable of advocating for a change to their status in society. Concurrently, it seeks also to identify practices that organizations might employ as they adopt social media tools to organize and seek social change that improves the lives of members of that marginalized community.

The seventeen findings begin to explain exactly how one social movement employed these tools in the context of traditional organizing and advocacy efforts to advocate for inclusion. The LGBT military community's effort demonstrates both the value and the challenges that this emergent technology provides across the lifecycle of a social movement. Social media provides a powerful tool set across the lifecycle of this social movement, and other marginalized groups might find a model to better organize and advocate to improve their own circumstances.

ACKNOWLEDGMENT

I want to thank the founders, board members and staff of OutServe/Servicemembers Legal Defense Network who made it possible for LGBT military personnel to serve openly and who continue to advocate for inclusion and fair treatment. This research would not have been possible without the many Servicemembers who contributed through participation in social media groups and agreed to share their experiences and insights. Dr. Eric Dimmitt, Ms. Bridget Wilson, and Dr. Preston Cosgrove also deserve special commendation and thanks for their guidance, and support.

This research received no specific grant from any funding agency in the public, commercial, or not-for-profit sectors.

REFERENCES

Allsop, B. (2016). Social media and activism: A literature review. *Social Psychology Review, 18*(2), 35–40.

Arredondo, P. (2008). Counseling individuals from marginalized and underserved groups. In *Readings in multicultural practice* (pp. 331–348). SAGE Publications Inc.

Bazeley, P., & Jackson, K. (Eds.). (2013). *Qualitative data analysis with NVIVO* (2nd ed.). Los Angeles, CA: SAGE Publications Ltd.

Blumer, H. (1969). Collective behavior. In A. M. Lee (Ed.), Principles of sociology (3rd ed.; pp. 65–121). New York, NY: Barnes & Noble Books.

Christiansen, J. (2009). Four stages of social movements. *EBSCO Research Starters*, 1–7.

Delany, C. (2016, January). *How to use the internet to win in 2016: A comprehensive guide for campaigns & advocates (version 4.1)*. Retrieved from Epolitics.com/Winning

Della Porta, D., & Diani, M. (2006). *Social movements: an introduction* (2nd ed.). Malden, MA: Blackwell Publishing.

Dobusch, L., & Schoeneborn, D. (2015). Fluidity, identity, and organizationality: The communicative constitution of Anonymous. *Journal of Management Studies*, *52*(8), 1005–1035. doi:10.1111/joms.12139

Earl, J., & Garrett, R. K. (2016). The new information frontier: Toward a more nuanced view of social movement communication. *Social Movement Studies*, 1–15.

EBSCO Information Services. (2018). *EBSCO LGBT life with full text*. Retrieved September 10, 2018, from https://www.ebsco.com/products/research-databases/lgbt-life-full-text

Fulton, B. S. (2013). Outserve: An underground network stands up. *Journal of Homosexuality*, *60*(2-3), 219–231. doi:10.1080/00918369.2013.744668 PMID:23414270

Gainous, J., & Wagner, K. M. (2013). *Tweeting to power: the social media revolution in American politics*. Oxford University Press. doi:10.1093/acprof:oso/9780199965076.001.0001

Garrett, R. K., Bimber, B., de Zuniga, H. G., Heinderyckx, F., Kelly, J., & Smith, M. (2012). New ICTs and the study of political communication. *International Journal of Communication*, *6*, 214–231.

Gerbaudo, P. (2018). *Tweets and the streets: Social media and contemporary activism*. Retrieved from http://tacticalmediafiles.net/mmbase/attachments/5000/Tweets__the_Streets_Introduction.pdf

Gladwell, M. (2010). Small change: Why the revolution will not be tweeted. *The New Yorker*, *4*(2010), 42–49.

Harfoush, R. (2009). *Yes we did! An inside look at how social media built the Obama brand*. New Riders.

Hopper, R. D. (1950). A frame of reference for the study of revolutionary movements. *Social Forces*, *28*(3), 270–279. doi:10.2307/2572010

QSR International. (2018). *NVIVO 12 Plus (Version 12.2.0.443 (64-bit))* [Windows 10 Home]. Burlington, MA: QSR International.

Kahn, R., & Kellner, D. (2004). New media and internet activism: From the 'Battle of Seattle' to blogging. *New Media & Society*, *6*(1), 87–95. doi:10.1177/1461444804039908

Kaplan, A. M., & Haenlein, M. (2010). Users of the world, unite! The challenges and opportunities of social media. *Business Horizons*, *53*(1), 59–68. doi:10.1016/j.bushor.2009.09.003

Lewis, K., Gray, K., & Meierhenrich, J. (2014). The structure of online activism. *Sociological Science*, 1–9. doi:10.15195/v1.a1

LexisNexis. (2018, September 10). *LexisNexis academic*. Retrieved September 10, 2018, from LexisNexis website: http://www.lexisnexis.com/hottopics/lnacademic

Lievrouw, L. (2011). *Alternative and activist new media* (1st ed.). Cambridge, UK: Polity.

Lincoln, Y. (2001). Varieties of validity: quality in qualitative research. In J. Smart (Ed.), *Higher education: handbook of theory and research* (Vol. 16). New York, NY: Agathon Press.

Macionis, J. J. (2001). *Sociology* (8th ed.). Upper Saddle River, NJ: Prentice Hall.

Maddow, R. (2010, October 13). *The Rachel Maddow Show*. MSNBC.

Marin, A., & Wellman, B. (2011). Social network analysis: an introduction. The SAGE Handbook of Social Network Analysis, 11.

Melluci, A. (1995). The Process of Collective Identity. In H. Johnston & B. Klandermans (Eds.), *Social Movements and Culture* (pp. 41–63). Minneapolis, MN: University of Minnesota Press.

Miles, M. B., Huberman, A. M., & Saldaña, J. (2013). Qualitative data analysis: a methods sourcebook (3rd ed.). Thousand Oaks, CA: SAGE Publications, Inc.

Miller, F. (1999). The end of SDS and the emergence of weatherman: demise through success. In J. Freeman & V. Johnson (Eds.), *Waves of protest : social movements since the sixties*. Lanham, MD: Rowman & Littlefield Publishers.

Morozov, E. (2011). *The net delusion: The dark side of internet freedom*. New York: PublicAffairs.

Mucciaroni, G. (2011). The study of LGBT politics and its contributions to political science. *PS, Political Science & Politics*, *44*(01), 17–21. doi:10.1017/S1049096510001782

Obar, J. A., & Wildman, S. S. (2015). *Social media definition and the governance challenge: an introduction to the special issue* (SSRN Scholarly Paper No. ID 2647377). Retrieved from Social Science Research Network website: https://papers.ssrn.com/abstract=2647377

Obar, J. A., Zube, P., & Lampe, C. (2012). Advocacy 2.0: An analysis of how advocacy groups in the United States perceive and use social media as tools for facilitating civic engagement and collective action. *Journal of Information Policy*, *2*, 1–25. doi:10.5325/jinfopoli.2.2012.0001

Onuch, O. (2015a). Euromaidan protests in Ukraine: Social media versus social networks. *Problems of Post-Communism*, *62*(4), 217–235. doi:10.1080/10758216.2015.1037676

Onuch, O. (2015b). Facebook helped me do it': Understanding the euromaidan protester 'tool-kit. *Studies in Ethnicity and Nationalism*, *15*(1), 170–184. doi:10.1111ena.12129

Onwuegbuzie, A. J., & Leech, N. L. (2007). Validity and qualitative research: An oxymoron? *Quality & Quantity*, *41*(2), 233–249. doi:10.100711135-006-9000-3

Puranam, P., Alexy, O., & Reitzig, M. (2014). What's "new" about new forms of organizing? *Academy of Management Review*, *39*(2), 162–180. doi:10.5465/amr.2011.0436

Rubin, H. J., & Rubin, I. S. (2011). *Qualitative interviewing: the art of hearing data* (3rd ed.). Thousand Oaks, CA: SAGE Publications, Inc.

Rutledge, P. (2010). *What is media psychology? And why you should care*. Media Psychology Research Center. doi:10.1037/e537062011-001

Scott, J., & Carrington, P. J. (2011). *The SAGE handbook of social network analysis*. London: SAGE Publications Inc.

Shirky, C. (2011). The political power of social media: Technology, the public sphere, and political change. *Foreign Affairs*, *90*(1), 28–41.

Tapscott, D. (2008). *Grown up digital: how the net generation is changing your world* (1st ed.). McGraw-Hill Education.

Tatarchevskiy, T. (2011). The 'popular' culture of internet activism. *New Media & Society*, *13*(2), 297–313. doi:10.1177/1461444810372785

Tufekci, Z. (2014). Big questions for social media big data: Representativeness, validity and other methodological pitfalls. *ICWSM*, *14*, 505–514.

Valenzuela, S. (2013). Unpacking the use of social media for protest behavior: The roles of information, opinion expression, and activism. *The American Behavioral Scientist*, *57*(7), 920–942. doi:10.1177/0002764213479375

Wald, K. D. (2000). The context of gay politics. In C. A. Rimmerman, K. D. Wald, & C. Wilcox (Eds.), The politics of gay rights (pp. 1–28). Chicago: University of Chicago Press.

KEY TERMS AND DEFINITIONS

Content Analysis: A qualitative research methodology focused on the interpretation of documents through a systematic process of coding the data in order to identify patterns and themes.

LGBT: (i.e., lesbian, gay, bisexual, transgender). This acronym is sometimes shortened to LGB, referencing those specific members of the community in cases that exclude the transgender community.

Marginalized Community: This phrase describes a group facing discrimination, repression, or exclusion based on "sociopolitical designations, unchangeable dimensions based on personal identities, or as a result of life circumstances that cause them to 'assume' a new status" (Arredondo, 2008).

Social Media: Internet-based applications whereby individuals and groups create user-specific profiles and generate content on a site designed to connect individuals and groups (Obar & Wildman, 2015). Content development can be "continuously modified by users in a participatory and collaborative fashion" (Kaplan & Haenlein, 2010).

Social Network Analysis: A research approach focused on identifying and mapping the organizational topology structure of a group. The effort focuses on identifying the relationships between organizations and how they interact.

Section 7
Using Ethical Principals and Conduct in Scientific Research

As instructors of research one of our goals is to teach ethical practices and principals to students. The importance of ethics for the conduct of research is especially essential since scientific researchers operate mainly the upholding of personal values and the process of peer review. Hence, researchers need to be trained in the practice of utilizing ethics when conducting scientific and scholarly inquiry.

Chapter 11
To Whose Benefit? At What Cost?
Consideration for Ethical Issues in Social Science Research

Aaliyah A. Baker
Cardinal Stritch University, USA

ABSTRACT

This chapter takes a conceptual approach to addressing issues of ethics in research with human participants. The author proposes preliminary questions at the onset of a research study that deal with the issue of addressing researcher responsibility. The chapter argues ethical considerations surround epistemology and impact when conducting mixed methods research. Moreover, defining the interaction between researchers and participants is crucial. The author challenges early career practitioners to ask the question 'To whose benefit is the research?' but more importantly 'At what cost when conducting research?' Recommendations for engaging in an applied social science methodology include understanding critical epistemological and philosophical perspectives and grappling with the potential impact and outcomes of research. This level of critical awareness enables research to display complex processes that address social, political, and moral ideals that resonate with and value human experience as knowledge.

DOI: 10.4018/978-1-7998-1025-4.ch011

Copyright © 2020, IGI Global. Copying or distributing in print or electronic forms without written permission of IGI Global is prohibited.

INTRODUCTION

Ethical concerns arise over the attempt to collect and codify research that deals with human subjects. However, social science research is uniquely positioned to be able to explore and illustrate complex processes encompassing, for example, social, political, and moral ideals that resonate with human experience. Considering the representation and mediation of multiple perspectives, the responsible researcher is called to explicitly unpack the intent of their research agenda. One way to do this is to invite participants to make well-informed decisions about their participation by way of ensuring that the research study adheres to the protection of human rights by way of internal and institutional review (i.e. IRB). The organic and procedural transactions embedded in establishing a doctrine of ethics in research resembles an explicit and implicit contract (Josselson, 2007). Taking a deeper look at the persistent concerns over managing ethical dilemmas and making ethically and intellectually sound decisions allows for awareness of the level of reflexive assessment necessary for establishing research responsibility. When the researcher positions oneself as a learner during the course of research, this position warrants a self-reflexivity and an 'ethic of care'. Care, as demonstrated by the researcher's concern and empathy for the participants' stories, that the research will a) cause no harm to the participant and b) embrace a commitment to standards that ensure that the research methods are trustworthy.

This chapter takes a conceptual approach to addressing issues of ethics in research with human participants. It is not meant to report findings from an empirical study. Rather, it serves as a discussion of the author's experiences reporting on empirical social science research and teaching research methods courses at the doctoral degree level. Much of the discussion stems from the author's experience addressing preliminary questions at the onset of a research study. This chapter is intended for anyone wishing to gain a bit more insight, and open-minded perspective, around ethical decision-making in research. The chapter argues for ethical considerations when conducting mixed methods research. Moreover, defining the interaction between researchers and participants is crucial. The author charges early career practitioners to ask the question 'to whose benefit is the research' but more importantly 'at what cost am I conducting this research'? Clandinin and Connelly (2000) reflect on the *relational responsibility* of the "ambiguous, shifting participant observation relationships" (Clandinin and Connelly, 2000, p. 9). They describe this relationship as "the study of an experience…participants are in relation, and we as researchers are in relation to participants" (p.189). To that end, Craig and Huber (2007) articulate the ethical concerns for hearing the stories of others:

we realized that our negotiation of morally and ethically responsible relationships within inquiries with them was a "relational responsibility" (Clandinin and Connelly, 2000, p. 177) that called us to be thoughtful about children's lives not only as we lived alongside them but as they continue to story and restory who they were becoming as their lives unfolded into the future (p. 258).

Thus, there exists the responsibility of the researcher to consider the intended *and* unintended outcomes as well as all repercussions long after the research study concludes. These repercussions and outcomes the author is referring to are "costs": not in terms of a monetary amount paid, but, in terms of a penalty of harm. Harm endured as an unintended outcome of research results in an insurmountable debt. The costs of conducting unethical research by way of a carelessness on behalf of the researcher can be everlasting.[1]

A number of books and articles have been published on topics that deal exclusively with the treatment and protection of children (i.e. Graue and Walsh, 1998). It does not come as a surprise to most researchers that children would be considered a protected population given the context of cultural and societal norms. This does not negate the need to use empirical methods for including the voices of experiences of those who have been left out of empirical social science research. Kozol (1991) reiterates this ideal in his research pertaining to children. He argues that the voices of children have been missing from the whole discussion of schooling. Kozol (1991) goes on to say "this seems especially unfortunate because the children often are more interesting and perceptive than the grown-ups are about day-to-day realities of life in school" (Kozol, 1991, p. 5). Young people bring as much knowledge and expertise to any discussion through their individual experiences. Weinstein (2018) employs this concept in her research that explores spoken word poetry through the inclusion of the voices of youth. There exists the need for early career scholars, emerging scholars, novice researchers, students committed to scholarly writing and many others to explore and address this chapter's title question by way of learning how to do and better understanding implications for research methodology.

Othering

The researcher/participant relationship can become dichotomous.[2] The *us vs. them* dichotomy is problematic. Given the imperialistic nature of traditional Western research (Smith, 1999), qualitative methods have a history of *othering* marginalized groups and participants being investigated (Fine, 1994).[3] Thus, Western assumptions in research are often passed on as universal truths which inadvertently marginalizes the voice of the participant. *Othering* acts as a way to reroute responsibility and accountability away from the infrastructure of schooling. Historically, the "*other*" has been perceived as a socially and culturally disadvantaged person unable to fit into a "normal" system of education (Bourdieu, 2000; Gordon, Gordon & Nembhard, 1994). Therefore, research can unintentionally perpetuate this dichotomous relationship. In order to avoid dichotomizing the relationship between the researcher and the researcher, the researcher must first address the question "to whose benefit? And, at what cost?" in connection to the theories explored, methods applied, conclusions and research implications.

The researcher assumes a certain amount of power and responsibility when conducting research:

Where there is power, there is resistance, and yet, or rather consequently, this resistance is never in a position of exteriority in relation to power (Foucault, 1990).

The researcher must insist on asking "who is the research intended for?" in order to deconstruct the already polarized dichotomy of essentialized notions of power dynamics in a research/participant relationship. To ask this type of question prior to conducting the research would suggest that the researcher does not have a set of predetermined outcomes to choose from; rather, the results and conclusions would be dependent upon the interaction. This might differ from that of traditional quantitative studies that approach a question with a particular hypothesis in which the study aims to prove.

Identity

One might be perceived as having an insider perspective to research when certain cultural and phenotypical characteristics resemble those of the participant pool. However, the researcher might be viewed as an outsider so long as the research is being conducted outside of the self. Borrowing from Gee's theory of social linguistics, considering the nature of the interaction, the discourse remains a mediation of sign systems and symbols, relationships, practices, identities, politics, connections, and significance (Gee, 2012). People are constantly negotiating identity and the social discourse surrounding identities present and thus may have to consider multiple objective perspectives given the nature of subjective interpretations…

Speaking for Others

Educational researchers tend to study groups who are marginalized and oppressed in order to better understand the complexities of the injustice. In order to challenge the *us vs. them* binary, the researcher can position oneself as the learner, thus keeping with the belief that the participant still owns his/her story (Creswell, 2005). Research that analyzes experiences of marginalized groups can illustrate how naming oppressive and hegemonic acts can lead to social justice only if the researcher has positioned oneself as the learner in order to maintain the integrity and validity of the stories told.

Although the researcher reports the data, the participant's voice is crucial in the process. Speaking for others warrants careful consideration for representation and authority. The researcher's honesty and authenticity is an integral component in order to preserve the sacredness of another's life story, thus enhancing the trustworthiness and fidelity of the research. Roof and Wiegman (1995) discuss the consequences of a lack of authenticity:

Persons from dominant groups who speak for others are often treated as authenticating presences that confer legitimacy and credibility on the demands of subjugated speakers; such speaking for others does nothing to disrupt the discursive hierarchies that operate in public spaces. (p. 99)

Extensive use of the participants' quotes and language is necessary in order to avoid restorying to the extent that the story is no longer the participants' own (Creswell, 2005). According to Creswell, the language of the participants "provide(s) a voice for seldom-heard individuals in educational research" (Creswell, 2005, p. 477).

The Role as the Researcher

The interpretation of the research implications must be validated by the lived experiences and accounts of the stories being told in order for the research to be beneficial to the participants. If done well, research that utilizes both qualitative and quantitative approaches can help break down barriers between epistemological camps and unify research methods – which in turn allows for a richer story to be told.

Among the thick descriptions of life histories and social processes one can become lost in the "reportedness" of it all. It can be difficult to decide on the inclusion of data based on the sensitive nature of information shared and the trust that gets established through relationships with participants. Guidelines are outlined within the IRB protocol. However, the desire to share as much of the story as possible is typical in research.

To add to the complexity of reporting on social science research, a reciprocal relationship between the research and the participant(s) might mean that researchers will share their own life stories during mixed methods data collection techniques. The question arises as to how much of this level of engagement is important to consider by way of building trust and establishing a trustworthy relationship. During a previous study on homeschooling, I wanted to engage in a conversation about raising children, culture, ethnicity, balancing career, etc.; yet some of the ways we have been trained as scholar-practitioners sometimes inhibits an organic sharing between researcher and participant. Research training might over shadow authenticity of interactions with participants. However, one might wish to take care for omitting life experiences and resisting to share as this might hinder the uniquely rich data collection process in mixed methods research.

Beyond Participation

After the interviews have concluded, the researcher has a responsibility to continue the relationships which were developed with participants, and more importantly, to continue the research. One might begin to reconsider whether authority has been granted to ask such research questions; whether the interpretation of participants' narratives would be accurate; and how to establish credibility through the generalizability of findings.

Geertz (1995) speaks to *change* in anthropological research: "Change is the hallmark" for Geertz (2000, p. 5). He emphasized the need to form contextual connections to loosely formed accounts of events, history, and stories. Acceptance and accountability are necessary for change to occur, which is similar to narrative inquiry research. In addition, Webster and Mertova (2007) verify narrative inquiry "requires the researcher to be brave enough to let the critical events arise out of the data, and resist the preliminary design of outcomes so firmly entrenched in other research traditions" (p. ix). Wolf (1992) also contends:

whether it was this "new" professional audience or the postmodern rhetoric on ethnographic authority that was responsible, my "findings" are more often tentative than they once were and my conclusions, I hope, more accessible to different interpretations. (p. 120)

Change, acceptance, and accountability are all interwoven in the iterative process of writing the report. In qualitative research, the researcher cannot be certain of the outcome of the research. As such, the interconnectedness of qualitative techniques embedded in the mixed methods approach to addressing research questions requires a process of reflection on these three ideals.

Research is often thought of outside of practice. Mixed methods research can allow research and practice to intersect. With respect to this intersection, Collins (1998) describes the movement through different social, political and economic groups best through her notion of the *outsider within*.[4] She describes "the location of people who no longer belong to any one group... describing individuals who found themselves in marginal locations between groups of varying power" (Hill-Collins,

1998). Hill-Collins' research focuses on how the researcher positions himself/herself with respect to the rest of the world. A mixed methods approach must also employ this notion. People are adaptable to many sociocultural groups. Using mixed methods research to delve into the social and cultural thought processes and events that lead to the decision to homeschool can help illustrate those marginal locations between and within groups of varying power relations in schools.

So, "to whose benefit? And, at what cost?"

Positioning research questions within a methodology that is rooted in an appropriately established interpretive framework is important. Due to a personally, socially, culturally, and historically rooted epistemological commitment to ethics in research, research that is conducted with the purpose of advocating for large-scale benefits (often rooted in social justice) and without harm or the intent to harm can have a profound impact on communities of practice at large. Therefore, the call is to ask oneself 'what benefit will the research promote and at what cost?' If in the answering of these fundamental questions, concerns arise then the study should revisit its ontological, epistemological, axiological and methodological perspectives (Creswell, 2018). In any mixed methods study that relies on qualitative techniques for part of the data collection, I offer two recommendations that can apply:

1. The researcher must be prepared to understand critical epistemological and philosophical perspectives across disciplines.
2. In order to bring knowledge to action, the researcher should engage regularly in conversations that challenge them to think about the sustainability, potential and impact of their research.

Research has the capacity to reach many lives if and when done well. Taking these questions, recommendations and challenges into consideration will position the work to display complex processes that address social, political, and moral ideals which resonate with human experience. Having an ethical attitude, by way of addressing the epistemological nature of a study's purpose, can only strengthen the approach to social science mixed methods research.

REFERENCES

Baker, A. A. (2013). *Black families' pedagogies: Pedagogical philosophies and practices surrounding black parents' decisions to homeschool* (Order No. 3604570). Available from ProQuest Dissertations & Theses Global. (1475253691). Retrieved from http://search.proquest.com.csu.ezproxy.switchinc.org/docview/1475253691?accountid=9367

Bourdieu, P. (2000). Cultural reproduction and social reproduction. In R. Arum & I. Beattie (Eds.), *The structure of schooling: Readings in the sociology of Education* (pp. 56–68). New York, NY: McGraw-Hill.

Clandinin, D. J. (Ed.). (2007). *Handbook of narrative inquiry: Mapping a methodology.* Sage Publications. doi:10.4135/9781452226552

Clandinin, D. J., & Connelly, F. M. (1994). Personal experience methods. In N. K. Denzin & Y. Lincoln (Eds.), *Handbook of qualitative research.* Thousand Oaks, CA: Sage.

Clandinin, D. J., & Connelly, F. M. (2000). *Narrative inquiry: Experience and story in qualitative research.* San Francisco: Jossey-Bass Publishers.

Clandinin, D. J., & Rosiek, J. (2007). Mapping a landscape of narrative inquiry: Borderland spaces and tensions. In D. J. Clandinin (Ed.), Handbook of narrative inquiry: Mapping a methodology. Sage Publications.

Collins, P. H. (1998). *Fighting words: Black women and the search for justice.* University of Minnesota Press.

Craig, C., & Huber, J. (2007). Relational reverberations: Shaping and reshaping narrative inquiries in the midst of storied lives and context. In D. J. Clandinin (Ed.), *Handbook of narrative inquiry: Mapping a methodology.* SAGE Publications. doi:10.4135/9781452226552.n10

Creswell, J. (2005). *Educational Research: Planning, conducting, and evaluating quantitative and qualitative research.* Pearson Education, Inc.

Creswell, J. W. (2018). *Research design: Qualitative, quantitative, and mixed methods Approaches* (5th ed.). Thousand Oaks, CA: Sage.

Fine, M. (1994). Working the hyphens: Reinventing self and other in qualitative research. In N. R. Denzin & Y. S. Lincoln (Eds.), *Handbook of qualitative research* (pp. 70–82). Thousand Oaks, CA: Sage.

Foucault, M. (1980). Power/knowledge. In C. Gordon (Ed.), *Selected interviews and other writings 1972-1977* (p. 153). Pantheon Books.

Foucault, M. (1990). The history of sexuality: Vol. I. *An introduction.* New York: Vintage.

Foucault, M. (1991). *Discipline and Punish: the birth of a prison.* London: Penguin.

Gee, J. P. (2012). *Social linguistics and literacies: Ideology in discourses* (4th ed.). New York: Routledge.

Geertz, C. (1973). Thick Description: Toward an interpretive theory of culture. In C. Geertz (Ed.), *The Interpretation of Cultures* (pp. 3–30). New York: Basic Books.

Gordon, E. T., Gordon, E. W., & Nembhard, J. G. G. (1994, Autumn). Social science literature concerning African American men. *The Journal of Negro Education*, *63*(4), 508–531. doi:10.2307/2967292

Gordon, E. W. (1999). The experiences of African American males in school and society. In V. C. Polite & J. E. Davis (Eds.), *African American males in school and society*. Teachers College Press.

Graue, M. E., & Walsh, D. (2012). *Studying children in context: Theories, methods, and ethics*. SAGE Publications.

Josselson, R. (2007). The ethical attitude in narrative research: principles and practicalities. In D. J. Clandinin (Ed.), Handbook of narrative inquiry: Mapping a methodology. Sage Publications. doi:10.4135/9781452226552.n21

Kozol, J. (1991). *Savage Inequalities*. New York, NY: Crown Publishers.

Reicher, S., Haslam, S. A., & Rath, R. (2008). Making a virtue of evil: A five-step social identity model of the development of collective hate. *Social and Personality Psychology Compass*, *2*(3), 1313–1344. doi:10.1111/j.1751-9004.2008.00113.x

Roof, J., & Wiegman, R. (1995). *Who can speak*. Urbana, IL: University of Illinois Press.

Smith, L. T. (1999). *Decolonizing methodologies: Research and indigenous peoples*. Zed Books Ltd.

Webster, L., & Mertova, P. (2007). *Using narrative inquiry as a research method: An introduction to using critical event narrative analysis in research on learning and teaching*. New York, NY: Routledge. doi:10.4324/9780203946268

Weinstein, S. (2018). *The room is on fire: The History, Pedagogy, and Practice of Youth Spoken Word Poetry*. SUNY Press.

ENDNOTES

[1] Stanley Milgram's obedience study of 1963 is an example of the everlasting consequences of the psychological, social, and emotional debt in which the author uses to describe as the high price to pay for the failure to consider ethical concerns in research.

2. Geertz's (1973, 1988, and 1995) work on anthropological research also helps to define narrative and narrative inquiry.
3. Psychoanalytic theory provides a conceptual framework for understanding how the social construction of race becomes affectively lived experiences and blackness and/or the perception of 'otherness' becomes feared. See works by Frantz Fanon, these works are beyond the scope of this paper.
4. Patricia Hill-Collins' research takes on a black feminist approach in describing how black women must negotiate different identities and allegiances as college academia.

Section 8
Conducting Research From Start to Finish

The numerous steps to be considered when conducting a research study can be daunting for an inexperienced researcher. Similarly, teaching these skills to students requires considerable thought as to how to best provide an integrated approach to teaching both strands and then combining this orientation. This section provides a step by step linear approach to the research process. The mixed methods researcher needs to manage numerous competencies starting with the philosophical assumptions underlying the use of mixed methods. Considerable data from each component and make meaningful inferences. In addition, a mixed methods study needs to integrate, link and connect the two strands of research in order to provide a comprehensive understanding of the issue under investigation.

Chapter 12
Developing the Research Study:
A Step-by-Step Approach

Mette L. Baran
Cardinal Stritch University, USA

Janice E. Jones
Cardinal Stritch University, USA

ABSTRACT

This chapter serves as a guideline for outlining the core characteristics of qualitative, quantitative, or mixed methods research (MMR) and the various steps researchers undertake in order to conduct a research study. While the focus is on MMR, the steps are similar for any type of research methodology. The purpose is to create a framework assisting the researcher with an outline following the seven steps to conducting research. It is important to note that MMR is not a limiting form of research. Researchers need a mixed method research question and a mixed methods purpose statement for the research project. This chapter will also help explain why MMR is one of the best approaches in answering a research question. Finally, the chapter includes a suggestion to the importance of adding a visual diagram of the mixed methods research project into the research project and into the final report.

INTRODUCTION

The following sub-sections present criteria to be used when selecting each of the four mixed methods designs: Parallel Convergent, Sequential Explanatory, Sequential Exploratory, and Embedded.

DOI: 10.4018/978-1-7998-1025-4.ch012

Copyright © 2020, IGI Global. Copying or distributing in print or electronic forms without written permission of IGI Global is prohibited.

Parallel Convergent Mixed Method Design

The parallel convergent mixed method design requires matching the design to the study's purpose and is best suited for group research work or when an individual researcher can collect only limited quantitative and qualitative data. This design is a good choice in the following cases: 1. Where there is limited time for data collection. 2. Collection of both data types is needed in one visit to the field. 3.The researcher feels that collection and analysis of both types of data would be of equal value in understanding the research problem. 4. When the researcher possesses expertise in both quantitative and qualitative methods of research or can manage extensive data collection and analysis.

Explanatory Mixed Method Design

This design is most useful in the following situations: 1. When the researcher wants to assess trends and relationships with quantitative data but also needs to be able to explain the mechanism or reasons behind the resultant trends. 2. In cases when the researcher, or research question itself, is more quantitatively oriented or the researcher knows the important research constructs and has quantitative instruments to measure these constructs. 3. When the researcher can perform a second round of qualitative data collection or can conduct research in multiple phases. 4. When the researcher has limited resources 5. The researcher develops new questions based on quantitative results and need qualitative data to answer these questions.

Sequential Exploratory Mixed Method Design

The sequential exploratory mixed method design is most useful in the following types of studies: 1. Where the qualitative exploratory results are to be generalized, assessed, or tested for their applicability to a sample and a population. 2. When the researcher needs to develop an instrument when one is not available (first explore, then develop instrument) 3. When the researcher needs to develop a classification or typology for testing or the researcher wants to identify the most important variables to study quantitatively when these variables are not known. 4. In cases where the researcher identifies new emergent research questions based on qualitative results that requires quantitative data, exploratory mixed method design would be a good choice.

Embedded Mixed Method Design

This design is an appropriate choice in the following situations: 1. For researchers investigating different questions requiring different types of data to enhance the application of a quantitative or qualitative design in order address the basic objective of the study. 2. When a researcher possesses expertise to rigorously implement the planned quantitative or qualitative design. 3. When the researcher possesses little experience in dealing with the supplementary method or does not have adequate resources to attach equal priority to both types of data. 4. In cases when emergent issues related to the primary research design (quantitative or qualitative) are discovered. the embedded mixed method design can help gain insight into these issues by using a secondary data set.

Starting the Research Journey

The following is a list of decisions researchers need to consider at the start of any research project. The various prompts are displayed in a logical step-by-step fashion which is the typical the outline followed when conducting empirical research. The authors envision practitioners completing each section and then building on the previous decisions when completing the worksheet. The information can then be compiled to be used in a master's thesis, dissertation, or any other type of research study.

USE THE GUIDING QUESTIONS BELOW TO DEVELOP YOUR RESEARCH PLAN

1. Reasons for Conducting Mixed Methods Research?
    a. The Compatibility of Quantitative and Qualitative Methods
    b. Strengths and Weaknesses of Mixed Methods Research
    c. Triangulation, Complementarity, Expansion
2. Characteristics of Quantitative Research
    a. Deductive data analysis
    b. Strength and Weaknesses of Quantitative Methods
1. Characteristics of Qualitative Research
    a. Inductive data analysis
    b. Strengths and Weaknesses of Qualitative Methods
2. Order of Methodology – Which comes first: Quantitative or Qualitative?
    a. Parallel Convergent: - Both quantitative and qualitative data sets are collected simultaneously
    b. Sequential Explanatory: - Quantitative data are collected first with qualitative data collection following
    c. Sequential Exploratory: -Qualitative data are collected first with quantitative data collection following

Developing the Research Study

Figure 1. Steps in Deductive Research

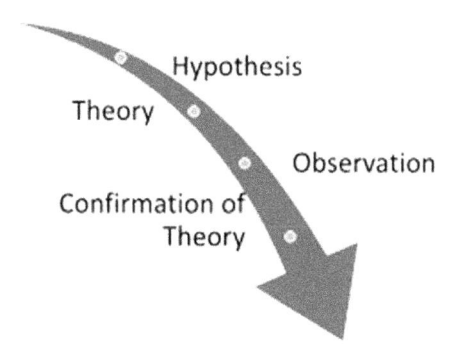

Hypothesis
Theory
Observation
Confirmation of Theory

Figure 2. Steps in Inductive Research

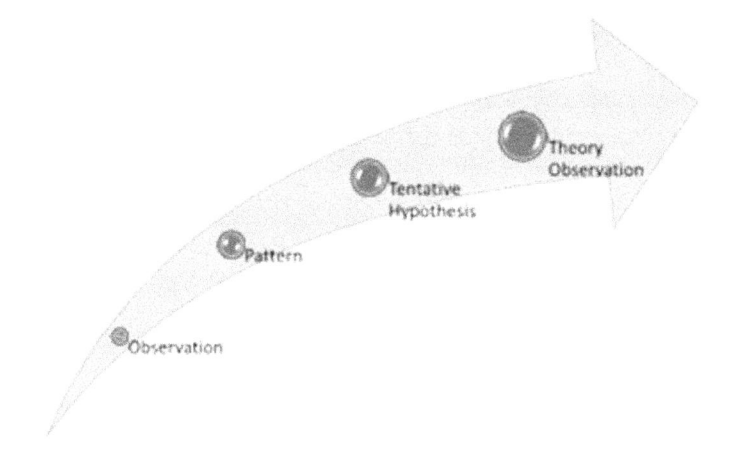

Theory
Observation
Tentative Hypothesis
Pattern
Observation

    d.   Descriptive: Either Quantitative or Qualitative comes first
    e.   Describe your methodology:
        i.   Assumptions that differentiate qualitative and quantitative studies
3. Epistemology
    a.   Qualitative researchers believe there are multiple realities represented by the participants' perspectives
    b.   Quantitative researchers believe a single, objective reality exists
4. Context
    a.   Qualitative researchers believe context is critical to understanding the phenomena being studied
    b.   Quantitative researchers do not believe context is an important factor
    c.   Describe your worldview and epistemology including researcher assumptions about the research:

i. Researcher bias
ii. Qualitative researchers believe the researcher's biases and perspectives must be understood to interpret the results
iii. Quantitative researchers believe researcher bias is controlled through the control of internal validity threats
d. Describe your bias towards the research study:

Steps in Conducting a Mixed Methods Research Study

The following 7 decision steps outlines the research path when conducting a research study as outlined in Figure 1 below.

1. Determine Purpose and problem statement.
2. Identify a rationale for a mixed methods study.
3. Identify data collection strategy and design including strategy and sequence.
4. Determine qualitative and quantitative research question or mixed methods questions? Is mixed methods the best approach?

Figure 3. Steps to conducting a Mixed Methods Research Study

Developing the Research Study

5. Collect qualitative and quantitative data
6. Analyze data concurrently or separately
7. Write report

Researcher Work Sheets using the 7 Decision Steps:

1. Determine Purpose and Problem Statement
   a. What is the purpose of the study?
   b. What is the problem statement?
2. Identify a rationale for a mixed methods study
   a. Describe your worldview and epistemological stance?
   b. Describe your theoretical framework?
3. Identify data collection strategy and design including strategy and sequence

Research design refers to the plan of action that links the philosophical assumptions to specific methods (Creswell, 2003; Crotty, 1998).

1. Quantitative Strategies:
   a. Experimental
   b. Quasi-Experimental
2. Qualitative Strategies:
   a. **Narrative:** Narrative research is a form of inquiry in with the researcher studies the lives of individuals and asks one or more individuals to provide stories about their lives. This information is then retold or re-storied by the researcher into narrative chronology. In the end, the narrative combines views from the participant's life with those of the researcher's life in a collaborative narrative.
   b. **Ethnography**: An in-depth description and interpretation of cultural patterns and meanings within a culture or social group with culture being a shared pattern of beliefs, normative expectations, behaviors, and meanings.
   c. **Phenomenology:** Describes and interprets the experiences of participants to understand their perspectives based on the belief that there are multiple ways of interpreting the same experience and the meaning of that experience is what constitutes reality.
   d. **Grounded Theory:** Grounded theory offers the researcher an opportunity to derive a general, abstract theory of a process, action, or interaction grounded in the views of participants in a study. This process involves using multiple stages of data collection and the refinement and interrelationship

of categories of information. Two primary characteristics of this design are the constant comparison of data with emerging categories and theoretical sampling of different groups to maximize the similarities and the differences of information.

    e. **Case Study:** An in-depth analysis of one or more events, settings, programs, groups, or other "bounded systems." Types of case studies:
        i. Historical organizational - focus on the development of an organization over time
        ii. Observational - study of a single entity using participant observation
        iii. Life history (i.e., oral history) - a first-person narrative completed with one person
        iv. Situation analysis - a study of a specific event from multiple perspective
        v. Multi-case - a study of several different independent entities
        vi. Multi-site - a study of many sites and participants the main purpose of which is to develop theory

3. Mixed Methods Strategies:
    a. Parallel Convergent
    b. Sequential (Explanatory or Exploratory)
    c. Embedded
4. Describe your research design?

DETERMINE QUALITATIVE AND QUANTITATIVE RESEARCH QUESTIONS OR MIXED METHODS QUESTIONS TO DETERMINE IF MIXED METHODS IS THE BEST APPROACH

Explain clearly and explain why MM is necessary. Provide a compelling reason why MM is needed and how a holistic understanding of the research problem will be gained through MM. Explain how both approaches make it possible to draw inferences that would have been different if only one approach or strand had been used.

Fill in:
Quantitative Research Question(s):
Null Hypothesis (es:)
Alternative Hypothesis(es):
Qualitative Research Question(s):
Mixed Methods Question(s):

Developing the Research Study

COLLECT QUALITATIVE AND QUANTITATIVE DATA

1. What data to use?
    a. Existing data:
    b. Archival data:
    c. Longitudinal data:
    d. Quantitative Data Collection:
        i. Who are your participants and how will they be selected and contacted?
        ii. Which research question will this data help answer?
    e. Qualitative Data Collection:
        i. Who are your participants and how will they be selected and contacted?
        ii. Which research question will this data help answer?

Observation (Unstructured in Nature)

1. Comprehensive - continuous over an extended period
2. Participant-observer role of the researcher
3. Continuum between complete participant and complete observer
4. Passive participant
5. Moderate participant
6. Active participant
7. Complete participant
8. Use of field notes to record observations
9. Two types of information
10. Descriptions of what occurred
11. Reflections of what the descriptions mean (i.e., speculations, emerging themes, patterns, problems)
12. Accuracy
13. Extensive nature of notes

Interviews (Unstructured in Nature)

1. Begins with a general idea of what needs to be asked and moves to specific questions based on what the respondent says
2. Types of interviews
    a. Key informant
    b. Life history

c. Tape recording and transcribing interviews afford the opportunity to study the data carefully

Focus Groups

1. Document analysis
2. Written records
    a. Print (e.g., minutes from meetings, reports, yearbooks, articles, diaries)
    b. Non-print (e.g., recordings, videotapes, pictures)
3. Types of sources
    a. Primary - original work
    b. Secondary - secondhand interpretations of original work
4. Commonly used to verify other observations or interview data

Mixed Methods Data Collection:

1. Who are your participants and how will they be selected and contacted?
2. Which research question will this data help answer?
3. Identify the research site(s).
4. Describe access to physical locations, participants, documents, physical locations, etc.:

Determine Sampling Techniques

1. Probability Sampling
2. Non-Probability sampling
    a. Use of purposeful sampling strategies to select "information rich" participants
    b. Purposeful sampling strategies
        i. Maximum variation - selecting individuals or cases to represent extremes (e.g., very positive or very negative attitudes, highest and lowest achieving students)
        ii. Snowball (i.e., network) - initially selected participants recommend others for involvement
        iii. Key informant - selecting an individual(s) particularly knowledgeable about the setting and or topic
        iv. Comprehensive - selecting all relevant individuals or cases
3. Describe your sampling technique:

Developing the Research Study

Reliability and Validity in Mixed Methods Research

This section covers reliability and validity issues that are apparent in MMR. The researcher needs to determine:

1. Define Validity:
2. Define Reliability:
3. Quantitative Validity & Reliability:
   a. Internal Validity
   b. External Validity
   c. Construct Validity
   d. Reliability
4. Objectivity

Qualitative Validity & Reliability

1. Credibility
2. Transferability
3. Dependability
4. Confirmability
5. Techniques to enhance validity & credibility
6. Triangulation
7. Prolonged and persistent field work
8. Copious field notes
9. Low inference descriptors
10. Mechanically recorded data
11. Member checking / Peer Review
12. Verbatim accounts
13. Abundant use of detail
14. Data collection in natural settings
15. Researcher's role as participant observer
16. Describe how you will address quantitative and qualitative validity and reliability in your research?

ANALYZE DATA CONCURRENTLY OR SEPARATELY

Analyzing Quantitative Data

Describe statistical procedures to be used:

1. Levels of Measurement
2. Hypothesis Testing
3. T-tests inferences concerning two means
4. ANOVA – Inferences using a one-way ANOVA
5. Correlational research

Analyzing Qualitative Data

Observations, interviews, and document analyses result in large quantities of narrative data
    Analysis includes critically examining, summarizing, and synthesizing the data
    Three stages of analysis

1. Transcription
2. Transcribe all your documents carefully and store in an organized fashion
3. Coding
   a. Organizing the data into reasonable, meaningful units that are coded with words or very short phrases that signify a category
   b. Use of major codes and sub-codes is common
   c. Summarizing the coded data
   d. Examining all similarly coded data and summarizing it with a sentence or two that reflects its essence
   e. Computerized sorting of data is common and effective
   f. Pattern seeking and synthesizing
   g. Synthesizing identifies the relationships among the categories and patterns that suggest generalization
   h. The researcher interprets findings inductively, synthesizes the information, and draws inferences

PATTERN SEEKING AND THEMES

1. Begins with the researcher's informed hunches and ideas
2. Tentative patterns are identified, and additional data collected to determine if they are consistent with those patterns
3. Characterized by enlarging, combining, subsuming, and creating new categories that make sense

ADDITIONAL DECISIONS PERTAINING TO DATA ANALYSIS

1. Timing (Sequencing)
2. Weight (Priority) of Data
3. Where and how to mix the strands
   a. **Concurrent Design**: How will the quantitative and qualitative data be merged? What strategies will be used if findings conflict or are contradictory from the two data. A strategy of resolving differences needs to be considered, such as gathering more data or revisiting the databases.
   b. **Sequential Design**: What results from the first phase will be used in the follow-up phase? Key issues surround the "point of interface" in which the investigator needs to decide what results from the first phase will be the focus of attention for the follow-up data collection.
4. Embedded Design:

WRITE REPORT

How Will you use Visual Modeling in Your Study?

1. Graphic representation of literature review (Chapter 2 of dissertation)
2. Graphic representation of Methodology (Chapter 3 of dissertation)
3. Graphic representation of Findings (Chapter 4 of dissertation)
4. Graphic representation of findings connecting with existing literature and/or new theory (Chapter 5 of dissertation)

CONCLUSION

This step-by-step framework is a tool for researchers in outlining their methodology and study design. The approach is useful whether the study is quantitative, qualitative, or mixed methods in nature. As research professors we use this framework in our courses, having students complete the various sections as parts of assignments. The various sections can be studied separately as the researcher builds knowledge or followed systematically building on previous decisions. We have found that the framework help novice students keep track of their research agenda as it forces them to consider every aspect and decision which are part of a rigorous study.

REFERENCES

Creswell, J. W. (2003). *Research design: Qualitative, quantitative, and mixed methods approaches* (2nd ed.). Thousand Oaks, CA: Sage.

Crotty, M. (1998). *The foundations of social research*. Los Angeles, CA: Sage.

Compilation of References

AECT. (n.d.). *The Handbook of Research for Educational Communications and Technology*. Retrieved from http://www.aect.org/edtech/ed1/41/41-01.html

AeraVibes. (2019). Retrieved from: https://www.areavibes.com/chicago-il/englewood/crime/

Aguinis, H., Pierce, C. A., & Quigley, B. M. (1995). Enhancing the validity of self-reported alcohol and marijuana consumption using a bogus pipeline procedure: A meta-analytic review. *Basic and Applied Social Psychology*, *16*(4), 515–527. doi:10.120715324834basp1604_8

Ajay, O. (2017). *Data visualization*. Hoboken, NJ: Wiley & Sons.

Akers, R. L., Massey, J., Clarke, W., & Lauer, R. M. (1983). Are self-reports of adolescent deviance valid? Biochemical measures, randomized response, and the bogus pipeline in smoking behavior. *Social Forces*, *62*(1), 234–251. doi:10.2307/2578357

Allaman, J. D., Joyce, C. S., & Crandall, V. C. (1972). The antecedents of social desirability response tendencies of children and young adults. *Child Development*, *43*(4), 1135–1160. doi:10.2307/1127504 PMID:4643767

Allsop, B. (2016). Social media and activism: A literature review. *Social Psychology Review*, *18*(2), 35–40.

Altheide, D., & Johnson, J. (1998). Criteria for assessing interpretive validity in qualitative research. In N. Denzin & Y. Lincoln (Eds.), *Collecting and interpreting qualitative materials* (pp. 283–312). Thousand Oaks, CA: Sage.

Andrews, P., & Meyer, R. G. (2003). Marlowe–Crowne social desirability scale and short form C: Forensic norms. *Journal of Clinical Psychology*, *59*(4), 483–492. doi:10.1002/jclp.10136 PMID:12652639

Aquilino, W. S. (1997). Privacy effects on self-reported drug use: Interactions with survey mode and respondent characteristics. *NIDA Research Monograph*, *167*, 383–415. PMID:9243571

Aquilino, W. S., Wright, D. L., & Supple, A. J. (2000). Response effects due to bystander presence in CASI and paper-and-pencil surveys of drug use and alcohol use. *Substance Use & Misuse*, *35*(6-8), 845–867. doi:10.3109/10826080009148424 PMID:10847214

Arnold, V. (2006). Behavioral research opportunities: Understanding the impact of enterprise systems. *International Journal of Accounting Information Systems, 7*(1), 7–17. doi:10.1016/j.accinf.2006.02.001

Arredondo, P. (2008). Counseling individuals from marginalized and underserved groups. In *Readings in multicultural practice* (pp. 331–348). SAGE Publications Inc.

Baker, A. A. (2013). *Black families' pedagogies: Pedagogical philosophies and practices surrounding black parents' decisions to homeschool* (Order No. 3604570). Available from ProQuest Dissertations & Theses Global. (1475253691). Retrieved from http://search.proquest.com.csu.ezproxy.switchinc.org/docview/1475253691?accountid=9367

Ballard, R. (1992). Short forms of the Marlowe-Crowne social desirability scale. *Psychological Reports, 71*(3), 1155-1160.

Barbour, R. S. (2001). Checklists for improving rigour in qualitative research: A case of the tail wagging the dog? *BMJ (Clinical Research Ed.), 322*(7294), 1115–1117. doi:10.1136/bmj.322.7294.1115 PMID:11337448

Bartlett, J. E., Kotrlik, J. W., & Higgins, C. C. (2001). Organizational research: Determining appropriate sample size in survey research appropriate sample size in survey research. *Information Technology, Learning and Performance Journal, 19*(1), 43.

Bashir, M., Afzal, M. T., & Azeem, M. (2008). Reliability and validity of qualitative and operational research paradigm. *Pakistan Journal of Statistical and Operation Research, IV*(1), 35–45. doi:10.18187/pjsor.v4i1.59

Bazeley, P. (2004). Issues in mixing qualitative and quantitative approaches to research. In R. Buber, J. Gadner, & L. Richards (Eds.), *Applying qualitative methods to marketing management research* (pp. 141–156). Palgrave Macmillan.

Bazeley, P., & Jackson, K. (Eds.). (2013). *Qualitative data analysis with NVIVO* (2nd ed.). Los Angeles, CA: SAGE Publications Ltd.

Bear, J. H. (2019, January 7). *Callouts are effective in print and web design*. Retrieved from https://www.lifewire.com/call-out-in-graphic-design-1074265

Bell, K. M., & Naugle, A. E. (2007). Effects of social desirability on students' self-reporting of partner abuse perpetration and victimization. *Violence and Victims, 22*(2), 243–256. doi:10.1891/088667007780477348 PMID:17479559

Bergman, M. M. (2010). On concepts and paradigms in mixed methods research. *Journal of Mixed Methods Research, 4*(3), 171–175. doi:10.1177/1558689810376950

Bettis, R. A., Ethiraj, S., Gambardella, A., Helfat, C., & Mitchell, W. (2016). Creating repeatable cumulative knowledge in strategic management: A call for a broad and deep conversation among authors, referees, and editors. *Strategic Management Journal, 37*(2), 257–261. doi:10.1002mj.2477

Biesta, G. (2010). Pragmatism and the philosophical foundations of mixed methods research. In A. Tashakkori & C. Teddlie (Eds.), *SAGE Handbook of Mixed Methods in Social & Behavioral Research* (2nd ed., pp. 95–118). Thousand Oaks, CA: Sage. doi:10.4135/9781506335193.n4

Birks, M., Chapman, Y., & Francis, K. (2008). Memoing in qualitative research: Probing data and processes. *Journal of Research in Nursing*, *13*(1), 68–75. doi:10.1177/1744987107081254

Blaikie, N., & Priest, J. (2019). *Designing social research: The logic of anticipation*. Hoboken, NJ: John Wiley & Sons.

Blumer, H. (1969). Collective behavior. In A. M. Lee (Ed.), Principles of sociology (3rd ed.; pp. 65–121). New York, NY: Barnes & Noble Books.

Booth-Kewley, S., Larson, G. E., & Miyoshi, D. K. (2007). Social desirability effects on computerized and paper-and-pencil questionnaires. *Computers in Human Behavior*, *23*(1), 463–477. doi:10.1016/j.chb.2004.10.020

Bourdieu, P. (2000). Cultural reproduction and social reproduction. In R. Arum & I. Beattie (Eds.), *The structure of schooling: Readings in the sociology of Education* (pp. 56–68). New York, NY: McGraw-Hill.

Bradburn, N. M., Sudman, S., Blair, E., Locander, W., Miles, C., Singer, E., & Stocking, C. (1979). *Improving interview method and questionnaire design: Response effects to threatening questions in survey research*. San Francisco: Jossey-Bass.

Bradburn, N. M., Sudman, S., Blair, E., & Stocking, C. (1978). Question threat and response bias. *Public Opinion Quarterly*, *42*(2), 221–234. doi:10.1086/268444

Brenner, P. S., & DeLamater, J. D. (2014). Social desirability bias in self-reports of physical activity: Is an exercise identity the culprit? *Social Indicators Research*, *117*(2), 489–504. doi:10.100711205-013-0359-y

Brenner, P. S., Serpe, R. T., & Stryker, S. (2014). The causal ordering of prominence and salience in identity theory: An empirical examination. *Social Psychology Quarterly*, *77*(3), 231–252. doi:10.1177/0190272513518337 PMID:27284212

Brodsky, A. E. (2008). Negative case analysis. In L. M. Given (Ed.), *The Sage encyclopedia of qualitative research methods*. Thousand Oaks, CA: Sage Publications.

Brown, J. S., & Druid, P. (1991). Organizational learning and communities of practice: Toward a unified view of working, learning, and innovation. *Organization Science*, *2*(1), 40–57. doi:10.1287/orsc.2.1.40

Bryman, A. (2006). Integrating quantitative and qualitative research: How is it done? *Qualitative Research*, *6*(1), 97–113. doi:10.1177/1468794106058877

Bryman, A. (2006). Paradigm peace and the implications for quality. *International Journal of Social Research Methodology Theory and Practice*, *9*(2), 111–126. doi:10.1080/13645570600595280

Burns, N., & Grove, S. K. (2005). *The Practice of Nursing Research: Conduct, Critique, and Utilization* (5th ed.). St. Louis, MO: Elsevier Saunders.

Burrell, G., & Morgan, G. (1979). *Sociological paradigms and organizational analysis*. Ashgate Publishing Limited.

Bygrave, W. D. (2007). The entrepreneurship paradigm (I) revisited. Handbook of qualitative research methods in entrepreneurship, 1748.

Byrne, D. (1961). The repression-sensitization scale: Rationale, reliability, and validity 1. *Journal of Personality*, *29*(3), 334–349. doi:10.1111/j.1467-6494.1961.tb01666.x PMID:13689584

Cameron, R. (2009). A sequential mixed model research design: Design, analytical and display issues. *International Journal of Multiple Research Approaches*, *3*(2), 140–152. doi:10.5172/mra.3.2.140

Campanelli, P. C., Dielman, T. E., & Shope, J. T. (1987). Validity of adolescents' self-reports of alcohol use and misuse using a bogus pipeline procedure. *Adolescence*, *22*(85), 7. PMID:3591505

Campbell, D. T., & Stanley, J. C. (1963). *Experimental and quasi-experimental designs for research*. Boston: Houghton Mifflin Company.

Caracelli, V. J., & Greene, J. C. (1993). Data analysis strategies for mixed-method evaluation designs. *Educational Evaluation and Policy Analysis*, *15*(2), 195–207. doi:10.3102/01623737015002195

Cater, J. J. III. (2012). The Pierre Part store: A case study. *Journal of Family Business Management*, *2*(2), 166–180. doi:10.1108/20436231211261899

Charoenruk, D. (2009). *Communication research methodologies: qualitative and quantitative methodology*. Available From: http://utcc2.utcc.ac.th/localuser/amsar/PDF/documents49/quantative and qualitative methodologies.pdf

Chenail, R. J. (2011). YouTube as a qualitative research asset: Reviewing user generated videos as learning resources. *Qualitative Report*, *16*(1), 229–235.

Chlosta, S. (2016). *Getting into methodological trouble. In A Research Agenda for Entrepreneurship and Context* (pp. 109–119). Cheltenham, UK: Edward Elgar. doi:10.4337/9781784716844.00013

Christiansen, J. (2009). Four stages of social movements. *EBSCO Research Starters*, 1–7.

Christiansen, N. D., Burns, G. N., & Montgomery, G. E. (2005). Reconsidering forced-choice item formats for applicant personality assessment. *Human Performance*, *18*(3), 267–307. doi:10.120715327043hup1803_4

City of Chicago Data Portal. (2019). *Selected socioeconomic indicators 2008 – 2014*. Retrieved from: https://data.cityofchicago.org/Health-Human-Services/Englewood/b352-9cxu

Clandinin, D. J., & Rosiek, J. (2007). Mapping a landscape of narrative inquiry: Borderland spaces and tensions. In D. J. Clandinin (Ed.), Handbook of narrative inquiry: Mapping a methodology. Sage Publications.

Clandinin, D. J. (Ed.). (2007). *Handbook of narrative inquiry: Mapping a methodology*. Sage Publications. doi:10.4135/9781452226552

Clandinin, D. J., & Connelly, F. M. (1994). Personal experience methods. In N. K. Denzin & Y. Lincoln (Eds.), *Handbook of qualitative research*. Thousand Oaks, CA: Sage.

Clandinin, D. J., & Connelly, F. M. (2000). *Narrative inquiry: Experience and story in qualitative research*. San Francisco: Jossey-Bass Publishers.

Cohen, L., & Manion, L. (1989). *Research methods in education* (3rd ed.). London, UK: Routledge.

Colli, A. (2012). Contextualizing performances of family firms: The perspective of business history. *Family Business Review*, *25*(3), 243–257. doi:10.1177/0894486511426872

Collins, K., Onwuegbuzie, A., & Sutton, I. L. (2006). A model incorporating the rationale and purpose for conducting mixed methods research in special education and beyond. *Learning Disabilities (Weston, Mass.)*, *4*(1), 67–100.

Collins, P. H. (1998). *Fighting words: Black women and the search for justice*. University of Minnesota Press.

Comrey, A. L. (1980). *Handbook of interpretations for the Comrey Personality scales*. San Diego, CA: EdITS.

Conger, A. J., & Jackson, D. N. (1972). Suppressor variables, prediction, and the interpretation of psychological relationships. *Educational and Psychological Measurement*, *32*(3), 579–599. doi:10.1177/001316447203200303

Connelly, B. S., & Chang, L. (2016). A meta-analytic multitrait multirater separation of substance and style in social desirability scales. *Journal of Personality*, *84*(3), 319–334. doi:10.1111/jopy.12161 PMID:25565409

Cook, T. D., & Campbell, D. T. (1979). *Quasi-experimentation: Design & analysis issues for field settings*. Boston: Houghton Mifflin Company.

Cote, J. A., & Buckley, M. R. (1988). Measurement error and theory testing in consumer research: An illustration of the importance of construct validation. *The Journal of Consumer Research*, *14*(4), 579–582. doi:10.1086/209137

Craig, C., & Huber, J. (2007). Relational reverberations: Shaping and reshaping narrative inquiries in the midst of storied lives and context. In D. J. Clandinin (Ed.), *Handbook of narrative inquiry: Mapping a methodology*. SAGE Publications. doi:10.4135/9781452226552.n10

Crandall, V. C., Crandall, V. J., & Katkovsky, W. (1965). A children's social desirability questionnaire. *Journal of Consulting Psychology*, *29*(1), 27–36. doi:10.1037/h0020966 PMID:14277395

Creswell, J. W., Fetters, M. D., Plano Clark, V. L., & Morales, A. (2009). Chapter 9, Mixed Methods Intervention Trials. In S. Andrew & E. J. Halcomb (Eds.), Mixed Methods Research for Nursing and the Health Sciences. Blackwell Publishing Ltd.

Creswell, J. (2005). *Educational Research: Planning, conducting, and evaluating quantitative and qualitative research*. Pearson Education, Inc.

Creswell, J. W. (1994). *Research design: Qualitative and quantitative approaches*. Thousand Oaks, CA: Sage.

Creswell, J. W. (1998). *Qualitative inquiry and research design: Choosing among five traditions*. London: Sage.

Creswell, J. W. (2003). *Research design: Qualitative, quantitative and mixed methods approaches* (2nd ed.). Thousand Oaks, CA: SAGE Publications.

Creswell, J. W. (2007). *Qualitative Inquiry and Research Design: Choosing among five traditions* (2nd ed.). Thousand Oaks, CA: Sage.

Creswell, J. W. (2009). Editorial: Mapping the field of mixed methods research. *Journal of Mixed Methods Research*, 3(2), 95–108. doi:10.1177/1558689808330883

Creswell, J. W. (2009). *Research design, qualitative, quantitative, and mixed methods approaches* (3rd ed.). London, UK: Sage Publications, Inc.

Creswell, J. W. (2014). *Research design: Qualitative, quantitative, and mixed methods approaches* (4th ed.). Los Angeles, CA: Sage.

Creswell, J. W. (2018). *Research design: Qualitative, quantitative, and mixed methods Approaches* (5th ed.). Thousand Oaks, CA: Sage.

Creswell, J. W., Fetters, M. D., & Ivankova, N. V. (2004). Designing a mixed methods study in primary care. *Annals of Family Medicine*, 2(1), 7–12. doi:10.1370/afm.104 PMID:15053277

Creswell, J. W., Klassen, A. C., Plano Clark, V. L., & Smith, K. C. (2011). *Best practices for mixed methods research in the health sciences*. Bethesda, MD: National Institutes of Health. doi:10.1037/e566732013-001

Creswell, J. W., & Miller, D. L. (2000). Determining validity in qualitative inquiry. *Theory into Practice*, 39(3), 124–130. doi:10.120715430421tip3903_2

Creswell, J. W., & Plano Clark, V. (2007). *Designing and Conducting Mixed Methods Research*. Thousand Oaks, CA: Sage.

Creswell, J. W., & Plano Clark, V. L. (2011). *Designing and conducting mixed methods Research* (2nd ed.). Thousand Oaks, CA: SAGE Publications.

Creswell, J. W., & Plano Clark, V. L. (2011). *Designing and conducting mixed methods research* (2nd ed.). Thousand Oaks, CA: Sage.

Compilation of References

Creswell, J. W., Plano Clark, V. L., Gutmann, M., & Hanson, W. (2003). Advanced mixed methods research designs. In A. Tashakkori & C. Teddlie (Eds.), *Handbook of mixed methods in social & behavioral research* (pp. 209–240). Thousand Oaks, CA: Sage.

Crotty, M. (1998). *The foundations of social research*. Los Angeles, CA: Sage.

Crotty, M. (1998). *The foundations of social research: Meaning and perspective in the research process*. London: Sage Publications.

Crowne, D. P., & Marlowe, D. (1960). A new scale of social desirability independent of psychopathology. *Journal of Consulting Psychology*, *24*(4), 349–354. doi:10.1037/h0047358 PMID:13813058

Crowne, D. P., & Marlowe, D. (1964). *The approval motive*. New York: John Wiley & Sons.

Crutzen, R., & Göritz, A. S. (2010). Social desirability and self-reported health risk behaviors in web-based research: Three longitudinal studies. *BMC Public Health*, *10*(1), 720. doi:10.1186/1471-2458-10-720 PMID:21092267

Daft, R. L. (1983). Learning the craft of organizational research. *Academy of Management Review*, *8*(4), 539–546. doi:10.5465/amr.1983.4284649

Dalton, D. R., Daily, C. M., & Wimbush, J. C. (1997). Collecting" sensitive" data in business ethics research: A case for the unmatched count technique (UCT). *Journal of Business Ethics*, *16*(10), 1049–1057. doi:10.1023/A:1017917904743

Dalton, D. R., Wimbush, J. C., & Daily, C. M. (1994). Using the unmatched count technique (UCT) to estimate base rates for sensitive behavior. *Personnel Psychology*, *47*(4), 817–829. doi:10.1111/j.1744-6570.1994.tb01578.x

Davidsson, P. (2004). *Researching entrepreneurship*. New York: Springer.

De Jong, M. G., Pieters, R., & Fox, J. P. (2010). Reducing social desirability bias through item randomized response: An application to measure underreported desires. *JMR, Journal of Marketing Research*, *47*(1), 14–27. doi:10.1509/jmkr.47.1.14

Delany, C. (2016, January). *How to use the internet to win in 2016: A comprehensive guide for campaigns & advocates (version 4.1)*. Retrieved from Epolitics.com/Winning

Della Porta, D., & Diani, M. (2006). *Social movements: an introduction* (2nd ed.). Malden, MA: Blackwell Publishing.

Denscombe, M. (2008). Communities of practice: A research paradigm for the mixed methods approach. *Journal of Mixed Methods Research*, *2*(3), 270–283. doi:10.1177/1558689808316807

Denzin, N. K. (1989). *The research act* (3rd ed.). Englewood Cliffs, NJ: Prentice Hall.

Denzin, N. K. (1989). *The research act: a theoretical introduction to sociological methods* (2nd ed.). Sage.

Denzin, N. K. (2006). *Sociological methods: a source book* (5th ed.). Chicago: Aldine Publication Company.

Denzin, N. K. (2009). The elephant in the living room: Or extending the conversation about the politics of evidence. *Qualitative Research*, *9*(2), 139–160. doi:10.1177/1468794108098034

Denzin, N. K. (2010). Moments, mixed methods, and paradigm dialogs. *Qualitative Inquiry*, *16*(6), 419–427. doi:10.1177/1077800410364608

Denzin, N. K., & Lincoln, Y. S. (2011). Introduction: The discipline and practice of qualitative research. In N. K. Denzin & Y. S. Lincoln (Eds.), *The SAGE handbook of qualitative research* (4th ed.; pp. 1–19). Thousand Oaks, CA: Sage.

Detrick, P., & Chibnall, J. T. (2008). Positive response distortion by police officer applicants: Association of Paulhus Deception Scales with MMPI-2 and Inwald Personality Inventory Validity scales. *Assessment*, *15*(1), 87–96. doi:10.1177/1073191107306082 PMID:18258735

Dewey, J. (1934). *Art as experience*. New York: Minton, Malach, and Co.

Dewey, J. (1966). *Logic: They theory of inquiry*. New York: Henry Holt.

Digenti, D. (1999). Collaborative Learning: A Core Capability for Organizations in the New Economy. *Reflections: The SoL Journal*, *1*(2), 45–57. doi:10.1162/152417399570160

Dobusch, L., & Schoeneborn, D. (2015). Fluidity, identity, and organizationality: The communicative constitution of Anonymous. *Journal of Management Studies*, *52*(8), 1005–1035. doi:10.1111/joms.12139

Dodaj, A. (2012). Social desirability and self-reports: Testing a content and response-style model of socially desirable responding. *Europe's Journal of Psychology*, *8*(4), 651–666. doi:10.5964/ejop.v8i4.462

Dodou, D., & de Winter, J. C. (2014). Social desirability is the same in offline, online, and paper surveys: A meta-analysis. *Computers in Human Behavior*, *36*, 487–495. doi:10.1016/j.chb.2014.04.005

Dohrenwend, B. S., Colombotos, J., & Dohrenwend, B. P. (1968). Social distance and interviewer effects. *Public Opinion Quarterly*, *32*(3), 410–422. doi:10.1086/267624

Donovan, J., Mills, N., Smith, M., Brindle, L., Jacoby, A., & Peters, T. (2002). Improving design and conduct of randomized trials by embedding them in qualitative research: Protect (prostate testing for cancer and treatment) study. *British Medical Journal*, *325*, 766–769. doi:10.1136/bmj.325.7367.766 PMID:12364308

Doyle, A. B., & Aboud, F. E. (1995). A longitudinal study of White children's racial prejudice as a social-cognitive development. *Merrill-Palmer Quarterly*, *41*, 209–209.

Earl, J., & Garrett, R. K. (2016). The new information frontier: Toward a more nuanced view of social movement communication. *Social Movement Studies*, 1–15.

EBSCO Information Services. (2018). *EBSCO LGBT life with full text*. Retrieved September 10, 2018, from https://www.ebsco.com/products/research-databases/lgbt-life-full-text

Edens, J. F., Buffington, J. K., Tomicic, T. L., & Riley, B. D. (2001). Effects of positive impression management on the Psychopathic Personality Inventory. *Law and Human Behavior*, *25*(3), 235–256. doi:10.1023/A:1010793810896 PMID:11480802

Edwards, A. L. (1957). *The Social Desirability Variable in Personality and Assessment and Research*. Ft Worth, TX: Dryden Press.

Edwards, J. R., & Berry, J. W. (2010). The presence of something or the absence of nothing: Increasing theoretical precision in management research. *Organizational Research Methods*, *13*(4), 668–689. doi:10.1177/1094428110380467

Egloff, B., & Schmukle, S. C. (2002). Predictive validity of an implicit association test for assessing anxiety. *Journal of Personality and Social Psychology*, *83*(6), 1441–1455. doi:10.1037/0022-3514.83.6.1441 PMID:12500823

Eisner, E. W. (1991). *The enlightened eye: Qualitative inquiry and the enhancement of educational practice*. New York: Macmillan.

Elo, S., Kaarlainen, M., Kanste, O., Polkki, T., Utriainen, K., & Kyngas, H. (2014, January-March). Qualitative content analysis: A focus on trustworthiness. *SAGE Open*, 1–10. doi:10.1177/2158244014522633

Emmanuel, A. (2018). *Chicago releases school ratings: Few make the top tiers*. Retrieved from:https://chalkbeat.org/posts/chicago/2018/10/26/chicago-releases-school-ratings-fewer-make-the-top-tiers/

Eysenck, H. J., & Eysenck, S. B. G. (1964). *The manual of the Eysenck Personality Inventory*. London: Univ. of London Press.

Fabrigar, L. R., Wegener, D. T., MacCallum, R. C., & Strahan, E. J. (1999). Evaluating the use of exploratory factor analysis in psychological research. *Psychological Methods*, *4*(3), 272–299. doi:10.1037/1082-989X.4.3.272

Faul, F., Erdfelder, E., Lang, A.-G., & Buchner, A. (2007). G*Power 3: A flexible statistical power analysis program for the social, behavioral, and biomedical sciences. *Behavior Research Methods*, *39*(2), 175–191. doi:10.3758/BF03193146 PMID:17695343

Feilzer, M. Y. (2010). Doing mixed methods research pragmatically: Implications for the rediscovery of pragmatism as a research paradigm. *Journal of Mixed Methods Research*, *4*(1), 6–16. doi:10.1177/1558689809349691

Fetters, M. D., Curry, L. A., & Creswell, J. W. (2013). Achieving integration in mixed methods designs—Principles and practices. *Health Services Research*, *48*(6pt2), 2134–2156. doi:10.1111/1475-6773.12117 PMID:24279835

Feuer, M. J., Towne, L., & Shavelson, R. J. (2002). Scientific culture and educational research. *Educational Researcher*, *31*(8), 4–14. doi:10.3102/0013189X031008004

Fielding, N. G. (2012). Triangulation and mixed methods designs: Data integration with new research technologies. *Journal of Mixed Methods Research*, *6*(2), 124–136. doi:10.1177/1558689812437101

Fielding, N. G., & Fielding, J. L. (1986). *Linking data: the articulation of qualitative and quantitative methods in social research*. Beverly Hills, CA: SAGE. doi:10.4135/9781412984775

Fine, M. (1994). Working the hyphens: Reinventing self and other in qualitative research. In N. R. Denzin & Y. S. Lincoln (Eds.), *Handbook of qualitative research* (pp. 70–82). Thousand Oaks, CA: Sage.

Finlay, L. (2002). "Outing" the researcher: The provenance, process, and practice of reflexivity. *Qualitative Health Research*, *12*(4), 531–545. doi:10.1177/104973202129120052 PMID:11939252

Fisher, R. J. (1993). Social desirability bias and the validity of indirect questioning. *The Journal of Consumer Research*, *20*(2), 303–315. doi:10.1086/209351

Fisher, R. J. (2000). The future of social-desirability bias research in marketing. *Psychology and Marketing*, *17*(2), 73–77. doi:10.1002/(SICI)1520-6793(200002)17:2<73::AID-MAR1>3.0.CO;2-L

Fisher, R. J., & Katz, J. E. (2000). Social-desirability bias and the validity of self-reported values. *Psychology and Marketing*, *17*(2), 105–120. doi:10.1002/(SICI)1520-6793(200002)17:2<105::AID-MAR3>3.0.CO;2-9

Flick, U. (1992). Triangulation revisited: Strategy of validation or alternative? *Journal for the Theory of Social Behaviour*, *22*(2), 175–197. doi:10.1111/j.1468-5914.1992.tb00215.x

Foucault, M. (1980). Power/knowledge. In C. Gordon (Ed.), *Selected interviews and other writings 1972-1977* (p. 153). Pantheon Books.

Foucault, M. (1990). The history of sexuality: Vol. I. *An introduction*. New York: Vintage.

Foucault, M. (1991). *Discipline and Punish: the birth of a prison*. London: Penguin.

Fowler, F. J. Jr, & Mangione, T. W. (1990). *Standardized survey interviewing: Minimizing interviewer-related error* (Vol. 18). Newbury Park, CA: Sage Publications. doi:10.4135/9781412985925

Freeman, M., deMarrais, K., Preissle, J., Roulston, K., & St. Pierre, E. A. (2007). Standards of evidence in qualitative research: An incitement to discourse. *Educational Researcher*, *36*(1), 25–32. doi:10.3102/0013189X06298009

Fulton, B. S. (2013). Outserve: An underground network stands up. *Journal of Homosexuality*, *60*(2–3), 219–231. doi:10.1080/00918369.2013.744668 PMID:23414270

Fusch, P., Fusch, G. E., & Ness, L. R. (2018). Denzin's paradigm shift: Revisiting triangulation in qualitative research. *Journal of Social Change*, *10*(1), 19–32.

Gainous, J., & Wagner, K. M. (2013). *Tweeting to power: the social media revolution in American politics*. Oxford University Press. doi:10.1093/acprof:oso/9780199965076.001.0001

Ganster, D. C., Hennessey, H. W., & Luthans, F. (1983). Social desirability response effects: Three alternative models. *Academy of Management Journal*, *26*(2), 321–331.

Garrett, R. K., Bimber, B., de Zuniga, H. G., Heinderyckx, F., Kelly, J., & Smith, M. (2012). New ICTs and the study of political communication. *International Journal of Communication*, *6*, 214–231.

Gee, J. P. (2012). *Social linguistics and literacies: Ideology in discourses* (4th ed.). New York: Routledge.

Geertz, C. (1973). Thick Description: Toward an interpretive theory of culture. In C. Geertz (Ed.), *The Interpretation of Cultures* (pp. 3–30). New York: Basic Books.

Gerbaudo, P. (2018). *Tweets and the streets: Social media and contemporary activism*. Retrieved from http://tacticalmediafiles.net/mmbase/attachments/5000/Tweets__the_Streets_Introduction.pdf

Gerty, J. L. M., Hox, J. J., & Heijden, P. (2005). Meta-analysis of randomized reponse research: 35 years of validation studies. *Sociological Methods & Research*, *33*(3), 319–348. doi:10.1177/0049124104268664

Giddings, L. S. (2006). Mixed-methods research: Positivism dressed in drag? *Journal of Research in Nursing*, *11*(3), 195–203. doi:10.1177/1744987106064635

Gittelman, S., Lange, V., Cook, W. A., Frede, S. M., Lavrakas, P. J., Pierce, C., & Thomas, R. K. (2015). Accounting for social-desirability bias in survey sampling: A model for predicting and calibrating the direction and magnitude of social-desirability bias. *Journal of Advertising Research*, *55*(3), 242–254. doi:10.2501/JAR-2015-006

Gladwell, M. (2010). Small change: Why the revolution will not be tweeted. *The New Yorker*, *4*(2010), 42–49.

Glaser, B. G., & Strauss, A. L. (1967). *The discovery of grounded theory: Strategies for qualitative research*. Chicago, IL: Aldine Publishing Company.

Golafshani, N. (2003). Understanding reliability and validity in qualitative research. *Qualitative Report*, *8*(4), 597–607.

Gordon, E. T., Gordon, E. W., & Nembhard, J. G. G. (1994, Autumn). Social science literature concerning African American men. *The Journal of Negro Education*, *63*(4), 508–531. doi:10.2307/2967292

Gordon, E. W. (1999). The experiences of African American males in school and society. In V. C. Polite & J. E. Davis (Eds.), *African American males in school and society*. Teachers College Press.

Gough, H. G. (1957). *Manual for the California Psychological Inventory*. Palo Alto, CA: Consulting Pschologists Press.

Graue, M. E., & Walsh, D. (2012). *Studying children in context: Theories, methods, and ethics*. SAGE Publications.

Greene, J. C. (2007). *Mixed methods in social inquiry*. John Wiley & Sons.

Greene, J. C. (2007). *Mixing methods in social inquiry*. San Francisco: Jossey-Bass.

Greene, J. C., & Caracelli, V. J. (1997). Defining and describing the paradigm issue in mixed-method evaluation. In J. C. Green & V. J. Caracelli (Eds.), *Advances in Mixed-Method Evaluation: The Challenges and Benefits of Integrating Diverse Paradigms* (pp. 5–18). San Francisco: Jossey-Bass. doi:10.1002/ev.1068

Greene, J. C., Caracelli, V. J., & Graham, W. F. (1989). Toward a conceptual framework for mixed method evaluation designs. *Educational Evaluation and Policy Analysis*, *11*(3), 255–274. doi:10.3102/01623737011003255

Greenwald, A. G., Poehlman, T. A., Uhlmann, E. L., & Banaji, M. R. (2009). Understanding and using the Implicit Association Test: III. Meta-analysis of predictive validity. *Journal of Personality and Social Psychology*, *97*(1), 17–41. doi:10.1037/a0015575 PMID:19586237

Greenwald, H. J., & Satow, Y. (1970). A short social desirability scale. *Psychological Reports*, *27*(1), 131–135. doi:10.2466/pr0.1970.27.1.131

Grimm, P., (2010). Social desirability bias. *Wiley International Encyclopedia of Marketing*.

Guba, E. C. (1990). The alternative paradigm dialogue. In E. C. Guba (Ed.), *The Paradigm Dialogue* (pp. 17–27). Newbury Park, CA: Sage.

Guba, E. G., & Lincoln, Y. S. (1989). *Fourth Generation Evaluation*. Newbury Park, CA: Sage.

Guest, G., Namey, E. E., & Mitchell, M. L. (2012). Collecting qualitative data: A field manual for applied research. *Sage (Atlanta, Ga.)*.

Hammersley, M. (2002). *Educational research, policymaking and practice*. London: Sage. doi:10.4135/9781849209083

Hancock, D. R., & Flowers, C. P. (2001). Comparing social desirability responding on World Wide Web and paper-administered surveys. *Educational Technology Research and Development*, *49*(1), 5–13. doi:10.1007/BF02504503

Hardesty, D. M., & Bearden, W. O. (2004). The use of expert judges in scale development: Implications for improving face validity of measures of unobservable constructs. *Journal of Business Research*, *57*(2), 98–107. doi:10.1016/S0148-2963(01)00295-8

Harfoush, R. (2009). *Yes we did! An inside look at how social media built the Obama brand*. New Riders.

Hartley, S., & Muhit, M. (2003). Using Qualitative Research Methods for Disability Research in Majority World Countries. *Asia Pacific Disability Rehabilitation Journal*, *103*(14).

Hathaway, S. R., & McKinley, J. C. (1951). *MMPI Manual*. New York: Psychological Corporation.

Hayashi, P., Abib, G., & Hoppen, N. (2019). Validity in qualitative research: A processual approach. *Qualitative Report*, *24*(24), 98–112.

Hays, D. G., & Singh, A. A. (2012). *Qualitative inquiry in clinical and educational settings*. New York, NY: The Guilford Press.

Hebert, J. R., Clemow, L., Pbert, L., Ockene, I. S., & Ockene, J. K. (1995). Social desirability bias in dietary self-report may compromise the validity of dietary intake measures. *International Journal of Epidemiology*, *24*(2), 389–398. doi:10.1093/ije/24.2.389 PMID:7635601

Heerwegh, D. (2009). Mode differences between face-to-face and web surveys: An experimental investigation of data quality and social desirability effects. *International Journal of Public Opinion Research*, *21*(1), 111–121. doi:10.1093/ijpor/edn054

Holbrook, A. L., Green, M. C., & Krosnick, J. A. (2003). Telephone versus face-to-face interviewing of national probability samples with long questionnaires: Comparisons of respondent satisficing and social desirability response bias. *Public Opinion Quarterly*, *67*(1), 79–125. doi:10.1086/346010

Holden, R. R., & Fekken, G. C. (2017). Balanced Inventory of Desirable Responding. Encyclopedia of personality and individual differences, 1-4.

Holden, R. R., & Kroner, D. G. (1992). Relative efficacy of differential response latencies for detecting faking on a self-report measure of psychopathology. *Psychological Assessment*, *4*(2), 170–173. doi:10.1037/1040-3590.4.2.170

Holden, R. R., Kroner, D. G., Fekken, G. C., & Popham, S. M. (1992). A model of personality test item response dissimulation. *Journal of Personality and Social Psychology*, *63*(2), 272–279. doi:10.1037/0022-3514.63.2.272

Holden, R. R., & Lambert, C. E. (2015). Response latencies are alive and well for identifying fakers on a self-report personality inventory: A reconsideration of van Hooft and Born (2012). *Behavior Research Methods*, *47*(4), 1436–1442. doi:10.375813428-014-0524-5 PMID:25381021

Holden, R. R., Starzyk, K. B., McLeod, L. D., & Edwards, M. J. (2000). Comparisons among the holden psychological screening inventory (HPSI), the brief symptom inventory (BSI), and the balanced inventory of desirable responding (BIDR). *Assessment*, *7*(2), 163–175. doi:10.1177/107319110000700208 PMID:10868254

Holtgraves, T. (2004). Social desirability and self-reports: Testing models of socially desirable responding. *Personality and Social Psychology Bulletin*, *30*(2), 161–172. doi:10.1177/0146167203259930 PMID:15030631

Hopper, R. D. (1950). A frame of reference for the study of revolutionary movements. *Social Forces*, *28*(3), 270–279. doi:10.2307/2572010

Hopper, T., & Hoque, Z. (2006). Triangulation approaches to accounting research. In Z. Hoque (Ed.), *Methodological issues in accounting research: theories, methods and issues* (pp. 562–569). London: Spiramus Press.

Hoque, Z., Covaleski, M. A., & Gooneratne, T. N. (2013). Theoretical triangulation and pluralism in research methods in organizational and accounting research. *Accounting, Auditing & Accountability Journal, 26*(7), 1170–1198. doi:10.1108/AAAJ-May-2012-01024

Howe, K. R. (1988). Against the quantitative-qualitative incompatibility thesis or dogmas die hard. *Educational Researcher, 17*(8), 10-16.

Hox, J., De Leeuw, E., Couper, M. P., Groves, R. M., De Heer, W., & Kuusela, V. (2002). The influence of interviewers' attitude and behavior on household survey nonresponse: An international comparison. *Survey Nonresponse*, 103-120.

Hubbard, R., & Lindsay, R. M. (2013). From significant difference to significant sameness: Proposing a paradigm shift in business research. *Journal of Business Research, 66*(9), 1377–1388. doi:10.1016/j.jbusres.2012.05.002

Hult, G. T. M., Keillor, B. D., & Lafferty, B. A. (1999). A cross-national assessment of social desirability bias and consumer ethnocentrism. *Journal of Global Marketing, 12*(4), 29–43. doi:10.1300/J042v12n04_03

Humm, D. G., & Wadsworth, G. W. Jr. (1935). The Humm-Wadsworth temperament scale. *The American Journal of Psychiatry, 92*(1), 163–200. doi:10.1176/ajp.92.1.163 PMID:14838148

Humphreys, M. M. (2013). Daughter succession: A predominance of human issues. *Journal of Family Business Management, 3*(1), 24–44. doi:10.1108/20436231311326472

Hussein, A. (2009). The use of triangulation in social science research: Can qualitative and quantitative methods be combined? *Journal of Comparative Social Work, 1*, 1–12.

Hyman, H. H. (1954). *Interviewing in social research*. Chicago: Chicago University Press.

Ibiamke, A., & Ajekwe, C. C. M. (2017). On ensuring rigour in accounting research. *International Journal of Academic Research in Accounting. Finance and Management Sciences, 7*(3), 157–170.

Ivankova, N. V., Creswell, J. W., & Stick, S. L. (2006). Using mixed-methods sequential explanatory design: From theory to practice. *Field Methods, 18*(1), 3–20. doi:10.1177/1525822X05282260

Jackson, D. N. (1967). *Manual for the personality research form*. University of Western Ontario.

Jackson, D. N. (1996). *Basic Personality Inventory manual* (2nd ed.). London, Canada: Sigma Assessment Systems.

Jackson, D. N., & Messick, S. (1961). Acquiescence and desirability as response determinants on the MMPI. *Educational and Psychological Measurement, 21*(4), 771–790. doi:10.1177/001316446102100402

Compilation of References

Jackson, D. N., Wroblewski, V. R., & Ashton, M. C. (2000). The impact of faking on employment tests: Does forced choice offer a solution? *Human Performance*, *13*(4), 371–388. doi:10.1207/S15327043HUP1304_3

Jacobson, L. I., Kellogg, R. W., Cauce, A. M., & Slavin, R. S. (1977). A multidimensional social desirability inventory. *Bulletin of the Psychonomic Society*, *9*(2), 109–110. doi:10.3758/BF03336944

Jaeger, R. M. (1997). *Complementary Research Methods for Research in Education* (2nd ed.). Washington, DC: American Educational Research Association.

James Cater, J. III, & Beal, B. (2014). Ripple effects on family firms from an externally induced crisis. *Journal of Family Business Management*, *4*(1), 62–78. doi:10.1108/JFBM-02-2013-0006

Janesick, V. J. (2011). *Stretching exercises for qualitative researchers* (3rd ed.). Thousand Oaks, CA: Sage. doi:10.1177/136078041101600402

Jick, T. D. (1979). Mixing qualitative and quantitative methods: Triangulation in action. *Administrative Science Quarterly*, *24*(4), 602–611. doi:10.2307/2392366

Johnson, B., & Gray, R. (2010). A history of philosophical and theoretical issues for mixed methods research. In A. Tashakkori & C. Teddlie (Eds.), *SAGE Handbook of Mixed Methods in Social & Behavioral Research* (2nd ed.; pp. 69–94). Thousand Oaks, CA: Sage. doi:10.4135/9781506335193.n3

Johnson, R. B., & Christensen, L. (2012). *Educational research: Quantitative, qualitative, and mixed approaches* (4th ed.). Thousand Oaks, CA: Sage.

Johnson, R. B., & Onwuegbuzie, A. J. (2004). Mixed methods research: A research paradigm whose time has come. *Educational Researcher*, *33*(7), 14–26. doi:10.3102/0013189X033007014

Johnson, R. B., Onwuegbuzie, A. J., & Turner, L. A. (2007). Toward a definition of mixed methods research. *Journal of Mixed Methods Research*, *1*(2), 112–133. doi:10.1177/1558689806298224

Johnstone, L. P. (2007). Weighing up triangulating and contradictory evidence in mixed methods organizational research. *International Journal of Multiple Research Approaches*, *1*(1), 27–38. doi:10.5172/mra.455.1.1.27

Jo, M. S. (2000). Controlling social-desirability bias via method factors of direct and indirect questioning in structural equation models. *Psychology and Marketing*, *17*(2), 137–148. doi:10.1002/(SICI)1520-6793(200002)17:2<137::AID-MAR5>3.0.CO;2-V

Jo, M. S., Nelson, J., & Kiecker, P. (1997). A model for controlling social desirability bias by direct and indirect questioning. *Marketing Letters*, *8*(4), 429–437. doi:10.1023/A:1007951313872

Jones, E. E., & Sigall, H. (1971). The bogus pipeline: A new paradigm for measuring affect and attitude. *Psychological Bulletin*, *76*(5), 349–364. doi:10.1037/h0031617

Josselson, R. (2007). The ethical attitude in narrative research: principles and practicalities. In D. J. Clandinin (Ed.), *Handbook of narrative inquiry: Mapping a methodology*. Sage Publications. doi:10.4135/9781452226552.n21

Kahn, R., & Kellner, D. (2004). New media and internet activism: From the 'Battle of Seattle' to blogging. *New Media & Society*, *6*(1), 87–95. doi:10.1177/1461444804039908

Kam, C., Risavy, S. D., & Perunovic, W. E. (2015). Using Over-Claiming Technique to probe social desirability ratings of personality items: A validity examination. *Personality and Individual Differences*, *74*, 177–181. doi:10.1016/j.paid.2014.10.017

Kaplan, A. M., & Haenlein, M. (2010). Users of the world, unite! The challenges and opportunities of social media. *Business Horizons*, *53*(1), 59–68. doi:10.1016/j.bushor.2009.09.003

Keillor, B. D., Owens, D., & Pettijohn, C. (2001). A Cross—Cultural/cross national Study of Influencing Factors and Socially Desirable Response Biases. *International Journal of Market Research*, *43*(1), 1–19. doi:10.1177/147078530104300101

Kepes, S., Bennett, A. A., & McDaniel, M. A. (2014). Evidence-based management and the trustworthiness of our cumulative scientific knowledge: Implications for teaching, research, and practice. *Academy of Management Learning & Education*, *13*(3), 446–466. doi:10.5465/amle.2013.0193

Kiersz, A. (2018). *Every U.S. state ranked from worst to best*. Retrieved from: https://www.businessinsider.com/state-economy-ranking-q1-2018-2#36-illinois-16

King, M. F., & Bruner, G. C. (2000). Social desirability bias: A neglected aspect of validity testing. *Psychology and Marketing*, *17*(2), 79–103. doi:10.1002/(SICI)1520-6793(200002)17:2<79::AID-MAR2>3.0.CO;2-0

Klassen, A. C., Creswell, J., Clark, V. L. P., Smith, K. C., & Meissner, H. I. (2012). Best practices in mixed methods for quality of life research. *Quality of Life Research: An International Journal of Quality of Life Aspects of Treatment, Care and Rehabilitation*, *21*(3), 377–380. doi:10.100711136-012-0122-x PMID:22311251

Knoll, B. R. (2013). Assessing the effect of social desirability on nativism attitude responses. *Social Science Research*, *42*(6), 1587–1598. doi:10.1016/j.ssresearch.2013.07.012 PMID:24090853

Koro-Ljungberg, M. (2008). Validity and validation in the making in the context of qualitative research. *Qualitative Health Research*, *18*(7), 983–989. doi:10.1177/1049732308318039 PMID:18552324

Kozol, J. (1991). *Savage Inequalities*. New York, NY: Crown Publishers.

Krauss, S. E. (2005). Research paradigms and meaning making: A primer. *Qualitative Report*, *10*(4), 758–770.

Compilation of References

Kroner, D. G., & Weekes, J. R. (1996). Balanced Inventory of Desirable Responding: Factor structure, reliability, and validity with an offender sample. *Personality and Individual Differences*, *21*(3), 323–333. doi:10.1016/0191-8869(96)00079-7

Krumpal, I. (2013). Determinants of social desirability bias in sensitive surveys: A literature review. *Quality & Quantity*, *47*(4), 2025–2047. doi:10.100711135-011-9640-9

Kuhn, T. S. (1962). *The structure of scientific revolutions*. Chicago: The University of Chicago Press.

Kuklinski, J. H., Sniderman, P. M., Knight, K., Piazza, T., Tetlock, P. E., Lawrence, G. R., & Mellers, B. (1997). Racial prejudice and attitudes toward affirmative action. *American Journal of Political Science*, *41*(2), 402–419. doi:10.2307/2111770

Lajunen, T., & Summala, H. (2003). Can we trust self-reports of driving? Effects of impression management on driver behaviour questionnaire responses. *Transportation Research Part F: Traffic Psychology and Behaviour*, *6*(2), 97–107. doi:10.1016/S1369-8478(03)00008-1

Lalwani, A. K., Shavitt, S., & Johnson, T. (2006). What is the relation between cultural orientation and socially desirable responding? *Journal of Personality and Social Psychology*, *90*(1), 165–178. doi:10.1037/0022-3514.90.1.165 PMID:16448316

Lanyon, R. I., & Carle, A. C. (2007). Internal and external validity of scores on the Balanced Inventory of Desirable Responding and the Paulhus Deception Scales. *Educational and Psychological Measurement*, *67*(5), 859–876. doi:10.1177/0013164406299104

Larsen, K. S., Martin, H. J., Ettinger, R. H., & Nelson, J. (1976). Approval seeking, social cost, and aggression: A scale and some dynamics. *The Journal of Psychology*, *94*(1), 3–11. doi:10.1080/00223980.1976.9921389

Lather, P. (2001). Validity as an incitement to discourse: Qualitative research and the crisis of legitimation. In V. Richardson (Ed.), *Handbook of research on teaching* (4th ed.; pp. 241–250). Washington, DC: American Educational Research Association.

Lather, P. (2004). This *IS* your father's paradigm: Government intrusion and the case of qualitative research in education. *Qualitative Inquiry*, *10*(1), 15–34. doi:10.1177/1077800403256154

Lather, P. (2007). Validity, Qualitative. In G. Ritzer (Ed.), *The Blackwell Encyclopedia of Sociology* (pp. 5169–5173). Malden, MA: Blackwell Publishing. doi:10.1002/9781405165518.wbeosv001

Lautenschlager, G. J., & Flaherty, V. L. (1990). Computer administration of questions: More desirable or more social desirability? *The Journal of Applied Psychology*, *75*(3), 310–314. doi:10.1037/0021-9010.75.3.310

Lave, C. A., & March, J. G. (1993). *An introduction to models in the social sciences*. Lanham, MD: University Press of America, Inc.

Lave, J., & Wenger, E. (1991). *Situated learning: Legitimate peripheral participation*. Cambridge, UK: Cambridge University Press. doi:10.1017/CBO9780511815355

Leech, N. L., & Onwuegbuzie, A. J. (2009). A typology of mixed methods research designs. *Quality & Quantity*, *43*(2), 265–275. doi:10.100711135-007-9105-3

Leech, N. L., & Onwuegbuzie, A. J. (2010). Guidelines for conducting and reporting mixed research in the field of counseling and beyond. *Journal of Counseling and Development*, *88*(1), 61–69. doi:10.1002/j.1556-6678.2010.tb00151.x

Leedy, P. D., & Ormrod, J. E. (2013). *Practical research: Planning and design* (10th ed.). Boston: Pearson.

Leedy, P., & Ormrod, J. (2010). *Practical research: planning and design* (9th ed.). Boston, MA: Pearson.

Lee, R. M. (1993). *Doing research on sensitive topics*. London: Sage Publications.

Lee, Z., & Sargeant, A. (2011). Dealing with social desirability bias: An application to charitable giving. *European Journal of Marketing*, *45*(5), 703–719. doi:10.1108/03090561111119994

Leite, W. L., & Beretvas, S. N. (2005). Validation of scores on the Marlowe-Crowne social desirability scale and the balanced inventory of desirable responding. *Educational and Psychological Measurement*, *65*(1), 140–154. doi:10.1177/0013164404267285

Leite, W. L., & Cooper, L. A. (2010). Detecting social desirability bias using factor mixture models. *Multivariate Behavioral Research*, *45*(2), 271–293. doi:10.1080/00273171003680245 PMID:26760286

Lelkes, Y., Krosnick, J. A., Marx, D. M., Judd, C. M., & Park, B. (2012). Complete anonymity compromises the accuracy of self-reports. *Journal of Experimental Social Psychology*, *48*(6), 1291–1299. doi:10.1016/j.jesp.2012.07.002

Lester, J. N., & O'Reilly, M. (2015). Is evidence-based practice a threat to the progress of the qualitative community? Arguments from the bottom of the pyramid. *Qualitative Inquiry*, *21*(7), 628–632. doi:10.1177/1077800414563808

Lewis, K., Gray, K., & Meierhenrich, J. (2014). The structure of online activism. *Sociological Science*, 1–9. doi:10.15195/v1.a1

LexisNexis. (2018, September 10). *LexisNexis academic*. Retrieved September 10, 2018, from LexisNexis website: http://www.lexisnexis.com/hottopics/lnacademic

Li, A., & Bagger, J. (2007). The Balanced inventory of desirable responding (BIDR) a reliability generalization study. *Educational and Psychological Measurement*, *67*(3), 525–544. doi:10.1177/0013164406292087

Lievrouw, L. (2011). *Alternative and activist new media* (1st ed.). Cambridge, UK: Polity.

Lincoln, Y. (2001). Varieties of validity: quality in qualitative research. In J. Smart (Ed.), *Higher education: handbook of theory and research* (Vol. 16). New York, NY: Agathon Press.

Compilation of References

Lincoln, Y. S. (1995). Emerging criteria for quality in qualitative and interpretive research. *Qualitative Inquiry*, *1*(3), 275–289. doi:10.1177/107780049500100301

Lincoln, Y. S. (2001). Varieties of validity: Quality in qualitative research. In J. C. Smart & W. G. Tierney (Eds.), *Higher Education: Handbook of Theory and Research* (pp. 25–72). New York: Agathon Press.

Lincoln, Y. S., & Guba, E. G. (1985). *Naturalistic Inquiry*. Newbury Park, CA: Sage. doi:10.1016/0147-1767(85)90062-8

Litwin, M. S. (2003). *How to assess and interpret survey psychometrics* (2nd ed.). Thousand Oaks, CA: Sage. doi:10.4135/9781412984409

Lodico, M. G., Spaulding, D. T., & Voegtle, K. H. (2010). *Methods in educational research: From theory to practice* (Vol. 28). John Wiley & Sons.

Lönnqvist, J. E., Paunonen, S., Tuulio-Henriksson, A., Lönnqvist, J., & Verkasalo, M. (2007). Substance and style in socially desirable responding. *Journal of Personality*, *75*(2), 291–322. doi:10.1111/j.1467-6494.2006.00440.x PMID:17359240

Lubke, G. H., & Muthén, B. (2005). Investigating population heterogeneity with factor mixture models. *Psychological Methods*, *10*(1), 21–39. doi:10.1037/1082-989X.10.1.21 PMID:15810867

Ludeke, S. G., & Makransky, G. (2016). Does the Over-Claiming Questionnaire measure overclaiming? Absent convergent validity in a large community sample. *Psychological Assessment*, *28*(6), 765–774. doi:10.1037/pas0000211 PMID:26372263

Macionis, J. J. (2001). *Sociology* (8th ed.). Upper Saddle River, NJ: Prentice Hall.

Maddow, R. (2010, October 13). *The Rachel Maddow Show*. MSNBC.

Malhotra, N. K. (2004). *Marketing Research: an Applied Orientation* (4th ed.). London: Prentice-Hall International.

Marin, A., & Wellman, B. (2011). Social network analysis: an introduction. The SAGE Handbook of Social Network Analysis, 11.

Mark, M. M., Feller, I., & Button, S. B. (1997). Integrating qualitative methods in a predominantly quantitative evaluation: a case study and some reflections. In J. Green & V. Caracelli (Eds.), Advances in mixed-methods evaluation. New directions for evaluations. San Francisco, CA: Jossey-Bass Publishers. doi:10.1002/ev.1071

Mashey, J. R. (1998). *Big data and the next wave of InfraStress* [PDF PowerPoint slides]. Retrieved from http://static.usenix.org/event/usenix99/invited_talks/mashey.pdf

Maxcy, S. J. (2003). Pragmatic threads in mixed methods research in the social sciences: The search for multiple modes of inquiry and the end of the philosophy of formalism. In A. Tashakkori & C. Teddlie (Eds.), *Handbook of Mixed Methods in Social & Behavioral Research* (pp. 51–90). Thousand Oaks, CA: Sage.

Maxwell, J. A. (2013). *Qualitative research design: An interactive approach* (3rd ed.). Thousand Oaks, CA: Sage.

Maxwell, J. A., & Loomis, D. M. (2003). Mixed methods design: An alternative approach. In A. Tashakkori & C. Teddlie (Eds.), *Handbook of Mixed Methods in Social & Behavioral Research* (pp. 241–271). Thousand Oaks, CA: Sage.

Maxwell, J. A., & Mittapalli, K. (2010). Realism as a stance for mixed methods research. In A. Tashakkori & C. Teddlie (Eds.), *SAGE Handbook of Mixed Methods in Social & Behavioral Research* (2nd ed.; pp. 145–162). Thousand Oaks, CA: Sage. doi:10.4135/9781506335193.n6

McCall, G. J., & Simmons, J. L. (1966). *Identities and Interactions*. New York: Free Press.

McGawley, J. (1982). *Thirty million theories of grammar*. Chicago: University of Chicago Press.

Meehl, P. E., & Hathaway, S. R. (1946). The K factor as a suppressor variable in the Minnesota Multiphasic Personality Inventory. *The Journal of Applied Psychology*, *30*(5), 525–564. doi:10.1037/h0053634 PMID:20282179

Melluci, A. (1995). The Process of Collective Identity. In H. Johnston & B. Klandermans (Eds.), *Social Movements and Culture* (pp. 41–63). Minneapolis, MN: University of Minnesota Press.

Meneses, R., Coutinho, R., & Carlos Pinho, J. (2014). The impact of succession on family business internationalisation: The successors' perspective. *Journal of Family Business Management*, *4*(1), 24–45. doi:10.1108/JFBM-01-2013-0004

Merriam, S. B. (2009). *Qualitative research: A guide to design and implementation* (3rd ed.). San Francisco: Jossey-Bass.

Mertens, D. M. (2010). *Research and evaluation in education and psychology: Integrating diversity with quantitative, qualitative, and mixed methods* (3rd ed.). Thousand Oaks, CA: Sage.

Mesmer-Magnus, J., Viswesvaran, C., Deshpande, S., & Joseph, J. (2006). Social desirability: The role of over-claiming, self-esteem, and emotional intelligence. *Psychological Science*, *48*(3), 336–356.

Messick, S. (1960). Dimensions of social desirability. *Journal of Consulting Psychology*, *24*(4), 279–287. doi:10.1037/h0044153

Mick, D. G. (1996). Are studies of dark side variables confounded by socially desirable responding? The case of materialism. *The Journal of Consumer Research*, *23*(2), 106–119. doi:10.1086/209470

Miles, M. B., Huberman, A. M., & Saldaña, J. (2013). Qualitative data analysis: a methods sourcebook (3rd ed.). Thousand Oaks, CA: SAGE Publications, Inc.

Miles, M. B., & Huberman, A. M. (1994). *Qualitative data analysis: An expanded sourcebook* (2nd ed.). Thousand Oaks, CA: SAGE Publications.

Milfont, T. L. (2009). The effects of social desirability on self-reported environmental attitudes and ecological behaviour. *The Environmentalist*, *29*(3), 263–269. doi:10.100710669-008-9192-2

Compilation of References

Miller, F. (1999). The end of SDS and the emergence of weatherman: demise through success. In J. Freeman & V. Johnson (Eds.), *Waves of protest : social movements since the sixties*. Lanham, MD: Rowman & Littlefield Publishers.

Mills, G. E., & Gay, L. R. (2015). *Educational research: Competencies for analysis and applications* (11th ed.). Boston: Pearson.

Mishler, E. G. (1990). Validation in inquiry-guided research: The role of exemplars in narrative studies. *Harvard Educational Review*, *60*(4), 415–442. doi:10.17763/haer.60.4.n4405243p6635752

Mitchell, M. L., & Jolley, J. M. (2010). *Research design explained* (7th ed.). Belmont, CA: Wadsworth.

Modell, S. (2009). In defence of triangulation: A critical realist approach to mixed methods research in management accounting. *Management Accounting Research*, *20*(3), 208–221. doi:10.1016/j.mar.2009.04.001

Modell, S. (2015). Theoretical triangulation and pluralism in accounting research: A critical realist critique. *Accounting, Auditing & Accountability Journal*, *28*(7), 1138–1150. doi:10.1108/AAAJ-10-2014-1841

Morf, M. E., & Jackson, D. N. (1972). An Analysis of Two Response Styles: True Responding and Item Endorsement 1. *Educational and Psychological Measurement*, *32*(2), 329–353. doi:10.1177/001316447203200210

Morgan, D. L. (1998). Practical Strategies for combining quantitative and qualitative methods: Applications for health research. *Qualitative Health Research*, *8*(3), 362–376. doi:10.1177/104973239800800307 PMID:10558337

Morgan, D. L. (2007). Paradigms lost and pragmatism regained: Methodological implications of combining qualitative and quantitative methods. *Journal of Mixed Methods Research*, *1*(1), 48–76. doi:10.1177/2345678906292462

Morgan, G., & Smircich, L. (1980). The case for qualitative research. *Academy of Management Review*, *5*(4), 491–500. doi:10.5465/amr.1980.4288947

Morozov, E. (2011). *The net delusion: The dark side of internet freedom*. New York: PublicAffairs.

Morse, J. (1991). Approaches to qualitative-quantitative methodological triangulation. *Nursing Research*, *40*(2), 120–123. doi:10.1097/00006199-199103000-00014 PMID:2003072

Morse, J. M., Barrett, M., Mayan, M., Olson, K., & Spiers, J. (2002). Verification strategies for establishing reliability and validity in qualitative research. *International Journal of Qualitative Methods*, *1*(2), 13–22. doi:10.1177/160940690200100202

Mosteller, F., & Boruch, R. F. (2002). *Evidence matters: Randomized trials in education research*. Washington, DC: Brookings Institution Press.

Mucciaroni, G. (2011). The study of LGBT politics and its contributions to political science. *PS, Political Science & Politics*, *44*(01), 17–21. doi:10.1017/S1049096510001782

Mühlenfeld, H. U. (2005). Differences between talking about and admitting sensitive behaviour in anonymous and non-anonymous web-based interviews. *Computers in Human Behavior*, *21*(6), 993–1003. doi:10.1016/j.chb.2004.02.023

Näher, A. F., & Krumpal, I. (2012). Asking sensitive questions: The impact of forgiving wording and question context on social desirability bias. *Quality & Quantity*, *46*(5), 1601–1616. doi:10.100711135-011-9469-2

National Center for Educational Statistics. (2019). *College navigator*. Retrieved from: https://nces.ed.gov/collegenavigator/?q=East+West+University&s=all&id=144883#expenses

National Child Care Information Center. (2011). *Qualitative research assessment tool*. Available From: http://www.researchconnections.org/childcare/datamethods/downloads/qualitativeresearchassesstool.pdf

Nederhof, A. J. (1985). Methods of coping with social desirability bias: A review. *European Journal of Social Psychology*, *15*(3), 263–280. doi:10.1002/ejsp.2420150303

New York University. (n.d.). *What is Research Design? The Context of Design*. Retrieved from http://www.nyu.edu/classes/bkg/methods/005847ch1.pdf

Newman, I., Ridenour, C. S., Newman, C., & Demarco, G. M. P., Jr. (2003). A typology of research purposes and its relationship to mixed methods. In A. Tashakkori & C. Teddlie (Eds.), Handbook of mixed methods in social and behavioral research (pp. 167-188). Academic Press.

Norwood, F. B., & Lusk, J. L. (2011). Social desirability bias in real, hypothetical, and inferred valuation experiments. *American Journal of Agricultural Economics*, *93*(2), 528–534.

O'Boyle, E. H. Jr, Rutherford, M. W., & Banks, G. C. (2014). Publication bias in entrepreneurship research: An examination of dominant relations to performance. *Journal of Business Venturing*, *29*(6), 773–784. doi:10.1016/j.jbusvent.2013.10.001

O'Donoghue, T., & Punck, K. (2003). *Qualitative educational research in action: doing and reflecting*. London: Falmer Press. doi:10.4324/9780203506301

Obar, J. A., & Wildman, S. S. (2015). *Social media definition and the governance challenge: an introduction to the special issue* (SSRN Scholarly Paper No. ID 2647377). Retrieved from Social Science Research Network website: https://papers.ssrn.com/abstract=2647377

Obar, J. A., Zube, P., & Lampe, C. (2012). Advocacy 2.0: An analysis of how advocacy groups in the United States perceive and use social media as tools for facilitating civic engagement and collective action. *Journal of Information Policy*, *2*, 1–25. doi:10.5325/jinfopoli.2.2012.0001

Olsen, W. (2004). Triangulation in social research: qualitative and quantitative methods can really be mixed. In M. Holborn (Ed.), Development in sociology. Causeway Press.

Ones, D. S., Viswesvaran, C., & Reiss, A. D. (1996). Role of social desirability in personality testing for personnel selection: The red herring. *The Journal of Applied Psychology*, *81*(6), 660–679. doi:10.1037/0021-9010.81.6.660

Ong, A. D., & Weiss, D. J. (2000). The impact of anonymity on responses to sensitive questions 1. *Journal of Applied Social Psychology*, *30*(8), 1691–1708. doi:10.1111/j.1559-1816.2000.tb02462.x

Onuch, O. (2015a). Euromaidan protests in Ukraine: Social media versus social networks. *Problems of Post-Communism*, *62*(4), 217–235. doi:10.1080/10758216.2015.1037676

Onuch, O. (2015b). Facebook helped me do it': Understanding the euromaidan protester 'tool-kit. *Studies in Ethnicity and Nationalism*, *15*(1), 170–184. doi:10.1111ena.12129

Onwuegbuzie, A. J., & Collins, K. M. (2007). A typology of mixed methods sampling designs in social science research. *Qualitative Report*, *12*(2), 281–316.

Onwuegbuzie, A. J., Collins, K. M., & Frels, R. K. (2013). Foreword: Using Bronfenbrenner's ecological systems theory to frame quantitative, qualitative, and mixed research. *International Journal of Multiple Research Approaches*, *7*(1), 2–8. doi:10.5172/mra.2013.7.1.2

Onwuegbuzie, A. J., & Corrigan, J. A. (2014). Improving the quality of mixed research reports in the field of human resource development and beyond: A call for rigor as an ethical Practice. *Human Resource Development Quarterly*, *25*(3), 273–299. doi:10.1002/hrdq.21197

Onwuegbuzie, A. J., & Leech, N. L. (2006). Linking research questions to mixed methods data analysis procedures. *Qualitative Report*, *11*(3), 474–498.

Onwuegbuzie, A. J., & Leech, N. L. (2007). Validity and qualitative research: An oxymoron? *Quality & Quantity*, *41*(2), 233–249. doi:10.100711135-006-9000-3

Open Science Collaboration. (2012). An open, large-scale, collaborative effort to estimate the reproducibility of psychological science. *Perspectives on Psychological Science*, *7*(6), 657–660. doi:10.1177/1745691612462588 PMID:26168127

Open Science Collaboration. (2015). Estimating the reproducibility of psychological science. *Science*, *349*(6251), aac4716. doi:10.1126cience.aac4716 PMID:26315443

Oswald, A. (2019). Improving outcomes with qualitative data analysis software: A reflective journey. *Qualitative Social Work: Research and Practice*, *18*(3), 436–442. doi:10.1177/1473325017744860

Pasick, R. J., Burke, N. J., Barker, J. C., Galen, J., Bird, J. A., & Otero-Sabogal, R. (2009). Behavioral theory in a diverse society: Like a compass on Mars. *Health Education & Behavior*, *36*(5), 11S–35S. doi:10.1177/1090198109338917 PMID:19805789

Patton, M. Q. (2002). *Qualitative research & evaluation methods* (3rd ed.). Thousand Oaks, CA: Sage.

Paulhus, D. L. (1986). Self-deception and impression management in test responses. In Personality assessment via questionnaires (pp. 143-165). Springer. doi:10.1007/978-3-642-70751-3_8

Paulhus, D. L. (1991). Measurement and control of response bias. In Measures of personality and social psychological attitudes (pp. 17-59). San Diego, CA: Academic Press. doi:10.1016/B978-0-12-590241-0.50006-X

Paulhus, D. L. (2002). Socially desirable responding: The evolution of a construct. In The role of constructs in psychological and educational measurement (pp. 49-69). Erlbaum.

Paulhus, D. L. (2017). Socially desirable responding on self-reports. Encyclopedia of Personality and Individual Differences, 1-5.

Paulhus, D. L. (2018). The Big Two dimensions of desirability. In Agency and communion in social psychology (pp. 79-89). Routledge. doi:10.4324/9780203703663-7

Paulhus, D. L., & Trapnell, P. D. (2008). Self-presentation of personality. Handbook of Personality Psychology, 19, 492-517.

Paulhus, D. L. (1984). Two-component models of socially desirable responding. *Journal of Personality and Social Psychology*, *46*(3), 598–609. doi:10.1037/0022-3514.46.3.598

Paulhus, D. L. (1988). Balanced inventory of desirable responding (BIDR). *Acceptance and Commitment Therapy Measures Package*, *41*, 79586–79587.

Paulhus, D. L. (1998). *Paulhus deception scales (PDS): the balanced inventory of desirable responding-7: user's manual*. North Tanawanda, NY: Multi-Health Systems.

Paulhus, D. L., Harms, P. D., Bruce, M. N., & Lysy, D. C. (2003). The over-claiming technique: Measuring self-enhancement independent of ability. *Journal of Personality and Social Psychology*, *84*(4), 890–904. doi:10.1037/0022-3514.84.4.890 PMID:12703655

Paulhus, D. L., & John, O. P. (1998). Egoistic and moralistic biases in self-perception: The interplay of self-deceptive styles with basic traits and motives. *Journal of Personality*, *66*(6), 1025–1060. doi:10.1111/1467-6494.00041

Paulhus, D. L., & Reid, D. B. (1991). Enhancement and denial in socially desirable responding. *Journal of Personality and Social Psychology*, *60*(2), 307–317. doi:10.1037/0022-3514.60.2.307

Paunonen, S. V., & LeBel, E. P. (2012). Socially desirable responding and its elusive effects on the validity of personality assessments. *Journal of Personality and Social Psychology*, *103*(1), 158–175. doi:10.1037/a0028165 PMID:22564012

Perinelli, E., & Gremigni, P. (2016). Use of social desirability scales in clinical psychology: A systematic review. *Journal of Clinical Psychology*, *72*(6), 534–551. doi:10.1002/jclp.22284 PMID:26970350

Peterson, R. A., & Kerin, R. A. (1981). The quality of self-report data: review and synthesis. In Review of marketing, (pp. 5-20). AMA.

Phillips, D. C., & Burbules, N. C. (2000). *Postpositivism and educational research*. Lanham, MA: Rowman & Littlefield Publishers, Inc.

Phillips, D. L., & Clancy, K. J. (1972). Some effects of "social desirability" in survey studies. *American Journal of Sociology, 77*(5), 921–940. doi:10.1086/225231

Pitman, M. A., & Maxwell, J. A. (1990). Qualitative approaches to evaluation. In M. D. LeCompte, W. L. Milroy, & J. Preissle (Eds.), *The Handbook of Qualitative Research in Education* (pp. 729–770). San Diego, CA: Academic Press.

Plano-Clark, V. I., & Badiee, M. (2010). Research questions in mixed methods research. In A. Tashakkori & C. Teddlie (Eds.), *SAGE Handbook of Mixed Methods in Social & Behavioral Research* (2nd ed.; pp. 275–300). Thousand Oaks, CA: Sage. doi:10.4135/9781506335193.n12

Polit, D. F., & Hungler, B. P. (1999). *Nursing Research: Principles and Methods* (6th ed.). Philadelphia: Lippincott.

Ponce, O. A., & Pagán-Maldonado, N. (2015). Mixed methods research in education: Capturing the complexity of the profession. *International Journal of Educational Excellence, 1*(1), 111–135. doi:10.18562/IJEE.2015.0005

Ponterotto, J. G. (2005). Qualitative research in counseling psychology: A primer on research paradigms and philosophy of science. *Journal of Counseling Psychology, 52*(2), 126–136. doi:10.1037/0022-0167.52.2.126

Popham, S. M., & Holden, R. R. (1990). Assessing MMPI constructs through the measurement of response latencies. *Journal of Personality Assessment, 54*(3-4), 469–478. doi:10.1080/00223891.1990.9674012 PMID:2348336

Pratt, N., & Woods, P. (2006). *Qualitative research*. University of Plymouth. Available from: http://www.edu.plymouth.ac.uk/resined/qualitative%20methods%202/qualrshm.htm

Preacher, K. J., & MacCallum, R. C. (2003). Repairing Tom Swift's electric factor analysis machine. *Understanding Statistics, 2*(1), 13–43. doi:10.1207/S15328031US0201_02

Presser, S., & Stinson, L. (1998). Data collection mode and social desirability bias in self-reported religious attendance. *American Sociological Review, 63*(1), 137–145. doi:10.2307/2657486

Puranam, P., Alexy, O., & Reitzig, M. (2014). What's "new" about new forms of organizing? *Academy of Management Review, 39*(2), 162–180. doi:10.5465/amr.2011.0436

QSR International. (2018). *NVIVO 12 Plus (Version 12.2.0.443 (64-bit))* [Windows 10 Home]. Burlington, MA: QSR International.

Randall, D. M., & Fernandes, M. F. (1991). The social desirability response bias in ethics research. *Journal of Business Ethics, 10*(11), 805–817. doi:10.1007/BF00383696

Ray, J. J. (1990). Acquiescence and problems with forced-choice scales. *The Journal of Social Psychology, 130*(3), 397–399. doi:10.1080/00224545.1990.9924595

Rea, L. M., & Parker, R. A. (2014). *Designing and conducting survey research: A comprehensive guide* (4th ed.). San Francisco: Jossey-Bass.

Reavey, P. (2011). *Visual methods in psychology: Using and interpreting images in qualitative research*. New York, NY: Psychology Press.

Reicher, S., Haslam, S. A., & Rath, R. (2008). Making a virtue of evil: A five-step social identity model of the development of collective hate. *Social and Personality Psychology Compass, 2*(3), 1313–1344. doi:10.1111/j.1751-9004.2008.00113.x

Reynolds, W. M. (1982). Development of reliable and valid short forms of the Marlowe-Crowne Social Desirability Scale. *Journal of Clinical Psychology, 38*(1), 119–125. doi:10.1002/1097-4679(198201)38:1<119::AID-JCLP2270380118>3.0.CO;2-I

Richman, W. L., Kiesler, S., Weisband, S., & Drasgow, F. (1999). A meta-analytic study of social desirability distortion in computer-administered questionnaires, traditional questionnaires, and interviews. *The Journal of Applied Psychology, 84*(5), 754–775. doi:10.1037/0021-9010.84.5.754

Roese, N. J., & Jamieson, D. W. (1993). Twenty years of bogus pipeline research: A critical review and meta-analysis. *Psychological Bulletin, 114*(2), 363–375. doi:10.1037/0033-2909.114.2.363

Roof, J., & Wiegman, R. (1995). *Who can speak*. Urbana, IL: University of Illinois Press.

Rothbaner, P. M. (2008). *Triangulation*. Available From: http://www.sage-ereference.com/research/Article_n468.html

Roxas, B., & Lindsay, V. (2012). Social desirability bias in survey research on sustainable development in small firms: An exploratory analysis of survey mode effect. *Business Strategy and the Environment, 21*(4), 223–235. doi:10.1002/bse.730

Rubin, H. J., & Rubin, I. S. (2011). *Qualitative interviewing: the art of hearing data* (3rd ed.). Thousand Oaks, CA: SAGE Publications, Inc.

Rubio, D. M., Berg-Weger, M., Tebb, S. S., Lee, E. S., & Rauch, S. (2003). Objectifying content validity: Conducting a content validity study in social work research. *Social Work Research, 27*(2), 94–104. doi:10.1093wr/27.2.94

Rutledge, P. (2010). *What is media psychology? And why you should care*. Media Psychology Research Center. doi:10.1037/e537062011-001

Ryan, G. W., & Bernard, H. R. (2000). Data management and analysis methods. In N. K. Denzin & Y. S. Lincoln (Eds.), *Handbook of qualitative research* (2nd ed.; pp. 769–802). Thousand Oaks, CA: Sage Publications, Inc.

Sackeim, H. A., & Gur, R. C. (1978). Self-deception, self-confrontation, and consciousness. In Consciousness and self-regulation (pp. 139-197). Springer. doi:10.1007/978-1-4684-2571-0_4

Samuels, M., & Samuels, N. (1975). *Seeing with the minds eye*. New York, NY: Randomhouse.

Sandelowski, M. (2000). Combining qualitative and quantitative sampling, data collection, and analysis techniques in mixed-method studies. *Research in Nursing & Health, 23*(3), 246–255. doi:10.1002/1098-240X(200006)23:3<246::AID-NUR9>3.0.CO;2-H PMID:10871540

Compilation of References

Sayer, A. (1992). *Method in social science: A realist approach.* London: Routledge.

Schaeffer, N. C. (2000). Asking questions about threatening topics: A selective overview. In The science of self-report: Implications for research and practice (pp. 105-121). Erlbaum.

Schmidt, F. L. (1996). Statistical significance testing and cumulative knowledge in psychology: Implications for training of researchers. *Psychological Methods*, *1*(2), 115–129. doi:10.1037/1082-989X.1.2.115

Schoderbek, P. P., & Deshpande, S. P. (1996). Impression management, overclaiming, and perceived unethical conduct: The role of male and female managers. *Journal of Business Ethics*, *15*(4), 409–414. doi:10.1007/BF00380361

Schoonenboom, J. (2018). Designing mixed methods research by mixing and merging methodologies: A 13-step model. *The American Behavioral Scientist*, *62*(7), 998–1015. doi:10.1177/0002764218772674

Schuessler, K., Hittle, D., & Cardascia, J. (1978). Measuring responding desirably with attitude-opinion items. *Social Psychology*, *41*(3), 224–235. doi:10.2307/3033559

Schwab, A., Abrahamson, E., Starbuck, W. H., & Fidler, F. (2011). Perspective— Researchers should make thoughtful assessments instead of null-hypothesis significance tests. *Organization Science*, *22*(4), 1105–1120. doi:10.1287/orsc.1100.0557

Schwandt, T. A. (1996). Farewell to criteriology. *Qualitative Inquiry*, *2*(1), 58–72. doi:10.1177/107780049600200109

Scott, J., & Carrington, P. J. (2011). *The SAGE handbook of social network analysis.* London: SAGE Publications Inc.

Seale, C. (1999). *The quality of qualitative research.* London: Sage. doi:10.4135/9780857020093

Shadish, W. R. (1995). The quantitative-qualitative debates: "Dekuhnifying" the conceptual context. *Evaluation and Program Planning*, *18*(1), 47–49. doi:10.1016/0149-7189(94)00048-3

Shadish, W. R., Cook, T. D., & Campbell, D. T. (2002). *Experimental and quasi-experimental designs for generalized causal inference* (2nd ed.). Boston: Houghton Mifflin Company.

Shannon-Baker, P. (2015). Making paradigms meaningful in mixed methods research. *Journal of Mixed Methods Research*, *10*(4), 1–16. doi:10.1177/1558689815575861

Sharp, J. L., Mobley, C., Hammond, C., Withington, C., Drew, S., Stringfield, S., & Stipanovic, N. (2012). A mixed methods sampling methodology for a multisite case study. *Journal of Mixed Methods Research*, *6*(1), 34–54. doi:10.1177/1558689811417133

Shaver, J. P. (1993). What statistical significance testing is, and what it is not. *Journal of Experimental Education*, *61*(4), 293–316. doi:10.1080/00220973.1993.10806592

Shenton, A. K. (2004). Strategies for ensuring trustworthiness in qualitative research projects. *Education for Information*, *22*(2), 63–755. doi:10.3233/EFI-2004-22201

Shepherd, D. A., & Zacharakis, A. (1999). Conjoint analysis: A new methodological approach for researching the decision policies of venture capitalists. *Venture Capital: An International Journal of Entrepreneurial Finance, 1*(3), 197–217. doi:10.1080/136910699295866

Shirky, C. (2011). The political power of social media: Technology, the public sphere, and political change. *Foreign Affairs, 90*(1), 28–41.

Shulruf, B., Hattie, J., & Dixon, R. (2011). Intertwinement of individualist and collectivist attributes and response sets. *Journal of Social, Evolutionary, & Cultural Psychology, 5*(1), 51–65. doi:10.1037/h0099275

Siggelkow, N. (2007). Persuasion with case studies. *Academy of Management Journal, 50*(1), 20–24. doi:10.5465/amj.2007.24160882

Silva, C. N. (2008). Review: Catherine Marshall & Gretchen B. Rossman (2006). Designing Qualitative Research [20 paragraphs]. Forum Qualitative Sozialforschung / Forum: Qualitative. *Social Research, 9*(3), 13. Retrieved from http://nbn-resolving.de/urn:nbn:de:0114-fqs0803137

Silverman, D. (2005). *Doing qualitative research* (2nd ed.). Thousand Oaks, CA: Sage Publications, Inc.

Simoni, J. M., Frick, P. A., & Huang, B. (2006). A longitudinal evaluation of a social support model of medication adherence among HIV-positive men and women on antiretroviral therapy. *Health Psychology, 25*(1), 74–81. doi:10.1037/0278-6133.25.1.74 PMID:16448300

Singer, E., Hippler, H. J., & Schwarz, N. (1992). Confidentiality assurances in surveys: Reassurance or threat? *International Journal of Public Opinion Research, 4*(3), 256–268. doi:10.1093/ijpor/4.3.256

Sirken, M. G. (1970). Household surveys with multiplicity. *Journal of the American Statistical Association, 65*(329), 257–266. doi:10.1080/01621459.1970.10481077

Slabbinck, H., & Kenhove, P. V. (2010). *Social desirability and indirect questioning: New insights from the Implicit Association Test and the Balanced Inventory of Desirable Responding*. ACR North American Advances.

Smith, L. L., Federer, W. T., & Raghavarao, D. (1974). *A Comparison of Three Techniques for Eliciting Answers to Sensitive Questions*. Academic Press.

Smith, J. (1990). Alternative research paradigms and the problem of criteria. In E. G. Guba (Ed.), *The paradigm dialogue* (pp. 167–187). Newbury Park, CA: SAGE.

Smith, J. K. A. (2013). *Imagining the kingdom: How worship works*. Grand Rapids, MI: Baker Academic.

Smith, L. T. (1999). *Decolonizing methodologies: Research and indigenous peoples*. Zed Books Ltd.

Sproull, L., & Kiesler, S. (1986). Reducing social context cues: Electronic mail in organizational communication. *Management Science, 32*(11), 1492–1512. doi:10.1287/mnsc.32.11.1492

St. Pierre, E. A., & Roulston, K. (2006). The state of qualitative inquiry: A contested science. *International Journal of Qualitative Studies in Education: QSE*, *19*(6), 673–684. doi:10.1080/09518390600975644

Stake, R. E. (1978). The case study method in social inquiry. *Educational Researcher*, *7*(2), 5–8. doi:10.3102/0013189X007002005

Stake, R. E. (1995). *The Art of Case Study Research*. Thousand Oaks, CA: SAGE.

Stavros, C., & Westberg, K. (2009). Using triangulation and multiple case studies to advance relationship marketing theory. *Qualitative Market Research*, *12*(3), 307–320. doi:10.1108/13522750910963827

Steenkamp, J. B. E., De Jong, M. G., & Baumgartner, H. (2010). Socially desirable response tendencies in survey research. *JMR, Journal of Marketing Research*, *47*(2), 199–214. doi:10.1509/jmkr.47.2.199

Stöber, J. (2001). The Social Desirability Scale-17 (SDS-17): Convergent validity, discriminant validity, and relationship with age. *European Journal of Psychological Assessment*, *17*(3), 222–232. doi:10.1027//1015-5759.17.3.222

Strahan, R., & Gerbasi, K. C. (1972). Short, homogeneous versions of the Marlow-Crowne social desirability scale. *Journal of Clinical Psychology*, *28*(2), 191–193. doi:10.1002/1097-4679(197204)28:2<191::AID-JCLP2270280220>3.0.CO;2-G

Strauss, A., & Corbin, J. (1990). *Basics of qualitative research: Grounded theory procedures and techniques*. London: Sage.

Stronach, I. (2006). Enlightenment and the "heart of darkness": (Neo)imperialism in the congo, and elsewhere. *International Journal of Qualitative Studies in Education: QSE*, *19*(6), 757–768. doi:10.1080/09518390600975982

Stryker, S. (1968). Identity salience and role performance: The relevance of symbolic interaction theory for family research. *Journal of Marriage and the Family*, *30*(4), 558–564. doi:10.2307/349494

Sudman, S., & Bradburn, N. M. (1974). *Response effects in surveys: A review and synthesis (No. 16)*. Chicago, IL: Aldine.

Sullivan, G. M. (2011). Getting off the "gold standard": Randomized controlled trials and education research. *Journal of Graduate Medical Education*, *3*(3), 285–289. doi:10.4300/JGME-D-11-00147.1 PMID:22942950

Sweetman, D., Badiee, M., & Creswell, J. W. (2010). Use of the transformative framework in mixed methods studies. *Qualitative Inquiry*, *16*(6), 441–454. doi:10.1177/1077800410364610

Symanzik, J., Fischetti, W. Z., & Spence, I. (2009). *Commemorating William Playfair's 250th birthday*. Utah State University.

Tapscott, D. (2008). *Grown up digital: how the net generation is changing your world* (1st ed.). McGraw-Hill Education.

Tashakkori, A., & Teddlie, C. (1998). *Mixed Methodology: Combining Qualitative and Quantitative Approaches in Applied Social Research Methods Series, 46*. Thousand Oaks, CA: Sage Publications.

Tashakorri, A., & Teddlie, C. (1998). *Mixed methods methodology: Combining the qualitative and quantitative approaches*. Thousand Oaks, CA: Sage.

Tashakorri, A., & Teddlie, C. (2010). Epilogue: Current developments and emerging trends in integrated research methodology. In A. Tashakkori & C. Teddlie (Eds.), *SAGE Handbook of Mixed Methods in Social & Behavioral Research* (2nd ed.; pp. 803–825). Thousand Oaks, CA: Sage. doi:10.4135/9781506335193.n31

Tatarchevskiy, T. (2011). The 'popular' culture of internet activism. *New Media & Society*, *13*(2), 297–313. doi:10.1177/1461444810372785

Teddlie, C., & Johnson, R. B. (2009a). Methodological thought before the 20th century. In C. Teddlie & A. Tashakkori (Eds.), *Foundations of mixed methods research: Integrating quantitative and quaitative approaches in the social and behavioral sciences* (pp. 40–61). Thousand Oaks, CA: Sage.

Teddlie, C., & Johnson, R. B. (2009b). Methodological thought since the 20th century. In C. Teddlie & A. Tashakkori (Eds.), *Foundations of mixed methods research: Integrating quantitative and qualitative approaches in the social and behavioral sciences* (pp. 62–82). Thousand Oaks, CA: Sage.

Teddlie, C., & Tashakkori, A. (2006). A general typology of research designs featuring mixed methods. *Research in the Schools*, *13*(1), 12–28.

Teddlie, C., & Tashakkori, A. (2009). *Foundations of mixed methods research: Integrating quantitative and qualitative approaches in the social and behavioral sciences*. Thousand Oaks, CA: Sage.

Teddlie, C., & Tashakkori, A. (2010). Overview of contemporary issues in mixed methods research. In A. Tashakkori & C. Teddlie (Eds.), *SAGE Handbook of Mixed Methods in Social & Behavioral Research* (2nd ed.; pp. 1–41). Thousand Oaks, CA: Sage. doi:10.4135/9781506335193.n1

Teddlie, C., & Tashakkori, A. (2011). *Mixed methods research. In The Sage Handbook of Qualitative Research*. Thousand Oaks, CA: Sage Publications.

Teddlie, C., & Yu, F. (2007). Mixed methods sampling: A typology with examples. *Journal of Mixed Methods Research*, *1*(1), 77–100. doi:10.1177/1558689806292430

Tellegen, A. (1982). *Brief manual for the Differential Personality Inventory* (Unpublished manuscript). University of Minnesota, Minneapolis, MN.

Compilation of References

Tellis, G. J., & Chandrasekaran, D. (2010). Extent and impact of response biases in cross-national survey research. *International Journal of Research in Marketing*, *27*(4), 329–341. doi:10.1016/j.ijresmar.2010.08.003

Terzi, T. (2017). *Detecting semi-plausible response patterns* (Doctoral dissertation). The London School of Economics and Political Science (LSE).

Thompson, B., & Daniel, L. G. (1996). Factor analytic evidence for the construct validity of scores: A historical overview and some guidelines. *Educational and Psychological Measurement*, *56*(2), 197–208. doi:10.1177/0013164496056002001

Tijjani, B. (2010). *Share valuation and stock market analysis in emerging markets: the case of Nigeria*. Adamu Joji Publishers.

Tourangeau, R., & Smith, T. W. (1996). Asking sensitive questions: The impact of data collection mode, question format, and question context. *Public Opinion Quarterly*, *60*(2), 275–304. doi:10.1086/297751

Tourangeau, R., & Yan, T. (2007). Sensitive questions in surveys. *Psychological Bulletin*, *133*(5), 859–883. doi:10.1037/0033-2909.133.5.859 PMID:17723033

Trapnell, P. D., & Paulhus, D. L. (2012). Agentic and communal values: Their scope and measurement. *Journal of Personality Assessment*, *94*(1), 39–52. doi:10.1080/00223891.2011.627968 PMID:22176265

Trochim, W. M. K. (2006). *Research Methods Knowledge Base. Deduction and Induction*. Retrieved from: http://www.socialresearchmethods.net/kb/dedind.php

Tsuchiya, T. (2005). Domain estimators for the item count technique. *Survey Methodology*, *31*(1), 41–51.

Tufekci, Z. (2014). Big questions for social media big data: Representativeness, validity and other methodological pitfalls. *ICWSM*, *14*, 505–514.

Tufte, E. R. (2001). *The visual display of quantitative information*. Cheshire, CT: Graphics Press.

Turner, S. F., Cardinal, L. B., & Burton, R. M. (2017). Research design for mixed methods: A triangulation-based framework and roadmap. *Organizational Research Methods*, *20*(2), 243–267. doi:10.1177/1094428115610808

U.S. Department of Health & Human Services. (2015). *The Nature and Design of Mixed Methods Research*. Retrieved from obssr.od.nih.gov/scientific_areas/methodology/mixed_methods_research/section2.aspx

Ullmann, L. P. (1962). An empirically derived MMPI scale which measures facilitation-inhibition of recognition of threatening stimuli. *Journal of Clinical Psychology*, *18*(2), 127–132. doi:10.1002/1097-4679(196204)18:2<127::AID-JCLP2270180206>3.0.CO;2-V PMID:13923691

Uziel, L. (2010). Rethinking social desirability scales: From impression management to interpersonally oriented self-control. *Perspectives on Psychological Science*, *5*(3), 243–262. doi:10.1177/1745691610369465 PMID:26162157

Valenzuela, S. (2013). Unpacking the use of social media for protest behavior: The roles of information, opinion expression, and activism. *The American Behavioral Scientist*, *57*(7), 920–942. doi:10.1177/0002764213479375

Van Burg, E., & Romme, A. G. L. (2014). Creating the future together: Toward a framework for research synthesis in entrepreneurship. *Entrepreneurship Theory and Practice*, *38*(2), 369–397. doi:10.1111/etap.12092

Van de Mortel, T. F. (2008). Faking it: Social desirability response bias in self-report research. *The Australian Journal of Advanced Nursing*, *25*(4), 40–48.

Van Harpen, G. (2015). *Connected to learn: A mixed methods study of professional learning for secondary school leaders in small districts and rural areas* (Unpublished dissertation). Cardinal Stritch University, Milwaukee, WI.

Vecchione, M., Alessandri, G., & Barbaranelli, C. (2013). Measurement and application of egoistic and moralistic self-enhancement. *International Journal of Selection and Assessment*, *21*(2), 170–182. doi:10.1111/ijsa.12027

Venkatesh, V., Brown, S. A., & Bala, H. (2013). Bridging the qualitative-quantitative divide: Guidelines for conducting mixed methods research in information systems. *Management Information Systems Quarterly*, *37*(1), 21–54. doi:10.25300/MISQ/2013/37.1.02

Venkatesh, V., Brown, S. A., & Sullivan, Y. W. (2016). Guidelines for conducting mixed-methods research: An extension and illustration. *Journal of the Association for Information Systems*, *17*(7), 435–494. doi:10.17705/1jais.00433

Victor, C. R., Ross, F., & Axford, J. (2004). Capturing lay perspectives in a randomized control trial of a health promotion intervention for people with osteoarthritis of the knee. *Journal of Evaluation in Clinical Practice*, *10*(1), 63–70. doi:10.1111/j.1365-2753.2003.00395.x PMID:14731152

Vispoel, W. P., & Kim, H. Y. (2014). Psychometric properties for the Balanced Inventory of Desirable Responding: Dichotomous versus polytomous conventional and IRT scoring. *Psychological Assessment*, *26*(3), 878–891. doi:10.1037/a0036430 PMID:24708082

Wald, K. D. (2000). The context of gay politics. In C. A. Rimmerman, K. D. Wald, & C. Wilcox (Eds.), The politics of gay rights (pp. 1–28). Chicago: University of Chicago Press.

Warner, S. L. (1965). Randomized response: A survey technique for eliminating evasive answer bias. *Journal of the American Statistical Association*, *60*(309), 63–69. doi:10.1080/01621459.1965.10480775 PMID:12261830

Webster, L., & Mertova, P. (2007). *Using narrative inquiry as a research method: An introduction to using critical event narrative analysis in research on learning and teaching*. New York, NY: Routledge. doi:10.4324/9780203946268

Compilation of References

Weinstein, S. (2018). *The room is on fire: The History, Pedagogy, and Practice of Youth Spoken Word Poetry*. SUNY Press.

Welter, F. (2011). Contextualizing entrepreneurship—Conceptual challenges and ways forward. *Entrepreneurship Theory and Practice, 35*(1), 165–184. doi:10.1111/j.1540-6520.2010.00427.x

Wiggins, J. S. (1959). Interrelationships among MMPI measures of dissimulation under standard and social desirability instruction. *Journal of Consulting Psychology, 23*(5), 419–427. doi:10.1037/h0047823

Wiggins, J. S. (1964). Convergences among stylistic response measures from objective personality tests. *Educational and Psychological Measurement, 24*(3), 551–562. doi:10.1177/001316446402400310

Wikipedia. (2011). *Triangulation: Social science*. Available From: http://en.wikipedia.org/wiki/triangulation_(social_science)

Wilkerson, J. M., Nagao, D. H., & Martin, C. L. (2002). Socially Desirable Responding in Computerized Questionnaires: When Questionnaire Purpose Matters More Than the Mode 1. *Journal of Applied Social Psychology, 32*(3), 544–559. doi:10.1111/j.1559-1816.2002.tb00229.x

Williams, J. A. Jr. (1964). Interviewer-respondent interaction: A study of bias in the information interview. *Sociometry, 27*(3), 338–352. doi:10.2307/2785623

Willig, C. (2008). *Introducing qualitative research in psychology: Adventures in theory and method*. London: Open University Press.

Willis, G. B., & Sirken, M. G. (1994). *The cognitive aspects of responses to sensitive survey questions*. Cognitive Methods Staff working paper series, US Department of Health and Human Services, Centers for Disease Control and Prevention, National Center for Health Statistics.

Winder, P. (1975). New Motivational Distortion Scales for the 16 PF. *Journal of Personality Assessment, 39*(5), 532–537.

Wolcott, H. (1990). On seeking–and rejecting–validity in qualitative research. In E. W. Eisner & A. Peshkin (Eds.), *Qualitative Inquiry in Education: The Continuing Debate* (pp. 121–152). New York: Teachers College Press.

Wolcott, H. F. (2009). *Writing up qualitative research* (3rd ed.). Thousand Oaks, CA: Sage. doi:10.4135/9781452234878

Yeasmin, S., & Rahman, K. F. (2012). Triangulation research method as the tool of social science research. Bangladesh University of Professionals Journal, 1(1), 154-163.

Yin, R. K. (1981). The case study crisis: Some answers. *Administrative Science Quarterly, 26*(1), 58–65. doi:10.2307/2392599

Yin, R. K. (2003). *Case study research, design and methods* (3rd ed.; Vol. 5). Thousand Oaks, CA: Sage.

Yin, R. K. (2003). *Case study research: Design and methods* (3rd ed.). Thousand Oaks, CA: Sage.

Yin, R. K. (2016). *Qualitative research from start to finish*. New York, NY: Guilford Press.

Yung, Y. F. (1997). Finite mixtures in confirmatory factor-analysis models. *Psychometrika, 62*(3), 297–330. doi:10.1007/BF02294554

Zahra, S. A., & Wright, M. (2011). Entrepreneurship's next act. *The Academy of Management Perspectives, 25*(4), 67–83. doi:10.5465/amp.2010.0149

Zerbe, W. J., & Paulhus, D. L. (1987). Socially desirable responding in organizational behavior: A reconception. *Academy of Management Review, 12*(2), 250–264. doi:10.5465/amr.1987.4307820

Ziegler, M., & Buehner, M. (2009). Modeling socially desirable responding and its effects. *Educational and Psychological Measurement, 69*(4), 548–565. doi:10.1177/0013164408324469

About the Contributors

Mette L. Baran completed her Ed.D. in Administrative Leadership and Supervision from DePaul University. She obtained an M.B.A. in International Business and a baccalaureate degree in Marketing from DePaul University. Dr. Baran is a tenured associate professor in the Doctoral Studies Department within the College of Education and Leadership at Cardinal Stritch University and teaches leadership, learning, higher Education, and research courses. Her background includes being a faculty member and senior executive at Robert Morris University in Chicago including the positions as campus director, director of education, and director of development. Dr. Baran's research interests and expertise include mixed methods research, looping, student attitudes and achievement, charter schools, middle school education, higher education administration and access, and international family policy. She is the author of several books and presents regularly at national and international conferences. She is an international consultant preparing U.S. professional for their overseas assignments. She is a member of the Board of Trustees to Robert Morris University.

Janice Jones is the Associate Dean of the College of Education and Leadership at Cardinal Stritch University in Milwaukee, WI. Janice earned her doctorate in Counseling Psychology from the University of Wisconsin-Milwaukee and has taught research in the Doctoral Leadership Studies department. Her research interests include children in out of home care, successful life transitions, and adult learning. Janice has published numerous articles, chapters and several books and enjoys collaborating with colleagues and students.

* * *

Aaliyah Baker is an Assistant Professor in the College of Education and Leadership at Cardinal Stritch University in Milwaukee, WI. She began her career in education as a classroom teacher with the Milwaukee Public Schools. Her research interests include critical race theory, multicultural education, sociocultural theories of learning, and the role of race, class and gender in educational achievement and experiences in schools. Dr. Baker has conducted research within the scope of education, society, culture and learning. She has presented research findings at regional, national, and international conferences. Dr. Baker maintains strong partnerships with K-12 schools by developing and supporting curriculum and instruction that meets the increasingly diverse needs of students and identifies pedagogical practices that build capacity for cultural competence and humility.

Todd Burton is a retired Army officer with over 30 years of service, serving as a Senior Policy Analyst in the Office of the Secretary of Defense where he focused on disaster response planning, military support to civilian law enforcement, and support to the Department of Homeland Security. He earned his Ph.D. in Leadership for the Advancement of Learning and Service from Cardinal Stritch University in 2019.

Preston B. Cosgrove is an Associate Professor in the School of Education at Concordia University Wisconsin, where he teaches research methods in the Leadership in Innovation and Continuous Improvement Doctoral Program. His research interests include social science epistemology, validity in qualitative inquiry, survey development and validation, adoption discernment and identity, and faith integration in Christian higher education.

Mindy Crain-Dorough is an Associate and Endowed Professor in the Department of Educational Leadership and Technology at Southeastern Louisiana University, teaches doctoral and masters research methods courses (quantitative, qualitative, and mixed methods) and has served as methodologist on over 70 dissertation committees. She completed a bachelor's degree in secondary mathematics education, a master's degree in applied statistics, a master's degree in educational research methodology, and a Doctorate of Philosophy in educational research methodology all from Louisiana State University. She was a Research Analyst at the Louisiana Department of Education for nine years in the areas of assessment, accountability, and data reporting. She has publications and presentations in varied areas (e.g., data-driven decision-making, accountability, research methods instruction) and has given numerous presentations to professional organizations, (e.g., AERA and MSERA). She has served as President of both the Mid-South Educational Research Association and the Louisiana Education Research Association and as Chair of the AERA Professors of Education Research SIG.

Ahmet Durmaz graduated from Turkish Naval Academy/Istanbul as an Electric/Electronics Engineer in 2010. He successfully acquired Maritime Logistics Management Master's Degree from Institute of Naval Sciences and Engineering. He is currently working as a logistics officer in Turkish Naval Academy and getting his 2nd Master's Degree on MBA from Gebze Technical University. He specializes in logistics mangement, supply chain management and marketing management.

Inci Dursun studied the MSc in Business Administration (2003-2006) and Ph.D. in in Business Administration specializing in marketing management (2006-2012) at Gebze Technical University (GTU). Then, between 2013-2018, she worked as an Assistant Professor in the Department of Management at Yalova University, Turkey. Recently she is working at GTU as an Assistant Professor. Her research interests are in the areas of social marketing, consumer behavior, and survey methodology. Specifically, she focuses on sustainable consumption and change of nonfunctional consumer attitudes and behaviors. She lectures on marketing management, consumer behaviors, research methodology and statistical data analysis.

Koholga Ormin is an Associate Professor with the Department of Accounting, Adamawa State University, Mubi, Nigeria. His research interest is financial reporting, accounting theory, accounting scandals, finance and research. He has published widely in local and international journals.

Pierre Sindambiwe currently works as Lecturer at School of Business, University of Rwanda (UR) and a PhD candidate in business administration at the Centre for Family Enterprise and Ownership (CeFEO), Jönköping International Business School (JIBS), Sweden. Pierre has MBA in Finance and a wide teaching experience from undergraduate to post-graduate courses in business and management areas. Pierre has a vast experience in the administration, curriculum development, consulting and training. Pierre is laureate of the "Global Leadership Academic Excellence Award" (2015) as well as "Global Leader Development Academic Excellence Award" (2016). In past, Pierre worked with different banks, occupied different administrative and academic positions in the University and different non-for-profit organizations. Pierre is currently working on his Doctoral thesis, with a seminar defended in June 2019. His research interest is in family business continuity in the context of developing countries. Besides, he has been interested in the areas of Entrepreneurship, Organizational Studies and research methods.

Carolyn Stevenson is a Veteran educator and qualitative research expert Carolyn Stevenson has over 18 years teaching and administrative experience in higher education. She currently serves as a full-time faculty member and faculty advisor at Purdue University Global. She holds a Master of Arts degree in Communication, Master of Business Administration, and Doctor of Education with an emphasis in Higher Education. Recent publications include a chapter entitled: "Leading across

Generations: Issues for Higher Education Administrators" published in the Handbook of Research on Transnational Higher Education Management, IGI Global; Technical Writing: A Comprehensive Resource for Technical Writers at all Levels, (Martinez, Hannigan, Wells, Peterson and Stevenson) Revised and Updated Edition, Kaplan Publishing, Building Online Communities in Higher Education Institutions: Creating Collaborative Experience (with Joanna Bauer), published by IGI Global, and Promoting Climate Change Awareness through Environmental Education (with Lynn Wilson), published by IGI Global.

Ebru Tumer Kabadayı is a professor of marketing at Gebze Technical University. She obtained her PhD in Marketing from Gebze Technical University in 2001. Her research interests focus on brand management, consumer behaviour and relationship marketing. Her researches have been published in Journal of Business Research, and in numerous Turkish-language scholarly journals.

Glady Van Harpen is an Assistant Professor in the Department of Educational Leadership and Policy at the University of Wisconsin Oshkosh. Glady has been involved in education and leadership for more than 25 years. Her experience includes work with early adolescents through adults in the public educational system. She has specialized teaching experiences in the juvenile corrections system, alternative high school, and outdoor education. Additionally, she has more than 16 years of school leadership experience at the middle and high school levels. Her academic interests include research on communities of practice (CoPs) and personal learning networks (PLNs), connected learning, and school leadership. The focus of her study is how school leaders, in small districts and rural areas, further their professional learning and increase school success. She is also involved in the International School Leadership Development Network (ISLDN) through the University Council of Educational Administration (UCEA). The ISLDN is a collaborative team of more than 40 researchers from over 20 countries. As part of the ISLDN team she is researching the challenges and success of school leaders at a high-needs urban school. Glady completed her Ph.D. at Cardinal Stritch University in Milwaukee, Wisconsin, M.A.E. at Northern Michigan University in Marquette, Michigan, and B.S. at the University of Wisconsin Stevens Point.

Index

A

Accounting 186, 188, 190, 193-197
Action Research 143

B

Balanced Inventory 160, 162-163
Between-Strategy 72, 85
Breadth and Depth 60, 74

C

Categories and Themes 91-92
Coding 71, 89-92, 96, 144, 222, 228-230, 244, 249
Confidentiality 143, 149, 152-153, 156, 168, 170
Conjoint analysis 209, 213
Consent 96, 114, 125-126, 143, 225
Content Analysis 71, 95, 144, 210, 219, 221, 227-228, 242-244, 249
Context 3, 13-14, 32, 34, 36, 54, 60, 89, 93, 96, 112, 124, 143-144, 147-149, 154-155, 159, 167-168, 171, 189, 196, 206-207, 209-211, 220, 229, 241-243, 245, 253

D

Data Analysis 27, 36-37, 40, 46-48, 55, 81-82, 85, 87-93, 95-97, 107, 113, 125, 144, 188, 196, 273

Descriptive Research 28
Desirable Responding Scale 163
Document Analysis 143

E

Epistemology 10, 14-16, 96, 251
Ethnography 33, 143
Explanatory Research 28-29
Exploratory and Confirmatory 73
Exploratory Research 26, 28-29, 49, 59, 73

F

Facebook Groups 235-236, 240
Field Observation 143-144
Framework Analysis 144

G

Graphics 107-109
Grounded Theory 34, 90, 144

H

Holistic 10, 13, 32, 34-35, 73, 82, 124, 144, 268

I

Immediate Research Purpose 57, 85
Infographics 108

Index

L

LGBT 216-217, 219-221, 224-225, 227, 230, 233-235, 237, 240-243, 245, 249

M

Marginalized Community 216-217, 220, 241, 244, 249
Marginalized Groups 242, 244-245, 253, 255
Memoing 90, 93
Mixed Methods Approach 35-37, 110, 204, 256-257
Mixed Methods Data Collection 38, 72, 85, 255, 270
Mixed Methods Design 27, 36-38, 46, 55-58, 63, 69, 80-82
Mixed Methods Research 1, 7-9, 13, 16, 26-27, 35-36, 48-49, 54, 56, 71, 90, 98, 188, 251-252, 256-257, 262, 266, 271
Mixed-Methods 2, 6-9, 16, 201, 204, 207, 210, 212

O

Ontology 14

P

Paradigm 1-2, 4-10, 16, 152, 187, 191, 219, 243
Photography 56, 119-120, 123, 126, 140
Poetry 119-120, 123, 140, 253
Presenting Data 107, 116, 123
Process 2-3, 6, 13, 15, 26-27, 31-34, 36, 42, 45-47, 54-58, 60, 63, 69, 78-80, 87-92, 94-97, 114, 123-125, 144, 149, 151, 153, 156, 162, 164, 169, 195, 210, 219-222, 225-226, 228-229, 234, 237, 241, 249, 255-256

Q

Qualitative Approach 16, 73, 210
Qualitative Data 27, 32, 36-37, 39-47, 56, 65-66, 72, 74, 78-79, 82, 85, 87-88, 90-95, 97-98, 108, 113, 115, 120, 123, 263, 272
Qualitative Design 32, 45-46, 123, 264
Qualitative Research 3, 6, 11, 13-16, 32, 34-35, 39, 43, 92-97, 108, 119, 123-124, 187-188, 209-210, 237, 249, 256
Quantitative Design 30, 46-47
Quantitative Research 1, 3, 11, 14, 30-31, 35, 44, 73, 108, 147, 186-187, 194, 209-210, 268

R

Reliability 27, 93, 162, 168, 186-187, 190, 202, 271
Remote Research Purpose 57, 60, 85
Replication 31, 201, 204, 206-208, 213
Research Design 9-10, 26-29, 33, 37, 42-43, 45-47, 49, 73, 75, 97, 159, 170, 187, 212, 237, 264, 267
Research Methods 31, 36, 49, 58-60, 119, 194, 196, 252, 255
Research Questions 4, 26, 28, 30, 35, 41, 43-44, 46-49, 55, 57-59, 61, 63, 69, 71, 73-74, 79-80, 82, 109, 113, 115, 195, 237, 256-257, 263, 268
Research Responsibility 252

S

Sampling 34, 36, 42, 54-55, 58, 75-81, 190, 212, 225, 241, 270
Scope 60-61, 63, 75, 85, 162, 240
Significance 12, 150, 201-210, 212-213, 254
Social Desirability Bias 146-148, 150-151, 160, 167

Index

Social Media 216-217, 219-222, 224-225, 227, 230, 233, 240-245, 249
Social Network Analysis 216, 227, 234-236, 240-241, 244, 249
Social Science 3, 12, 28, 33, 108, 121, 146-147, 186-188, 193, 197, 251-253, 255, 257
Social Science Research 3, 108, 146-147, 186-188, 193, 251-253, 255
Sources of Qualitative Data 88
Statistical power 201-202, 212
Strand 56, 73, 78, 82, 85, 268

T

Transferability 7, 60, 144, 187
Triangulation 14, 39, 42, 46, 82, 94, 144, 186-197, 240-241

U

Unit of Analysis 56, 85, 124, 213

V

Validity 1, 10-16, 27, 60, 93, 144, 146-147, 157-163, 165, 168-170, 186-188, 190-191, 196, 206-207, 237, 240, 255, 271
Visual Data 108, 120
Visualization 108-109

W

Within-Strategy 64, 72-74, 78, 85

Purchase Print, E-Book, or Print + E-Book

IGI Global's reference books can now be purchased from three unique pricing formats:
Print Only, E-Book Only, or Print + E-Book.
Shipping fees may apply.

www.igi-global.com

Recommended Reference Books

Premier Reference Source
Research Data Access and Management in Modern Libraries

ISBN: 978-1-5225-8437-7
© 2019; 325 pp.
List Price: $195

Premier Reference Source
The Role of Knowledge Transfer in Open Innovation

ISBN: 978-1-5225-5849-1
© 2019; 397 pp.
List Price: $195

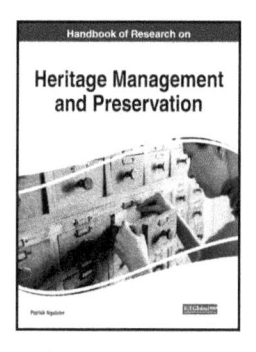

Handbook of Research on
Heritage Management and Preservation

ISBN: 978-1-5225-3137-1
© 2018; 508 pp.
List Price: $265

Premier Reference Source
Research 2.0 and the Impact of Digital Technologies on Scholarly Inquiry

ISBN: 978-1-5225-0830-4
© 2017; 343 pp.
List Price: $185

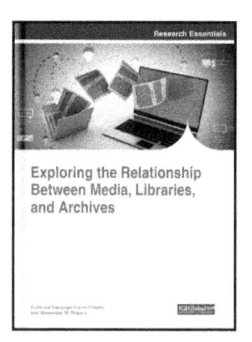

Research Essentials
Exploring the Relationship Between Media, Libraries, and Archives

ISBN: 978-1-5225-5840-8
© 2019; 263 pp.
List Price: $175

Premier Reference Source
Effective Knowledge Management Systems in Modern Society

ISBN: 978-1-5225-5427-1
© 2019; 391 pp.
List Price: $195

Looking for free content, product updates, news, and special offers?
Join IGI Global's mailing list today and start enjoying exclusive perks sent only to IGI Global members.
Add your name to the list at **www.igi-global.com/newsletters**.

Publisher of Peer-Reviewed, Timely, and Innovative Academic Research

IGI Global
DISSEMINATOR of KNOWLEDGE

www.igi-global.com   Sign up at www.igi-global.com/newsletters   facebook.com/igiglobal   twitter.com/igiglobal

Ensure Quality Research is Introduced to the Academic Community

Become an IGI Global Reviewer for Authored Book Projects

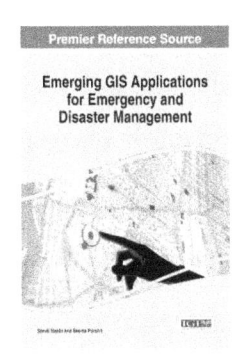

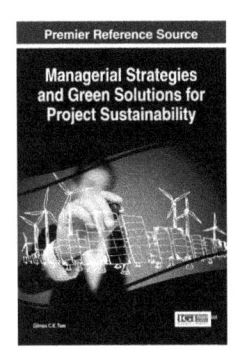

The overall success of an authored book project is dependent on quality and timely reviews.

In this competitive age of scholarly publishing, constructive and timely feedback significantly expedites the turnaround time of manuscripts from submission to acceptance, allowing the publication and discovery of forward-thinking research at a much more expeditious rate. Several IGI Global authored book projects are currently seeking highly-qualified experts in the field to fill vacancies on their respective editorial review boards:

Applications and Inquiries may be sent to:
development@igi-global.com

Applicants must have a doctorate (or an equivalent degree) as well as publishing and reviewing experience. Reviewers are asked to complete the open-ended evaluation questions with as much detail as possible in a timely, collegial, and constructive manner. All reviewers' tenures run for one-year terms on the editorial review boards and are expected to complete at least three reviews per term. Upon successful completion of this term, reviewers can be considered for an additional term.

If you have a colleague that may be interested in this opportunity, we encourage you to share this information with them.

IGI Global Proudly Partners With eContent Pro International

Receive a 25% Discount on all Editorial Services

Editorial Services

IGI Global expects all final manuscripts submitted for publication to be in their final form. This means they must be reviewed, revised, and professionally copy edited prior to their final submission. Not only does this support with accelerating the publication process, but it also ensures that the highest quality scholarly work can be disseminated.

English Language Copy Editing

Let eContent Pro International's expert copy editors perform edits on your manuscript to resolve spelling, punctuaion, grammar, syntax, flow, formatting issues and more.

Scientific and Scholarly Editing

Allow colleagues in your research area to examine the content of your manuscript and provide you with valuable feedback and suggestions before submission.

Figure, Table, Chart & Equation Conversions

Do you have poor quality figures? Do you need visual elements in your manuscript created or converted? A design expert can help!

Translation

Need your documjent translated into English? eContent Pro International's expert translators are fluent in English and more than 40 different languages.

Hear What Your Colleagues are Saying About Editorial Services Supported by IGI Global

"The service was very fast, very thorough, and very helpful in ensuring our chapter meets the criteria and requirements of the book's editors. I was quite impressed and happy with your service."

– Prof. Tom Brinthaupt,
Middle Tennessee State University, USA

"I found the work actually spectacular. The editing, formatting, and other checks were very thorough. The turnaround time was great as well. I will definitely use eContent Pro in the future."

– Nickanor Amwata, Lecturer,
University of Kurdistan Hawler, Iraq

"I was impressed that it was done timely, and wherever the content was not clear for the reader, the paper was improved with better readability for the audience."

– Prof. James Chilembwe,
Mzuzu University, Malawi

Email: customerservice@econtentpro.com

www.igi-global.com/editorial-service-partners